NATIONS OF THE MODERN WORLD

ENGLAND	W. R. Inge
ISRAEL	Norman Bentwich
SA'UDI ARABIA	H. St John Philby
FRANCE	P. E. Charvet
SOUTH AFRICA	J. H. Hofmeyer *Revised by* J. P. Cope
THE SUDAN	Sir Harold MacMichael

SCOTLAND

SCOTLAND

By the late

SIR ROBERT RAIT
C.B.E. M.A. LL.D.

and

GEORGE S. PRYDE
M.A. PH.D.

SECOND EDITION
Revised throughout by
GEORGE S. PRYDE

LONDON
ERNEST BENN LIMITED

First Published 1934
Second Edition 1954

Published by Ernest Benn Limited
Bouverie House · Fleet Street · London · EC4
Printed in Great Britain

Contents

	Preface	ix
1	The Medieval Kingdom	11
2	Reformation and Union	48
3	From the Union to the First Reform Act	84
4	Political Life since the First Reform Act	110
5	The Government of Scotland	155
6	Economic Conditions	187
7	Social Life	226
8	The Churches Yesterday and To-day	259
9	Scottish Education	284
10	Arts and Letters	303
	Bibliographical Note	323
	Index	331

Maps

Counties, Cities and Large Burghs of Scotland   185

Economic Map of Scotland   219

Distribution of Population, 1951   246–7

Preface

MUCH has happened in the twenty years that have elapsed since the publication of the first edition of this book. The political and economic conditions, the social and intellectual life of the nation have undergone profound changes, while the story of Scotland's past has been elucidated along new or novel lines, and our appraisal of present problems, for example, in constitutional and cultural matters, is utterly different from that of the 1930s. In the pages which follow an endeavour has been made to trace the more important recent developments and to reflect the findings of modern historical and other writers.

The late Sir Robert Rait's portion of the book (now forming the first two chapters) has been lightly revised; here and there some of his matter has been condensed, in order to make way for a few supplementary passages, but the political narrative down to 1707 is still in all essentials his work. The remainder of the book has been entirely re-written. I hope, rather than expect, that errors of fact have been avoided throughout. The opinions which are expressed (and for which the responsibility is now mine alone) will not, I fear, please every reader; I can only plead the impossibility—and perhaps the undesirability—of avoiding them in a work of this scope and nature.

It is by the kind permission of Lady Rait, as executrix of Sir Robert Rait, that *Scotland* appears in a new edition; to her my sincere and respectful thanks are offered.

GEORGE S. PRYDE

The University, Glasgow
1954

Chapter 1

The Medieval Kingdom

THE historical kingdom of Scotland emerged from an amalgamation of four peoples: Picts, Gaels, Britons, and Angles. When the Romans invaded Scotland they found a people whom they described as Caledonians, including a race of Gaels or Goidels, and the mysterious Picts, who, in historical times, spoke a Gaelic tongue, but whose origin has been a matter of persistent controversy. Roman invasion and occupation left only a slight impress upon the country, and after the abandonment of the wall of Antoninus Pius between Forth and Clyde, about the year A.D. 180, there is a long interval during which we know nothing about the course of events, except for punitive expeditions by the Emperor Severus in 208 and by Theodosius (father of the first emperor of that name) in 368. Before the Romans left Britain, Christianity had been introduced into what was to become Southern Scotland by St. Ninian (died c. 432). It used to be assumed that the influence of St. Ninian and his disciples was confined to the south-west and that it was short-lived, but recent discussions have attributed more widespread and more persistent effects to the teaching of the first Scottish missionary.

The conquest of South Britain by the Angles and the Saxons led to the settlements in the northern portion of the island. The Britons were driven westward by the invaders into the long narrow region between the Clyde and the Mersey, and the conquering Angles, about the middle of the sixth century, founded the kingdom of Bernicia, which extended from the Tees to the Forth, along a coast where Teutonic immigration had been in progress for some time. Somewhat earlier, at the beginning of the sixth century, bodies of Gaels or Goidels came from Ireland to what is

now Argyll, and founded a kingdom of Dalriada or Scot-land.
The political importance of the Scots was enhanced by
the mission of St. Columba, who landed in the island of
Iona in 563. His work prepared the way for an ultimate
union of the Picts and Scots, and that union made possible
the existence of a kingdom of Scotland.

In the time of St. Columba, the most probable future of
North Britain might well have seemed to be a division
into three kingdoms. Picts and Scots would unite to form
one kingdom of Pictland or Scotland north of Clyde and
Forth; the British in Strathclyde would form part of a great
western kingdom, stretching from the Clyde to the Bristol
channel, and the Lothians would remain part of the great
Anglian kingdom. Only the first part of such a forecast
came true. After many years, the invasions of the Northmen led to a union of Picts and Scots under the king of
Dalriada, Kenneth MacAlpin, to form the new kingdom
of Alban (844). But the chance of the emergence of a great
British kingdom was destroyed in the first quarter of the
seventh century by the Angles' capture of Chester and the
consequent separation of the Britons of Cumbria and
Strathclyde from the Britons of Wales. Thus isolated, the
Britons had to meet the military power of Northumbria
at its height, and they had also to fight the Picts and the
Northmen. A separate Strathclyde state persisted for many
years, though often in dependence upon one of its neigh-
bours, until, in 1018, Duncan, the heir to the throne of
Alban, succeeded to the throne of Strathclyde.

A separate kingdom of the Angles existed until the same
memorable year, 1018. At one period, it seemed as if the
Angles were to penetrate much farther north, but the defeat
of Ecgfrith, king of Northumbria, by Brude, king of the
Picts, at Dunnichen (Nectansmere) in Angus, in 685, was
the deathblow to Northumbrian greatness. Finally, at the
battle of Carham-on-Tweed, in 1018, Malcolm II, king of
Alban, overthrew the Northumbrians and annexed the
Lothians to Scotland. Malcolm's grandson, Duncan, the
Duncan of *Macbeth*, was the first king of Scots in the historical
sense of the term. He ruled Dalriada, Pictland, Strath-

clyde and Lothian, although the Northmen had occupied the islands, made settlements on the coasts, and secured Caithness and Sutherland. Duncan's reign over Scotland (1034–40) was brief and unlucky, and he was slain by his own general, Macbeth, who succeeded him on the throne. Macbeth appears to have ruled competently until, in 1057, Malcolm, a son of Duncan, with English help, defeated and slew him at Lumphanan in Aberdeenshire. The long reign of Malcolm III (Canmore) witnessed the initiation of profound changes in the history of Scotland.

The outstanding fact in the history of Scotland is the fundamental change which, in the course of two centuries, converted the population of the Lowlands into an English-speaking community whose social and political life was organized on the model of the Anglo-Norman kingdom of England. It is true that, long after the reign of Alexander III, when this process may, for practical purposes, be regarded as complete, the Gaelic tongue lingered in regions which are geographically Lowland, but the battle between English speech and civilization on the one hand, and the Gaelic language and a Celtic organization on the other hand, was fought and won between the marriage of Malcolm Canmore and the death of Alexander III. So complete was the English victory that historians have accounted for this social and political revolution by the assumption that the Gaelic population was displaced and that the Lowlands of Scotland were colonized by a people of English blood. Outside the Lothians, which, as we have seen, were for a long period part of an English kingdom, there is no evidence of a popular immigration, though some English traders (as well as Flemings) settled in the burghs on the east coast. But the theory of a racial displacement had an attraction both for poetry and for history. It suited the purpose of Sir Walter Scott in *The Lady of the Lake* to portray a racial cleavage between Saxon and Celt in Scotland:

'These fertile plains, that softened vale
Were once the birthright of the Gael;
The stranger came with iron hand
And from our fathers reft the land.'

The assumption possessed an appeal for English historians like Freeman and Green, to whom the Lowland Scots were 'stout Northumbrian Englishmen' and Edward I was consequently the champion of his nation's greatness and the saviour of its unity.

The process by which a revolution in manners, customs, organization, law and language was accomplished is easily traceable, and it constitutes the history of Scotland for two centuries. It was begun by the English princess Margaret, sister of Edgar the Atheling, who married Malcolm Canmore about the year 1070, but Margaret herself was able to achieve very little. An Englishwoman who had been educated on the continent of Europe, she had small respect for Celtic customs and institutions, but her husband's life, as we shall see in another connexion, was largely spent in warfare with England, and he showed no tendency to adapt the institutions of his Celtic kingdom to the organization which the Norman conqueror of England was engaged in establishing there. Malcolm himself owed something to England; he had found shelter there during the reign of Macbeth, and had received Northumbrian help on the occasion of at least one of his invasions of Scotland. But the England which he knew was not the England of the Normans, and, with some ingratitude, he chose to avenge the wrongs of the Saxon house upon the north of England, which had much better reason to hate the Normans than he could profess.

Such changes as Queen Margaret achieved were in the Church. She was a devout woman, who would gladly have taken the veil, and her enthusiasm for the Roman Church was so much stronger than her antipathy to the Normans that she regarded herself as the daughter in the Lord of Lanfranc, Norman archbishop of Canterbury. She found in Scotland an ill-organized Church, its original monastic constitution destroyed, and its episcopal constitution ineffective. The abbots were frequently laymen who hired secular priests or Culdees to perform the services. The clergy were not celibate—this, of course, was common all over Europe until the Lateran Council of 1139—and there was a marked tendency for ecclesiastical offices to become hereditary. The queen was shocked by certain unfamiliar practices in matters of detail—one of them was an old-fashioned method of calculating the beginning of Lent—and there is no reason to suspect the existence of heresy. Our information is derived from a biography of Queen Margaret, written by her Saxon confessor, Turgot, prior of Durham. He describes how the queen persuaded the Scottish Church to abandon the celebration of 'masses in I know not what barbarous rite, contrary to the custom of the whole Church,' and 'other practices contrary to the rule of faith and the observances of the Church.' If the divergence from ecclesiastical canons had been anything so violent as the celebration of mass in the Gaelic tongue, Turgot could scarcely have failed to mention the circumstance, for his object was to exalt the greatness of his lady's achievement. What we do learn from him shows that the Scottish Church had fallen out of touch with Roman custom and Roman organization, but that it did not reject Roman doctrine.

The reformation of these points of detail was only the beginning of a process which Queen Margaret did not live to complete. The conditions of the time were not propitious, and her husband was content to allow her to follow her own bent without either help or hindrance. His reign was largely spent in invasions of England which brought retaliations from William the Conqueror and William Rufus. One of these raids provoked a counter-invasion in 1072, when the Conqueror, granting to Malcolm some lands in England, received from him an undefined homage; the last of them, in 1093, was the occasion of Malcolm's own death. He fell in a skirmish at Alnwick, and his eldest son, Edward, was mortally wounded in the same fight. Margaret survived her husband and son for only a few days.

The English queen had roused in Celtic Scotland—and Scotland was still Celtic outside the Lothians—a deep-rooted suspicion and antagonism. Malcolm's people foresaw, and tried to prevent, a process of Anglicization in church and state. On his death, they rejected the claims of the sons of Malcolm and Margaret, whose English Christian names were a sign and symbol of the revolutionary changes contemplated by their mother, and, following an ancient custom, chose as king a brother of Malcolm named Donald. At the same time, they drove out of Scotland the Englishmen who had come to Margaret's court, just as the English, at the time of the revolt of Earl Godwin, had driven out the Confessor's Norman favourites. The effort was made in vain. By his first wife, Ingibjorg, Malcolm had a son, Duncan, who had been living in England, a hostage given by Malcolm to William I. With English help, he overthrew Donald in 1094. Duncan II promised that he would receive neither Saxons nor Normans, but within six months he fell a victim to an alliance between Donald and Edmund, a son of Malcolm and Margaret. They divided the country, Donald ruling north of the Forth and Edmund south of it, and for three years it seemed as if Celtic Scotland was to remain a separate kingdom, though the Celts of Strathclyde and Galloway were not included in it and seem to have lived in provincial independence. In 1097, however, Edgar, one of the four sons of Malcolm and Margaret who bore the names of Saxon kings, defeated Donald and Edmund with the help of an English army. He reigned for over nine years, making Edinburgh, instead of Dunfermline, his favourite residence, living peaceably in English Scotland, and allowing the Norwegians to confirm their possession of all the western islands and of Kintyre.

Edgar's brother, Alexander, who succeeded him in 1107, was a man of another type. He allowed a younger brother, David, to govern the Lothians and Galloway, and made a home for himself at Invergowrie in Perthshire, in the heart of Celtic Scotland. He suppressed so vigorously a revolt of the men of Moray and the Mearns that he became known as Alexander the Fierce. David succeeded him in 1124, and continued and developed his policy. It was in David's long reign (1124–53) that the process of Anglicization or Anglo-Normanization came to be definitely accepted outside the western and northern Highlands. The court, the church, the law, the institutions of the kingdom and its commerce, were alike subjected to English influence.

Edgar, Alexander and David had all lived at the English court, David for many years. Their sister Matilda was married to Henry I in 1100; Alexander's wife is said to have been a natural daughter of the same English sovereign, and David married the widow of a Norman baron who was also the heiress of the old English earls of Northumbria and Huntingdon, and brought with her claims to wide English lands. The Church, in the reigns of Alexander and David, came to be divided into dioceses as elsewhere in Europe. The Celtic Church had suffered from lack of organization, and there was no machinery to keep it in touch with western Christendom. Nine Scottish dioceses —St. Andrews, Dunkeld, Moray, Glasgow, Ross, Caithness, Aberdeen, Dunblane and Brechin—were founded or re-founded between 1107 and 1153; a tenth—Argyll or Lismore —was to follow in the thirteenth century. Galloway or Whithorn (Candida Casa) was for long subject to the arch-bishopric of York, while the two other sees of Orkney and the Isles owed obedience to the Norwegian archbishopric of Trondhjem. The establishment of the see of St. Andrews in 1109 was the occasion of much controversy, for both the English archbishops claimed jurisdiction over Scotland. Two successive appointments were ineffectual because the first bishop, Turgot, Margaret's confessor, acknowledged the pretensions of York, and the second, Eadmer, the historian and the biographer of St. Anselm, declared that not for all Scotland would he renounce being a monk of Canterbury; and it was not until after the death of Eadmer that Alexander, at the close of his life, was able to make a successful nomination to St. Andrews. Before 1153, however, every district of Scotland had a recognized ecclesi-astical ruler, who could communicate with Rome and whose business it was to secure the proper observance of the order and discipline of the Roman Church. The institution of dioceses had a profound political importance. Every bishop was a landowner and a magnate of the realm, and all the bishops, in virtue of their position, were necessarily

supporters of the crown and the royal policy, and enemies
of Celtic institutions and customs, ecclesiastical and secular
alike. The early occupants of the new sees were, for the
most part, Englishmen, and in the rare instances in
which a new bishop bore a Celtic name we may be
sure that he was a Scotsman who had identified himself
with the new influences and, unlike the clergy found by
Queen Margaret in Scotland, could speak the English
tongue.

To the political influence of the dioceses there must be
added that of the monasteries. Queen Margaret had found
in Scotland a form of conventual life which had been in
use since the ninth century. The Culdees represented a
development from ascetics who, in early Ireland, lived in
isolated cells; in Scotland they were religious communities
not belonging to any of the recognized orders. Malcolm
and Margaret had shown them favour, and Turgot had
described them as 'men who lived in the flesh, but not
according to the flesh, and even on earth lived the life of
angels.' But the Culdees were conservatives who maintained
traditional Celtic custom, and it was essential for the royal
policy that they should yield place to religious who belonged
to one or other of the monastic orders. Even before the
death of Margaret, a great Benedictine house was founded
at Coldingham, but this was in English Scotland. Her
sons established monasteries in the country north of the
Forth. Some of these, like the mother house of Canons
Regular or Austin Canons, founded by Alexander I at
Scone in 1114, were independent foundations; others were
originally colonies from Lothian houses. David I, for
example, re-founded a Benedictine monastery at Kelso in
1128, from which were planted houses in the Celtic parts
of Scotland—Kilwinning in Ayrshire, Lesmahagow in
Lanarkshire, Lindores in Fife, Arbroath in Forfarshire, and
Fyvie in Aberdeenshire. Similarly, David's great foundation
of Canons Regular at Holyrood came to be closely associated
with the south-west of Scotland, owing to the accident that,
in the reign of Malcolm IV, a rebellious prince of Galloway,
defeated in an effort to resist Anglicization, became a canon

of Holyrood, endowed it with lands in Kirkcudbrightshire, and founded the daughter house of St. Mary's Isle.

The monasteries, like the bishops, were landowners, and their abbots or priors ranked with the great men of the realm. The early monks were Englishmen (David I, for example, brought monks from Canterbury to Dunfermline in 1128), and they and their successors, drawn chiefly from great Scottish families, were necessarily upholders of English influence. James I afterwards complained that his ancestor, David I, had attained the honour of popular canonization by being 'a sair sanct for the Crown,' but there was policy as well as piety in the lavish grants of land made by Alexander I and his successors to diocesan and monastic establishments. These grants were made during a great period of monastic revival in Europe, and were doubtless rendered easier of accomplishment by this circumstance: it was natural that the king of Scots should do what princes were doing elsewhere. The new monasteries replaced the Culdee establishments, though some of these lingered until after the War of Independence. It should be remembered that monks not only prayed—they worked. The great Border abbeys of Jedburgh, Kelso, Melrose, Dryburgh and Coldingham owned large sheep farms and conducted a brisk trade in wool through Scotland's chief port, Berwick; and the monks of Newbattle and Dunfermline, pioneers in coal-mining, worked the surface seams near the firth of Forth.

A new system of land tenure, in accordance with which bishoprics and religious houses were endowed, was itself a potent instrument for the establishment of English influence. The sons of Queen Margaret introduced feudalism into Scotland. The old Celtic method of land tenure was not, as has been sometimes imagined, communal. The land was held by the chief and his near kindred, and the generality of a tribe had nothing to lose by feudalization. Nor was there, except in a few rebellious areas, any racial displacement, nor even any actual dispossession of existing holders of land. The system, when it came to be applied to the Scotland of David I, was well developed, and large grants of land were a feature of the time in England and other European countries. When David I made to his friend, Robert de Brus, a member of a great Anglo-Norman family, a gift of some 200,000 acres in Annandale, or to the FitzAlans, afterwards the royal Stewarts, a district comprising the modern county of Renfrew and a large portion of Kyle in Ayrshire, he deprived no man of his heritage. The newcomers, however, received rights and privileges which were presumed to have belonged, not to the occupants of the land, but to the crown, and these rights and privileges placed the tenants in a position of dependence upon their new lords. They held their lands from Bruce or FitzAlan, and some of them owed him not only money rents, but actual services rendered at seed-time or harvest, in the carriage of goods, in the making of roads, and in the maintenance of the lord's mill, to which they had to bring their grain for grinding and to pay 'multure.' Besides the free tenants of varying social rank, there were occupants of the land who were bondsmen, and these serfs and their offspring were often granted in the deeds of gift. Serfs could not, as a rule, be sold away from the land to which they belonged, but, if they escaped from it, the law provided for their being brought back to it by force. Charters conveying land and jurisdiction over the occupants of land were conferred by the crown not only upon the Anglo-Norman friends of the sovereign, but also upon Scottish chiefs who adopted the new ways of the court and were glad to possess written evidence of their old customary rights and to have these rights enlarged in written charters. For example, Malcolm, earl of Fife, had his earldom confirmed by Alexander II in 1225, with precise land rights and with the customary feudal jurisdiction.

Thus there grew up in the Lowlands the characteristically Scottish institution of the family, while in the Highlands the old tribal system developed into the clan. The division of Scotland into clans and families marks the distinction between Celtic Scotland and Anglicized Scotland. The clan, in its historical form, cannot be traced to an earlier date than the end of the fourteenth century; it represents the natural development of Celtic institutions and civilization. The family, dating from the twelfth century, was the direct result of the land system introduced by David I. The recipients of his charters became supreme in their own districts and had the right of granting land and privileges to under-tenants. These were often members of their own families—the rise of some hundred and fifty Gordon families in Aberdeenshire after a grant of land to a Gordon in the early fourteenth century is an excellent illustration—but, as the use of surnames became frequent, the tenants and dependents of a great house adopted its family name, and the family became a unit comparable to the clan; it possibly derived some of its cohesion from the same Celtic tradition that inspired the loyalty of clansmen to their chief.

Along with feudalism as a system of land tenure, David I and his successors introduced into Scotland the political institutions associated with feudal monarchies. The royal household came to be an administrative unit and to include such great officers of state as the chancellor, the chamberlain, the justiciar, the constable, the marshal and the steward. The laws were based on English exemplars, and the office of sheriff, English in name and origin, was established. At a later date, many Scottish sheriffdoms became hereditary and therefore independent of the crown, but, originally, the sheriff, in Scotland as in England, was the king's representative, charged with the maintenance of his interests in matters of justice and finance. The net-work of sheriffdoms that David I and his successors stretched over the entire kingdom marks the slow and painful spread of the rule of law on the new model. A great council of the realm, based upon English precedent, came into existence, consisting in theory of all tenants-in-chief. To these councils the king summoned bishop, abbot and prior, as well as earl and baron.

Finally, the development of commerce gave a fresh impulse to English influence. Commerce was chiefly with England, and an expansion of trade under David I and his successors brought into the towns a new population of English and Flemish merchants, many of the Flemings coming to Scotland via England. Thus was introduced into Scotland the institution of the burgh; Scottish burghs were founded on English precedents, and the whole system of burghal law and custom was derived from English models. The king's burgh served as the seat of his sheriffdom and was generally protected by one of his castles, under the charge of a castellan or captain; and to this day Edinburgh, Linlithgow, Stirling, and Dumbarton remind us vividly of a close association, which once held good also of places like Berwick, Roxburgh and Peebles, Lanark, Ayr and Dumfries, Perth, Forfar and Aberdeen, Banff, Elgin, Nairn and Inverness. Bishops, too, had their burghs, like St. Andrews and Glasgow, as had the abbots of Holyrood (Canongate), Kelso, Arbroath, Dunfermline (Musselburgh) and Lindores (Newburgh). A few burghs, finally, belonged to the greater baronial families—Prestwick to the FitzAlans, Kirkintilloch to the Comyns, Dunbar to the earls of March, Crawford to the Lindsays, and Urr, in Galloway, to the Balliols. All of them were centres of local trade and handicrafts.

Thus, during the twelfth and thirteenth centuries, the influences of the church, the court, the law, and of political and commercial institutions, all combined to bring about, in the Scottish Lowlands, a change of speech and civilization, unaccompanied by any racial displacement. The nobility became Anglo-Norman, partly by the introduction into Scotland of Anglo-Norman families and partly by the intermarriage of Anglo-Normans with the old Celtic houses; the ancient line of the lords of Galloway, for example, ended with three co-heiresses, daughters of Alan FitzRoland, himself the son of a marriage between a Celtic chief and a daughter of the family of de Moreville. These co-heiresses married, respectively, the earl of Winchester, John Balliol, and William of Aumale. There was also an infiltration of English blood into the burghs, but there is no evidence of such an expulsion of the Gael as Scott assumed in *The Lady of the Lake*. The facts were known to the medieval Scottish historians. 'Those of us who live on the borders of England,' wrote Hector Boece, 'have forsaken our own tongue and learned English, being driven thereto by wars and commerce. But the Highlanders remain just as they were in the time of Malcolm Canmore, in whose days we began to adopt English manners.'

This revolution was not entirely peaceful. The Celtic reaction which followed the death of Malcolm Canmore was only the first of a long series of revolts against the sons of Malcolm and Margaret. Alexander I, David I, Malcolm IV, William the Lion and Alexander II had all to face serious rebellions of the Gaelic population in various parts of Scotland. The revolt of Angus, earl of Moray, and his brother, Malcolm MacHeth, in the reign of David I, lasted for some five years and was suppressed only with the help of the king's Anglo-Norman friends in the north of England; ultimately, the Celtic earldom was suppressed, the lands were distributed among new proprietors, and religious houses — Kinloss, Pluscardine, Urquhart — were founded in the district, in accordance with the methods of the time. William the Lion had to deal with rebellions both in Galloway and in the north. The last of the Galloway revolts (1234) may be said to mark the end of Celtic resistance. Its cause was the unwillingness of the Galwegians to pass under the jurisdiction of the Anglo-Norman husbands of the heiresses to whom we have already referred. They begged Alexander to annex the lordship of Galloway to the crown and to rule them directly. The development of feudal ideas may, perhaps, be illustrated by the remark of the contemporary writer of the *Melrose Chronicle*. 'The king,' he says, 'was too just to do this.' Two campaigns were needed to compel obedience to the new families. The suppression of these revolts hastened the process of the supersession of the ancient nobility by strangers or the parallel process of the acceptance of the new polity by the old lords. In one of William the Lion's northern campaigns he was assisted by the Celtic lord of Galloway, and in another by the Celtic earls of Fife and Atholl.

During these two centuries, while English influence was becoming predominant in Lowland Scotland, political relations between Scotland and England were not always friendly, but there is a marked distinction between the hostilities of this period and subsequent Anglo-Scottish warfare. From the death of Malcolm Canmore to the death of Alexander III, alike when Englishmen fought in Scotland and when Scotsmen fought in England, they did so as the allies of one side or another in a civil conflict. English rebels obtained Scottish aid against their sovereigns; Scottish kings received English help against their rebellious subjects. From the accession of Edgar, with English military support, in 1097, to the outbreak of the War of Independence in 1296, there were, in fact, only three periods of conflict. The most notable of these, and the only military episode remembered by the name of a battle, belongs to the reign of David I. His intervention in the civil war that followed the death of Henry I (1135) was undertaken on behalf of his niece, Matilda, against her rival, Stephen, but no Anglo-Scottish quarrel was involved. David claimed, in the name of his eldest son, the earldom of Northumbria, the heritage of his English queen. It is not a heroic story. At the battle of the Standard, near Northallerton, in August, 1138, he led to defeat his army of Anglo-Normans, Scots and Galwegians; among his opponents was a baron who had been his ally, a few years earlier, in suppressing a Celtic rising in Moray. He ultimately secured a few concessions in Northumbria.

In the next series of hostilities, a Scottish king was also fighting in an English cause, for William the Lion, in his unlucky invasion of 1174, to which we shall refer in another connexion, was the ally of the rebellious son, and of the rebellious barons, of Henry II. The only other period of actual fighting was when the young Alexander II aided the English barons in their struggle for the Great Charter. John retaliated by capturing Berwick-on-Tweed, and boasted that he would 'hunt the red fox cub from his lair,' but this was no mere English invasion of Scotland, for a great, and ultimately victorious, English party was in sympathy with the Scottish king. From 1216 until the outbreak of the War of Independence, a period of eighty years, there were no hostilities between Scotland and England. These peace-

ful relations, and the existence of something like a community of feeling between the two countries, aided the
victory of the royal policy. Many Scottish magnates, like
the Bruces and the Balliols, held territory in both England
and Scotland, and, as time went on, the influence of these
newcomers increased, and they ceased to be strangers in
the land. The royal family continued to intermarry with
England. The heir of David I, who predeceased his father,
was earl of Huntingdon, in right of his mother, and he had
claims to the earldom of Northumberland. He married
Ada, daughter of William, earl of Warenne and second
earl of Surrey, and had three sons and some daughters;
the latter were the ancestresses of the claimants to the
crown after the death of Alexander III. The eldest son,
Malcolm the Maiden, succeeded his grandfather, David I,
in 1153, and died, unmarried, in 1165. The third son,
David, succeeded to the earldom of Huntingdon and lived
as an English baron. The second son, William the Lion,
succeeded his brother Malcolm as king in 1165, and reigned
for nearly fifty years. He married, late in life, Ermengarde,
a cousin of Henry II of England, and by her he had a son,
Alexander II, who was king of Scots from 1214 to 1249.
Alexander's first wife, Joanna, was a sister of Henry III of
England, and Alexander III (1249-1286) also married an
English princess (Margaret, daughter of Henry III), though,
like his father, he brought a second bride from France.

During these two centuries there were two serious subjects
of dispute between the monarchs of England and Scotland.
We have seen that both Canterbury and York claimed
jurisdiction over the Scottish Church, and that Alexander I,
in spite of his general policy of Anglicization, was adamant
in his refusal to admit any such claim. The papacy declined
to grant the request of more than one Scottish king for the
creation of a metropolitan see in Scotland, and, when
William the Lion, in circumstances about to be described,
acknowledged Henry II of England as his feudal superior,
the Treaty of Falaise admitted the subordination of the
Scottish to the English Church, but, fortunately, left un-
settled the rival claims of Canterbury and York. This

rivalry involved an appeal to Rome, and the papacy, after a violent dispute with William over an election to the bishopric of St. Andrews, issued a bull in 1192 declaring the Scottish Church to be the spiritual daughter of the see of Rome, 'with mediation of none.' In 1225, permission was given to the Scottish clergy to hold an annual provincial council, but it was not until 1472 that the bishop of St. Andrews was given the dignity of a metropolitan.

The other cause of dispute was an English claim to the overlordship of Scotland. Entries in the *Anglo-Saxon Chronicle*, relating to temporary alliances between England and Scotland against the Norsemen, were interpreted, after the Norman Conquest, as constituting records of a legal and permanent dependence of Scotland upon England, and inventive chroniclers embroidered the entries of the *Chronicle* until they created the mythical tale of the English monarch Edgar, holding a golden rudder, being rowed upon the river Dee by eight vassal kings. The position was complicated by the circumstance that, from the time of Malcolm Canmore, the kings of Scots possessed lands in England, for which they did homage to the kings of England. William I gave lands to Malcolm, and Malcolm's son, David I, married a great English heiress, who brought to the Scottish crown actual possession of the earldom of Huntingdon and claims upon Northumberland. The nature of the homage done for English lands by Scottish kings was not defined; Malcolm IV, for example, became the man of Henry II 'in such fashion as his grandfather had been the man of Henry I,' and each king could interpret these words as he wished. But, when William the Lion was captured at Alnwick in 1174, while aiding the rebellious son of Henry II, he was forced to consent to the Treaty of Falaise, by which he became the liegeman of Henry II expressly for Scotland. For fifteen years Scotland was actually in feudal subjection to England, and the relationship was felt to be, in the words of a contemporary Scottish chronicler, a 'grievous yoke of slavery,' so grievous that in 1189 the Scots, at a great price, purchased their freedom from Richard I. Richard's bargain with William freed the Scottish

king 'from all conventions and compacts which my father
King Henry extorted from him by new charters and by his
capture, so that he do to me fully and entirely what Malcolm,
king of Scots, his brother, did to our predecessors of right
and of right ought to have done.' The ambiguity of this
formula was pleasing to both parties. Richard could claim
that Malcolm had done homage for Scotland (though, if
this was so, what were the Scots paying money for?) and
William did claim that Malcolm 'of right ought to have done'
homage for Northumberland, denied to him and his successor by the English. During the reigns of Alexander II
and Alexander III, the ambiguity of the homage done by
the monarchs of Scotland for lands which they held in
England persisted, and on the last occasion upon which
this homage was done (1278) the evidence about what
actually happened is conflicting; the records of the chroniclers
on both sides may well have been manipulated after the
great controversy broke out a few years later.

Although the English claim to overlordship was thus a
standing menace, the relations between Scotland and her
neighbour were on the whole friendly. During more than
two hundred years there were only four periods of
hostility—the ravages of Canmore, David I's intervention in
England's civil war, William the Lion's rash adventure,
and Alexander II's invasion in the interests of the English
barons in their struggle with John (1215–16). Scotland was
prosperous, and the descendants of Malcolm Canmore
succeeded in consolidating the kingdom. An organized
central government was beginning to exercise authority
even in the north and in Galloway, and the territory which
had been lost to Norway in the reign of Edgar was recovered.
The Norsemen had helped Celtic resistance to the Anglo-
Norman policy of the kings of Scots, and it was not until
the latter had entirely subdued the opposition of their own
subjects that they began to make headway against the
Norwegians. In the end of his reign, Alexander II asserted
his right to the Hebrides, and, at his death on the island of
Kerrera in 1249, he was engaged in an expedition against
the Norse. His son, Alexander III, reasserted the claim,

which was resisted by Haco of Norway and Magnus, king of Man, who brought a great armament to the shores of the firth of Clyde. A storm wrecked the Norse fleet, and the invaders were defeated at the battle of Largs in 1263. Haco retired to the Orkneys, where he died in the following winter, and Alexander extorted a submission from Magnus and sent an expedition to the Hebrides. In 1266 Eric of Norway ceded the western islands to Scotland for a money payment. Orkney and Shetland remained in the hands of the Norsemen until, in 1469, they were given as a pledge for the dowry of Margaret of Denmark on her marriage to James III and became part of the kingdom of Scotland.

Scotland in 1286 was not yet a fully unified state, but rather a series of communities possessing a common and distinctive organization, and gradually coming to recognize a central power and a national law. Its internal history for a hundred years had been not more disturbed than that of England, which had passed through the strain of the Barons' Wars and had seen the monarchy, first under John and then under Henry III, temporarily rendered impotent by successful rebellions. The authority of the Scottish crown had survived the minority of Alexander III, but his closing years were clouded with tragic destiny. His English queen died in 1275, his younger son, David, a boy of eight, in 1281, his only daughter, Margaret, queen of Norway, in 1283, and Alexander, his elder son, aged twenty, in 1284. Margaret left a baby girl of her own name who, in 1284, was acknowledged as heir-presumptive to her grandfather. In October 1285, Alexander married a second wife; in March 1286, in his forty-fifth year, he was killed by a fall from his horse near Kinghorn in Fife.

If there had been an adult male of the royal house closely related to the late king, the claims of an infant girl, foreign by birth, might have been ignored, but Alexander III left neither nephew nor cousin of legitimate blood. So the succession of the Maid of Norway was accepted, though not without opposition, and guardians of the kingdom were appointed. They welcomed the support of Edward I of England, who made no assertion of the rights of an overlord

but negotiated for a marriage between the little queen and
his son and heir, afterwards Edward II. After prolonged
deliberations, and the receipt of a papal dispensation—
the children were cousins—a treaty entirely satisfactory to
Scotland was made, the nation's consent being given by the
guardians, prelates and barons of the kingdom, assembled in
'parliament' at Brigham-on-Tweed in March 1290. Six
months later the queen, only eight years old, died on her
way to Scotland. The nearest heirs were descendants of
David I's youngest grandson, David, earl of Huntingdon,
whose three daughters had married into the Anglo-Norman
nobility of Scotland. The grandson of the eldest was John
Balliol, the son of the second was Robert Bruce. The latter
was a man of seventy-six, and about fifty years earlier he
had been acknowledged as heir-presumptive before the
birth of Alexander III. Balliol, belonging to a younger
generation, was about forty. By later rules of strict primo-
geniture, the grandson of an elder daughter has a prior
claim to that of the son of a younger daughter, but these
rules had not yet been established. The Bruces, rivals of
the Balliols and their relatives, the Comyns, had long been
pro-English, and the present Robert was ready to accept
Edward's terms, including overlordship.

Edward was too wise—from his own point of view—to
make a bargain of this kind with any of the competitors
for the Scottish throne. The Balliols and the Comyns
would have raised the standard of independence, and
organized a patriotic party. The English king was determined to secure an admission of his supremacy from all
the competitors and their supporters. After an investigation
of the historical evidence for the English claims, he asserted
his just right to be lord paramount of Scotland. Summoning
conferences of the Scottish magnates to Norham-on-Tweed
in May and June 1291, and making some display of force,
he got what he wanted from the competitors, who, thirteen
in number, presented their claims at Berwick in August.
A protest against Edward's suzerainty was made on behalf
of 'the community of the realm of Scotland,' but, in view
of the community's lack of organization and the want of a

true parliament, it is not easy to say just what the phrase means.

The lord paramount's first duty was to choose between the claimants, or to decide that the kingdom had lapsed to the overlord in default of heirs, a threat intended to secure the new-born allegiance of the Scottish nobility. With the regard for legal claims which characterized him, he ordered an elaborate investigation, and on November 17, 1292, at Berwick, he announced his decision in favour of John Balliol. For four years, Balliol ruled as a vassal king. Edward's treatment of him suggests that he aimed at driving him into rebellion in order to justify an annexation of Scotland, for he spared no pains to render his position ignominious. On the other hand, if this was his object, he chose an unfortunate time for a Scottish war; he had a French war and a Welsh rebellion to deal with, and his over-taxation was rousing opposition among clergy and people in England. At the end of 1295, Balliol, sacrificing his English lands, renounced his allegiance. He made a treaty with France, and this marks the beginning of the 'auld alliance,' which was to endure for over 260 years. At the moment, however, the accursed rivalry of Bruces and Balliols deprived the king's resistance of any chance of success. Robert Bruce, the claimant, had died, but his son, Robert, the father of the future king, was holding Carlisle for the English.

Edward I led an army to Scotland in person, took the town of Berwick, and was guilty of a merciless massacre of the citizens, the first act of war after nearly a century of peace, and the prelude to a long and ferocious conflict. There was little resistance, and in the summer of 1296 Edward made a triumphal march through Scotland. He went home in the early autumn, after sending to Westminster Scotland's coronation stone and leaving the country under a military occupation. Within a year a popular rising under Sir William Wallace regained Scottish independence by the battle of Stirling Bridge (September 11, 1297); his army included Celts from Galloway, Highlanders from Moray and Badenoch, and Scots from north of the

Forth. His success was the result of his own military skill and his power of leadership, working upon a widespread popular devotion to Scottish independence. For a brief period Wallace governed Scotland as guardian for John Balliol, but in 1298, deserted by some of the nobles who had supported him, he was defeated by Edward at Falkirk and he resigned his guardianship. But the desire for independence was still strong enough to continue resistance, and it was not until 1305 that Edward could again regard Scotland as a conquered country. In that year, Wallace was captured —betrayed, according to tradition—and Edward took a cruel revenge upon the man who, in the words of John Richard Green, will live in history as 'the first to assert freedom as a national birthright': the noblest and the purest of his country's heroes.

Edward proceeded to undertake the task of devising a permanent administrative system for the government of Scotland as a province of England, but the interval between hostilities was very short. Robert Bruce, grandson of the original competitor, was crowned king of Scots at Scone in March 1306. A few weeks earlier he had slain John Comyn, the representative of the Balliol claim. The rivals, who some years before had been at each other's throats in the council of guardians, arranged a meeting which can scarcely have had any other purpose than an adjustment of their claims as a prelude to further resistance. The murder was certainly unpremeditated, for Bruce had made no preparations for a leadership to which his rash deed inevitably committed him; there could be no mistaking the significance of the meeting and its result. He had also incurred the guilt of sacrilege, for Comyn was killed in a church at Dumfries, and the excommunication that must (and did) follow might well have deprived Bruce of the support of the clergy, who had been staunch upholders of the cause of independence. The responsibility thus thrust upon Robert Bruce by his own act changed him from a self-seeking baron into a great national leader, but the murder made the Balliols, the Comyns and all their adherents devoted champions of the English king, for there was a blood feud between them and the man-slayer upon whom rested the hopes of his country's freedom.

If a popular determination that Scotland should be a free country was shown when the Scots placed themselves under the command of a simple country gentleman in 1296, it was shown even more clearly when, in the hour of national humiliation, they gathered round the standard of Robert Bruce, ten years later. Their resolve was at once subjected to a stern test. The king was defeated in June 1306 at Methven, near Perth, and again in August at Dalry, in Argyll. He became a hunted and excommunicated fugitive; his supporters, including some of his brothers, were captured, and hanged and quartered as traitors to King Edward; his wife and daughters were prisoners. Barbour tells that the confidence of the people in their new leader was shaken and that they began to submit to the English, but he adds that a little experience of 'thraldome' led them to yearn for good news of the Bruce.

In the spring of 1307 Robert tried again, and in May he won a victory at Loudoun hill, in Ayrshire. This was the turning-point in his career, and fortune favoured him by removing the man whose ambition was the cause of centuries of bloodshed. Edward I died at Burgh-on-Sands, near Carlisle, on July 7, and his death left the English party in Scotland without support and without any definite plan of campaign. Edward II did a little ravaging, and left Scotland in August. King Robert was thus free to deal with his Scottish enemies in detail. Within three years he accomplished his task, and in February 1310 the Scottish clergy, meeting at Dundee, took a solemn oath of fealty to their excommunicated monarch. By 1311 the character of the war changed. Robert was no longer fighting his Scottish enemies, most of whom had sought refuge in England. He was able to invade Northumberland and to expel the English garrisons from Scottish strongholds. In the summer of 1313, his brother Edward made with the English governor of Stirling castle a chivalrous and foolish bargain that the castle should be surrendered if it was not relieved within a year. This was a reversal of Robert's military

policy, for it forced him to stake his fortunes, and the
fortunes of Scotland, upon the issue of one great battle,
in which the English were bound to enjoy a superiority
of numbers. But fortune was again kind, and on the field
of Bannockburn (June 24, 1314) King Robert proved
himself a great soldier. The independence of Scotland was
secured, and, in the years which intervened between the
victory and the recognition of its results by the regents
for Edward III, the Scots engaged in offensive warfare
both in the north of England and in Ireland. In 1320,
from Arbroath, the Scots barons sent Pope John XXII
their famous letter, acknowledging Robert as their king
and pledging themselves to resist England to the death.
The letter may well have had some effect, for papal recognition of Robert as king came in 1323. In the same year
Edward II sought a truce, and, though there were further
hostilities in 1327, the treaty of Northampton was made
in the following year between two independent sovereigns;
it arranged for the marriage of Robert's heir, David, to the
sister of the young English king.

Robert died in 1329, his life work apparently crowned
with success. Soldier, patriot and hero, he was a shrewd
judge and born leader of men, in peace as in war. He put
his trust in the fighting qualities of Sir Thomas Randolph
and Sir James Douglas, and he was not disappointed.
The first he made earl of Moray and lord of Annandale;
the second was granted Ettrick forest, Jedburgh forest,
and many other lands in south Scotland. It is not so well
known that King Robert had an equally reliable adviser
for the ordinary affairs of the state; here he depended on
the outstanding talents of Bernard de Linton, abbot of
Arbroath and chancellor for almost the whole of the reign.
The reform and consolidation of land tenures, carried out
soon after Bannockburn, were to serve the state for centuries
to come. Over sixty surviving charters from this period
show that the barony, generally owing knight service or
archer service in the royal army, but sometimes held for a
money rent or 'in free alms,' was from now on the basic
unit of land held from the crown. This reorganization,

B

aimed at strengthening both the defence and the justice of the realm, was in all probability the work of Abbot Bernard; and Lord Cooper has recently shown that he was almost certainly responsible for the impassioned patriotism, the polished eloquence, of the Arbroath letter. It is possible, too (the evidence is ambiguous) that Robert should be regarded as the true founder of the Scots parliament, for burgesses may have been present at a meeting of the 'three estates' at Cambuskenneth in 1326. Finally, it was during this reign that the crown began the process of setting its burghs in feu to the burgesses themselves; Aberdeen in 1319 and Edinburgh in 1329 achieved 'feu-ferme' tenure, and in due course all the king's burghs attained, in a similar manner, their aim of financial autonomy.

There is an inglorious epilogue to the story, for the freedom of Scotland, seemingly secure in 1329, was again in jeopardy during the reign of a boy who grew up to be a worthless man. The iron will of Edward I had made the subjection of Scotland a cardinal point for the honour of England and had given his young and ambitious grandson a precedent which he might well consider it ignoble to disregard; the ignominy of the reign of Edward II demanded a revival of English military glory. Scotland was now governed by successive regents for the young David II, and the struggle was renewed with an invasion by Edward Balliol, the heir of John Balliol. The help given him by England was at first unavowed, but, after a Scottish defeat at Dupplin moor, near Perth, in August 1332, Balliol was crowned at Scone as the acknowledged vassal of Edward III of England. He was almost immediately driven out of Scotland, but the intervention of the English king and his victory at Halidon hill, outside Berwick, in July 1333, brought about a temporary restoration. David was sent to France for safety. Edward III's abandonment of his grandfather's final policy of annexation was only partial, for in 1334 Balliol ceded to his liege lord the counties of Edinburgh, Haddington, Linlithgow, Peebles, Roxburgh, Selkirk, Berwick and Dumfries. English officials began again to administer the land between Tweed and Forth.

The worst seemed to have happened, but the English partisans began to quarrel about the restoration of their lands, new Scottish leaders arose, and the ambitions of Edward III were transferred from Scotland to France. Scottish forces gained some minor successes, and, when Edward invaded the country in person, he was not given the chance of fighting a pitched battle. By 1341 Perth, Stirling and Edinburgh were again in Scottish keeping, and it was deemed safe to bring home David II, then a boy of seventeen.

The struggles of these years left their mark upon the history of Scotland. Although the tract of country ceded by Edward Balliol was largely recovered within a brief period, revivals of hostilities were inevitable, and it took nearly 130 years to expel the English from the south of Scotland. The powerful lord of the Isles had made terms with Balliol and had been granted a large territory, part of which belonged to Robert the Steward, grandson of Robert I through his daughter, Marjory Bruce, and heir-presumptive to the young king. David II at once cancelled these grants and forfeited some of the original possessions of the lord of the Isles. The grievance thus created led to frequent intrigues between successive lords of the Isles and the English. Further, it was during these years that the Franco-Scottish alliance came to be a factor of some importance in European politics. The French had given some encouragement to the Scots at the beginning of the struggle with England. The help that was rendered in the early years of David II, and the English attack upon the French, starting in the year 1337, gave Scotland and France a bond of union and a common interest. While the English held French and Scottish soil, a Franco-Scottish alliance was inevitable. On many occasions, the English tried to detach the Scots from the French, but it is difficult to blame Scottish statesmen for retaining a conviction that, if France were defeated, Scotland could not long remain safe.

Declining such blandishments in 1346, the Scots invaded England and were defeated at Neville's Cross, near Durham, where David II was captured. As a result of the battle, the

English reoccupied part of the Scottish territory which they had lost. Only in 1357, during a truce between England and France, was David II released, in return for the promise to pay an exorbitant ransom (part of which was never paid). David, who had been well treated during his captivity, paid a visit to London in 1363, and agreed to a treaty of perpetual peace with England and to the recognition of an English prince as the heir to the throne of Scotland. The Scots indignantly refused to sanction such a bargain, and the nation patiently continued its task of recovering territory held by the 'auld enemy.'

The main interest of the last fourteen years of David's reign lies, not in the fluctuating and indecisive military struggles against England, but in the constitutional developments brought about by the impoverished state of the country and the efforts made to pay off the ransom. Meetings of parliament and of the less formal general council were frequent, and burgesses, forming (after prelates and barons) the 'third estate,' were certainly present in the latter from 1357 and in the former from 1366; for their concurrence in the levying of taxes and in the quadrupling of the king's or great custom was deemed essential. To save members' time, the expedient was adopted of delegating parliamentary powers to commissions and committees, which were much smaller bodies, and this device was to become a leading, and an unfortunate, feature of constitutional development.

David's death was followed by the feeble reigns of the elderly Robert II (1371–90) and Robert III (1390–1406), the first kings of the house of Stewart. Intermittent warfare continued. There were invasions and counter-invasions in 1385, when a French force, under John de Vienne, assisted the Scots. The Douglases, stoutest defenders of the border, defeated the Percys at the battle of Otterburn, in 1388. The English gained two victories in 1402, at Nesbit moor and Homildon hill. Robert III, by now senile and ineffective, lost his elder son, David, duke of Rothesay, in 1402, in circumstances which pointed firmly to foul play; but he probably did not live long enough to hear of the capture by the English, at sea, of his other son, James, in 1406.

Robert, duke of Albany, brother of Robert III (who had repudiated his own unlucky name of John), was regent for the captive king, James I, from 1406 until his own death in 1420. He had to face a rebellion, in 1411, by Donald, lord of the Isles, who, in alliance with Henry IV of England, sought by force of arms to make good his claim to the earldom of Ross. His defeat at Harlaw obliged him to come to terms with the regent. Albany was succeeded in the title and the regency by his son, Murdoch Stewart, who brought the Franco-Scottish alliance to its climax by sending Scottish troops to aid the French against Henry V. John Stewart, earl of Buchan, a son of the elder Albany, with his Scottish soldiers, won the victory of Baugé in 1421, the first hope of a reversal of the verdict of Agincourt. Buchan was made constable of France, and he had some further successes in the war until he was killed, in 1424, at Verneuil, where he and Archibald, fourth earl of Douglas, who fell with him, held the centre of the French position with persistent courage.

James I was ransomed and released in 1424, and he returned to Scotland determined to introduce law and order—in his own words 'to make the key keep the castle and the bracken bush the cow.' He adopted a policy of merciless repression, and at once put to death the regent, the younger Albany, and two of his sons, imprisoned the lord of the Isles, and confiscated the estates of some Lowland magnates. Scottish troops continued to give valued assistance to the French in their efforts to oust the English from their land. In recognition of their services, the French king, Charles VII, instituted the famous corps of Scots Guards. At home, most of the south of Scotland was recovered by 1430, but the English still held Roxburgh castle and the coveted town of Berwick. Just before his murder at Perth, in 1437, at the hands of a group of noble malcontents, James put an end to a series of truces with England and made an effort to recover Roxburgh castle.

James did much to restore the power and prestige of the

monarchy, now sadly lapsed. A stern, almost a despotic, ruler, he was still in some sense a constitutionalist. Parliament met frequently and was used by the king for the overhaul and improvement of the machinery of government. A statute of 1426 decreed that the chancellor and certain discreet persons chosen from each estate should sit three times a year and determine all causes. Many acts in a similar sense were to follow, but over a century was to pass before an organized supreme court, with proper financial support, emerged. As with justice, so with parliamentary representation: James's legislation is a foreshadowing rather than an achievement. Another act of 1426 directed all freeholders of the crown, great and small, to attend parliament and general council in person. Then, in 1428, reversing his policy, the king decreed that only the greater tenants-in-chief would be summoned by writ, the other barons and freeholders being excused from attendance, provided they chose two commissioners to represent each shire (one only from Clackmannan and from Kinross); these commissioners were to elect a speaker on the English model. Both acts were inoperative, but that of 1428 resulted, in this and the following reigns, in the development of a new peerage, comprising the earls and the 'lords of parliament,' who owed attendance in person; while long after—in 1587—James's ideas in the matter of shire representation were finally carried out. Much useful, or at least well-intentioned, social and economic legislation was passed during the reign. 'Wappinschaws' (musters-in-arms) and the practice of archery were ordered, while football and poaching were forbidden. Costume and prices were regulated, and the interests of a mainly rural society are reflected in the statutes decreeing the hunting of wolves and the sowing of peas and beans.

James's policies and reforms were inspired, partly by his determination to foster the material well-being of his subjects, partly by his aim of asserting the authority of the crown over the greater barons, who had become, during four successive reigns of weak or absent kings, petty monarchs in their own domains. To them he hoped to find counter-poises in his own power, in the rule of law, in the politically-inclined lairds, and in a contented commonalty; but to their envy and pride he fell a victim at the end. Most notable among them were the Douglases, whose strength, growing steadily under the early Stewarts and spreading through the whole of the south of Scotland, was now such as to challenge that of the monarchy itself.

James II, like all the royal Stewarts down to James VI, succeeded to the throne while a minor. During his minority a grave blow was dealt at the Douglases by the regents, who murdered the young (sixth) earl and his brother, and thus brought about a division of the vast Douglas estates. But William, the eighth earl, married the heiress of such Douglas lands as he did not himself inherit, and the Douglas power seemed to be as great as ever when the young king began to govern in person. The inevitable trial of strength followed. James himself stabbed the eighth earl in 1452, when the Scottish Parliament took the view that the earl 'was guilty of his own death by resisting the king's gentle persuasions,' and he finally crushed the Douglases and their allies at Langholm in 1455. The central power was now stronger than it had been since the days of Robert I.

The last enterprise of the short life of James II was the siege of the castle of Roxburgh, the last English possession in Scotland except the town of Berwick. In August, 1460, as the king was watching the effect of a piece of artillery, the gun exploded, and he was killed, while still in his thirtieth year. The castle was taken a few days after his death, and its fall marks the end of the War of Independence, for no English garrison, except that of Berwick, was left on Scottish soil. It also marks the end of the period during which the Franco-Scottish alliance was a necessity for either country. The English had been expelled from France as well as from Scotland, and the kingdom of France was about to become, once again, a great European power. While both countries were struggling for freedom from a common invader, their interests were similar and their methods of co-operation were simple, but, when France developed into a great and aggressive power, with many interests of which the small

Scottish nation could know nothing, the alliance could be maintained only if Scotland were to become completely dependent upon France. The long tradition of the alliance persisted for exactly a century after 1460, led the Scots into one unhappy adventure, and afforded them protection at more than one period of danger, but its real significance belongs to the years between the death of Robert I in 1329 and the death of James II in 1460, when it played an important part in securing the freedom of both countries.

The influence of France during the later middle ages profoundly affected the development of Scottish civilization. Up to the War of Independence, Scotland had derived its legal and administrative systems from England, as also its manners and customs, and its architecture. Except for literature, the influence of England, after the War of Independence, was replaced by that of France. The record of Scottish progress during the War of Independence, if we regard it as covering the whole period from 1296 to 1460, is very remarkable. The country was able to wage almost continuous warfare, to pay (in part) heavy ransoms, to build, or rebuild, great religious houses, cathedrals and other churches, royal palaces, and baronial and episcopal castles. Learning was advanced by the foundation of two universities—St. Andrews in 1412 and Glasgow in 1451—and by the end of the fifteenth century a third, Aberdeen, was added to the number (1495). Trade and commerce were maintained and the towns began to recover a modest prosperity.

The reign of James III, which followed the fall of the house of Douglas and the recovery of Southern Scotland, was troubled and unhappy, but neither Scottish independence nor the Stewart dynasty was in danger. The years of the minority were unusually fortunate, partly because England was absorbed in the Wars of the Roses, and partly because, for five years after the death of James II, the regent was one of the few great statesmen whom Scotland produced in the middle ages—James Kennedy, bishop of St. Andrews, and the founder of St. Salvator's College in that university. The reconquest of the south of Scotland was completed by the surrender of Berwick, which was again a Scottish town from 1461 to 1482. James began his active reign in 1469 with fair prospects. Orkney and Shetland were annexed to the crown in 1472, in default of payment of the dowry of James's queen, Margaret of Denmark. In 1476 the king was able to put an end to the attempt of the last lord of the Isles to play at being an independent sovereign.

The troubles of the reign were connected with the personality of James III and with the disloyalty of his brother, Alexander, duke of Albany. James 'was one that loved solitariness, and desired never to hear of wars nor the fame thereof, but delighted mair in music and policy of building than in the government of his realm.' He made friends with musicians and architects, and quarrelled with his brothers, Albany and Mar. The latter died in prison and the former escaped to France in 1479, made a bargain with Edward IV of England, and invaded Scotland to claim the crown as a vassal king. In the course of this invasion the duke of Gloucester (afterwards Richard III) recovered Berwick-on-Tweed, in the summer of 1482, and it was while James was preparing to meet Albany that the Scottish nobles seized and hanged the royal favourites on Lauder bridge. Albany invaded the country again in 1484, in alliance with Richard III and the last earl of Douglas, who had been an exile in England. The attempt failed, Albany again escaped to France, and Douglas was captured and died a prisoner. The king remained unpopular, and he was slain in the course of another rebellion in the summer of 1488. His enemies professed loyalty to the house of Stewart, and asserted that they were merely trying to restrain a misguided monarch, and they brought his son and heir into their camp as evidence of their good intentions. The circumstance that, after their victory, they thought it necessary to obtain parliamentary approval of their conduct and to explain to the people of Scotland and to foreign nations that they had not been guilty of rebellion, indicates an increase in the prestige of the monarchy and of the dynasty since 1437.

The authority of the crown still further increased in

the reign of James IV (1488–1513), the Golden Age of Scotland after the War of Independence. James made the central power a reality even in the Highlands and Islands, and deprived the lord of the Isles of that title, which was annexed to the crown. He encouraged trade and commerce, and the report of a Spanish agent emphasizes the prosperity of the country in his time; the foreigner was impressed by the Edinburgh houses and their furniture and by the abundance of food (chiefly fish and mutton). Towards the end of his reign, James created a powerful Scottish navy. He played a considerable part in European politics. In his early years he adopted the cause of the pretender, Perkin Warbeck, and invaded England, but he ultimately married Margaret, elder daughter of Henry VII. The marriage treaty involved an English recognition (the first since 1328) of the independence of the Scottish crown, and it brought about, a century later, the Union of the Crowns of England and Scotland.

A marriage of a Scottish king to an English princess was not in itself a guarantee of peace, but the 'Union of the Thistle and the Rose' was felt to be an event of considerable significance. A people generally clings persistently to a traditional foreign policy, and no one could doubt that the French alliance had been, in the past, of crucial importance for the independence of Scotland. Was it still of such importance? When Henry VIII began to prepare for war with France, he wished, as his predecessors had wished, to obtain an assurance of Scottish neutrality. He and his brother-in-law had many causes of dispute. There were troubles in the Borders; English and Scottish sailors were in the habit of fighting at sea without much regard to diplomatic agreements; and Henry had failed to pay to his sister, Queen Margaret, a legacy left her by her father. On all these points, Henry was willing to give way, but James, remembering the past, was convinced that, if France were conquered, Scotland would immediately be attacked. It is easy for us to realize that France was in no such danger as he imagined; within a very brief period, Henry's sister was to marry the French king. But the European combination against France was formidable enough, and it is scarcely fair to blame James for going to war. The really remarkable thing is that there were Scottish statesmen who had begun to doubt whether it must always be in the interests of Scotland to ally with France against England, and that these opponents of the royal policy included the greatest Scotsman then living, William Elphinstone, bishop of Aberdeen, and the founder of its university, who himself owed much to France. It was a dispute between the older and the younger advisers of James IV; the voice of the young men was for war, and James listened to the words of the young men. In May 1513 a French ambassador brought from the French queen the famous message to her knight and a turquoise ring which was to be found on James's dead hand. Attempts, described in *Marmion*, were made to work upon his superstitious nature, but without avail, and on August 22 he led a great Scottish army to defeat. James fell at Flodden on September 9; in the words of a contemporary, 'God gave the stroke, and he was no more regarded than a poor soldier, for all went one way.' For Scotland, it was indeed the stroke of fate, but the valour displayed upon the stricken field saved the country from the extremity of disaster. Edinburgh prepared for a siege and ordered the townsmen to have their arms ready, and the women to cease weeping and wailing in the streets and to go to the churches to pray. But the victorious army was in no condition to undertake a siege. Flodden was, in one sense, the greatest of many Scottish defeats, and its dead were mourned for many a day. It deeply affected the internal history of the country, but its importance in international affairs is slight; the war dragged on until May 1515, but nothing happened more serious than border raids. The doubts entertained before Flodden as to whether it was necessarily in the interests of Scotland to fight for France against England survived the battle and the defeat. They were expressed in the *History of Greater Britain*, published in Paris in 1521 by the great

Schoolman, John Major, a Scotsman who owed much to France. 'The Scots,' he wrote, 'ought to prefer no king to the English king in the marriage of an heiress (of the crown), and I am of the same opinion as to the English in a similar case. In this way alone would two hostile kingdoms, flourishing in the same island, of which neither can subdue the other, be united under one king,' and he went on to expound the advantages of union. Major's view cannot have been generally held, but it indicates a new stage in Anglo-Scottish relations.

The death of James IV at the age of forty, and the accession of James V in his second year, heralded another disturbed minority. In 1514 the queen-mother and regent, Margaret Tudor, married the earl of Angus, the head of a cadet line of the house of Douglas, which had risen to power on the ruin of the elder branch. The French offer to send to Scotland the duke of Albany, the son of the traitor duke of the reign of James III, was accepted in 1515. Margaret and Angus fled to England, where she bore to Angus a daughter who was brought up in that country, married the earl of Lennox, and became the mother of the unfortunate Darnley. Albany was an unsatisfactory regent, and was often absent from the country. He finally left Scotland in 1524, and Angus, long estranged from the fickle queen-mother, came into power in 1526, the year in which he ceased to be her husband. The severance of their marriage did not diminish her hatred, and in 1528 James V, still a boy of fifteen, undertook the government and banished Angus, forfeiting his estates. The young king thus began his rule by offending a powerful section of the nobility, and the measures which he took to establish law and order in the course of his short reign made for him many more enemies among his nobles. Alienated from the nobility, he relied upon the support of the bishops, whom he employed in great offices usually held by laymen. It was a fateful decision, for it committed the Scottish crown to the support of the powers of tradition and reaction against the forces of religious revolution that were gathering, or about to gather, throughout Christendom. It marks, as accurately as any single measure can mark, the end of the middle ages for the kingdom of Scotland.

To an unusual degree, the progress and well-being of the medieval state and nation were bound up with the personality of the reigning monarch. In one respect, the Stewart dynasty was extremely unlucky, for, while the two Roberts were senile and ineffective, each of the five Jameses succeeded as a minor and met a violent death in the prime of manhood. They did, however, enjoy good fortune in that the line of succession was clear and undisputed; though thin, it held, and the royal house did not suffer the embarrassment of throwing off collateral branches to challenge, generation after generation, the central power of the kingdom. It is, moreover, easy to dwell too much on the baronial feuds and the disturbed minorities, and to forget the enduring elements of strength in the state and the solid advances in the rule of law. Each of the boy-kings did, after all, survive his minority; and in turn the Albanys, the Douglases and the lords of the Isles were humbled by their royal masters.

The machinery of government was developed and improved towards the close of the middle ages. The full parliament or a general council (just beginning to be called a convention of estates) was at least consulted on important affairs of state—legislation, taxation and *haute justice*. The three estates (prelates, nobles and burgesses) attended regularly, though it is true that they committed most of their powers to the lords of the articles. (The parliamentary records are defective, but it would seem that the characteristic device of cross-election, whereby the nobles chose the six or eight prelates, while the clergy chose the same number from the nobility, was in use by 1525 for the election of the lords of the articles.) The nation was not wealthy, and the accepted theory was that 'the king should live of his own'; a 'stent' or tax was rarely granted, and then the clergy paid one-half, the nobles one-third, and the burghs one-sixth. It was a papal grant to the crown that made possible the institution, in 1532, of the Court of Session or College of Justice, comprising a president and fourteen other lords, and exercising supreme jurisdiction in civil cases.

Medieval Scotland made advances in other directions. Cultural achievement will be considered later (see Chapter 10); but the reorganization of the Scottish Church is a reminder that baronial turbulence and sudden death do not tell the whole story. St. Andrews was made a metropolitan see by a papal bull of 1472, which also brought the bishoprics of Orkney, the Isles and Galloway into the Scottish system. Twenty years later Glasgow likewise became an archbishopric, and the final arrangement incorporated Galloway, Argyll and the Isles within its provincial jurisdiction.

Progress in the arts of peace is indicated by the introduction of the printing press and the establishment of the Royal College of Surgeons, both dating from James IV's reign. The increasing importance of trade and industry is reflected in the regulation and definition of burghal privilege. The royal burghs—the style dates only from the fifteenth century—paid the burghal share of stents and formed the burgess estate; in return, they engrossed the exclusive right to foreign trade. Numbering some 45 by the early sixteenth century, they developed their own deliberative and legislative assembly, the Convention of Royal Burghs. Meanwhile, the lesser sea-ports and market towns were being recognized, in a series of royal charters commencing in 1450, as 'burghs in barony' (later 'burghs of barony'). By the mid-sixteenth century there were about a hundred of this subsidiary class of municipality, which, with their craftsmen, weekly markets and annual fairs, met, in some degree, the economic needs of rural and semi-rural Scotland.

The total population of the country in 1500 may be guessed at something like 750,000. The towns were not large. Edinburgh, much the biggest of them, may have had about 20,000 inhabitants; but Arbroath is estimated to have had only 1,000 in 1517, Stirling not more than 2,000 in 1544, and Glasgow about 4,500 in 1560, though

these three were among the twenty largest burghs. It
follows that a majority of the ancient burghs had only
a few hundred inhabitants. Yet trade was maintained,
despite civil commotions, with the Low Countries, with
the Baltic and French ports, and with England and Ireland.
From Leith, Dundee, Aberdeen, Inverness, Ayr and other
ports, wool and wool-fells, skins and hides, cloth, salmon
and herring were shipped, and occasionally sea-coal and
grain; return cargoes included timber, iron, tar and salt,
flax and hemp, wines, spices, and dyestuffs, fine cloths,
silk and manufactures. The picture that presents itself
is that of a small, remote, and not naturally fertile country
making a gallant and not unsuccessful effort to maintain
a civilized and satisfactory way of life, while manfully
defending its right to national independence.

Chapter 2

Reformation and Union

BEFORE James V assumed personal rule, Scotland had witnessed a few protests and revolts against the Church. James Resby, an English Wycliffite, had been burnt as a heretic in 1407, as had Paul Crawar, a Hussite, in 1433. James IV had laughingly dismissed the thirty 'Lollards of Kyle' in 1494, but in 1528 Patrick Hamilton, abbot of Ferne, met his death as a Lutheran critic of the established order. What evoked the denunciations of these men was the inordinate wealth of a Church which had, in many ways, departed from spiritual grace. In a poor country, the greater abbeys and bishoprics afforded rich livings to the favoured few, who were generally well-born and whose ambitions were often entirely secular; meanwhile, the country parishes were served by under-paid curates and the bulk of the parochial revenues were diverted elsewhere, particularly through the 'appropriation' of rents and teinds for the maintenance of monasteries, cathedrals and collegiate churches. The ground was thus prepared for a violent change.

In the 1530s, as James V decided in favour of a pro-clerical policy, contemporary events in England brought fresh elements into Scottish politics. Henry VIII broke with the Pope and enriched himself and many of his subjects from the spoils of the monasteries. Isolated in Europe, he urged his nephew to follow his example. The Scottish nobles liked the English precedent, but the clergy became enthusiastic advocates of the French alliance. James declined the hand of his cousin, Mary Tudor, and married, first, a daughter of Francis I and, after her death, another French lady, Mary of Guise. Relations with England became strained. Henry VIII began to invite his nephew to personal meetings on

English soil, his object being to kidnap him. James, who had been kidnapped in his youth and may have suspected his uncle's benevolent designs, refused to go to discuss the possibility of suppressing the monasteries. Their revenues were large, and might well have been a temptation, for, though the kings of Scots possessed wide tracts of land, they were far from rich. They depended upon crown lands, feudal dues, great customs, and burgh fermes (or rents). Henry despised a relative who was blind to the Providence which put money within his grasp, and he lost patience, broke off friendly relations, and sent an army to invade Scotland.

The first effect of the Reformation movement was thus to render the Scottish government more dependent than ever upon the French alliance. But, when James proposed to make a counter-invasion of England, he found that his nobles declined to support him in what they called a French war. Their opposition does not find an adequate explanation either in personal resentment or in jealousy of the influence exercised over the king by Cardinal Beaton and the clergy, and by an unpopular favourite, Oliver Sinclair. The dissolution of the English monasteries, and James's defence of the Scottish religious orders, were probably the most potent causes of the alienation of the nobles from the sovereign. Reformed doctrine had by this date made some headway in Scotland, but the Scottish nobles of 1542 were not devout Protestants; their eyes were fixed on the spoils of the Church. Ignorant of Henry's real intentions, they blamed James for not going to York to meet his uncle, and left him to depend on the troops furnished by Beaton and the ecclesiastical party. James, in bad health, did not accompany the small Scottish force to the field. Enclosed between the river Esk and Solway moor, it was routed (November 24, 1542). James returned to Falkland, where he died on December 14, at the age of thirty. Six days earlier, his daughter Mary had been born at Linlithgow. 'It came wi' a lass and it will gang wi' a lass,' said the dying king, remembering how the crown had come to his unhappy house.

The gradual spread of reformed doctrine and the temptaiton to seize the church lands gave a great, and misused, opportunity for English diplomacy. James V's will, appointing Cardinal Beaton as one of the regents, was declared to be forged, and the regency was conferred upon the earl of Arran, as heir-presumptive to the baby queen. Arran was known to incline to Protestantism, and he was a greedy noble eager to improve the fortunes of his family. Under Arran's influence, Parliament passed an act legalizing the circulation of the scriptures 'in the vulgar tongue,' and agreed to a treaty for the marriage of the queen of Scots to the prince of Wales (1543). But Henry, behaving with foolish insolence, threatened violence, and Arran recanted his Protestant opinions and was reconciled with Beaton. An encounter between English and Scottish ships afforded an excuse for denouncing the marriage treaty (1544).

Even yet, if Henry had been patient, he might have won in the end. Arran and Beaton were not likely to continue to be friendly, the inducement to dissolve the monasteries during a minority of the crown remained very powerful, and the spread of the Reformation was creating a new link with England. But Henry at once made the breach complete and for that generation irrevocable, and he incidentally determined Mary's fate by securing that she should grow up a Frenchwoman. He sent the earl of Hertford (afterwards Protector Somerset) to crush resistance ruthlessly, and English armies ravaged Scotland in 1544 and 1545. The French alliance again became essential for the safety of the country, and when, in 1546, a body of Scottish Protestants murdered Cardinal Beaton in revenge for the martyrdom of George Wishart, and seized his castle of St. Andrews, they held it with English help until it was retaken for the Scottish government, in July 1547, by a force largely composed of French troops.

Henry VIII had died in the preceding January, but Somerset, against his own better judgment, carried on the policy of his master, and employed force in an attempt to sever the Franco-Scottish league. In this aim he completely failed, though he won some military reputation by his victory at Pinkie in September 1547, the last of the old battles between England and Scotland. An appeal to the Scots for a union with England, made after the battle, was naturally rejected, and Arran arranged a marriage between the child-queen and the Dauphin, afterwards Francis II, and in August 1548 sent her to France, where she remained for thirteen years. Meanwhile French troops helped the Scots to recover strongholds occupied by English garrisons until, in 1550, Scotland was included in a peace between France and England. The French had saved Scotland from a grave danger, and the Auld Alliance seemed to be cemented more firmly than ever. But Scotland now needed France so much more than France needed Scotland that there could be no real alliance; the small country must be dependent upon the great one. Further, the cartloads of Bibles which the English invaders are recorded to have brought with them gave a fresh impetus to Scottish Protestantism, and the traditional unpopularity of French troops in Scotland was increased by the German mercenaries whom they brought with them.

In July 1553 Mary Tudor succeeded to the English throne, and in April 1554 the queen-mother, Mary of Guise, became regent for her daughter. If these two ladies, both devout Roman Catholics, could have made an Anglo-Scottish alliance, the current of history might have been changed, but Mary of England was a Spaniard and the enemy of France. The persecution in England created a fresh bond of sympathy between English and Scottish Protestants, and made the latter determined to bring about a religious revolution while the Scottish queen was still in France. The queen-mother was surrounded by French advisers, and a Frenchman shared the chancellorship with the earl of Huntly. It was useless for Parliament to legislate against slanderers of the regent and of the allies who had come 'for the common weal and suppressing the auld enemies.' There were popular outbreaks against the French garrisons, and the nobles forced Mary of Guise to disband a French army assembled for an invasion of England. The marriage of Queen Mary to the Dauphin in April 1558 rather injured than helped the French cause. The crown matri-, monial—a French conception—was conferred upon Francis, and there was a suspicion, now known to have been well-founded, that Mary had been induced to sign agreements inimical to Scottish independence. The Protestant party found 'Scotland a province of France' a potent argument against the regent.

By 1557, the Scottish Protestants had grown so strong that they formed themselves into a militant league, known as the Congregation, and drew up the first National Covenant for the establishment of the reformed faith. There were isolated attacks upon church buildings in 1558, but hostilities did not begin until the following year. By that time, Elizabeth was on the English throne, and Francis and Mary, who became king and queen of France in the summer of 1559, had antagonized her by putting forward Mary's claim to the English crown as the senior legitimate representative of the line of Henry VII. The Protestants could therefore look to England for help, and in 1559 they secured a great leader by the return of John Knox to Scotland. Mary of Guise chose this moment for denouncing the Protestant leaders as heretics, and they took up arms against her. Assured of English help, they declared that she was deposed from the regency, and published a Latin manifesto asserting that the main ground of their action was 'the insolence and intolerable oppression' of the French. But religion was by that date the real point at issue, and religious zeal had so far overcome the ancient enmity to England that the Protestants invited Elizabeth to 'accept the realm of Scotland into her protection and maintenance,' for their preservation during the time of their queen's marriage. Such protection was guaranteed by the treaty of Berwick (February 1560), which completed the diplomatic revolution and was the prelude to the entry into Scotland of the English forces as friends and allies.

The death of Mary of Guise in June led to a truce, deprived the crown of any real authority, and transferred political power to the militant Protestants. The lords of the Congregation saw their opportunity and resolved to obtain parliamentary sanction for the reformed faith. The Parliament of August 1560, irregularly convened, was still representative of a large and insistent body of public opinion, and its acts became the effective law of the land. It abolished the authority of the Pope, forbade, under an ultimate penalty of death for a third offence, the celebration of mass, and recognized Protestantism as the only legal form of belief. A Confession of Faith drawn up by John Knox and his colleagues was ratified by Parliament, but the problems of the organization of the Church and of the destination of ecclesiastical property, much of which had been already secularized, were left for future settlement. A Convention of Estates refused in January 1561 either to sanction the constitution of the Church as submitted in the First Book of Discipline or to transfer to it any substantial share of the old ecclesiastical revenues, for which there were many eager claimants. The result was disastrous for the Scottish Parliament. The Church, not yet presbyterian, developed an organization under a supreme court known as the General Assembly. Such an assembly was the natural successor of the old provincial councils of the Church in Scotland, but the new General Assembly differed from them in including laymen in its membership and in the possession of supreme authority. The Assembly was more closely in touch with public opinion than the Parliament, with its feudal constitution, could possibly be, and its subjects of debate were those which, for many years to come, most interested the people of the Lowlands. The refusal of the Convention of 1561 to concede the demands of the Church was regarded as a betrayal by Knox and his followers, and it created a definite breach between the Assembly and the Parliament.

In August 1561, Mary, a young widow, returned to Scotland and had no alternative to a recognition of the ecclesiastical and diplomatic revolutions. Her great ambition was the union of Scotland and England through her succession to Elizabeth (who was nine years her senior). But Elizabeth took full advantage of the situation. Fearing that Mary might marry into the house of Hapsburg and thus invite a Spanish attack upon England, she warned her that the Scottish succession would be barred in the event of an undesirable marriage, and she held out hopes of a recognition if she married in accordance with her wishes. Elizabeth's mastery is shown by the fact that for four years she prevented Mary from marrying anybody.

During these years, Mary acted with the Protestant party and was guided by the advice of her illegitimate half-brother, whom she created earl of Moray. Any attempt to restore papal authority, as the English Mary had done, was out of the question. The nobles were not likely to surrender the church lands or to resign the pensions with which Elizabeth bribed them in order to please their girl sovereign, and the utmost that Mary could seriously hope for was the toleration that Knox was determined to prevent. Yet the fascination of her personality was creating a queen's party in Scotland when she made an unhappy marriage which alienated many who might have been her friends. Her cousin, Henry, lord Darnley, stood next to herself in the succession to the English crown, and after the Hamiltons in the succession to the crown of Scotland, but her decision to marry him (July 1565) was dictated by passion rather than policy.

Elizabeth at once declared herself offended, and Moray raised a rebellion. The people rallied to Mary's side and Moray fled to England to be disowned and supported by Elizabeth, who was attempting to bring about her 'dear sister's' ruin. A year later she had another opportunity. Darnley, a petulant and sulky boy, was offended by his wife's refusal to give him the crown matrimonial, and, friendless in Scotland, he blamed all on the influence of Mary's private secretary, an Italian named David Rizzio. Darnley entered into a conspiracy with a group of Scottish nobles. Rizzio was to be murdered and Mary imprisoned, Moray and his fellow-exiles were to return and Darnley was to govern Scotland. Elizabeth well knew, what Darnley was foolish enough not to understand, that the nobles had no intention of removing Mary to make way for her detested husband. Only two of the objects of the conspiracy were actually carried out. Rizzio was brutally murdered in the presence of the queen, then far advanced in pregnancy. She was duly imprisoned, but she obtained an interview with her husband,

and persuaded him that he had nothing to expect from his accomplices, and together they escaped from Holyrood (March 1566). Again public opinion and public support rallied to the queen, and the Rizzio murderers fled to Elizabeth. Moray and his friends had arrived in Edinburgh the morning after the murder, and her brother made his peace with Mary.

Mary was fully aware of her husband's treason, and the birth of their son, James, in June 1566 failed to reconcile the unhappy parents. Mary would not seek an annulment of her marriage, since this might jeopardize her baby's claim to the English throne. Darnley had incurred the bitter enmity of the nobility, and there was a widespread conspiracy against him. His destruction was inevitable, but it need not have involved the ruin of his wife, if she had not married the earl of Bothwell in May 1567, some three months after the murder of Darnley, in which he was known to have taken an active share. Mary's guilt or innocence is a matter of biographical rather than historical importance. There were those in Scotland who were determined to get rid of her as well as of Darnley; if there was an under-plot in the form of a domestic intrigue between Mary and Bothwell, the queen was unconsciously fulfilling the aims of her worst enemies. The 'Casket Letters' are the only (and dubious) evidence for this; it may be that Mary knew merely that her nobles were engaged in a plot against the husband whom she had good reason to hate, and that she had no reason to suspect Bothwell of larger guilt than the rest of them. One thing is certain—that the device of a gunpowder explosion was adopted in order to advertise to the country and the world that Darnley had been murdered. He was recovering from a serious illness and poison (about which that age knew something) would have been the natural resort of a guilty wife and her paramour, if they alone were concerned. Long afterwards, the nobles accused each other of a share in the murder, and one of them, the earl of Morton, suffered for it on the scaffold.

Mary was, however, discredited by the Bothwell marriage, and, when Moray raised another rebellion, she was without support. In June 1567 she surrendered to her enemies at Carberry hill, near Musselburgh. Imprisoned in Loch Leven castle, she was forced to abdicate and to nominate Moray as regent for her son. Escaping in the summer of 1568, she found herself at the head of an army in which there were many Protestants; but, defeated by Moray at Langside, on the outskirts of Glasgow, and misled by a previous invitation by Elizabeth, she took refuge on English soil, to find herself a prisoner for life. But there was still a queen's party in Scotland, and civil war continued through the regencies of the earl of Moray, who was assassinated in January 1570, the earl of Lennox (Darnley's father), who was killed in a skirmish at Stirling in September 1571, and the earl of Mar, who died in October 1572. Mar was succeeded by Morton, who, with English help, ended the war by capturing Edinburgh castle, the queen's last stronghold (May 29, 1573). All the regents were dependent upon English support, for Elizabeth could always threaten to release Mary. This was probably her main reason for imprisoning the Scottish queen, a decision dishonourable to the woman who had invited her, and without justification except as a matter of English policy. But the English Roman Catholics, who had submitted peacefully to the rule of a heretic, found their patience strained when the usurper imprisoned the lady whom they regarded as their rightful sovereign, and, from the time of Mary's captivity, Elizabeth had to face conspiracy and rebellion.

During the regency of Morton, the dispute between Church and State in Scotland, to the origin of which we have already referred, underwent a significant development. While the civil war was in progress, the king's party was dependent upon the elements in the nation most deeply interested in the security of the Protestant faith. The first parliament which met (December 1567) after the deposition of Mary, ratified the ecclesiastical legislation of 1560, recognized the jurisdiction of the Protestant church courts, and promised to define that jurisdiction and to make financial provision for the ministry. Partly in order to secure the revenues of the old dioceses, and partly in order to establish a system of local ecclesiastical administration, the reformed Church developed a tendency towards a modified form of episcopacy; the bishops were to be administrative officers and not a superior order of clergy. Morton feared the use which an adequately endowed church might make of the powers it claimed to possess. It held ecclesiastical authority, the power of the keys, to be distinct in its nature and operation from the office of the civil magistrate, 'not having a temporal head on earth.' The establishment of a theocracy was a real danger when ecclesiastical questions were the politics of the day, and Morton not only wished to prevent this development, but also, as a greedy and unscrupulous baron, was anxious to use the episcopal revenues as endowments for the great families, a purpose they had served before the Reformation. His exercise of ecclesiastical patronage convinced the Church that claims on bishoprics which would be merely appanages of the nobility were not worth preserving, and about the same time a new ecclesiastical leader appeared in the person of Andrew Melville. He taught the essential 'parity' of all ministers, denounced the episcopal office as unscriptural, and, adapting precedents familiar in reformed churches on the Continent, urged upon the Church the establishment of the court known as the presbytery or classical assembly (the assembly of a classis or division) to supply an efficient system of local ecclesiastical administration. The Melvillian policy was accepted by the General Assembly, and from about 1581 the Church in Scotland became Presbyterian; but there remained a minority who desired to have some kind of episcopacy, and on this issue the long battle between Church and State was to be fought.

Morton had been a doubtful friend to the Church, but his forced resignation in 1578 was regarded as a blow to the Protestant cause, the full force of which was brought home when the late regent was beheaded in June 1581. The king, a precocious lad of fifteen, had meanwhile assumed the government and fallen under the influence of a kinsman, Esmé Stewart, who had been brought up in France as a Roman Catholic. The king conferred upon him the title of duke of Lennox, announced his favourite's conversion to the reformed faith, and invited signatures to a new National Covenant, which was known as 'the King's Confession' and was directed against the 'usurped authority of that Roman Antichrist' (January 1581). Suspicion was not allayed, and a group of Protestant nobles, with the full approval of the General Assembly, seized the king's person in the Raid of Ruthven (August 1582). James eluded his captors in the summer of 1583, and at once took up the Assembly's challenge. He accused Andrew Melville of treason and persuaded an obedient parliament to pass the 'Black Acts' of 1584, which gave the crown authority over the Church, forbade the meeting of ecclesiastical courts without royal leave, and assigned administrative duties to bishops selected by the crown. The king's victory followed the suppression of a rebellion, and in the course of the next ten years he lost ground in his struggle with the Assembly. He was very poor, and in 1585 he made a league with England in return for a pension. In view of the menace from Spain, Elizabeth was anxious about the attitude of Scotland, whose harbours might serve as a base for a Spanish Armada; it is true that she chose this moment for putting his mother to death (February 1587), but she did so only after ascertaining that James would 'digest' the insult and give the world an example of manly resignation. His main interest, like his mother's, was the English succession; he realized that the Scottish claim would be ignored if Mary should be its representative when Elizabeth died, and the health of the English queen did not promise the longevity to which she ultimately (and, in James's view, unnecessarily) attained.

Friendship with England tended towards the establishment of better relations with Scottish Protestantism, and the poverty of the crown inspired James to take a step which he soon came to regret. In 1587 he annexed all ecclesiastical property to the crown, including episcopal revenues. As his bishops possessed no episcopal orders and had no commission from the Church, even as administrators, the seizure of diocesan property amounted, as James afterwards understood, to 'the indirect abolition of the estate of bishops.' Having thus dealt a blow to his own ecclesiastical policy, he entered into a series of intrigues with Catholic powers which aroused grave suspicion in Scotland and might have prevented his accession to the English throne. His opponents gained strength, and, when James left Scotland for some months in 1589, to bring home a Danish bride, he depended upon the Church for the preservation of peace and order. On his return, there were further intrigues with Spain, the crown fell into disrepute, and the Church was strong enough to extort from James in 1592 a statute, known as the Golden Act, by which parliamentary sanction was given for the first time to the presbyteries, and the royal supremacy was limited by a recognition of 'the privilege that God has given to the spiritual office-bearers in the Kirk.'

James, however, was biding his time and probably felt that he was giving his opponents rope enough. At the end of 1596 the Church leaders adopted an extreme and, indeed, untenable position, and James took full advantage of his opportunity. A Convention of Estates reasserted the royal supremacy over the Church, and James in 1597 enjoyed his first success in attempting to manipulate the Assembly itself. He obtained from a body of commissioners of the Church a request that the clerical estate should be represented in parliament, and he summoned a parliament to give effect to the demand. The act which followed ordered that 'such pastors and ministers . . . as at any time his majesty shall please to provide to the office, place, title, and dignity of a bishop, abbot, or other prelate, shall at all times hereafter have vote in parliament.' The 'abbots' of the period were lay grantees of monastic revenues, many of whom found their way into the peerage; the importance of the act lay in the legal recognition of the rights of a bishop. The 'bishops' whom James appointed had no episcopal orders, but he persuaded a General Assembly to confer upon them, under the title of 'commissioners,' some administrative authority. Thus, before his accession to the throne of England, James had laid the foundation of the ecclesiastical policy which he was to live to see triumphant over the parity on which Melville and his followers insisted.

The Union of the Crowns greatly increased the prestige of the monarchy in Scotland (March 25, 1603). Appreciating the worth of the Tudor device of government by council, James VI and I applied the lesson to his native kingdom, where the Privy Council became the sole executive and, to some extent, the legislature. Parliament almost always respected his wishes, and its traditional subservience was confirmed by the king's deft manipulation of the Lords of the Articles, a small and manageable 'business committee' with a composition not unlike that of the Privy Council. To exercise the functions of a local magistracy, he imported the English office of justice of the peace in 1609. Already the Borders had become 'the Middle Shires,' patrolled by mounted police and administered by an Anglo-Scottish commission (1605). In 1609, too, the Statutes of Icolmkill bound many island chiefs to accept the reformed faith, disarmament, Lowland education, and the duty of maintaining order within their districts. Even the earldom of Orkney was annexed to the crown, the last Stewart earl being beheaded in 1615. Beyond the seas, the plantation of Ulster by Scottish Presbyterians began in 1610, and an even more ambitious colonial scheme, the settlement of Acadia or Nova Scotia, was launched in 1621, though it is true that it was frustrated by French claims and French power, and had as its chief result the institution of Nova Scotia baronetcies.

Profiting from the security and resources afforded by his residence in London, James thus enjoyed greater powers than any of his ancestors and was able to deal with subversive elements which had too often triumphed over earlier monarchs. He realized from the first that the regal union ought to be followed by a union of the kingdoms. 'Those two kingdoms,' he said, 'are so conjoined that, if we should sleep in our beds, the union should be, though we would not.' In his first speech to an English Parliament, he urged a complete union of the two countries, and commissioners were appointed to discuss the question. The opposition came mainly from England; one of the Scottish commissioners, the great feudal lawyer, Sir Thomas Craig, has left on record

that, in his talks with his English colleagues, he found them
'frankly indignant that our countrymen should have equality
in honours and employment, their own reputation and
resources being so much the greater.' For a century, this
English attitude remained the stumbling block over which
successive negotiations came to grief—in 1604, in 1670, and
in 1702. All that James could obtain from his English
Parliament was the repeal of the laws which treated Scotland
as a hostile country; by a judicial decision, based upon the
prerogative of the crown, he secured that Scotsmen born
after March 24, 1603, were not aliens in England, and the
Scottish Parliament made a similar concession for the king's
English subjects. By proclamation he assumed the title of
King of Great Britain, and by a further use of the prerogative
he gave Scottish trade something like commercial freedom in
England.

His ambition of uniting the two kingdoms made James the
more anxious to establish uniformity of church government
by the introduction of a real episcopacy into Scotland, and
he pursued his conflict with the General Assembly. He
proscribed its meetings and he found a pretext for depriving
it of its leader, Andrew Melville, who, after being kept for
some years in restraint in England, was allowed to go into
exile in tolerant France, as a professor in the University
of Sedan. Parliament revoked the Act of 1587, annexing
episcopal revenues to the crown, and re-asserted the royal
prerogative over all persons and causes, ecclesiastical as well
as civil. The Linlithgow Assembly of 1606 accepted the
king's plan of naming each bishop as 'constant moderator'
of his synod, and in 1609 Parliament restored the ancient
episcopal jurisdiction in spiritual causes. These measures
were defended as essential for the proper execution of the
penal laws against Roman Catholics, and they were approved
by a nominated Assembly, which stipulated only that the
bishops should be subject to its censure, though they could
not be dismissed without the royal consent. The Assembly
at the same time appointed a penalty of deprivation for any
minister who preached on the parity of the clergy, the central
tenet of Presbyterianism.

Up till now the Scottish bishops had been merely administrative officials, but in 1610 James introduced an episcopal succession from England. There had always been in the Church of Scotland a party favourable to a modified form of episcopacy, and it was only a modified form that James, by a series of clever and unscrupulous tricks, succeeded in introducing. The provincial synod became a diocesan synod, and the General Assembly was rarely summoned; its authority had been in great measure transferred to the bishops and to a Court of High Commission on the English model. But the local church courts—the kirk session and the presbytery—still met and still exercised adequate authority within their own bounds. The ritual of the early reformed Church was maintained, and no attempt was made to interfere with the use of John Knox's Book of Common Order or to prohibit extemporary prayers. James had grafted bishops on to a presbyterian system. The clergy were indignant at the loss of their power, but laymen were content with the familiar local courts of the Church and with the retention of their traditional ritual. If no further steps had been taken, there is every indication that the Jacobean compromise would have endured. The younger ministers, as they grew up, were less vehemently opposed to the existence of bishops than the older generation, which had witnessed the long struggle and the royal triumph.

Some years later, James endangered the success of his policy by an attempt to introduce, by the Five Articles of Perth, some modifications of presbyterian ritual. These included the adoption of a kneeling posture at communion, and the observance of Christmas, Good Friday, Easter, Ascension Day, and Whitsunday. A nominated Assembly, which met at Perth in 1618, sanctioned these innovations, and its decisions were confirmed by Parliament. In the north-east of Scotland, where, alone in the Lowlands, the episcopal party was strong, the Articles were observed; elsewhere, they led to irreverent wranglings in church, and to the deprivation of ministers and the prosecution of recusant laymen. The Court of High Commission could not secure obedience to the law. James's attempt to legislate for the Church on points of ritual had re-opened the old quarrel on an untenable ground. In spite of some explosions of the royal temper, there are indications that he realized his mistake, and, in his last years, refusals to conform to the Five Articles were frequently ignored.

Charles I's reign opened on a note of drastic change. His Act of Revocation (October 1625), though in traditional form, was unusually comprehensive. It threatened the resumption by the crown of all grants of land made by it since 1542, and these included most of the gifts of old church lands. The king's plans also called for a reformation of the system of 'teinds' or tithes, now largely in the hands of lay owners or 'titulars,' and for the provision from the teinds of a 'competent maintenance' for the ministry. In 1626 he began the legal process of 'reducing' or annulling many titles to ecclesiastical lands and teinds. In 1629, after prolonged negotiations, the nobles and other 'lords of erection' were confirmed in the possession, under crown superiority, of their lands, and provision was made for buying up the titulars' rights. A minimum stipend of 8 chalders of victual or 800 merks was proposed in 1627 and approved in 1633, when, also, Charles adopted the device (started by James in 1617) of naming a parliamentary commission, drawn from the four estates, for the valuation of teinds and the plantation of kirks. These great changes were, in part at least, statesman-like in conception and, from the point of view of the Church, of enduring worth, but Charles's revolutionary aims and brusque methods had gone far to alienate his natural supporters, the nobles. This is in marked contrast to the cautious wisdom of his father, who had used the lands at the disposal of the crown to ensure the loyalty and subservience of the great landowners.

Charles's taste for sweeping reforms grew with his experience of authority. The privy council and the bench of bishops were now his to command, and his visit to Scotland in 1633 convinced him of the need to remodel the liturgy of the Church and to remove the remaining elements of presbytery from its constitution. His measures to this end culminated in the publication of a book of canons in 1635–36 and of a prayer book in 1637; both were issued by royal authority and without the sanction of the Assembly, which had not met since 1618. The canons assumed a fully episcopal government and the disappearance of kirk session and presbytery, for the duties of which other provision was made; and they prohibited, under penalty of deprivation, the use of extemporary prayer. The new Scottish Prayer Book was based on the English Book of Common Prayer, but included alterations that were regarded in Scotland as 'plain proofs of Popery.' The changes in ritual and government were deeply disliked by laity as well as clergy, and they were resented as being English in origin and Popish in spirit, and as being forced by the State upon the Church. The reading of the prayer book in St. Giles' Cathedral, in Edinburgh, on Sunday, July 23, 1637, produced a riot which was the beginning of a revolution.

No revolution is explicable by a single formula, and there are other considerations which account for the significance of what might have been an isolated outbreak. Noblemen, lairds, judges and merchants had all been alienated by the earlier events of the reign, and opposition to the king's will was encouraged by the situation of his affairs in England, and by the gradual formation of an alliance between the Scottish Presbyterians and the English Puritans. The riot in St. Giles was followed by the enthusiastic signature of the National Covenant, a revival of the covenants of 1557 and 1581, and Charles was compelled to assent to the meeting of a 'free' General Assembly, in Glasgow, in November 1638. The Assembly was free only in the sense that it was not nominated by the crown: instead, it was dominated by the Covenanters. The Assembly defied the king and deposed the bishops, and in the spring of 1639 sent the young earl of Montrose to enforce the Covenant upon the reluctant inhabitants of Aberdeenshire. Alexander Leslie, a veteran of the wars of Gustavus Adolphus, was placed in command of an army on the Borders. Charles's raw English levies were unable to meet a body of trained soldiers, many of whom had fought in Germany, and a truce was negotiated. Another Assembly defied the king, and in August 1640 Leslie and Montrose dispersed a royalist force at Newburn and seized Newcastle. In the interval, the meeting, and the dissolution, of the Short Parliament had proved that the king's English opponents sympathized with the Scots, and that Charles could not hope to obtain parliamentary sanction for raising troops to suppress the Scottish rebellion. The presence of a Scottish army in England was, for the moment, not resented; it was regarded as a guarantee of English liberties, and it compelled Charles to summon the Long Parliament in order to get rid of it, by payment or by fighting.

As the struggle between king and parliament developed in England, Charles resolved to attempt to obtain Scottish support against his English opponents, and in the summer of 1641 he visited Edinburgh, gave way on all the points at issue with such facility as to arouse suspicion of his intentions, and loaded his Scottish enemies with honours. Meanwhile, Scottish commissioners resident in London became convinced that England desired the establishment of presbytery, and they adopted the ideal of James and Charles—compulsory uniformity of church government in the two kingdoms. The opportunity of carrying out this policy came in the autumn of 1643, when the English Parliament was in desperate need of help in the civil war. By this time the covenanting leaders were beginning to realize that what the English wanted was, in Robert Baillie's words, a 'civil league' and not a 'religious covenant.' But the Scots would send an army only on condition that the English Parliament should establish presbyterian church government. The representation of English Presbyterians in the Long Parliament was out of all proportion to their numbers and influence in the kingdom; even so, it was with reluctance that the Commons assented to the terms of the Solemn League and Covenant, and summoned an Assembly of Divines to determine the revised constitution of the Church.

The policy of the Solemn League was doomed from the first to the failure which it deserved. The Scottish army distinguished itself in the victory of Marston moor in 1644, but a large portion of it had to be recalled to Scotland to meet

c

the attack of Montrose, who, disgusted with the policy of the covenanting leaders, had adopted the royalist cause. In June 1645 Oliver Cromwell's triumph at Naseby put an end to organized royalist resistance in England, and in September the king's last hope was crushed by Montrose's defeat at Philiphaugh, after a brilliant series of victories. The English army, not the English parliament, had beaten the king, and the army was composed of Independents who hated presbytery as much as they hated episcopacy. The Parliament could keep its bond to the Scots only by passing statutes which it was powerless to enforce. The Scottish Church accepted a Confession of Faith, Catechisms, a Directory for Public Worship, and a new metrical version of the Psalms in agreement with the English Assembly of Divines, which had met at Westminster, and the English Parliament duly ordered the reception of these documents and the establishment of presbytery throughout England. But Cromwell and the army demanded toleration for the Independents, a demand inconsistent with the Solemn League and Covenant.

Fresh hopes were aroused by the surrender of Charles to the Scottish army in May 1646. If king, parliament, and Scots could agree, they might be able to contend with the army. But Charles, though he had accepted five years earlier the establishment of presbytery in Scotland, would not undertake to force it upon England and so betray the Church of England, whose members had been the mainstay of the royalist cause. The Scottish army was by this time extremely unpopular in England, and it was essential to evacuate Newcastle as soon as the English Parliament defrayed the expenses of the Scottish troops in accordance with the agreement made in 1643. The Parliament offered to pay a fraction of its debt in return for the surrender of the royal person, and the Scots assented to the bargain. But the Parliament, which had bought the king, was not strong enough to keep him; he was captured by the army, was unwise enough to decline surprisingly favourable terms, and was imprisoned in the Isle of Wight. In this extremity he again turned to the Scots and offered to establish presbytery in England, as an experiment, for three years. The suggestion was an insult to what the Scots held to be the only divinely appointed form of church government, but indignation at the failure of the king's English enemies to fulfil the obligations undertaken in the Solemn League was so strong that they entered into the agreement known as the Engagement and again invaded England, this time as a royalist force, in the summer of 1648, to meet with a crushing defeat at Preston, in July.

The Engagement had been carried by a large majority in the Scottish Parliament in defiance of the General Assembly, and the defeat at Preston was a victory for the Assembly, which dominated the Parliament for the next two years, until its authority was, in turn, destroyed by another English victory on the battlefield. Parliament and Assembly proscribed all their opponents who had taken the Engagement, and were entering into friendly relations with Cromwell and the Independents, when the execution of King Charles produced a violent reaction. Charles II was at once proclaimed king of Great Britain, France, and Ireland, in defiance of the English commonwealth; he was brought to Scotland from Holland and compelled to take the Solemn League and Covenant. Cromwell's victory at Dunbar, on September 3, 1650, destroyed the authority of the Assembly, and the balance of power in Scotland was changed by an influx of royalist soldiers to the standard of the young king. It was with an army that was largely royalist in sympathy that he marched into England, in 1651, and, if that army had returned victorious, or even if it had returned at all, the Scottish Parliament and the General Assembly might well have shared the experience of the Long Parliament in England, and have found themselves superseded by an army which fought in their name. As it was, Cromwell's 'crowning victory' at Worcester, on the first anniversary of Dunbar, left Scotland at the mercy of the English army, and there was some talk of annexing it as a conquered country.

Wiser counsels prevailed, and the terms of a nominally voluntary union were arranged. Events in England delayed the sanction of the agreement by an English Parliament, but Scotland became part of the Commonwealth and sent representatives to the Parliaments of the Protectorate. It is true that this representation was in fact ludicrously inadequate, since English army officers sat for many of the Scottish constituencies. Yet the paper constitutions of the time have more than an academic interest, for some of their arrangements foreshadowed and suggested those that were adopted by agreement in 1707 and even, to some extent, those that are observed in the parliamentary representation of Scotland to-day. Of the thirty members given to Scotland in 1654 as its share of the combined legislature, twenty went to the thirty-three shires and ten to fifty-seven of the burghs. Only eleven shires were allowed a member apiece, the remainder being grouped in pairs or in threes as single-member constituencies. Of the burghs, Edinburgh was to return two members, and the others were allocated to eight districts, varying between three and thirteen burghs and each returning one member. Double-county seats and districts of burghs thus began under the Cromwellian union.

In administration and justice Scotland gained much from the firm rule of the Protectorate, though the military establishment was costly and taxation high. The real boon was the grant of free trade with England; though it is commonly thought that the country was too impoverished to reap the full benefit, it is not easy to be sure on this point. Dutch wars certainly impeded Scotland's commerce, for Holland was the chief customer and the chief supplier of the Scottish merchants, but there is evidence of activity and growth as well as of stagnation and decay. Thomas Tucker, an English excise officer, visited Scotland in 1655-56 and reported fully on its trade and sea-ports. His impressions were mixed. While the smaller towns seemed to him mere villages, others found favour in his eyes. Leith, 'the most eminently mercantile and trading place of the whole nation,' possessed advantages that ought to have induced the inhabitants of Edinburgh 'to descend from their proud hill into the more fruitful plain, to be filled with the fulness and fatness thereof.' Borrowstounness, the port of Linlithgow, and the centre of the coal and salt trade of the upper estuary of the Forth, he reckoned the second port of the kingdom, and this opinion is borne out by the customs and excise returns of the time. These statistics show, too, that third place was now taken by Glasgow, which, with its four streets 'handsomely built in form of a cross, is one of the most considerablest burghs of Scotland, as well for the structure as trade of it,' though 'checked and kept under by the shallowness of her river.' Dundee, Montrose and Aberdeen still exported salmon and plaiding; but Dundee had suffered from 'domestic commotions,' which 'have much shaken and abated her former grandeur.' Burntisland, Kirkcaldy and Anstruther were beginning to engross the sea-borne commerce of Fife, to the loss of the smaller burghs. As for Inverness, 'the towne is a small one, though the chief of the whole North,' while Ayr's 'pretty trade' with Ireland was diminishing 'by reason of their harbours being clogged and filled up with sand.' War added to the normal hazards of shipping; Culross, for example, had lost three of its five ships. It seems clear, at all events, that, with larger ships coming into use, commerce was tending to concentrate in the ten or twelve principal seaports of the country.

To the Church, hopelessly divided by quarrels which had originated in the Engagement, Cromwell's rule brought an imposed peace but no harmony. The General Assembly was forcibly dissolved in 1653 and was not allowed to meet again, though the lower courts of the Church were left unmolested. Independents were tolerated and even encouraged, and Cromwell insisted that he had given the Scots liberty of conscience, but would give them no liberty to bind other men's consciences; from this liberal formula, Episcopalians and Roman Catholics were, of course, excluded. The Cromwellian rule which, however efficient, was military and English, could not be popular in Scotland, but in the interregnum which followed the death of the great Protector the Scots merely watched the progress of events in England. The Restoration was an English movement, though there is every indication that it was welcomed in Scotland.

Covenanting hopes were raised again during the year 1660, when many Scots chose to forget that, to the great majority of the English people, the Solemn League and Covenant was a wicked and rebellious document, and remembered only that Charles II was 'a covenanted king,' who must surely be true to his sacred oath. When, as late as September 1660, the king promised to 'protect and preserve the government of the Church of Scotland as it is settled by law,' they recalled that presbytery was legally established by royal consent. Disillusion came quickly. In the following spring, a sub-servient Scottish Parliament rescinded all legislation since 1633, and episcopacy thus became 'the government of the Church of Scotland as it is settled by law.' Scottish bishops were appointed and received Anglican orders, but there was no attempt to re-introduce the Book of Common Prayer. The lower church courts were permitted to meet, but they were placed under the direct control of the bishops, and the more rigid Presbyterians refused to acknowledge their authority. Lay patronage, which had been abolished in 1649, was automatically restored by the repeal of the legis-lation of that year, and every minister inducted into a parish since 1649 was ordered to apply for a presentation from the patron of his living and for a collation from the bishop of his diocese. Nearly three hundred ministers refused to do so and were ejected from their parishes; in the synod of Glasgow and Ayr, eighty-seven ministers were deprived and only thirty-five remained. Both the National Covenant and the Solemn League and Covenant were denounced by Act of Parliament as unlawful and rebellious bands, and anyone admitted to office of any kind was required to abjure them. Penalties were prescribed for preaching, or for praying (in public), against the episcopal government of the Church.

Force of circumstances threw the Scots back from the Solemn League, with its propaganda of proscription and persecution, to the National Covenant which had originated in a struggle for freedom. They still demanded the Solemn League, and insisted that it was binding for all time upon the two nations and their posterity, but after 1660 it ceased to be a matter of practical politics, and, in spite of their own assertions, the Scottish covenanters of the reign of Charles II would have acquiesced peaceably in a settlement that gave them the toleration which they described as the Devil's masterpiece. The government, on its side, brought new repressive measures into force. The expulsion of parish ministers led inevitably to meetings for worship elsewhere than in the churches, and acts were passed imposing fines for non-attendance in the parish churches, a device borrowed from the Elizabethan penal code in England. Troops were quartered in non-conformist districts to collect the fines, and the episcopal clergy were instructed to report delinquents. These measures failed to prevent the growth of conventicles, and the Privy Council ordered that no ejected minister might reside within twenty miles of his former parish, or within six miles of a cathedral city, or within three miles of a royal burgh.

A small rebellion in 1666, known as the Pentland rising, gave no serious trouble to the government, but the Privy Council took the revenge of men whom terror had made insensible of their cruelty. Of about 100 prisoners, ten were hanged on one gibbet at Edinburgh, and thirty-five were sent to be hanged at their own doors; others were subjected to the torture of the boot. They refused to save themselves, by renouncing the Covenants, and the royal commissioner, the earl of Rothes, described them as 'damd fules and incorrigeable phanaticks,' but he had made the Covenants the sole alternative to an enforced episcopacy; those who wished to worship as Presbyterians must worship as covenanters. Men of good will, the most famous of whom was Archbishop Leighton, tried in vain to mediate, and the government twice proclaimed an 'indulgence' under which presbyterian clergy might be inducted to parishes without repudiating the Covenants. But acceptance of the offer meant acceptance of episcopacy, and of a complete royal supremacy over the Church, and very few took advantage of it. Meetings for worship in private houses or on the hillsides became more and more frequent. Conventicles in the former were harmless from the point of view of the government, because the worshippers must necessarily be few in numbers; to the field conventicles arms were carried. Yet an act was passed increasing penalties for worship in private houses, and the consequent growth of field conventicles was met by a

ferocious statute which appointed a death penalty for the
offence of expounding scripture or praying at a field conventicle, the definition of which was extended to include a
house so crowded as to necessitate the doors being kept open.
Men who attended conventicles in arms were outlawed, and
outlawry was the punishment for giving food or shelter to
an outlaw.

The duke of Lauderdale, who governed Scotland from
1667 to 1679, recognized that his policy must produce a
rebellion, and he even welcomed the prospect. 'Would to
God,' he once wrote, 'they would rebel, that so I might bring
over an army of Irish Papists to cut all their throats.' When
the rebellion came, it was on a surprisingly small scale, and
was confined to the south-west. On May 3, 1679, James
Sharp, an ecclesiastic who had betrayed the presbyterian
cause and had become archbishop of St. Andrews, was
brutally murdered as he was driving across Magus moor in
Fife. The crime was regarded with horror by Presbyterians
in general, but the cruelties of the government had driven
men to despair, and on Restoration day, 1679, a body of
covenanters, most of them already outlaws, proclaimed at
Rutherglen their defiance to the king, and took up arms.
They collected a small army, defeated John Graham of
Claverhouse at Drumclog on June 1, and for three weeks they
held the country round Hamilton. The rising was suppressed
by the duke of Monmouth, at Bothwell bridge, on June 22,
and about a thousand prisoners were confined, without
shelter, in Greyfriars churchyard in Edinburgh, from June
to November. Lauderdale was replaced by the heir to the
throne, the duke of York. He seems to have had some ideas
of moderation and he made friends by his encouragement of
trade, but the years of his rule (1680–82) belong to what is
known as the Killing Time. The extreme covenanters, in
fanatical desperation, disowned Charles II for his 'perjury
and breach of covenant.' They were occasionally able to
fight a small action, but, for the most part, they were hunted
by Claverhouse and his dragoons and might be shot at sight.
New penal laws were enforced against them, and an oath was
imposed upon all persons in public trust, by which they were

required to approve the Confession of Faith of 1560 and also
the royal supremacy over the Church, which was inconsistent
with the Confession. Eighty of the episcopal clergy were
ejected from their livings for refusing to take this oath, and
the earl of Argyll, who took it 'as far as it is consistent with
itself,' was condemned to death for treason as a defamer of
the king's laws. After the duke of York left Scotland in 1682,
the atrocities of the Killing Time became even fiercer, and
the thumbscrew was invoked to vary the torture of the boot.

When Charles II died, in February 1685, the country was
ripe for rebellion, but, once again, the rebellion was on a
very small scale. Argyll, who had escaped to Holland,
invaded Scotland in the spring of 1685, and was captured
and executed under his old sentence. An obsequious parliament made mere attendance at a conventicle a capital
offence. Then, with the development of the English policy
of James VII and II, there was an entire change in the
conduct of affairs. Subservient as the Scottish parliament
was, it refused to legalize the toleration for Roman Catholics
upon which the king's heart was set, and he determined to
carry out his projects by unflinching use of the royal
prerogative. The Killing Time came to an end with his
Letters of Indulgence in 1687. They were received with
satisfaction, but the discovery that James was bent upon
achieving much more than toleration for Roman Catholics
soon aroused a widespread alarm. Roman Catholics were
appointed to the privy council, in defiance of the laws, and
the chancellor, the earl of Perth, announced his conversion.
Burgh elections were suspended, or, when they were permitted, the town councils (as in England) were filled with
royal nominees. Holyrood became a centre of Roman
Catholic worship and propaganda. A man was hanged for
expressing approval of an anti-Popish riot and for drinking
'confusion to Popery.' The printing of Protestant pamphlets
was practically prohibited by an order that all publications
must pass the chancellor's censorship.

The Revolution, like the Restoration, was an English
movement; Scotland was ready but was quiescent until the
English Revolution had begun. When the prince of Orange

meditated his invasion, he sent proclamations to Scotland, and on December 10, 1688, there was a riot in Edinburgh in which Holyrood was sacked and some members of its small garrison were murdered. There were attacks upon the Edinburgh Roman Catholics, and gangs of ruffians roamed the countryside, destroying the property of the episcopal clergy. Early in 1689 the prince of Orange issued summonses for the election of a Convention of Estates, which, in April, declared that King James had forfeited the throne and offered it to the prince and princess of Orange, who were already king and queen of England. The offer included a declaration that 'prelacy and the superiority of any office in the Church above presbyters is and hath been a great and insupportable grievance, and trouble to this Nation and contrary to the inclinations of the generality of the people.' These words are a significant indication of a coming development which was to divest Scottish Presbyterianism of its spirit of rigid intolerance, and to imbue it with the spirit of freedom which characterizes it to-day, but they were deeply resented in 1689. The 'generality' of Presbyterians at that date regarded presbytery as the only form of church government which could claim a scriptural warrant, and believed that they were bound, by a solemn and irrevocable covenant with the Almighty, to extirpate all other systems; the Church of Scotland to-day is content to hold that presbytery is warranted by the word of God and acceptable to the 'generality of the people.' The State in 1689 was wiser than the Church, when it refused to base the claim of Scotland to determine its own method of church government either upon the Solemn League and Covenant or upon current controversies about the evidence for the existence of a classical assembly or presbytery at Ephesus in the days of St. Paul. The extremists would be content with nothing but the Solemn League and urged that the omission of any demand for it involved the whole nation in fearful perjury, but the statesmen of the day were too sagacious to attempt to repeat the experiment of a covenanted king. The established Church of Scotland ceased to be episcopal in 1689, but the final settlement was delayed by a civil war, in which

Claverhouse, now Viscount Dundee, championed the cause
of James VII. Dundee was slain in the hour of victory at
Killiecrankie on July 27, 1689, and the rule of William and
Mary met with little further resistance.

The religious settlement was made in 1690. Parliament
restored the survivors of the presbyterian ministers, ejected in
1661, ratified the Westminster Confession of Faith, re-enacted
the Golden Act of 1592 (*cf.* p. 59), and abolished lay patronage. The two Covenants were, however, ignored, to the
indignation of the followers of Richard Cameron, who during
the Killing Time had founded a sect of Reformed Presbyterians. The Cameronians, as they were called (though they
themselves repudiated the title), formed the first of the
seceding churches. William insisted upon a toleration for
Episcopalians in Scotland, and episcopal clergy who took the
oath to the new government were permitted to retain their
livings, though they were deprived of any vote in the courts
of the Church. A considerable number took the oaths, and
in the north-east it was not until after 1716 that the
parishes generally were filled with ministers of presbyterian
sympathies. In the Highlands, a still longer period elapsed.

After the Restoration, Scottish commerce had suffered
severely from the operation of the English Navigation
Acts. Free trade with England came to an end with the
cessation of the Cromwellian union, and Charles II was
unable to secure for Scotland the privileges enjoyed after
the accession of King James to the English throne. In 1667,
there were negotiations for a commercial treaty between the
two countries, but the English representatives refused to
exempt the Scots from the operation of the Navigation Acts.
After the failure of this attempt, Charles II found among the
papers of his grandfather, King James, a recommendation
to his successors to persevere in 'the endeavour to establish
a firm Union betwixt England and Scotland,' and both
Parliaments complied with the royal wish that they should
appoint commissioners to treat of union. The commissioners
sat at Westminster for two months in the autumn of 1670,
adjourned, and never re-assembled; the Scots demanded that
the existing number of members of the Scottish Parliament

should be retained in a Parliament of Great Britain, and the English declined to consider the suggestion. At the date of the Revolution, the Scots were acutely conscious that their trade was being gravely handicapped by the restrictions placed upon it by their fellow-subjects in England. The disabilities suffered by the Scots merchants were rendered more onerous by the circumstance that the Restoration had made no difference to two adverse trends that had already shown themselves in Cromwell's time—the naval and mercantile rivalry between England and Holland (the main focus of Scotland's continental trade), and the increasing concentration of deep sea shipping in the larger Scottish ports, with the consequent decay of the lesser coastal burghs. It was thus, in a commercial sense, a difficult and puzzling time, and it was tempting, both now and later, to blame England for all the troubles that afflicted the Scottish economy.

The Scottish statesmen who, in their Claim of Right, had followed English precedent in demanding wide powers for a Parliament which, four years earlier, had gloried in 'the solid, absolute authority with which' the kings of Scots 'were invested by the first and fundamental Law of our Monarchy,' must have been conscious that a personal union of the crowns was a practicable method of governing the two nations only when the sovereign exercised the ultimate power of decision. A limited monarchy, in which the real authority rested with two separate parliaments, could not long survive serious disputes between the representatives of the two countries. From the date of the Revolution, the choice lay between union and separation. The Scottish Convention, at the opening of the new reign, recognized the implication of the Claim of Right, and appointed commissioners 'to treat the terms of an entire and perpetual union betwixt the two kingdoms, with reservation to us of our Church government, as it shall be established at the time of the Union,' and they offered to accept King William as arbiter in any dispute about the terms of the union. William welcomed the suggestion, but his English Parliament refused to appoint commissioners to meet the Scots.

A great opportunity was lost, and never again in William's reign would the Scottish Parliament have invited his arbitration. Many causes combined to render William personally unpopular and to embitter feeling against England. Chief among them were the massacre of Glencoe and the Darien scheme. The massacre of Glencoe was a crime which, alike in its conception and in its execution, was the work of William's Scottish advisers. There were precedents for it under the regents Moray and Morton, and under James VI, but it was differentiated from these precedents by an inhuman treachery which aroused sympathy in the Lowlands for a Highland sept. The criminals were Scotsmen—the master of Stair, the earl of Breadalbane, and Campbell of Glenlyon— but the king, who cannot have been aware of the details of the diabolical plot, had given his consent to 'the extirpation of that sect of thieves' and, three years later, in 1695, when the Scottish Parliament made an inadequate effort to secure the punishment of the murderers, William, by what Macaulay admits to have been 'a great breach of duty,' was content with dismissing Stair from his post as secretary of state. The history of the investigation into the massacre shows that William, who was not naturally fitted for the position of a constitutional monarch, was exercising an influence which, if unchecked, would have brought about the reversion of the Scottish Parliament to its old status of a court of registration.

A check to this tendency followed the failure of the Darien company, and that failure itself proved that there existed for Scotland a choice between war and union with England. In 1695, the Scottish Parliament received the royal assent to an act establishing a company to trade with Africa and the Indies, and subscriptions were secured in England as well as in Scotland. But the proposal aroused the jealousy of the English merchants who still believed that prosperity could be attained by one country only at the expense of another. The House of Commons ordered the prosecution of the English directors, the English subscriptions were withdrawn, and the Scots, who had themselves raised the astonishingly large sum of £220,000, were compelled to restrict the proposed activities of the African company to a settlement upon the isthmus of Darien or Panama. The expedition sailed in the summer of 1698, with great hopes of concentrating the trade of the New World in the new Scottish colony. That generation could not have realized the unhealthy character of the isthmus or the danger to European settlers, but they must have known, and apparently chose to ignore, the circumstance that Spain claimed sovereignty over the Darien territory. They could not have selected a more unlucky time for a quarrel with Spain, for William was engaged in the effort to prevent a European war by negotiating the partition treaties for the Spanish empire. William, as king of England, issued in 1699 orders to the governors of the English colonies in North America, in the Barbados, and in Jamaica, prohibiting his subjects from rendering any assistance to his Scottish subjects in their effort to colonize Darien. The Scottish Parliament retorted in 1700 by resolving that 'our Colony of Caledonia in Darien is a legal and rightful settlement in the terms of the Act of Parliament 1695,' to which the royal assent had been given. Already an issue had arisen upon which the two Parliaments of a nominally constitutional monarch were hopelessly and bitterly divided; the situation was an object lesson in the impossibility of maintaining a mere union of the crowns after an absolute monarchy had ceased to exist. William could only plead, as an excuse for adjourning the Scottish Parliament, that, if it had maintained this attitude, it would have 'infallibly disturbed the general peace of Christendom and brought inevitably upon that our ancient Kingdom a heavy war, wherein we could expect no assistance.'

A war between Scotland and Spain, or a Scottish repudiation of the authority of King William, was prevented by the news of the irretrievable failure of the Darien project. The settlers of 1698 had been carried off by disease and famine; a second expedition, which arrived in 1699, was equally unfortunate; a third expedition gained a victory over some Spanish troops in February 1700, but large Spanish forces arrived and offered honourable terms for the evacuation of Darien. The terms were accepted in April, but most of the Scottish adventurers perished in the return journey. Apart from its political implications, the enterprise had been from the start ill-conceived and sadly mismanaged. The recent verdict of a sympathetic American historian (Dr. Wallace Notestein, in *The Scot in History*) is worth quoting: 'the Scots were to blame themselves. They had been extraordinarily simple-minded when they put their money into such a project.' When the Scottish Parliament met again in October 1700, it had to admit that 'the business of Caledonia is now but a shadow,' and it refrained from adding to the difficulties of the king at a critical time in the history of the two kingdoms and of Europe. William, on his side, assented to an Act against 'wrongous imprisonment'—the Scottish Habeas Corpus Act—and promised to remedy other grievances.

A peace had been patched up, but William recognized that the position of the monarchy was impossible. At the very height of the controversy, in February 1700, he urged his English Parliament to appoint commissioners to treat of union; the House of Lords accepted the recommendation, but the House of Commons declined to do so. The subject was again discussed in the Lords in the following year, and, in the spring of 1702, William sent from his deathbed a royal message to the Parliament at Westminster, urging that 'nothing can contribute more to the present and future peace, security, and happiness of England and Scotland than a firm and entire union between them.' Queen Anne, on her accession, endorsed this recommendation and a commission sat from October 1702 to February 1703. Its deliberations were once more fruitless; English objections to free trade between the two countries proved to be insuperable.

Besides the commercial and constitutional arguments for union, there was another practical issue of grave importance. Both Parliaments had agreed in 1689 that the crown of each country should pass to the children of William and Mary, then to Anne and her children, and then to the children of William by a later marriage. When William died, Anne stood alone in the succession, and she was not likely to bear another child. The English Parliament, after the death of the duke of Gloucester, the only survivor of Anne's many children, had settled the succession to the English throne upon the house of Hanover, but the Scottish Parliament had taken no action in the matter, and in the session of 1702 a strong opposition had been offered to a proposal to exact from all men in public office an oath abjuring the Stewart claimant, who, in his French exile, had taken the title of James VIII and III. A Stewart restoration in Scotland would put in grave jeopardy the Protestant succession in England, and, with that succession, the limitations which had been placed on the monarchy at the Revolution. The English Whigs had, therefore, a strong inducement to make sure that, in Queen Anne's lifetime, the Scots should irretrievably commit themselves to the Hanoverian succession. The only adequate security was an incorporating union—the 'firm and entire union' of King William's dying words. Any form of federal union would have left open the possibility of secession, for such a union was regarded, in the political thought of the day, as a loose league between sovereign states, a temporary alliance that might at any time be denounced by one of the contracting parties; it is significant that Clerk of Penicuik refers to the contrasting type of union as 'incorporating and perpetual.' It seems to have been dimly realized by Scottish statesmen that Scotland's only chance of influencing the course of British politics lay in sharing fully in the national life through the medium of a completely united kingdom. Many years were to pass before it could be said in this matter that wisdom had been justified of her children, but there is, at all events, since the first Reform Act, ample evidence of the part played by Scotsmen in all departments of public life.

If the English ministers perceived the necessity of union, their Whig supporters, in spite of their anxiety about the Protestant succession, were unwilling to make the necessary sacrifice of admitting the Scots to equal privileges of trade with England and the English colonies, until the course of events forced their hand. On the other side, the Scottish Parliament seized every opportunity of emphasizing the difficulties of the existing relationship between the two countries. Queen Anne was at war with Louis XIV, and

Scottish soldiers were fighting under Marlborough, but neither the Scottish Parliament nor the queen's Scottish ministers had borne any share in the responsibility for the outbreak of hostilities. In 1703, an act was passed declaring that no future sovereign should have power to make war or peace without the consent of the Scottish Parliament, and another act admitted French wines, duty free, into Scotland. Anne gave her consent to these measures but withheld it from the famous bill, known as the Act of Security, which threatened rupture of the union of the crowns, after Anne's death, unless a satisfactory constitutional and commercial agreement should be negotiated in the interval. These measures were not inspired by an ambition to force England to consent to a union; a powerful faction, which called itself the Patriot or Country party, contemplated complete separation from England. Among its supporters were the Jacobites, whose main object was to prevent a recognition of the Electress Sophia of Hanover as the heiress of the Scottish crown. In 1704, the queen assented to the Act of Security, which included provisions for the training of a military force for the defence of the country.

The English Parliament recognized the real menace of the Act of Security, which lay in the postponement of the settlement of the succession in Scotland until, possibly, the throne should actually be vacant; the Act contained a provision that, failing an earlier agreement with England, the Scottish estates should, on the death of the queen without issue, name a successor from the Protestant descendants of the royal house. The English ministers determined to bring the question to an immediate issue, and in the spring of 1705 passed what was known as the Aliens Act, which provided that, unless the Scots accepted the Hanoverian succession by the following Christmas, all Scotsmen should be legally aliens in England and severe restrictions should be laid upon Scottish trade. But the Act also empowered the queen to nominate English commissioners to meet Scottish commissioners duly authorized to negotiate a treaty of union.

The Scottish Parliament met in June, and for a few weeks it seemed that a rupture between the two kingdoms was inevitable, but the project of a treaty of union was gaining support, and in September the Parliament not only agreed to the appointment of commissioners but also resolved to leave their selection to the queen. The latter decision was made on the suggestion of the Jacobite leader, the duke of Hamilton, whose motives were, and remain, inexplicable. It went considerably further than the general sense of the house, which had come to believe that a treaty of union deserved serious consideration as a solution of the problems of the constitutional and commercial relations between the two kingdoms. The practical effect of Hamilton's motion was to secure that the Scottish commissioners would be selected from the advocates of union and that there would not be an adequate representation of the minority—one Jacobite was, in fact, nominated as a commissioner, but he took little part in the proceedings. A protest was made against the minatory clauses of the English Aliens Act, and these clauses were repealed by the English Parliament in November.

The joint commission met in London on April 16, 1706, and almost immediately came to an agreement on three main points. Both sides accepted an incorporating union; the English gave guarantees of complete freedom of trade; the Scots undertook to recognize the Electress Sophia, and the heirs of her body, being Protestants, as the successors to Anne as queen of Scots. Further agreements about taxation and the jurisdiction of the Scottish law-courts soon followed. The question that produced the sharpest difference between the two bodies of commissioners concerned the number of the Scottish representatives in the future British House of Commons. While the Scots asked for fifty, the English suggested thirty-eight, but they ultimately proposed forty-five, together with sixteen representative peers in the House of Lords, and the offer was accepted. These numbers remained, for over a century, a blot on the scheme of union and constituted an ungenerous treatment of the smaller country by the larger. There was also considerable discussion about the capital sum payable by England as an 'Equivalent' for the future share of Scotland in the English national debt; it was fixed at £398,085 10s., the precise amount having been calculated by two distinguished Scottish mathematicians. On July 22, the articles of union were signed and sealed by the commissioners, and the Scottish Parliament met in October for their discussion.

The Treaty was ratified by the Scottish estates on January 16, 1707, by 110 votes to 68, over 40 members refraining from voting. There were many indications of popular disapproval, and protests were made by counties, burghs, parishes and presbyteries. But the protests were themselves indications that the anti-union feeling was diminishing; only 14 counties out of 34, only 19 burghs out of 66, only 60 parishes out of 938, and only 3 presbyteries out of 68, sent anti-union addresses to Edinburgh. There was, however, no lack of vehemence in the opposition; troops had to be brought into Edinburgh to quell riots in the streets. Accusations of bribery were brought by the Jacobites, to whose hopes of a restoration the Union was a fatal blow; the charge has been investigated by Hill Burton and Hume Brown, and, at considerable length, by Professor James Mackinnon, whose verdict (in his *Union of Scotland and England*) thus sums up the evidence: 'The historian, while premising that the charge of bribery rests on mere suspicion and assumption, and believing that the Union was, with some exceptions, the work of honest conviction, is amply justified in saying that there is at least as much evidence that members were bribed to oppose, as there is for the statement that they were bribed to support incorporation.'

The Treaty of Union itself contained no guarantees for the maintenance of the Church of Scotland as established in 1707, but Acts for the security of the Churches of Scotland and England were passed by the respective Parliaments and were inserted in their Acts ratifying the Treaty.

On May 1, 1707, the Act of Union came into force, and on October 23 the first Parliament of Great Britain met at Westminster.

Chapter 3

From the Union to the First Reform Act

WHEN Scotland entered the Union in 1707, the political life and political thought of the nation, though vigorous and at times turbulent, had not reached the stage of systematic organization: there were no recognized parties in any modern sense. The relations between members of the Scots Parliament tended to be governed by personal considerations rather than by their varying attitudes to public questions. The ties of kinship counted for much, and so did the need for working as harmoniously as possible with the ministry of the day, for opposition brought neither profit nor glory. Thus, when a Hamilton and an Ogilvie fell out in 1703, it was assumed that the duke of Hamilton and the earl of Seafield would act the parts of paternal arbitrators; and, three years later, the same Hamilton, though opposed to union, made no secret of his ambition to serve on the commission for drafting the Treaty. Nevertheless, the importance of the issues raised during the reigns of William and Anne, and the deep interest aroused by the parliamentary debates of the time, impelled men to sort out their ideas and to formulate their policies, and the Estates, awakening to full life during their last seventeen years, were at least evolving towards a true party system.

The adherents of the Revolution settlement came, for the most part, to accept both the need for the Hanoverian succession and the desirability of union with England. They were regarded, and spoken of, as the Court party, the Courtiers, or the Revolutioners; and they were accustomed to being called upon to form the administration and to fill the great offices of state—those of commissioner, chancellor, secretary, keeper of the privy seal, treasurer-depute and others. Those who were critical of the office-holders—there was little else that held them together—called themselves the Patriot party, the Country party, or the Countrymen. Both groups were virtually dissolved as a result of the disputes over the succession and the union, and three or four new combinations emerged. The Old party, led by the dukes of Argyll and Queensberry, the earls of Mar and Seafield, comprised those who worked with the English Whigs to ensure acceptance of the Protestant succession and of the Treaty. The New party, including the duke of Roxburghe, the marquis of Tweeddale and George Baillie of Jerviswood, also came, albeit reluctantly, to admit the inevitability of union; by 1707 they had assumed the exotic title of *Squadrone Volante*, as a symbol of their parliamentary policy and tactics of swift and untrammeled manœuvre, always in support of whichever side stood, at the moment, for the national interest. The *Squadrone* formed, in effect, an alternative ministerial group. The most prominent and eloquent member of the Country party, Andrew Fletcher of Saltoun, federalist, republican at heart, and sincere though impractical patriot, retired from public life in disgust at the passing of the Treaty. Most of the remaining Countrymen, notably the dukes of Hamilton and Atholl and George Lockhart of Carnwath, were openly Jacobite in sympathy and unlikely to move a finger in the cause of Anglo-Scottish amity, so long as that cause remained tied to the Union and the Hanoverian succession. In the language of the day, they were styled Episcopals or Cavaliers as well as Jacobites.

Thus Parliament House's legacy to Westminster comprised three parties, two of them, the not very different Court party and *Squadrone*, holding by a belief in the Union tempered by a lively sense of Scotland's own interests, and the third, the Jacobites, sincere or half-fearful advocates of a treasonable design to overturn the settled succession in favour of the exiled Stewarts. The picture is, however, incomplete unless allowance is made for the fact that most politicians (in Scotland even more than in England) played for safety by maintaining some kind of contact with both Hanover and St. Germains.

The last seven years of Anne's reign were a testing time for the new arrangements, and the uneasy opening of Anglo-Scottish partnership goes far to prove that union was in one way or another distasteful to a majority of both peoples, and that only the pressure of events had made it at all acceptable. Brought together in the united Parliament, the handful of Scots were quick to suspect and resent injustice, and the overwhelming English majority saw to it that they had ample cause for anxiety. Some of the quarrels that arose will be considered later in connexion with constitutional and ecclesiastical changes; all of them lent themselves to the polemical warfare of the day. As early as the summer of 1707 differences developed over the new methods of collecting customs and excise, over the delay in the delivery of the Equivalent, and over the quick profits obtained by smart merchants ready to take advantage of the low tariffs that operated in Scotland before the inception of the Union on May 1. These were, however, mere 'teething troubles'; more serious grievances appeared during the sittings of the first united Parliament in 1707–08. The act for abolishing the Scottish Privy Council and increasing the powers of the justices of the peace was opposed by Queensberry and his followers, as also by Godolphin's ministry generally. But the *Squadrone* supported the measure (which was easily carried), and the objections must be discounted as those of interested parties, for the Privy Council, as the governmental instrument for controlling elections, had been very useful to the cliques of ruling nobles. Moreover, its abolition was at least hinted at in the Treaty as a future possibility. Meanwhile the Jacobites were restive but undecided. There had been rumours of a rising in 1707, but the only real plans were those of the French king. His credulous emissaries spoke of universal dissatisfaction, but the issue showed that neither leaders nor followers were as yet prepared to rise. The exiles abroad and the conspirators at home were each disposed to wait until their allies were definitely committed, and, when a French fleet set out in March 1708, with troops and stores, nothing was to be done until a successful landing should be effected. Wretched seamanship marred the venture, and the English, coming on the French ships in the firth of Forth, drove them home without a fight. None of the Jacobite leaders compromised themselves over the affair, and all that it achieved was a revulsion of feeling in favour of the Court party, which, at the parliamentary election of 1708, gained from both *Squadrone* and Jacobites and got commanding majorities of both peers and commoners. The new Parliament, by substituting the English treason law for that of Scotland, united all Scottish parties in an unsuccessful opposition, but here again there were mixed motives; the penalties under the new code were indeed savage, but it was probably the near prospect of territorial losses that frightened the Scots nobles, many of whom had been in treasonable correspondence with the Pretender.

Although during these early years of union some want of tact had been shown in the handling of Scottish affairs, it might be thought that Anglo-Scottish friction had arisen from transient causes, and that common sense and mutual charity would overcome the difficulties. The hope was not to be realized. Towards the end of 1710 court intrigues and another general election installed in power a Tory government and a Tory Parliament, and the change placed Scotland at the mercy of an unsympathetic and anti-unionist party. The Scottish elections greatly reduced the Court party, almost wiped out the *Squadrone*, and gave the Jacobites and Tories control. In less than four years enough was done to alienate the greater part of the nation. In 1711 the House of Lords, reversing on appeal a Court of Session decision, found in favour of James Greenshields, an Edinburgh pastor who had challenged the Presbyterian order by conducting Anglican services. The consternation of the Kirk was heightened by the Act of Toleration, which sanctioned Episcopalian worship (1712). In the same year, the restoration of lay patronage, thought to have been finally abolished in 1690, roused fears for the Establishment itself and shook the strong unionist faith of the Presbyterian clergy and laity. Though it is far from true that nothing good can be said for patronage,

and though much of the subsequent strife and suffering
had deeper roots than any parliamentary statute, the Act
was still a breach of the Treaty, in the spirit even more
surely than in the letter. These measures were passed by a
combination of the English Tories (who were meanwhile
curtailing the liberties of the English dissenters) and the
Scots nobles, who, for the most part Episcopalians, listened
readily enough to the promptings of the mischievous Jacobite,
Lockhart of Carnwath.

In 1711, the Lords' ruling, in the case of the duke of
Hamilton and Brandon, that no British title could confer on
a Scots noble the right to a seat in the House, was deeply
and justly resented as a national affront. The imposition, in
1711, of an export duty on the staple Scottish manufacture—
linen—and the enactment, in 1713, of the principle of equal
taxation for Scottish malt (made largely from low-grade
'bere') and for the rich barley-malt of England, hardly
implied 'due regard to the circumstances and abilities' of
the northern nation. Disillusionment and disgust led to the
anomalous peers' debate of 1713, when the English Tories
barely contrived to defend the Union against an attack by
its authors, the English Whigs and the Scots nobles. The
motion for repeal, in so far as it was anything more than
a tactical move to gain a party advantage by forcing the
government to champion an unpopular measure, was less
a repudiation of union itself than a vote of censure on the
Tories' exploitation of their opportunities for creating dis-
harmony. In 1714 Bolingbroke's Jacobite plots miscarried,
and there followed, in rapid succession, the death of the
queen, the peaceful accession of George I, his contemptuous
dismissal of all the ministers, the formation of Townshend's
Whig government, and a great Whig victory in both English
and Scottish elections.

With the Whigs in power for the next forty-five years and
the Tories utterly discredited, the Jacobites' position was
critical. Denied all hope of peacefully realizing their aims,
and practically barred from public life, they must decide
whether the cause was worth rebellion. To many of them,
as the event showed, it was so. The story of the risings,

around which has grown a literature as great in volume and in depth of feeling as about Queen Mary, is too well known to call for more than a few general comments.

The prospects for the 1715 rising seemed bright. The Tories regretted their lost power and there were those who had expected a last-minute declaration for the Pretender, the titular 'James VIII and III.' Many gave the impression of being so dissatisfied with the effects of the Union as to be ready to support the project of changing the dynasty. Memories of Killiecrankie and Glencoe would reinforce the appeal of the exiled royal family to the traditional loyalty of the Highlanders. Actual results were disappointing. Mar's army, unable to move far beyond its base at Perth, fought only the ingloriously drawn battle of Sheriffmuir with Argyll's much smaller force, and had to give way when the melting of the snows allowed the well-equipped loyal troops to advance. The Jacobites of Cumberland and Dumfries-shire, from whom much was hoped, found the country apathetic or hostile and, though reinforced by the column under Mackintosh of Borlum detached by Mar, came by way of a rather aimless wandering to a fighting finish at Preston. The Chevalier did not arrive until his dispirited army was on the way to its disbandment around Montrose and Aberdeen, but it is far from clear that his absence was a material loss to his cause. The attempt of 1719 was a side-issue of the Anglo-Spanish war and, in the absence of any special domestic grievance, appealed only to the irreconcilable clans of the west. Even they were none too enthusiastic and wholly in the dark as to methods and aims, and, at Glenshiel, Wightman's small force of regulars and loyal clansmen scattered them at the first charge, the Highlanders dispersing and the unfortunate Spanish soldiers capitulating.

During the long internal peace associated with Walpole's name, Wade's fine roads were built for the express purpose of enabling troops and military stores to be moved quickly from one part of the Highlands to another, the Black Watch were formed to police the disaffected areas, and Fort Augustus was built as a supplement to Fort William. Despite all these precautions the insurrection of 1745 achieved a degree of success that is in striking contrast to the earlier failures. The French, again at war with Britain, promised help and, after an expedition in 1744 which was reminiscent of the fiasco of 1708, did send money, supplies and a few troops; but this aid was of slight importance. Of more significance is the fact that the Lowlands were becoming less martial; and, while the loyal clans are said to have obeyed the disarming acts, the unruly ones retained their effective weapons, surrendering only old and useless pieces. These handicaps were increased as a result of the government's initial slackness. The raising of loyal volunteer forces was at first forbidden, and this, in view of the general prevalence of pacific habits and the war-time absence of most of the regular troops, made the rebels' path easier. Cope's defence of Scotland offers a classic example of military ineptitude. Instead of holding Stirling as a rallying-point and confining the rising to north of Forth, as Argyll had done thirty years before, he went (too late in any case) into the Highlands, timorously avoided the hostile clans when there, and opened up the road to the south. The Prestonpans defeat (September 21, 1745) and the flight of the Hanoverian forces were the logical result of strategy of this kind. It has been suggested (by Sir James Fergusson in *Argyll in the Forty-Five*) that the fumbling indecision that marked the measures of defence at this time was due in part to the fact that the government's generals, with one notable exception (the duke of Cumberland), were very old men. By comparison, the Jacobites were fortunate in possessing a dashing leader in Prince Charles, an able administrator in Murray of Broughton, and a sound general in Lord George Murray. It was personality and leadership, sustained by Highland courage and hardihood, and aided by some good luck (which often attends these other qualities), that carried the Jacobites as far as Derby, for this great achievement, made possible by skilful avoidance of their numerically superior opponents, really flattered their strength.

The Jacobite area during both risings may be defined as including most of Ross, almost all Inverness-shire, the

hilly interior of Banffshire and Aberdeenshire, the braes of
Angus, the Perthshire highlands, the desolate tract around
the braes of Balquhidder, and parts of northern Argyll.
Thence came the Jacobite regulars—Mackenzies, all the
mainland Macdonalds, Camerons, the Clan Chattan,
Gordons, Ogilvies, Murrays, Robertsons of Struan, Drummonds, Macgregors, Stuarts of Appin, and their clients and
dependents. Clans on the fringes were of doubtful allegiance,
like the Frasers, held back by Simon in 1715 and treacherously
sent out under his son in 1745. This governmental loss was
offset by Duncan Forbes of Culloden's success in restraining
the Macdonalds of Sleat and the Macleods, who were out
in the 'Fifteen. Grants and Macleans rose only as irresponsible individuals or small scpts. Outside there was indifference
or hostility. Inverness and Inveraray were loyalist strongholds. Sutherlands, Munroes, Rosses and Mackays were
steadfast in their allegiance, holding Inverness during the
greater part of each rising, and enabling Lord Reay in the
second to bring off a brilliant coup which meant nothing less
than disaster to the Jacobites—the seizure of a French sloop
with £12,000 intended for the prince and the defeat of the
earl of Cromartie's endeavours to recover the booty. The
Campbells, of course, were equally staunch. The earl of
Islay (who was to succeed as third duke of Argyll) was strong
enough in 1715 to prevent the western clans from attacking
Inveraray, and he later sent reinforcements to his brother
at Stirling. In the 'Forty-five the earl of Loudoun (head of
another branch of the Campbells) raised 2,000 Highlanders
for service in the north, and the west Highlands were defended in masterly fashion, despite crippling lack of supplies
and official discouragement and inertia, by General John
Campbell of Mamore (afterwards fourth duke of Argyll).
The people from the towns and the Lowlands were almost
uniformly anti-Jacobite. True, the master of Sinclair, Lord
Elcho and a few others provided squadrons of cavalry, but
this arm, not very effective in 1715, never numbered 500
in 1745, and by Culloden had dwindled almost to vanishing
point. Even the feeble southern rising of 1715 had no
counterpart in the later enterprise; with the Lowlands in his

power, Charles Edward got only the Edinburgh regiment, composed of volunteers and deserters from Cope. Glasgow was very loyal, sending three battalions to Argyll at Stirling, and, along with Paisley, Dumbarton, and neighbouring places, equipping the Loch Lomond expedition against the outlawed Macgregors. The Fife townsfolk resisted the Jacobite cess-gatherers, and the burning of Auchterarder, Crieff, Blackford and other villages in dead of winter, to impede Argyll's advance, rallied civilian sentiment against the perpetrators of the stupid and pointless outrage. Less martial in 1745, Lowlanders still showed where their sympathies lay. The financial straits of the Jacobites again led them to impose taxation that was inevitably unpopular. Baggot's Hussars were hated in Aberdeen and Banff for their horse and money levies, and Glasgow parted most unwillingly with its thousands and its supplies of clothing. Lord George Murray admits—'were it not for our maroding, I believe we would be welcome guests.' England was utterly barren soil. Thomas Forster's petty rising of 1715 was doomed from the start, and the only result of the invasion in 1745 was the recruiting of the Manchester regiment of about 300 men, foolishly left in Carlisle to be mopped up by Cumberland.

Jacobite sentiment was thus strong only in the central Highlands. Agents spoke of raising between 30,000 and 40,000 soldiers, but such an estimate was wildly optimistic. The event showed that solid support could be drawn only from mainland Ross, Cromartyshire and mainland Inverness-shire, with smaller numbers from adjoining areas. Now, the unofficial census compiled by Webster in 1755 gave these three shires (less the royal burghs situated in them) a total population of just under 78,000. The entire adult male population, fit and unfit for war, cannot be computed at more than one-fourth of the whole, or nearly 20,000; and the non-Jacobite elements of the three shires may be taken as balancing the men who came from other counties. In this connexion it is interesting that Cumberland reckoned all the clans' fighting strength (a different matter from the adult males) at 20,000, including 6,000 loyal men. Thus the hopeful calculations made before the rising must have rested on illusory expectations from the Lowlands. Actually, Mar's numbers, if they ever totalled 12,000, soon fell away, and at no time could Charles Edward command a force of even that size. He had about 7,500 for the march to England, under 9,000 at Falkirk, and perhaps 5,000 at Culloden. Desertion, like finance, was a real problem to the Jacobites (as it is to most non-professional armies), and records show the Macdonalds of Keppoch, the Atholl brigade and the Glengarry regiment losing half their strength, or more, in a matter of days.

Most of the clans, whether organized on 'feudal' or 'patriarchal' lines, were military as well as political units, subject to common and compulsory service; the voluntary element was negligible, and the muster was backed by potent threats. 'For God's sake,' wrote Lord George Murray to Atholl, 'cause some effectual method be taken about the deserters; I would have their houses and crops destroyed for an example to others, and themselves punished in a most rigorous manner.' All depended on the chiefs. In 1715, the Frasers, uncertain which side to take, as soon as they heard Simon was for the government, left the rebel army, and most of the Glengarry men went home after Falkirk, because of the accidental death of one of the sons of their chief. Something like a mass levy of the readily available men, willing and unwilling, had been enforced—there were boys of sixteen and men over seventy among the Jacobites, and the average height seems to have been five feet four inches. That such an army marched and fought, endured and died as it did says much for the innate martial qualities of the Highlanders. The element of compulsion, and the incidence of desertion, are found also among Loudoun's levies and Mamore's Argyll men; on both sides what mattered was that military duty was habitual and in effect inescapable.

Thus the romantic aspects of the Jacobite movement are largely apocryphal; one must seek them in the songs of Lady Nairne rather than in the contemporary Atholl papers. The chieftains, the mainstay of the risings, included not only the brave and selfless Lochiel, but also Lovat who strove to keep safe while sending the clan out under his son. There was, indeed, little to inspire such devotion and loyalty as appeared at their best after Culloden. Mutual distrust cancelled out the good qualities of the leaders, and adversity revealed in Charles Edward the characteristic defects of his family. Weak, self-willed obstinacy led him to garrison Carlisle, to besiege Stirling castle, to offend the chiefs by favouring unworthy Irish officers. Though much was made of the alien character of the Hanoverian dynasty, the eighteenth century Stewarts, restored by French, Spanish, or any other foreign aid, would have been no different in this respect. And, in the end, Prince Charles chose not to 'die, sword in hand, at the head of his brave Highlanders'; as Professor J. D. Mackie has written, 'it is hard to justify . . . the mentality which demanded so much in the name of loyalty, and gave so little in return.' It is among his faithful but deluded followers that we must seek the real and only heroes of the risings.

The chiefs, like most of their followers, were either Episcopalians or Romanists, and resentment over Presbyterian dominance may have reinforced their traditional allegiance to the house of Stewart and their instinctive hostility to its opponents. In so far as their response to the call to arms had a political motive, they obeyed the summons, whether as patriarchal chiefs or as feudal landlords, because they sensed a growing threat to their power, their prestige, their way of life, in the great Whig achievements—the Revolution settlement, the Union and the Hanoverian succession.

During the reigns of George I and II, the schemes of the Jacobites rather than the proceedings in Parliament were the focus of Scottish political life. The Tories were seemingly harmless at Westminster, and no such concerted attack on Scotland's rights as had been mounted between 1710 and 1714 was to be expected from the Whigs, now in a commanding position. The Scottish people and its representatives were neither sufficiently powerful nor sufficiently interested to play much of a part in British politics and were only roused over their own concerns. Secondary adjustments of the Union, the imposition of fresh taxation, and the punitive measures which followed the rebellions, were the matters that engaged their attention. If their outlook seems limited, the limitations were imposed on them alike by their present condition and their past experiences. In Scottish parliamentary life, even during its best days between 1690 and 1707, the administration had been all-important; it could confer benefits and make bargains, and therefore was to be supported rather than opposed. Now, with the Scottish members in a small minority at St. Stephen's, and the government of the day controlling patronage, posts and pensions, their own and their country's welfare seemed to them to point to the advisability of making a general rule of voting with the ministry. They could still, when their prejudices were ruffled, 'bolt the party,' even led by the Scottish secretary or the lord advocate (who would not necessarily lose office on that account), but they did vote Whig fairly consistently as long as the Whigs were in power. Their habitual support (despite the constitutional argument in favour of 'weighting' a majority verdict) naturally caused bitter resentment in the ranks of the English opposition, and helped to foster the belief, which came to be widely held, in the meanness and servility of the Scot. This sentiment was strengthened by the rivalry between the two Scots parties, which were prepared to support the Whigs at a price. The Argathelians or Court party, led by the second duke of Argyll and his brother Lord Islay (who became third duke), were now separated from the *Squadrone Volante* rather by personal ambition than by questions of policy. If their manœuvres were thereby divested of any large claim to dignity or significance, it can be said that the English Whigs were in similar condition—so undeniably the masters that Townshend could struggle with Stanhope, Carteret with Walpole, over place rather than principle.

For eleven years of George I's reign the *Squadrone* were the more favoured party, Montrose (1714–15) and Roxburghe (1716–25) being in turn Scottish secretaries. There was fairly general agreement among Scotsmen that the punishments meted out to those implicated in the 'Fifteen were too harsh. Most of the chiefs and nobles had made good their escape, and only Kenmure and Derwentwater, two of the leaders of the southern rising, were executed. Acts for disarming the Highlands and forfeiting the rebels' estates were passed, but practically the whole nation, including judges and lawyers, offered a passive resistance to the attempts to punish rank-and-file Jacobites and to make good the government's right to the rents. National pride, coupled with suspicion of England, can be pleaded on behalf of the Scots in this matter, but it was only abject submissiveness to the ministry that induced Argyll, Roxburghe and the other fourteen peers to support Stanhope's unsuccessful plan of perpetuating the Whig oligarchy, at the expense of the Commons, through the notorious Peerage Bill of 1719, by which England's quota was to be fixed at its existing number, while that of Scotland should be altered from sixteen representative to twenty-five hereditary peers.

During Walpole's long tenure of power (1721–42), his talents were often overlooked by Scotsmen in their general hostility to his fiscal measures, for the idea of heavy indirect taxation was still repugnant. On two occasions discontent led to rioting and bloodshed. In 1725 the prime minister insisted on new revenue, whether by beer-excise or malt-duty, to the amount of £20,000 annually. In Glasgow the mob, having wrecked the house of the local M.P. (suspected of favouring the detested impost), attacked the soldiers and forced them to fire, while in Edinburgh the brewers struck work as a protest; in both cases Duncan Forbes, the new lord advocate, was largely responsible for inducing the people to submit, albeit in bitterness of heart. The *Squadrone* being involved in the national resistance, Walpole sundered his connexion with it and dismissed Roxburghe from the secretaryship. Argyll and Islay were henceforth the men who mattered in Scots affairs, their skill in 'managing' elections proving a real asset to Walpole. In 1736 the Edinburgh populace, in the most orderly fashion, executed 'lynch law' on Captain Porteous for his temerity in opening fire during what was in effect a public demonstration in favour of two condemned smugglers. The government, despite opposition from Argyll and Forbes, wished to penalize the corporation of Edinburgh heavily for its complicity or slackness, but parliamentary concern for municipal rights obtained substantial alterations in the bill, so that the city was merely fined £2,000 and its provost disqualified. Walpole's efficient work, including the construction of Wade's roads and forts to open up the Highlands, was forgotten by the people, Argyll sided with his English and Scottish critics, the 1741 election was a great triumph for the *Squadrone*, and the revived Scottish secretaryship was given to their leader, Tweeddale, in 1742, when Carteret's ministry took office.

The means adopted to ensure internal peace after the 'Forty-five provoked further dissatisfaction. Exception could hardly be taken to the execution of leaders like Lovat or Balmerino, and nothing but contempt could be felt for the double traitor Murray of Broughton, whose miserable life was spared. Entirely in agreement, too, with reason and progress was the major constitutional reform effected, the abolition of heritable jurisdictions, which broke the too often rebellious forces of feudalism. Common sense dictated the stricter supervision of the Episcopal clergy, whose loyalty to the reigning house had been ambiguous, though the act of 1748, requiring them to be ordained by an Anglican bishop, hampered their legitimate activities and put a stigma of inferiority on their sect. The disarming of the Highlands was necessarily more severe than on previous occasions, though the statute of 1752 disposing of the forfeited estates—their revenues went to improving Highland farms, setting up schools and planting forests—was a credit both to its author, Lord Advocate Grant, and to the British Parliament. But the belated offer of a few material benefits could not efface the memory of Cumberland's foolish atrocities, the occasion for which need never have arisen had the government adopted the Scottish suggestion of entrusting the work of disarmament and pacification to formations of loyal clansmen or Lowlanders, who could understand, without condoning, the motives behind the rising. Further cause for regret was given by the proscription of the tartan, as a badge of sedition and an essentially military garb. The truth is that Englishmen

D

did not realize that Jacobitism after 1746, far from being a live issue, was a mere sentiment or perhaps oftener a fashionable but hypocritical pose, and their distrust led them to reject Forbes's plan of enrolling the clansmen for foreign service under English colonels and Highland officers. It was almost by accident that the Black Watch, patrols of loyal Highlanders incorporated in 1726 to help in Wade's work, reached full regimental stature in time to play a distinguished and gallant part in the battle of Fontenoy (May 1745), and it was left to Pitt, during the Seven Years' War (1756–63), to make proper use of the splendid fighting material available in the glens. Not until 1782 was Highland dress legalized, and the policy of suppression and petty persecution contributed to the great exodus, during the generation after Culloden, from the homeland to the American colonies, especially to North Carolina, where Flora Macdonald, among many others, took part in a second lost cause by declaring for King George in the Cross Creek rising, which was suppressed in February 1776. Suspicions of Scotsmen's loyalty were responsible for the refusal to give them a militia, like that established in England in 1757, but in fairness it must be admitted that there was no unanimity on the subject, counter-arguments dwelling on the expense involved, the disturbance of civilian life, and doubts as to the supply of gentlemen officers.

With the final eclipse of Jacobitism, there followed for Scotland a period of deepest political apathy, the more surprising in that in other ways this half-century was perhaps the most brilliant in all her history. The absence of any stirring cause, together with grave defects in the constitutional machinery (to be examined in a later chapter), left the nation almost unconcerned and voiceless in public affairs. Meanwhile, with the change from Whig rule to that of the Tories under George III, the Scots M.P.s transferred their support to the new favourites. This step was made easier through George's choice of the earl of Bute as his first prime minister and the man to break the Whig tradition. Personal dislike of Scotsmen grew as positive distrust of their allegiance waned, and this in turn brought them closer to the king in his autocratic policies. The bulk of the nation as well as its representatives approved of the war undertaken against the American colonists in 1775, and the one issue that evoked the furious hostility of both was the proposal to emancipate the Roman Catholics. Riots in Edinburgh and Glasgow in 1779 revealed the depth of popular prejudice and anticipated by a year a similar outburst in London—the Lord George Gordon riots. Otherwise the Scottish members were unmoved by the proceedings of Lord North and his royal master, which so deeply provoked the English Whigs, and, when Dunning's famous motion against the power of the crown was tabled in 1780, only seven of the forty-five voted for it, twenty-three were against it, while fifteen did not trouble to attend!

The appointment of Henry Dundas as lord advocate in 1775 brought to the front the classic example of Scots 'managers.' Marshalling his fellow-members behind the government, he was able to disregard the minority sentiment against the war of 1775–83, during which loyal enthusiasm was keen enough to cause volunteer companies to be raised for home defence and to bring Scottish recruits to the army at a rate which has been estimated as 10,000 per annum. After the fall of North in 1782, Scotsmen were indifferent to English party manœuvrings, arguing that, since the king's government must be carried on, it was their place to make what arrangements were possible with the group in power. Dundas proved his foresight by following Pitt, to whom his almost unchallenged control of forty-five members rendered him invaluable, and their close co-operation ushered in a half-century of Tory dominance in Britain.

Yet there are signs that towards the end of the eighteenth century part of the nation was beginning to stir from its political lethargy. Radical opinions, once strongly held among the fellow-countrymen of Knox and Buchanan, had never quite disappeared, and, as early as 1724, the enclosure of common fields in Galloway led to an uprising of evicted tenants who were 'levellers' of other things besides dykes. The later social changes, which followed the agrarian and industrial revolutions and entailed much hardship and want, did not pass unchallenged. Some of the newer types of workers, no longer dependent on hereditary landlords, were of a critical or even republican temper. The war against the colonists drove others to espouse the unpopular and 'pro-American' Whig cause. Before long, too, the 'wild' or Evangelical party in the Church began to make headway against the Moderates, who had controlled the General Assembly for over a generation. The Evangelical ministers championed the rights of the people against the autocratic claims of the patrons of livings: what more natural than that their flocks should apply similar principles in secular affairs? As a result of the ferment, the questions of parliamentary and municipal reform drew much attention during the 1780s, and it looked as though Pitt and Dundas, who both professed interest, would introduce liberal changes. When, however, they found that the existing system buttressed their parliamentary power, they dropped the project (1785); nevertheless, the revival of interest in public affairs is marked in the years before 1789.

The first reaction to the outbreak of the French Revolution, in Scotland as in England, was sympathetic. The Dundee Whig club addressed a moderately worded letter of congratulation to the French national assembly, and Tom Paine's *Rights of Man* was widely read. Soon, however, reform was denounced as the prelude to revolution, and French excesses stiffened the attitude of the British authorities. After 1791, with Dundas installed at the Home Office (then responsible for Scotland) and his nephew, Robert Dundas, lord advocate, there could be no effective parliamentary opposition to the 'Dundas despotism.' Accordingly, from the start of its activities in 1792, the Society of the Friends of the People, advocating the constitutional achievement of such aims as manhood suffrage, and holding popular meetings in many towns, incurred the disapproval of landowners, M.P.s, and lawyers, and this in turn played into the hands of the wilder elements of what was in the main an orderly and law-abiding organization. In 1793, the outbreak of war with France and the inception of the Reign of Terror supplied the little more that was needed to incite persecution. The state trials that followed were travesties of justice, and the sentences imposed on the relatively mild leaders of the reform movement showed that judges like Lord Braxfield, the justice clerk, feared a repetition in Scotland of what had been perpetrated in France. Late in 1793, Thomas Muir, a prominent lawyer with progressive views, was sentenced to transportation for fourteen years, while a Methodist clergyman, Fysshe Palmer, was given seven years; the penal system then in use was such as to ensure untold misery and exposure for the sufferers. Early in 1794, three further sentences of fourteen years' transportation were pronounced after farcical sedition trials, and, later in the same year, two death sentences were passed (though a reprieve was granted in one case) for what was deemed treason. The legislature helped the courts in their work of suppression by suspending the English Habeas Corpus Act and the similar Scots Act of 1701 'for preventing Wrongous Imprisonment' (1794), and by defining treason and sedition in such a way as to ensure almost unhampered governmental control of public meetings (1795).

The new day was slow to dawn, but when, in 1796, his Whig sympathies caused the deposition of Henry Erskine from the deanship of the Faculty of Advocates (in theory an annual office but normally bestowed for life), the opposition gained an eminent lawyer as a leader. Henceforth the Scottish Whigs, under Erskine, Francis Jeffrey and some of the Popular party in the Church, set about the tasks of overthrowing the Tory government and obtaining constitutional reforms. In 1797 Parliament, expecting a French invasion, passed a Scots Militia Act, but the embittered masses suspected a design to press them into foreign service, and disliked the exemption of their wealthier fellow-citizens of the 'volunteer companies.' Rioting broke out, eleven were killed at Tranent by the soldiers, and four sentences of fourteen years' transportation were imposed. Opposition was driven underground, but the law reached in to seize George Mealmaker, one of the leaders of the 'United Scotsmen,' a secret society linked with the United Irishmen, who had been clamouring for independence since 1791.

Never exceeding a few hundreds in membership, societies of this kind were suppressed in 1799 and are not heard of after 1802, by which time a better tone had come over public life.

The period of repression coincided with the closing years of Scotland's greatest poet. Burns was profoundly stirred by the new democratic spirit, and even at the height of the French scare his ardent patriotism (and he, like Scott, was a 'volunteer')—

> 'For never but by British hands
> Maun British wrangs be righted.'—

did not blind him to the claims of the masses:

> '. . . while we sing *God save the King,*
> We'll ne'er forget the People.'

But *Does Haughty Gaul Invasion threat* was a topical and transient piece; as for his share in the conflicts between Whig and Tory, with 'the warmest admiration for individuals of both parties,' he either affected the pose of an onlooker—

> 'He sees and hears the distant war,
> A cool spectator purely;'—

or allowed his attitude to be determined by personal considerations. It is in other ways, in deeper senses, that Burns responded to the aspirations and movements of his age. His awareness of social and political discontents showed itself from the start of his work, as in *The Twa Dogs*:

> '. . . our gentry care as little
> For delvers, ditchers, an' sic cattle;
>
> .   .   .   .
>
> Poor tenant bodies, scant o' cash,
> How they maun thole a factor's snash:
>
> .   .   .   .
>
> There's monie a creditable stock
> O' decent, honest, fawsont folk
> Are riven out baith root an' branch,
> Some rascal's pridefu' greed to quench.'

His election ballads could on occasion strike the same note:

> 'A Lord may be a lousy loon,
> Wi' ribban, star, and a' that.'

His championship of popular rights, his sympathy with the common man, his knowledge of the peasantry whence he sprang, and his insistence on personal integrity apart from birth, rank and wealth, are of the essence of his best work— of *Hallowe'en*, of *Tam o' Shanter*, and of *The Jolly Beggars*; the same qualities inform *The Cottar's Saturday Night*, which, though more laboured and artificial than his greatest poems, had a tremendous influence on his fellow-countrymen. Towards the end of his life, his association with 'sons of sedition' was injudiciously intimate, and he delighted too freely in low company, but 'his Muse' was still inspired by liberal and radical ideas. The plan of *Scots Wha Ha'e* was conceived in 1793 and was suggested, not only by Bannock- burn, but also by 'some other struggles of the same nature *not quite so ancient*,' while *Is There for Honest Poverty* (1795) also owed something to the French Revolution, with its pathetic vision of universal peace and goodwill:

> 'It's comin' yet for a' that,
> That man to man the world o'er
> Shall brithers be for a' that.'

By the end of the century the wave of persecution had passed, so that Parliament was able to concern itself with worthier matters than the shipping of its critics to the Antipodes: time was found in 1803 for the provision of better salaries for schoolmasters. Whig attacks on the government were given a powerful medium of expression with the founding of the *Edinburgh Review* in 1802, but Dundas was still able, in that year, to nominate 43 out of the 45 M.P.s. His impeachment for peculation, three years later, was therefore a political sensation; though he was acquitted, and though he retained hosts of friends and admirers in Scotland, he was a less autocratic 'manager' in his last years than in the 1790s. The episode discredited his party and his methods. There was a brief Whig interlude under the 'Ministry of All the Talents' in 1806–07, when one notable reform reached the statute book with the abolition of the slave trade; in this administration Henry Erskine served as lord advocate. But the country, deeply involved in the struggle against Napoleon, was in no mood for political experiments, and the Tories came back in 1807 for a further long spell of rule. The régime was now, however, more benign, and the second Viscount Melville, who was manager from his father's death in 1811 until 1827, wielded a control over the election and conduct of the Scottish members that was much less strict than had been that of 'King Harry the Ninth' at the height of his power.

Whig ideas meanwhile made steady progress, especially among the leading Edinburgh lawyers, and the *Edinburgh Review* won many friends in England as well as Scotland. 'Cultured' as to life and letters, it was Whig in politics, and 'moderate,' even irreverent, towards religion. With *The Scotsman*, founded as a Whig weekly newspaper in 1817, it helped to create, among men of substance and education, a mental climate favourable to constitutional change. The challenge to the party in power was met by the establishment in 1817 of *Blackwood's Magazine*. *Blackwood's* fought the enemy with its own weapons, well-informed gravity and outrageous flippancy; from sheer contrariety it championed the Evangelical side in the Church. The journalistic activities of the time reveal the reborn Scottish concern with political controversy. A great meeting was held in Edinburgh in July 1814 for the purpose of petitioning Parliament against West Indian slavery. Henry Cockburn, whose *Memorials of his Time* provide the most vivid and authentic picture of the period, declares that 'this was the first assembling of the people for a public object that had occurred here for about twenty years,' but admits that, had the meeting been called for 'a purely political matter,' it could not have been held in Tory-ruled Edinburgh: 'it was only made safe and respectable by the attendance of the humane and the pious of all politics.' In February 1816, however, he records the convening of a public meeting 'for the avowed purpose of controlling Government on a political matter'; this time a petition was presented for the withdrawal of the property and income tax.

After Waterloo depression and industrial dislocation led to a revival of revolutionary societies, and seditious meetings were forbidden in 1817 and 1819. The Glasgow weavers, more turbulent reformers than the sedate Edinburgh lawyers, demanded annual parliaments and adult suffrage. Speech-making was still liable to lead to an appearance in court, but the penalties were much less severe than formerly: six months' imprisonment might be imposed, and 'not guilty' verdicts were sometimes pronounced. Persistent hardships impelled the workers to a bolder step in April 1820, when a general strike was to instal a provisional government which should frame a new and equitable constitution. Soldiers had to deal with this 'Radical War' at Glasgow and Carron. Out of 47 prisoners taken, 24 were condemned to death (of whom, however, only three were hanged), two were found not guilty, and 21 were never brought to trial. In December of the same year a large public meeting was held by the Edinburgh Whigs, in defiance of municipal authority, in order to petition for the ministry's removal. In 1822, as a result of an inquiry into the need for burgh reform, Parliament gave the Scottish Exchequer some control over burgh finance; though warped judicial interpretations rendered this statute almost inoperative, it may be taken as a straw in the wind.

Change was in the air, but one fact remained unchanged—the sturdy national spirit of the Scots and their readiness to resist an affront. Over-speculation induced a severe financial crisis in England in 1825, and the government, as one of its measures for the relief of distress, proposed to prohibit the issue of Scottish as well as English bank-notes. Sir Walter Scott led the opposition in the *Letters of Malachi Malagrowther*, and the withdrawal of the suggestion was the happy and sensible result of the outcry; for the Scottish banks had weathered the storm. In 1827 the more liberal-minded of the Tories came into power under Canning as premier, and the 'office' of manager for Scotland was laid aside in response to agitation over ministerial responsibility for the northern kingdom. Catholic emancipation was advocated by the Scottish Whigs for some years before it was granted by Wellington and Peel (1829).

At long last, in 1830, a Whig ministry, pledged to

parliamentary reform, took office, with Francis Jeffrey as
lord advocate and Henry Cockburn as solicitor-general. They
had, as the latter expressed it, 'come upon the public stage in
a splendid but perilous scene'; if they but did their duty,
they 'cannot fail to do some good to Scotland. In the abuses
of our representative and municipal systems alone, our
predecessors have left us fields in which patriotism may
exhaust itself.' The struggle for reform, which followed
immediately, did indeed give Jeffrey and Cockburn ample
scope for patriotic endeavour, for it evoked such depth of
feeling among the masses, despite the cautious nature of the
change involved in the proposed £10 household suffrage,
that the ministers had qualms about their ability to hold in
check their more excitable followers. To the douce but
persistent lawyers who saw their early dreams come true, the
first Reform Act of June 1832 was a triumph, complete in
itself; to many of their supporters (who would still lack the
vote) it was merely the prelude to further advances.

Thus the new patriotism found itself and found its work.
The electoral change closed one era and ushered in another,
and the attitude to reform became the touchstone of Scottish
politics. Long before 1832 the Union, accepted by all as an
implicit condition of public life, had ceased to arouse controversy or to require a champion: Burns and Scott, poles apart
on the need for reform, were at one on this point; as were
the many Scots who, singly or in their thousands, were
contributing courageously to the building of the Empire,
from the explorers of central Africa, James Bruce (1768–73)
and Mungo Park (1795–1806), to the United Empire
Loyalists, who moved from New York to Canada in 1786.
It was, indeed, a highly exceptional occurrence, like the
banking crisis of 1825, that divided Scotsman from English-
man and produced an explosion of the national temper;
otherwise, none doubted that the main duty of the Scottish
voter, as of other British citizens, was to answer the paramount questions of the day—were reforms necessary, and,
if so, how far should they go?

The period between the Union and the first Reform Act
divides sharply at the year 1789. The political apathy of the

nation before the French Revolution may be shown by a consideration of the ministerial appointments that were then made. The Scottish secretaries, between 1709 and 1746, were as a matter of course Scotsmen, but not many others, then or for a long time after, attained high office in the state. Viscount Dupplin acted for two years under the elder Pitt as paymaster-general of the forces, Bute was a secretary of state and prime minister for two years (1761–63), and Viscount Stormont (later earl of Mansfield) was in North's ministry and the Fox-North coalition. This record—three cabinet ministers, apart from the Scottish secretaries, in 82 years—is the reverse of impressive; yet a glance at the part played by members of the northern nation in diplomacy and in the fighting forces dispels any notion either of Scottish inferiority or of reluctance to enter a competitive British service.

By George III's reign Scotsmen were securing one out of every seven diplomatic appointments, including a share of the highest posts available. Noteworthy in the annals of the service were the embassies of Sir Robert Murray Keith at Vienna (1772–92), of Sir Andrew Mitchell (1756–71) and Joseph Ewart (1788–91) at Berlin, and of Sir William Hamilton at Naples (1764–1800); and there were many others. They 'took their appointments,' says Dr. D. B. Horn (in *Scottish Diplomatists, 1689–1789*), 'more seriously than many of their English competitors;' hard-headed 'career men,' they had often prepared themselves consciously for their chosen profession by following the broad curricula, practical as well as cultural, offered by the Scottish universities. Their aptitude for foreign languages was perhaps their outstanding asset.

The record is similar for the army and the navy. Each of the wars saw more and more Scotsmen advanced to positions of command and trust. The Campbells of Argyll themselves span the military history of the century, for the second duke had served under Marlborough and the fifth duke (who had been 'Colonel Jack' in the 'Forty-five) became a field-marshal in 1796; between them, the fourth duke had been a brigadier at Dettingen (1743), long before he succeeded, as a lieutenant-general, to the title. Another of Marlborough's generals, the second earl of Stair, lived to become, in his seventieth year, commander-in-chief (under George II) and victor of Dettingen; he had, incidentally, served as ambassador at several of the courts of Europe, as did, in his time, a successor, the sixth earl (while Lord Dalrymple). The Seven Years' War saw James Murray serving as a brigadier under Wolfe at the capture of Quebec and later becoming governor of Canada, while Admiral Sir James Douglas captured Dominica in 1761. The War of American Independence found Admiral Sir Charles Douglas relieving Quebec (1776), General Sir Hector Munro capturing Pondicherry (1778), and, above all, Sir George Eliott winning immortality by his defence of Gibraltar (1779–82). During the times of Admiral Duncan, victor of Camperdown (and how sorely a victory was needed in the year 1797!), Sir Ralph Abercromby, the effective liberator of Egypt from Napoleon's grip (1801), Sir James Craig and Sir David Baird, successive captors of Cape of Good Hope (1795 and 1806), and Sir John Moore, the hero of Corunna (1809), Scotland's contribution to military, naval and imperial history is too well known to require emphasis; but it is not always remembered that distinction had been reached by Scottish soldiers and sailors long before 1789.

It was, therefore, in marked contrast to what was happening in other branches of public service that fuller Scottish participation in political life is to be dated only from about the year 1789. The record of ministerial appointments again clarifies the position. The earl of Mansfield (already noticed as a politician in Lord North's time) served under the younger Pitt. Two Scotsmen reached the highest post in England's legal hierarchy, that of lord chancellor—the Tory Lord Loughborough and the Whig Lord Erskine. Henry Dundas, who played the leading role in Scottish parliamentary affairs for a generation, occupied many posts under Pitt, and his son, the second Viscount Melville, was at the Admiralty under Liverpool and Wellington. The duke of Montrose headed the Board of Trade in Pitt's last administration, and Charles Grant (who was to become Lord Glenelg) held cabinet posts both as a Canningite

Tory and as a Whig. In addition to Melville and Grant, Wellington had no fewer than three other Scots in his administration—Sir George Murray, the earl of Rosslyn, and the earl of Aberdeen (himself destined for the premiership). Within a space of 43 years, Scotland had supplied ten cabinet ministers; while this figure was still disproportionately small in relation to her share of the population of Great Britain, it shows a great improvement on the barren period that went before, and illustrates the political awakening that had taken place since 1789.

Chapter 4

Political Life since the First Reform Act

THE tumultuous approval by the Scottish people of the first Reform Bill was confirmed by the outcome of the general election held later in the year on a wider franchise and with a fairer distribution of seats. The Liberals won 43 of the 53 Scottish constituencies, the Conservatives only ten, and this result strikes the keynote of the parliamentary history of Victorian Scotland. The political genius of the nation, for long thwarted by reason of the defective machinery of the state, now found its proper outlet; and, from gratitude and conviction, it expressed itself in steady support of the party of reform. The period between the first and third Reform Acts (1832–85) was thus the heyday of Scottish Liberalism. Not that the record of nineteenth-century reforms is one of continuous Liberal triumphs; it was Peel who emancipated the Catholics and abrogated the corn laws, and Shaftesbury who inspired the factory legislation, while Gladstone's double rebuff over Irish home rule was the biggest political failure of the century. Yet the Tories were unable to enlist the sympathies of any large number of Scotsmen, who for the most part spurned their doctrines as the obstructive or negative creed of the privileged few. On the other hand, extreme left-wing movements had not the power, wealth, or organization to challenge the Liberals' championship of popular rights. The Chartists, it is true, anticipating by a generation or two the march of reform, had a substantial Scottish following about 1840, Socialist orators in the coal mines and at street-corners were creating mild consternation from the 'fifties onwards, and later still the trade unions taught the working man to ask for much more than even an advanced politician was prepared to concede. These movements, however, had negligible political results until very late in the century, so that, from 1832 to 1885, the Scots Liberals had little to fear from either right or left.

Their staunchest supporters were the Presbyterian members of the middle classes enfranchised by the Reform Act. In the early years of Victoria's reign the relations of Church and State were hotly debated; while half of the adherents of the Church of Scotland were jealous of State interference, the numerous dissenters were Whig to a man. The bias towards Liberalism was already almost irresistible, and Peel's failure to avert disruption in 1843, if (as is claimed) it left every remaining manse a Tory stronghold, confirmed an opposite trend in the laity. To many, a free church and free schools, a free press and free trade seemed but facets of the Christian philosophy. It was easy and natural for the church-goer to be a politician, and to impart a moral content to his view of the secular issues of the day.

Party discipline was loose enough to allow freedom of judgment and of action, so that the term 'Liberal' might be applied in a general way to men whose political views diverged widely. Apart from the hybrid politicians who styled themselves 'Liberal-Conservatives,' there were two main divisions, the 'Old Whigs' or 'Reform Whigs,' who were satisfied with the changes made in the 'thirties, and the Independent Liberals and Radicals, who were bent on further political and social reforms. Already in 1839 the more advanced section had set up the Reform Union, to press for a wider franchise and to keep the Whigs true to their function as a progressive party. The different aims of the two wings may be studied in the correspondence of T. B. Macaulay (member for Edinburgh in the years 1839–47 and 1852–56) with some of the more vehement and outspoken of his constituents; they were highly critical of their member, but there was room inside the party for all of them. By contrast to the wide spread of the Liberals, the appeal of the Tories lay primarily to the landlord and the farmer, whose relative importance was diminishing as the townsfolk advanced in numbers and influence. Moreover, the Conservative split, after 1846, into Protectionists and Peelites, and the fact that the latter were closer in spirit to the Liberals than to anyone else, brought a great accession of strength to the already dominant party.

There was a marked contrast between English and Scottish political trends during these years. The Tory opposition won the general election of 1837 as regards England and Wales with a majority of 20, but the Irish and Scottish results converted this into a minority of 34 and kept the Whig ministry in power; the experience was to be by no means unique in the annals of Conservatism. Ireland, whether it voted Liberal, Radical, 'Repealer' or Irish Nationalist, could be depended upon not to vote Tory. Scotland was equally barren ground for that party, and the hostile Irish and Scottish *blocs* could on occasion reverse the English verdict. As a result, only Peel in 1841 and Disraeli in 1874 were returned with Conservative majorities, despite the fact that their party did as well in England, on the whole, as did their opponents. Never once did the Liberals look like failing to carry Scotland at a general election. Their smallest majority of Scottish seats was nine, in 1841; thereafter it rose steadily, to reach 31 in 1865. The second and third Reform Acts, enlarging the electorates and increasing the number of members, raised the margin in favour of the Liberals still more, to 46 in 1868, and eventually to 52 in 1885.

The election returns show that it was the burghs' vote that ensured the nation's constant support of one party and its rejection of the other. The Liberals unfailingly carried all or almost all the burgh seats. Occasionally they dropped one or two—at most (in 1874), three;—at four successive general elections, between 1857 and 1868, they made a clean sweep of all the burgh constituencies. There were actually in 1885 more burgh seats with unbroken records of Liberal representation than without. The county results were not nearly so one-sided. The shires may be divided into three roughly equal groups, of which one, including most of the northern counties, was predominantly Liberal, one, including many southern seats, was mainly Conservative, whilst in the third group the contest was a fairly even one. On the whole, it may be said that until 1865 the two parties were equally matched in the counties; thereafter the Liberals had a definite, sometimes a very great, advantage, though never to the same extent as in the burghs.

The Liberalism of the towns was in part a natural reaction against the irresponsibility and extravagance of the un-reformed municipal corporations (which had been defended by the Tories); in part, too, it had an economic basis, for free trade, the heart of the Liberal programme, served the interests of the townsfolk, who craved cheap bread as strongly as they detested indirect taxes. The shire voters, on the other hand, besides being more familiar with the idea of a dominant territorial aristocracy, gave a better hearing to the party that stood as the protector of their particular economic interest—agriculture; but even here the Liberals could count on many supporters. Towards the end of the period, the habit of reading daily newspapers spread widely in the towns, and to a lesser extent in the country districts; and the Liberal tone of the two leading journals, the *Scotsman* and the *Glasgow Herald*, which served as models for the provincial press, helped to mould and confirm the prevailing trend in politics.

The voters in Victorian Scotland thus made a substantial contribution, and one that was disproportionate to their parliamentary representation, to the great series of British political and social reforms: their fidelity to the Liberal cause hastened the enactment of the several reform measures. Nor were the electors' interests conceived in any narrow or pro-vincial sense. State regulation of commerce, parliamentary and local reform, and budget proposals were considered on general principles, not for their impact on Scottish or regional affairs; these matters, along with imperial policy and the conduct of war, now engaged the close attention of the voters.

The first period of Whig rule was largely taken up with the reform of parliament (1832) and of the Scottish burghs (1833)—each to be examined in its place—and with the improvement of the English poor law (1834) and the English boroughs (1835), while colonial slavery was abolished in

1833 and the only less abhorrent slavery of British children was prohibited or restricted by the Factory Act of the same year. These statutes represent the Liberal programme, translated into action by the use of the normal constitutional means. From the late 1830s, however, two other movements, having aims that were social and economic as well as political, and being conducted largely outside of Parliament, attracted as much notice as the proceedings at Westminster—namely, the activities of the Chartists and the agitation of the Anti-Corn Law League.

For two years (1837–39) the efforts to win support for adult male suffrage, the secret ballot, payment of members, and the other points of the 'People's Charter' were mostly English efforts, directed from London and Birmingham, while the final phase of the movement (1842–48) was dominated by Irish leaders and Irish methods; between them lay the period (1839–42) when the Scottish variant of Chartism was the most vital element in the three kingdoms. Under leaders (mostly of good sense and moderation) like Patrick Brewster, Alexander Campbell and Abram Duncan, Scottish Chartism became a vigorous and distinctively national movement, with its roots in native traditions, and with ramifications into other fields of progressive idealism— temperance, total abstinence, pacifism, factory regulation, the abolition of capital punishment, and non-intrusion in the Church. For a short time Chartist churches and Chartist schools were maintained, and periodicals—*The True Scotsman*, the *Scottish Patriot* and the *Chartist Circular*—were published in Scotland, but from 1842 the impetus died away, took other forms, or moved to other places.

The struggle for the repeal of the Corn Laws was the major conflict of the late 'thirties and early 'forties. The project commanded, it is said, even wider support in Scotland than in England, and from the first public meeting, held in Edinburgh in January 1839, there was little doubt as to where the people stood. Cobden and Bright found their ablest and most useful ally in a rising Independent Liberal of 'advanced' views, Duncan McLaren, who soon became prominent in the Anti-Corn-Law League's work in both countries. By collecting, classifying and digesting statistics, disseminating propaganda, arranging meetings, organizing financial expedients and preparing monster petitions, he made the Scots nearly unanimous in supporting the demand for abolition; 'the late meetings,' Bright wrote in December, 1843, 'and all your printing must have saturated the Scotch mind with Free Trade doctrines.' Most spectacular of all his moves was the convening of no fewer than 801 ministers of the Secession, Relief, Congregational, Baptist and other Churches to denounce 'the sinfulness and injustice' of the Corn Laws. In some localities the bitterness of the struggle drove a wedge between Old Whigs and Independent Liberals, and, repeal having been passed in 1846, the Edinburgh electors showed their dissatisfaction with Macaulay, who seemed to them lukewarm in this matter, by refusing to re-elect him.

By 1848, while free trade had been adopted as the guiding principle of the British economy, it seemed that Chartism had failed completely and irrevocably. Its ideas did not, in fact, die. All of them, with the exception of annual parliaments, were eventually written into the constitution; and all of them continued to influence radical thought, particularly in Scotland, for two generations. Thus, in the very long run, the Chartists were justified by events; they had denounced free trade propaganda as a middle-class device to divert attention from the true radical objectives—and free trade lasted only until 1932.

The ferment in political ideas worked also to bring about changes in the relations of Church and State; while the Disruption of 1843 was by far the greatest consequence of the operation of the radical leaven, the less dramatic developments of the time have their importance. Besides organizing Sunday schools and home and foreign missions, the ministers and the laity, inside and outside the establishment, helped to found and run temperance groups, from 1829, and total abstinence societies, from 1836. Controversy raged around the merits of voluntary poor relief and compulsory assessments, until, in 1845, Peel in effect settled the matter by establishing parochial boards, which were empowered (though not obliged) to levy poor's rates. Amid so much that was novel and revolutionary, one ancient prejudice—the traditional Scottish antipathy to Roman Catholicism—remained strong. In 1845 Peel's act recognizing and endowing Maynooth College for the training of Irish priests had been passed with Whig help, despite opposition from the Tory ranks and much popular misgiving. In Scotland the grants from public funds for such a purpose were denounced, but not (it is fair to note) from partisanship alone: the 'voluntaries' opposed the 'concurrent endowment' of the denominations as heartily as they did the establishment principle. In 1850 the cry of 'Papal aggression' was raised over the plan to give territorial titles to English bishops of the Roman Church, and this evoked a wide response in Scotland (which was not directly concerned). Lord John Russell's prohibitory act of 1851 gave satisfaction, public alarm was allayed, the act was not enforced, and it was quietly repealed twenty years later.

Temperance was a worthier cause for the Liberal and the Christian, for drunkenness was a notorious vice in Scotland at that time. In 1852, when Duncan McLaren was lord provost of Edinburgh, the problem was tackled locally. Sunday drunkenness was punished by the city magistrates more severely than week-day offences, and the publicans began to close down voluntarily, with beneficial effects. Fired by the success of this experiment, Parliament in the following year passed the Forbes-Mackenzie Act, which has governed the conduct of Scottish licensed houses ever since. Drinking on the premises was limited to the hours between 8 a.m. and 11 p.m., grocers were allowed only an 'off-licence,' whilst on Sundays no public houses could open, and hotels or inns could supply drink only to residents or to bona fide travellers. A general improvement in social conditions was the result. In 1853 leading free-traders like Bright, Cobden and McLaren, faced by the impending Crimean War, found that consistency obliged them to be pleaders in the cause of international peace. The 'Peace Party,' a comprehensive movement including those who denounced all war and favoured intergovernmental arbitration, others who feared the baneful influence of a military caste and others again who wished reduction of armaments for economy's sake, attracted the sympathetic interest of Scottish Liberals. Dissenters, now powerfully reinforced by the large following of the Free Church, were especially interested in temperance and peace policies; their activities in these matters reveal the politico-religious support which meant so much to Liberalism.

From 1853 onwards the methods of conducting Scottish business began to provoke adverse comment. The work, it was asserted, was too varied to be efficiently discharged by the lord advocate, under the loose control of the home secretary; the results were waste, irresponsibility and a small share of the national expenditure. The criticism was sound, but some time elapsed before real interest was aroused. In any case, minor issues were now overshadowed by the question of further parliamentary reform. Radicals like John Bright and Duncan McLaren spoke of a ratepayer-and-lodger franchise, the secret ballot and a wholesale redistribution (the last point being of special concern to Scotland, still grossly under-represented at Westminster). Nothing, however, could be done in Parliament until after Palmerston's death in 1865. Already in the elections of that year the Edinburgh radicals had scored a great triumph by returning their champion McLaren at the head of the poll, against both Tory and Old Whig opposition, and in the debates over the second Reform Bill in 1867 he played a big part, not only by going over with his fellow-radicals to support Disraeli's burgh household suffrage, but also by his masterly presentation of the case for an increased Scottish quota. He showed that, while Scotland, with a population between one-ninth and one-tenth of that of the British Isles, contributed between one-eighth and one-ninth of the national taxation, she got, with 53 members out of 658, well under one-twelfth of the representation; to allow her 68 members would be an act of mere justice. Disraeli, possibly influenced by the tactical consideration that adding to Scotland's members meant adding to the opposing party, grudgingly raised the 53 to 60. The secret ballot was left over, to be enacted by Gladstone four years later, while votes for women, also advocated by the radicals, were to wait for another half-century.

The election of 1868 swept Gladstone into power with a majority of well over one hundred, thanks entirely to the Scottish and Irish vote. Of all his reforms, what made the biggest impression in Scotland was that affecting education. In the 1830s the schools, still run by the Church, had begun to receive state grants, and in 1839 these were made dependent on regular inspection. The Disruption, meanwhile, had changed the position, for the Free Church, embodying the educational fervour that had marked the old Evangelical party, was soon equipped throughout the land with its own schools, as rivals to the parish schools; the United Presbyterian Church, founded in 1847, was a good third. The Act of 1872 substituted a national scheme for independent denominational control. School boards were to have full authority in each parish and, although religious instruction was available, the 'conscience clause' enabled parents to decide whether their children should take it. The adoption of the principle of popular election for the school boards gratified Scottish Liberals, who felt that the same plan should apply over the whole field of local government. Already in 1870 Henry Campbell (later Sir Henry Campbell-Bannerman), member for Stirling burghs, and Duncan McLaren had proposed the setting up, in the counties, of responsible, elective bodies in place of the commissioners of supply, who, they felt, had long outlived their usefulness.

Ecclesiastical affairs continued to bulk large in the politics of the day. The year 1870 saw the end of a dispute which, though purely local in nature, had been for thirty-six years a national *cause célèbre*. The annuity-tax, exacted from householders in Edinburgh and Montrose for the upkeep of the Church of Scotland ministry in these towns, was detested as a financial grievance and a badge of servitude by Liberals and dissenters alike, who welcomed the statute by which it was directed to be compounded. The disestablishment of the Episcopal Church in Ireland, in 1869, encouraged the Scottish dissenters to press for a similar measure for Scotland; though the most severe critic could hardly claim that the cases were parallel, disestablishment became a favourite topic among Scottish Liberals. The most striking personality among them was that of Duncan McLaren, who, by his exact and masterly knowledge and lucid exposition of all Scottish questions, as well as by his sincere, enlightened and active patriotism, won for himself the sobriquet of 'Member for Scotland.'

Disraeli's return to power in 1874 was in a sense an English triumph over the changeless Liberalism of the sister countries, and yet the new ministry did something to earn Scotland's gratitude by abolishing Church patronage (that hoary grievance), removing road-tolls and consenting to fortify Inchkeith. Consequently Gladstone's victorious Midlothian campaign of 1879 and his party's success in the general election of the following year were a great disappointment to the Conservatives. The ninth decade of the century opened with the Liberals holding 53 of Scotland's 60 seats, and seemingly as firmly entrenched as ever; but divisive forces were at work within their party, which were to split it asunder and, within little more than a generation, to reduce it almost to impotence. On the need for a really wide franchise, a thorough-going redistribution of seats, and a system of elective local councils, Liberals were in agreement; but the case with Irish home rule was utterly different. That issue pitted its advocates against its opponents, and thousands of both categories were to be found within the Liberal ranks: it threatened to cut the party in two, and to show it for what it really was—a loose alliance of men who were essentially moderate and men who were essentially radical. Yet the day of decision, unpleasant as it must be, could not be for ever postponed; already during the 'seventies the Irish clamour was fierce enough to push home rule into the front rank of all outstanding questions.

The great achievement of Gladstone's second administration was the introduction of manhood suffrage under the third Reform Act (1884–85); and no difficulty was made about conceding Scotland's demand for fair representation. The raising of her quota of members from 60 to 72 gave her, for the first time since 1707, her proper share by population, and was a belated recognition of the accuracy of the figures put forward by McLaren in 1867. Another grievance, equally well founded, related to the maladministration of, and ministerial irresponsibility for, Scottish affairs. Action was deferred simply because of Gladstone's lack of real interest in Scotland (which gave him his seat as well as an invaluable body of supporters) through his preoccupation with Ireland. Since McLaren's resignation in 1881, Scotland's most effective spokesmen were two talented and patriotic Liberal peers, the young earl of Rosebery and the elderly duke of Argyll. Both were convinced that only a Scottish secretaryship could remedy the existing ills and assuage the general indignation, which was already such that, according to Rosebery, 'the words Home Rule have begun to be distinctly and loudly mentioned in Scotland.' Rosebery was given the under-secretaryship of home affairs, with Scotland as his special charge, and his uneasy tenure of an office which he deemed worthy neither of his country's dignity nor of his own deserts merely confirmed his views. Time was wasted and tempers were frayed over arguments as to what should be done; it all seems singularly barren and unreal to us to-day. Gladstone was out and Salisbury in before Rosebery's bill became law, so that it was under a Conservative ministry, though by a Liberal house, that the office of secretary for Scotland was instituted.

The general election held in November 1885 gave the Liberals 62 out of the 72 Scottish seats, and the returns show that rather more than two out of three voters had supported them. It was a fitting climax to 53 years of unbroken success at the polls—success, as we have seen, that was due as much to the content of moral righteousness in their creed as to considerations of political expediency. Not that they had a monopoly of the Christian virtues: a number of valuable reforms had come from the Conservatives, who, strong in rural England, had taken delight that was in part malicious in pointing to the evils of the urban factory system and in promoting humanitarian legislation. On the whole, however, the Conservatives' policy had been imprecise, frivolous, or opportunist. They could exploit Liberal mistakes, particularly in the foreign and colonial departments, and could offer an alternative administration, free from such blunders; but their essentially negative appeal made little impression on progressive and enterprising Scotland. It is easy nowadays to assess the Liberals' shortcomings—to note, for example, how, dazzled by the economic merits of the doctrine of *laissez-faire*, they either overlooked its social flaws or trusted that, in the long run, happiness and well-being would inevitably flow from freedom and self-government. If their understanding of the human consequences of an unplanned Industrial Revolution was imperfect, their aims and ideals were just and noble, and their steadfast political faith does credit alike to their strength of mind and their sincerity of purpose. It is well, in the twentieth century, to recognize these facts, for it can truly be said that our modern parties, Conservative, Liberal and Labour, have a common ancestor in the Liberals of Victorian times.

Meanwhile, the Irish troubles, and to a lesser extent Scotland's own ills, prompted many to speculate on the need to review the terms of the Union, and from this time most of the Scottish Liberal members spoke in favour of home rule for their own country, as well as disestablishment of the national Church. Not that they were separatists in a narrow sense: what was in their minds was a comprehensive scheme of devolution, whereby the control of local affairs would go to parliaments representative of the three, or even four, nations—for Wales was sometimes put on an equality with the others. McLaren, now a retired politician, approved of 'a measure of Home Rule which would apply equally to each of the three kingdoms, and have a tendency to unite them more and more in one friendly bond of brotherhood.' That the Scottish Liberals, from about 1884, were actuated by such general principles, and not merely by a resentful awareness of the deficiencies in their country's parliamentary representation and executive government, is shown by the fact that their agitation (mild as it was) did not cease with the remedying of these abuses in 1885. Many of them, indeed, joined the Scottish Home Rule Association, formed in the year 1886.

When, in April 1886, Gladstone announced his Irish home
rule plan, the Scottish question paled into insignificance
beside it. Opinion in Scotland, as in England, was rather
evenly divided upon it. The Conservatives, of course, were
against it to a man. Most of the Liberals approved, but there
was a powerful minority of dissentients. Some—heirs of the
old 'Reform Whig' tradition—objected to any meddling
with the legislative union of the kingdoms. Others, who
favoured the principle of home rule for all three nations,
saw in the Gladstonian scheme only abject surrender to
Irish intimidation and disbelieved in, or were dissatisfied with,
the premier's promise of a similar measure for Scotland.
Among these last was Duncan McLaren, 'advanced' Liberal
and home ruler as he was; already on his death-bed, he wrote
to the greatest of the recalcitrant English Liberals, John
Bright, 'If I had the health and strength which I possessed in
Anti-Corn Law times, I would be prepared to do what you
and other noble patriots did, and to do what our ancestors
used to call "to testify" against the proposed injustice.'
Thousands of Gladstone's Scottish followers turned against
him; the Liberal Unionists, as the opponents of the scheme
were called, were numerous in the cities and towns; and,
worst of all, the influence of the major organs of the press
was thrown to the other side, for both *Scotsman* and *Glasgow
Herald* adopted the Unionist position.

The ensuing general election (July 1886) showed how
wide was the breach in the Liberal ranks. Gladstone's
opponents gained enough support to put Salisbury in
office with a majority of over a hundred. In Scotland the
Liberal poll dropped by well over 100,000 votes, more
seats were lost than at any time since 1832, and the party's
margin in Scotland dropped from 52 to 14. No fewer
than nine burgh constituencies rejected Gladstonian candidates, eight of them in favour of Liberal Unionists. The
defection was serious and permanent, for the loss, at one
stroke, of the loyal support of the burghs and the sympathy
of the press was never made good. In Scotland, as in
England, Liberal Unionists happily co-operated with Conservatives, and, abandoning their intention of maintaining

their identity, ultimately merged with them. The new allies (many of them already fired by Disraeli's concepts of empire and patriotism) could appeal to the unionist faith of both nations as champions of the solidarity of the United Kingdom.

Another threat, less obvious at first but no less real, began to appear at the same time on the Liberals' left flank. Many of their candidates had for long had working-class supporters whose ideas were more revolutionary than their own, and relations had sometimes been strained between member and voters. Duncan McLaren had made enemies among his trade union followers, for he was too much of an in-dividualist to allow what they claimed to be their right to 'picket' during strikes; and at one meeting (1874) the dissatisfied workers had carried a vote of no confidence in their normally popular member. The malcontents were as yet few in number, and they were not ready to break away from the party that had fought their fights in the past. Candidates who called themselves 'Labour' or 'socialist' were, indeed, indistinguishable from the more radical of the Liberals, and they were encouraged to enter the party and to contest constituencies that had a large proportion of factory workers, mill-hands, or miners. Thus, in 1886, while Keir Hardie, the most dynamic of the Scottish socialists, was organizing the country's miners in a strong trade union, Cunninghame Graham, who not long after became the first chairman of the Scottish Parliamentary Labour party, won North-west Lanarkshire; but he won it as a nominal Liberal. Labour speakers, besides advocating purely socialist ideas like nationalization of industry, national insurance and abolition of the House of Lords, took over such Liberal policies as home rule and disestablishment. Twenty years were to elapse before Labour won a Scottish seat in its own name; there was no sign that it would one day steal the Liberals' thunder, but its appearance on the political stage is a portent.

The Salisbury administration went far towards satisfying the demand for local government reform by its establishment in 1889 of popularly elected county councils; save for the anomalous retention of commissioners of supply, it was a bold and thorough change. Something was being attempted at the same time in the way of relieving distress in the Highlands, where high rents and ejections had induced an ugly temper among the crofters. The Crofters' Holdings Act of 1886, sponsored by the first Liberal secretary for Scotland, Sir George Trevelyan, had sought to fix fair rents, guarantee security of tenure, enlarge existing holdings and allow compensation for improvements. Unrest, disturbance and rioting continued for several years, while, in accordance with the act, commissioners toured the northern counties endeavouring to alleviate hardships and settle disputes. The commission continued to visit and report annually until 1913, reducing rents in the aggregate by 25 per cent. and cancelling arrears up to 67 per cent.

The English elections of 1892 gave the Conservatives another majority, but Scotland and Ireland again reversed the verdict; Liberals won 50 Scottish seats and lost 22. Gladstone took office for the fourth time, only to give way in 1894 to his brilliant and erratic lieutenant, Rosebery; in the interim Irish home rule had encountered its second defeat. (Rosebery was only the third Scotsman in nearly two centuries to reach the premiership; but, of his eight successors during 40 years, four were fellow-countrymen of his—Balfour, Campbell-Bannerman, Bonar Law and Ramsay MacDonald.) It was during the Rosebery administration that the nineteenth-century local reforms were completed by the establishment of popularly elected parish councils and of a local government board to co-ordinate their activities (1894). The details of the act were worked out under a new procedure whereby all Scottish members were included in a Scottish Grand Committee. This was a concession to the demand for devolution—a demand which, from 1889 to 1895, underlay a perennial motion in favour of a separate parliament for Scotland. As regards relations between church and state, disestablishment was now not only reaffirmed by the United Presbyterian Church, but was also adopted as Free Church policy. Whether home rule and disestablishment helped or hindered the Liberal cause in Scotland is not easy to determine with certainty. Liberals would inevitably have dominated a Scottish parliament, and the greater part of their support came from Presbyterian dissent; but, though they asserted that there was a general desire for these changes, that desire was at all events not a compelling motive in men's minds. The questions were rather academic, and the attention they received came largely by way of a sympathetic response to the Irish agitation. And they may well have been a political liability, since they gave the Conservatives and Unionists the chance to speak and act as the defenders of church and state against untried change and factious schism.

The 1895 election results give point to these considerations. The Unionists obtained a larger majority than any recorded since 1832, and the Liberal majority in Scotland touched the unusually low figure of six. As the century drew to its close local issues were dwarfed by an all-pervading imperialism. The queen's diamond jubilee (1897) focussed the growing sense of pride in Britain and the empire, and this was kept alive by war and rumour of war in the Sudan (1896–98). The outbreak of the Boer War in October 1899 and the early reverses and disasters suffered by the British armies evoked a great outburst of military and patriotic fervour, and the government, in the 'khaki election' of October 1900, was confirmed in office with a margin just short of that of 1895. Scotland, swept along with the tide, broke with the tradition of two generations to give the Conservatives and Unionists a majority of four seats. Glasgow's seven constituencies, which had sent seven Liberals to parliament 15 years before, now returned seven Unionists, while Orkney and Shetland, a 'safe' Liberal seat throughout the queen's long reign, likewise changed its allegiance.

The Liberals were now, and for some time afterwards, weakened by divided opinions as to the justice of war. Rosebery, Asquith, and the Liberal League (formed in 1902) were converts to imperialism, while Campbell-Bannerman, Morley and the pacifists of the Young Scots Society (organized in the same year) had contrary ideas, which were not shared by Scotsmen generally. The government was able to please national sentiment, and to have regard to the needs of strategy, by authorizing the country's first naval base at Rosyth and by planning a permanent military camp at Stobs. But Unionist popularity was in turn undermined by internal dissension over Joseph Chamberlain's proposals for tariff reform (1904), by-elections told heavily against the party in power, and the government took the unusual step of resigning in 1905. The general election of January 1906 was a decisive victory for free trade, for the Liberals got a clear majority without help from their Irish and Labour allies. Unionists retained only twelve of the 72 Scottish seats; Glasgow returned two, instead of the seven of 1900, and those two were free traders. (The *Glasgow Herald*, while remaining Unionist, opposed Chamberlain and tariffs.) Dundee and the Blackfriars division of Glasgow gave Scotland her two first Labour members. Even now, however, the defeated Unionists polled nearly two out of five votes cast in Scotland.

After their years in the wilderness, the Liberals came back to power under Campbell-Bannerman (1905–08) and Asquith (1908–15) in a mood for radical change. In 1906 the new government, reversing the policy of its predecessor, proposed to remove the Scots Greys to England, on the grounds of expense and the lack of accommodation in Scotland, but the threatened extinction of the country's last remaining cavalry regiment aroused sufficient resentment to bring about the building of the Redford barracks, near Edinburgh. The concentration of by far the most important elements of Presbyterian dissent within the United Free Church, formed in 1900, had strengthened the old demand for disestablishment; and the Lords' decision in 1904 in favour of the vestigial Free Church's claim to the whole property of that sect seemed to many to supply yet another argument against state control. In 1906 the Scottish Liberal Federation included disestablishment in its programme, and in 1908 this was repeated, along with a plea for Scottish home rule. On these and other points, Labour generally supported the Liberals. There was a local understanding between the two parties at Dundee, a double-member constituency which was held by them jointly for twelve years (1906–18) against the Unionists. Such a concordat, had it been extended to the whole country, might have benefited both groups, by giving the one fresh vigour and the other political experience; but the opportunity, if it existed, passed, so far as Scotland was concerned, in 1906, when, by 55 votes against 34, the Scottish Liberal Federation resolved to oppose all socialist candidates for parliament— so that the Dundee arrangement stood as the sole exception to the national rule.

The reformist zeal of the Liberal administration was shown by the institution of old age pensions (1908), the reform of the House of Lords (1911), and the establishment of compulsory national insurance (1912), while the main legislative proposal from 1912 was that of home rule for Ireland. The intransigence of the strongly Tory House of Lords gave the Liberals a rousing war-cry in 'Peers *versus* People,' and the two general elections of 1910 renewed their mandate for reform: the Scottish results showed little net difference after nearly five years.

From 1909 onwards the Church of Scotland and the United Free Church were discussing the basis of reunion, and by 1914 (when a draft constitution was published) the principle of disestablishment had been abandoned. Meanwhile, home rule, the Liberals' other legacy from the Victorian age, remained among their aims. In 1907 Campbell-Bannerman had resuscitated the Scottish Grand Committee for dealing with Scottish bills; it was a concession to nationalist sentiment, as well as to sound legislative method, but the feeling remained that measures desired by the Scottish people, such as temperance and land reforms, were unduly delayed or side-tracked. As a result, in June 1910, some twenty Liberal M.P.s formed themselves into the Scottish Nationalist Committee, to demand Scottish control of Scottish affairs. They urged on Asquith the claim for devolution, but, as in Gladstone's time, the Irish question took precedence. Motions and bills were introduced, favourably received, and forgotten; in 1912 the House, by a small majority, approved a resolution to grant equal treatment to Scotland and Ireland.

In 1913 the Temperance (Scotland) Act was passed, to enable the electors in each district to control or prohibit the local liquor business by voting for 'No Change,' 'Limitation,' or 'No Licence.' The delay of four years in enacting this measure played into the hands of the home rulers, who, however, found the Liberal ministers (with Ireland engaging their attention) only vaguely benevolent. In 1913, therefore, and again in 1914, parliamentary time was refused for a specific Government of Scotland Bill. The plan was to entrust Scottish administration to the lord high commissioner and a revived privy council, and legislation to a parliament of 140 members, based on the existing constituencies, but without the universities; all 72 Scottish M.P.s would be retained at Westminster. Balfour and the Unionists condemned the proposal as unwanted; the Liberals (though some of them were suspected of lukewarmness) gave it their blessing. The near prospect of civil war gave the Irish question an urgency that could not be affirmed in Scotland's case; but it is just possible that, if home rule had been put into effect in Ireland in or after 1914, the Liberal government would have done the like for Scotland. But the outbreak of the first World War in August 1914 postponed both problems to a more convenient time.

The pre-war generation had seen political changes which (when every allowance is made for the swing of the pendulum) amounted to a large accession of strength to the Unionists at the expense of the Liberals, especially in their former strongholds, the burghs. Nevertheless, the electorate of 1914 was still more than half Liberal, less than half Unionist. On the left wing, Labour was just coming into prominence, with not quite one-eighth of the voting power of the Liberals. Closely associated with the trade unions, Scottish Labour candidates were often extreme radicals, acting as a 'ginger group' in the British movement; some of them had entered municipal politics (up till then concerned with local and non-party issues) and won a few seats on the councils of cities and burghs with a large working-class population, such as Glasgow, Paisley and Falkirk. In parliament, West Fife had joined Dundee and Blackfriars in December 1910, to give them three seats.

From August 4, 1914, to November 11, 1918, the nation's energies were devoted to the winning of the struggle for survival in its varied aspects—the raising (by voluntary recruiting until 1916, thereafter by conscription) of large armies, the seemingly endless test of endurance in the trench warfare of the western front, the defeat of the enemy's threats (especially by submarine) to our naval and mercantile strength, the defence or conquest of overseas territories, and, at home, the production of munitions of war and the acceptance of enforced shortages of food, clothing and housing. That the world-wide conflict was no time for the continuance of the normal party warfare was recognized by the admission of Conservatives and others to the Coalition governments formed by Asquith in May 1915 and by Lloyd George in December 1916. The personal rivalry between these two Liberal chiefs introduced another element of discord among their followers, and the Conservatives, already favoured by experience and tradition for war-time leadership, were bound to benefit from the weakness and discomfiture of their opponents. In spite, therefore, of the party truce, in spite also of Lloyd George's ability, pugnacity and eloquence, there was in fact a 'drift to the right' during the war years both in parliamentary affairs and in the thoughts of the people.

The other, and much more obscure and localized, war-time trend was in a contrary direction. The exigencies of war production led to much overtime working, the abrogation of trade union regulations, and the 'dilution' of labour (especially the employment of women for the simpler tasks, in order to release the skilled men for key positions). These changes made many of the men truculent and suspicious, and the shop stewards' committees championed their claims along lines of extreme socialism. The Clyde Workers' Committee was set up with the aims of superseding the existing trade unions, fostering industrial unions in their stead, and seizing governmental power by direct action. Though driven underground, the movement survived the war and lasted until about 1922; it can be taken as foretelling not only a general post-war 'drift to the left'

E

(also a normal feature of British political history), but also the revolutionary ideas that were to give birth to the term 'Red Clydeside.'

In December 1918, the month following the conclusion of the armistice, and long before the signing of the peace treaties, the government appealed to the country as a continuing coalition of the major parties. Female suffrage had been advocated, prior to 1910, by constitutional means, and, between 1910 and 1914, in a militant and often disorderly manner; it was conceded by an act passed earlier in 1918, and, for the first time, women voted in an election. The emotions engendered by the war had not yet found release, it was asserted that a national emergency still existed, and the election was a poor test of political feeling. The Coalition, supported by all but a few Conservatives, most of the Liberals (though not Asquith and his adherents, who were in opposition) and a small fraction of the Labour party, got a large majority; in Scotland it won 60 seats and lost only 14—half to Labour, half to independent Liberals.

Government by coalition went on for a further period of nearly four years. For Britain, saddled with huge war debts and faced by a gigantic task of economic and social reconstruction, those were trying years. Their hopes for international friendship were enshrined in the foundation of the League of Nations; their reality was more accurately reflected by the great coal strike of 1921, the general trade depression and the mounting figures of unemployment. Scotland, chiefly dependent on heavy industry, was hit with special severity, and her economic plight overshadowed all other cares. In domestic politics, the treaty that set up the Irish Free State as a self-governing dominion (December 1921) closed a long and stormy chapter of history, and incidentally removed from the path of the Conservatives a permanent *bloc* of parliamentary opponents.

The first general election that can be regarded as a guide to post-war political developments came in November 1922. It showed that the Conservatives had gained greatly from Liberal misfortunes and mistakes, for Bonar Law was returned to power with a majority of more than 80 over all other parties, whilst Labour advanced to chief place in the opposition. The triumph of the Conservatives depended on the English results, for they took third place in Scotland with only 15 seats. The 28 Liberal candidates who were successful comprised equal numbers of the 'national' and 'independent' groups, 30 Labour members were returned, and one constituency (Motherwell) sent a Communist to parliament for the first time. In little over a year another election was held over Baldwin's conviction that British trade required protection in a world that was becoming increasingly nationalist in the economic sense. The people did not endorse his proposal to reinstate tariffs, and the election resulted in a stalemate. Though the Conservatives led the other two major parties over the whole of Britain, Scotland's vote was utterly different, for Labour captured 35 seats, Liberals 23 and Conservatives 16; thus the main change from a year earlier was a further net gain for Labour from the Liberals.

There were not many constitutional precedents for the proper interpretation of these election returns (December 1923), but the fact that they involved a rebuff to the existing government was deemed paramount, and Ramsay MacDonald, forming the first Labour administration, reached 'office without power' (January 1924). The importance of Scotland's contribution to this event was acknowledged by the allocation of five of the 23 cabinet posts to Scotsmen; besides the premier himself, Lord Haldane was lord chancellor, Arthur Henderson home secretary, William Adamson secretary for Scotland, and John Wheatley minister of health. The very existence of a minority Labour government spelled further trouble for the Liberals, who, weakened by divided leadership and predisposed to take divergent views on public issues, must now answer the delicate question of how to act as a small party of the centre holding the balance between the two stronger forces to right and to left. Sympathetic towards some socialist tenets, distrustful of others, they could give only wavering support to the government, and their conduct in this dilemma was conducive neither to their unity nor to their repute. Their internal differences were no secret, and there were many defections to the other parties. When, in October 1924, after an adverse Liberal vote, the government felt impelled to appeal to the electorate, the inevitable consequence was seen in the swamping of the Liberal candidates: only nine of them were successful in Scotland, 41 in the whole country. The Conservatives scored a great victory, with a majority of some 220 in the new House, but in Scotland (where they got 38 of the 74 seats) the contest was much closer. Thus, in the short space of six years, the Liberals had been reduced to the status of a minor parliamentary group, without real hope or prospect of ever again forming its own administration, and forced into the undignified position of continuing to exist, and to exercise some influence, by way of understandings, central or local, with one or other of its greater rivals.

Several administrative and electoral reforms affecting Scotland were passed during the Baldwin administration (1924–29). The Scottish secretary became a secretary of state (1926); the admission of women voters to equal rights with men raised the total number of those qualified for the franchise in Scotland to well over three millions (1928); and the entire system of local government was overhauled (1929). But the most important political activity of the time occurred outside of parliament, when the general strike of May 1926 was proclaimed in support of the coal miners. The general council of the Scottish Trades Union Congress directed the strike in Scotland, while a Scottish Emergency Organization, headed by the lord advocate, supervised the local arrangements for the provision of essential food and fuel supplies and such restricted transport facilities as were available. The stoppage was at first reported to be complete, but voluntary labour soon filled up the main gaps and even daily newspapers of a sort were regularly obtainable. A few riots occurred and police charges were made in Glasgow and Edinburgh, but, as in England, there was surprisingly little disturbance or destruction, in view of the serious nature of the conflict; the end came on May 12, with the calling-off of the strike after only eight days.

Towards the end of the Conservative administration interest in the subject of Scottish self-government was revived.

Home rule bills had been presented in Parliament on several occasions between 1919 and 1927, only to be laid aside and forgotten. A scheme of devolution had been adopted by the Scottish Liberal Federation in 1924 and reaffirmed in subsequent years; it visualized a parliament for the United Kingdom—in which Scotland would still be represented—with control of war, defence, foreign and imperial affairs, currency, customs and excise, and another for Scotland, based on the existing constituencies and responsible for internal government, social services, education, transport and direct taxation. Official inaction bred distrust of moderate methods, and from 1927 more extreme ideas were being put forward; outright independence was the aim of the Scots National League. In a brief but vitriolic book, *Albyn*, Mr. C. M. Grieve pled for complete national regeneration to arrest the process of provincialization and decay which, in his view, resulted from the union with England. A companion volume, *Caledonia*, by Mr. G. M. Thomson, as forcefully argued that the nation must reassert itself against the alien Irish in its midst. Moreover, the country's economic ills convinced many of the need for drastic change. From varied elements like these, linked by agreement on the claim for a separate parliament, and supported by the literary group concerned mainly with a cultural renaissance, was born, in 1928, the Scottish Nationalist party, headed by R. B. Cunninghame Graham, Mr. R. E. Muirhead and Mr. J. M. MacCormick. Its interpretation of history and its analysis of fiscal relationships were spirited rather than accurate, and it did better to stress the congestion of business, and the difficulty of promoting legislation, at Westminster. It drew the attention of the press and won the warm sympathy of many writers and publicists.

The general election of 1929—the first to be contested on adult suffrage—saw Labour emerge as the strongest party in Britain, though still short of a clear majority. That majority it did obtain in Scotland, with 38 seats against the Conservatives' 22 and the Liberals' 14. The Communists' total vote rose to nearly 25,000 and the Scottish Nationalists made an unimpressive start, fighting two seats, getting 3,300 votes and forfeiting two deposits. Again, as in 1924, Scotsmen were prominent in the Labour administration of Ramsay MacDonald, with four out of the 19 cabinet positions. But the extreme socialists of Glasgow and Clydeside were displeased over their omission from the government: one of their number, John Wheatley, had been minister of health in 1924. They were further estranged over the failure of the ministry, dependent on Liberal support in the Commons, to achieve 'Socialism in our Time.' The Independent Labour party, always strong in and around Glasgow, became more critical of official Labour and more disposed to break away.

In the late summer of 1931 Britain was hit by the most severe and widespread of the post-war depressions. The government, its expert advisers, and the great majority of the people admitted the need for economies to avert the threat of an unbalanced budget and a 'flight from the pound.' Unable to carry their colleagues with them over their proposals to make really drastic cuts in expenditure, the Labour leaders, Ramsay MacDonald and Philip Snowden, combined with their Conservative and Liberal rivals to form a National government, pledged to a sound economy, a balanced budget and a stable currency. The new government, backed by almost all the Conservatives, most of the Liberals and a minority of Labour, and opposed by the bulk of the Labour party and a small body of Liberal independents, appealed to the country in October 1931. The verdict of the people was unmistakable. The government secured the record majority of 491 in a House of 615 members. Though it failed to carry Wales, it succeeded in 'radical' Scotland only slightly less strikingly than in Conservative England; even Dundas, with bribery, patronage and a narrow electorate at his disposal, could scarcely have bettered its showing of 67 seats won out of 74. The non-party, as well as the Liberal and Conservative, votes had gone to the government, to give a two-to-one victory at the polls and a ten-to-one victory in representation, and to leave to the opposition only seven socialist strongholds in and around Glasgow.

One or two features of this highly exceptional election are

worth noticing. The Scottish contingent of government adherents comprised no fewer than 50 Conservatives, alongside a mere 16 Liberals and a solitary 'National Labour'
member. On a former and comparable occasion, the Lloyd
George Coalition, in December 1918, had won (as we have
seen) 60 Scottish seats, but these had included 27 'Coalition
Liberals,' and there had then been seven Liberal M.P.s in
the opposition; now, in 1931, Liberal 'independency' was
reduced to one unsuccessful candidate (in the Roxburgh and
Selkirk division). These figures serve to illustrate the sharp
decline in the party's fortunes, particularly when we remember that it was favoured, as a component of the
'National' alliance, with the utmost goodwill of the Conservatives, and, indeed, was able to obtain the return of its
16 candidates only by virtue of the votes of its ancient
rivals. The Communists' 31,000 votes, spread over seven
constituencies, meant mostly forfeited deposits. The Scottish
Nationalists, who had been making little progress either in
by-elections or in municipal contests, but had, earlier in 1931,
achieved a non-parliamentary success with the election of
Mr. (later Sir) Compton Mackenzie as rector of Glasgow
University, and had thereby broken a tradition of Conservative rectors, fought five seats in the general election; the
results were disappointing for them, since their candidates
averaged under 4,200 votes and two of them forfeited their
deposits. The rebellious tendencies of the Clydeside left-wing
socialists were fomented by the victory of one of their group,
as an 'independent' in opposition to official Labour, at
Shettleston; before long these men became the nucleus of
a reorganized Independent Labour party, led by James
Maxton, member for Bridgeton and an outstanding parlia-
mentarian. The I.L.P. claim was that the regular Labour
party members were too timid to speak boldly and truthfully
on behalf of the workers, and, though the 'Red Clydeside'
M.P.s gave much offence by their rabid and fanatical
presentation of the 'proletarian' cause, they won the warm
admiration and devotion of thousands in the industrial
centres.

The National government, faced by economic malaise of a

severity without precedent, adopted drastic remedial measures. Historically, the most far-reaching of these was the
reversal, in 1932, of the policy of free trade which had been
in force since 1846. Of the economic aspects of this fundamental change more will be said in a later chapter; here
its political consequences must be noted. Once more the
Liberals, delicately poised between the protectionist right and
the socialist left, had to make an awkward choice; since the
matter at stake touched on a cardinal article of their creed,
indeed the basic tenet of Liberalism, any decision was almost
bound to lead to a further split. Sir Herbert Samuel and
other ministers led the Liberals out of the government in
1932 and into actual opposition in 1933; but Sir John Simon
and the right-wing National Liberals continued, now and
later, to support what had become a predominantly Conservative coalition. In 1934 the Unemployment Assistance
Board was set up, to administer centrally, instead of locally,
'transitional benefits' (paid to the long-term unemployed)
and able-bodied relief; another act of the same year provided
for an Exchequer grant to finance, through Scottish and
English commissioners, schemes of economic rehabilitation
and social improvement in the 'depressed' or 'special' areas
(which included the central industrial belt in Scotland).

Prolonged distress and poverty, symbolized by the 'means
test' imposed upon, and bitterly resented by, the unemployed,
gave point to socialist attacks upon the government. The
Labour party showed that, despite its crushing defeat in 1931,
it was by no means a spent force. Barred for the moment by
its great numerical inferiority from effective parliamentary
action, it found itself much more favourably situated in
another field of political endeavour. For years it had been
building up its strength in the municipal elections, and, in
November 1933, for the first time, it won a majority of the
seats in Glasgow town council (though its triumph was shared
with its insurgent wing, the I.L.P.), and it also gained
control at Greenock and Dunfermline. A year later the party
made two further captures—Motherwell and Wishaw, and
Port Glasgow; such minor victories put fresh heart into the
critics of the 'National' system.

Meanwhile, the movement for self-government was also gathering its forces. The moderate home rulers, who had stood aside from the Nationalist party, and who were led by the duke of Montrose and Sir Alexander MacEwen, formed the Scottish party, which advocated a parliament for Scottish affairs, but renounced the idea of separation from England and reaffirmed loyalty to crown and empire (September 1932). The Scottish Nationalists and the Scottish party, after co-operating at the Kilmarnock by-election in November 1933, combined in the next year to form a new and larger Scottish National party.

The general election of November 1935 was fought under the shadow of the Italo-Abyssinian war and the threat, still distant, of the vaster conflict with Hitler's Germany. The government, under Stanley Baldwin as premier, appealed to the electors for a renewal of its mandate as a ministry of national unity; despite its title, however, it could now count as adherents only the Conservatives and two small groups of their allies who had broken away from the Liberal and Labour parties. Though Labour gained over 100 seats in Britain, the 'National' forces, with a majority of over 240, scored a very substantial triumph. Scotland reverted to its earlier habit of voting further 'left' than England, returning 46 government candidates—37 of them Conservatives, eight 'National Liberal,' and one 'National Labour': all of these, whatever their party label, may be regarded as owing their election mostly to Conservative votes. The opposition was also 'fractionated' at this time of political confusion and blurred lines of demarcation. There were twenty Labour M.P.s, representing the cities, burghs and industrial centres, and also (a new gain) the Western Isles; four Glasgow seats fell to the I.L.P.; the Liberals were a minority holding only three seats (Caithness and Sutherland, one of the Dundee seats, and Paisley); and Mr. William Gallacher won West Fife for the Communists. Eight Scottish Nationalist candidates got between them nearly 30,000 votes in all.

The Parliament thus elected was destined to attain a record span of life—four months short of ten years—in the political history of the United Kingdom, and to face the gravest threat ever offered to the very existence of the state. Almost at once the war clouds started to gather. The years 1935–39 saw the aggressive ambitions of the European dictators being realized in one quarter after another—in the Italo-Abyssinian war, the Spanish civil war, the remilitarization of the Rhineland, and the seizure of Austria and Czechoslovakia. From 1936 rearmament was adopted as the nation's basic policy, and economic recovery may be dated from the next year. The veteran politician, Stanley Baldwin, gave way in May 1937 to the well-meaning but ineffectual Neville Chamberlain, who, despite his pathetic devotion to peaceable ways, felt obliged, two years later, to adopt conscription. At last, on September 1, 1939, the German invasion of Poland laid all doubts at rest, and the nation was obliged to bend all its energies to the tasks, first of mere survival, then of winning the second World War.

Although the main preoccupation of the administration between 1935 and 1939 turned on the approach of war, some of the routine legislation of the time is noteworthy. Farm workers were brought into the scheme of unemployment insurance in 1936, and from 1938 it was made possible for 'black-coated' workers (with incomes up to £400 a year) to acquire state pension rights as voluntary contributors. Responsibility for trunk roads was transferred in 1936 from the county councils to the Ministry of Transport. The decision, taken in that year, to raise the school-leaving age to fifteen was frustrated by the march of events and the conspicuously unfortunate choice of date for putting the change into effect (September 1, 1939); on the other hand, the plan, settled in 1938, to nationalize the coal royalties from July 1, 1942, was in fact to be implemented despite the posture of public affairs on the due date.

The conflict between the two major parties was as sharp as ever almost up to the beginning of hostilities, with Labour showing a marked 'pacifist' tendency long after their rivals had become reconciled to the necessity of preparing for possible war. The ten Scottish by-elections held between the general election and the end of the uneasy peace resulted in two Labour gains from the government, both of them in

1936—at Greenock and Dumbartonshire. These changes reduced the 'National' majority of Scottish seats to 14 (44–30), and showed that Labour was not quite as weak as might be surmised from the fact of its prolonged exclusion from office. Moreover, the municipal elections of the time offer a corrective to the parliamentary figures. Labour won control of Dundee in 1936, only to lose it next year; at Greenock, captured by Labour in 1933, the Moderates regained a majority in 1936, but lost it again in 1938. With only minor fluctuations, Labour remained in power at Glasgow, while strengthening its opposition at Aberdeen.

During the inter-war period, the political scene in Scotland had undergone a remarkable transformation. The once great Liberal party, bruised and battered by the hammer of Conservatism upon the anvil of Labour, had been reduced almost to impotence. Voters in their thousands had forsaken it for one or other of its rivals. Within the burghs and cities Labour had benefited most from these defections, while the Liberals in the county constituencies had tended most often either to become outright Conservatives or to merge with their ancient enemies and, under the label of 'National Liberal,' to sink their separate identity in an anti-socialist alliance. By the close of the period, therefore, only Paisley among the burghs, only Caithness and Sutherland among the shires, could be claimed as Liberal strongholds in any real sense—that is, seats that could be held by one of their candidates campaigning, unaided, against all comers; in Orkney and Shetland, too, Liberal 'independency' was still vigorous.

Typical of the former Liberal seats that had taken the 'National Liberal' path to the right were Dumfries, East Fife, Inverness, and Ross and Cromarty, and, among the burghs, Greenock, Leith and the Montrose district (the two last-named having unbroken Liberal records since 1832). In rather more cases, however, constituencies that had once been regarded as safely Liberal had, by the 1930s, become Conservative—all the shire divisions of the north-east, from Forfar to Nairn, Argyll, both Perthshire seats, both Renfrewshire seats, Galloway, and Roxburgh and Selkirk. By a tacit understanding, too, the four universities returned two Conservatives and one Liberal or National Liberal.

It was the cities and burghs that showed most clearly the political trends of the times. With the exceptions already noted (Paisley, Greenock, Leith and the Montrose burghs), and with the proviso that, by another implicit agreement of an entirely different kind from that which was observed in the years 1906–18, the Dundee Unionists and Liberals combined to fight the double-member constituency against socialist opposition, the burgh contests all came to be waged simply between Conservatives and Labour. Glasgow's Liberal tradition died out in the 1920s. One of its 15 divisions, Partick, was held by the Liberals in 1922, but lost to Labour in the following year; thereafter, the party that had held all its divisions in 1885 played no significant part in the city's politics. A nearly similar position was reached in Edinburgh by 1924, although a National Liberal held the Eastern division from 1931 to 1935. From the early 1920s, too, independent Liberalism had all but disappeared as a force worth reckoning from such districts of burghs as Dumbarton, Dunfermline, Kirkcaldy, and Stirling and Falkirk.

The growing impulse towards fixity of political loyalties, towards a constant party 'colour,' arose from economic and social conditions. Urban divisions, and even whole burghs, tended to fall into zones, to be either predominantly industrial and working-class, or predominantly residential and sub-urban, and the townsfolk in the main backed the party that championed, or seemed to champion, their sectional interests. The distinction could be seen at its clearest between Conservative Hillhead or Pollok and socialist Gorbals or Govan; but it was also sharp between the Ayr burghs, with a strongly middle-class and 'resort' flavour, and the Dumbarton burghs, with shipbuilding at the base of their economy. Apart from the exceptional elections of 1918 and 1931, Labour, on balance, did better in Glasgow, the Conservatives in Edinburgh; the contests were not uneven in Dundee and Aberdeen, and the smaller burghs leaned rather to the left than to the right. The picture is much the same for the shire divisions of the central lowland belt, which differed little, in economic and social matters, from the neighbouring towns. The Liberals lost, to Labour, the Kilmarnock division of Ayrshire, and Berwick and Haddington, in 1923; thereafter, in all contests in the 20 seats of the region, they either did not put forward a candidate or made a poor third. Here, too, economic determinism was most influential in shaping political affiliations. The gap was widest between Bute and Northern Ayrshire, unfailingly Conservative throughout the twenty-one years, and the Hamilton division of Lanarkshire, with an equally steady socialist record (extending even to the abnormal years 1918 and 1931). Between these extreme limits the party conflict fluctuated, with a slight balance in favour of Labour, which was able, for example, to carry all seven Lanarkshire divisions in 1929.

The greatest advance during the inter-war years had been made by the Labour party. Solidly entrenched in the working-class districts, it could command half, or nearly half, of the city and burgh seats, and about a third of the shires (all in the central industrial belt); though, on the left, the I.L.P. and, to a lesser extent, the Communists impaired the solidarity of the movement. The Conservatives, aided by the National Liberals, could count with some confidence on holding the other half of the urban divisions, and well over half of the shires; the latter included the farming areas of the south, the mainly residential or agricultural regions in the lowlands, and most of the midland and northern counties (where their gains had been most substantial). The Liberals, almost squeezed out of the burghs, were being driven back to the northern fringes; and the Scottish Nationalists had done little more than make a beginning. One formula, which accords tolerably well with all the general election returns of the period, is this: out of every six Scottish votes, two went to the Conservatives, two to Labour, one to the Liberals, and the sixth was the 'floating' or non-party vote, the winning of which was vital for success at the polls. It was the support of all, or nearly all, the non-party voters that swept the Coalition, in 1918, and the National government, in 1931, into office with such commanding and abnormal majorities; at other times their suffrages were more evenly distributed.

As was the case in 1914–18, purely political considerations were relegated to a subsidiary role during the years 1939–45, when men's thoughts and lives were occupied with the conduct of military and naval operations, air attacks on Britain and from Britain, war production and problems of supply, the maintenance of sea-borne commerce, and diplomatic relations with allied and neutral states. As early as September 26, 1939, the three main parties, through the whips, came to an understanding that they would not contest by-elections in the usual way, but that the party in possession of any seat would be allowed to fill a casual vacancy in it; in the following month a statute suspended all local elections for the duration of the war. At 'the darkest hour,' when Neville Chamberlain resigned and Mr. Winston Churchill succeeded as premier, the ranks were closed still tighter, for the government, hitherto little more than a Conservative administration, became 'National' in fact as in name through the full participation of the Labour and Liberal parties (May 1940). For five years this broad-bottomed ministry was responsible for managing affairs under an elder statesman who, to the admiration of the whole free world, reached his full stature under the challenge of the nation's deadly peril and became certainly one of the greatest—perhaps the greatest—of war leaders in its history.

Fifteen by-elections were held in Scotland during the war. The electoral truce was scrupulously observed by the three parties, but independents, unofficial candidates and members of minor political organizations often contrived to provide some sort of contest. During the early years the government's nominee usually won easily, though at Argyll in 1940 a Scottish Nationalist polled over 7,300 votes, to be defeated by 5,000. Towards the end of the war the pattern changed in such a way as to suggest some restiveness in the localities over what was deemed dictation by party headquarters. Thus at Northern Midlothian in 1943 'Common Wealth,' a short-lived 'splinter' group of progressives, ran within 900 votes of the Conservative victor, and next year, in the Labour stronghold of Kirkcaldy, a Scottish Nationalist lost by fewer than 1,700. This tendency culminated in the two by-elections held in April 1945, on the eve of the European victory. Sir John Boyd Orr, as an independent, had a resounding win over his 'Liberal National' opponent in the Scottish Universities; even more surprisingly, Dr. Robert McIntyre, a Scottish Nationalist, ousted Labour from Motherwell, to give his party its first seat in parliament.

Certain war-time enactments, decisions and reports had weight and significance as pointing the way to much of the post-war planning. In 1940 a royal commission, under Sir Montague Barlow as chairman, recommended, *inter alia*, the dispersal of industry from congested urban areas, balanced industrial development throughout all regions, and economic diversification, including the encouragement of trading estates; national action should be taken to ensure such planned location of industry. The main railway systems were taken over by the government on January 1, 1942, and 'vesting day,' six months later, saw the Coal Commission taking over all colliery leases and nationalizing the industry so far as royalties were concerned. On December 1, 1942, came the Beveridge report on social insurance, the most influential of the documents of the period. Sir William Beveridge proposed an unified scheme of social insurance, national assistance and workmen's compensation, to be administered centrally by a new ministry, a comprehensive medical service for all, under the health departments, great increases in the range and value of benefits, the inclusion of wives, and the provision of children's allowances; his broad aim—'to make want under any circumstances unnecessary'— fired the imagination of the whole nation and set new standards for social welfare. Following the report of a committee appointed to consider the development of Highland water power for the generation of electricity (December 15, 1942), a statute of 1943 set up the North of Scotland Hydro-Electric Board, empowered to promote the general economic development and social improvement of the Highlands, as well as the production of electric current. In 1944, Mr. R. A. Butler's Education Act raised the English school-leaving age to fifteen and visualized a great extension of 'further education' beyond that age; the 'pay-as-you-earn' principle was introduced in respect of the income tax of all salaried and wage workers; and the Speaker's conference led to the appointment of boundary commissions and foretold a redistribution scheme after the war (by which Scotland should not suffer any material reduction in representation).

It is always difficult to assess the political record of the immediate past; as the perspective shortens, objectivity and assurance elude the commentator. In the post-war period the pattern of event and achievement becomes more than usually obscure, for the policies, the decisions and the enactments of those years are still live issues as this book goes to press, and whether the legislation of, say, 1947 or 1948 is to be regarded as permanent is uncertain in 1954; so, too, the forlorn hope of yesterday may be the shining triumph of to-morrow. Yet the task of recounting those annals, at least in outline, and of making a brief and provisional evaluation, is worth attempting, for only so is it possible to discern any relationship between the problems of to-day and the experiences of the past.

Just after the end of the war with Germany (May 8, 1945), the National coalition having collapsed through the withdrawal of Mr. Attlee and his colleagues, a general election was fought on normal party lines (July). Winning nearly 400 seats out of 640, against 213 for the late government, Labour at last obtained, by a handsome margin, complete control of the machinery of state. The extent of its victory may be attributed in part to war-weariness and a sharp reaction against discipline and authority as exercised between 1939 and 1945, in part to public readiness to give a trial to the avowed socialist aims of nationalizing large sectors of the economy, and in part to suspicions as to whether the Tories really believed in, and would put into effect, state planning, the Beveridge proposals, universal medical service and a vigorous housing programme. Rightly or wrongly, such opinions and sentiments had induced some twelve million voters to give Labour its opportunity for responsible government. In Scotland the Conservatives and their associates won 32 seats, Labour 37 and the I.L.P. three (all in Glasgow), while the Communists retained West Fife in a close fight, and the Universities elected one independent along with two of Mr. Churchill's supporters. In the counties, the increasingly firm hold of the Conservatives on the northern, Highland, midland and southern regions had counter-balanced their losses in the central plain, where a solid Labour belt now stretched from southern Ayrshire to Berwick and Haddington, including (as in 1929) all seven Lanarkshire divisions; in the burghs Labour had a marked advantage, with two gains in Edinburgh, two at Dundee, and one each in Glasgow, Leith and Paisley. One striking— and, to many, lamentable—feature of the returns was the total elimination of the Liberals from the representation of Scotland (except, of course, for the 'Liberal National' allies of the Conservatives); contesting 23 seats, they received 136,000 votes but no single success came their way, though it was by small (or very small) margins that they failed in Orkney and Shetland, Caithness and Sutherland, the Western Isles, Kincardine and West Aberdeenshire, and Roxburgh and Selkirk. It seemed like a sorry ending to their record of 113 years of electioneering, during 80 of which they had held a clear majority of the Scottish constituencies. On this occasion the Scottish Nationalists fought eight seats and polled just over 30,000 votes; their one sitting member, Dr. McIntyre, ran second to his Labour opponent at Motherwell, but elsewhere their candidate finished third or worse. Their progress since 1935 had thus been infinitesimal.

The third Labour administration—and the first to enjoy real power—began at once to pass into law a massive programme of legislation. The Bank of England, the coal industry, and the imperial communications system (cable and wireless) were nationalized by acts passed in 1946, and it was provided that new towns be set up under specially appointed development corporations. The most far-reaching changes were those introduced under legislation of this and the following years, whereby social security, universal medical and dental services, and national assistance, centrally administered and taking the place of the old local poor relief or public assistance, all went into force, substantially on the lines of the Beveridge plan, but with a stronger element of state control and with little room for voluntary efforts, from July 5, 1948. The school-leaving age in Scotland was at last (from April 1, 1947) raised to 15. The legislation of that year nationalized electricity, the railways, and part of road transport, gas supply was dealt with in the same way in 1948, and the iron and steel industry in 1949; so controversial was the last-named measure, however, and so bitterly opposed by the House of Lords, that the operative date was postponed until January 1, 1951, at the earliest, to give the government an opportunity to appeal to the country for a renewed mandate, with special reference to this basic proposal. Bound up with it, therefore, was the Parliament Act, 1949, which limited the Lords' suspensory veto upon legislation to two sessions, and, in time, to a period of thirteen months from the Commons' second reading during the first session; this Act became law only under the provisions of the 1911 Parliament Act, that is, after, and in spite of, two rejections by the peers. Other Labour enactments of a constitutional rather than political or economic nature, such as the Representation of the People Act, 1948 (which abolished the university and business votes and gave Scotland 71 M.P.s out of 625), and also the statutory orders of the same year, which greatly extended the powers of the Standing Committee on Scottish Bills, will be treated in some detail in the following chapter.

The general election of February 1950 was disappointing to both major parties, for the pendulum, swinging in the traditional manner, came to rest near the centre instead of passing to the other side. Labour won 315 seats, Conservatives and their associates 297, Liberals (with 475 candidates) only nine, and Communists (with 100 candidates) none. From Scotland (where the changes from the 1945 position were not marked) Mr. Attlee got 37 supporters, Mr. Churchill 32; against the tide that was flowing in England and Wales, two Liberal M.P.s were returned (for Orkney and Shetland, and for Roxburgh and Selkirk). The elimination of Communist and I.L.P. representation, and the failure of the Scottish Nationalists (with 12,400 votes from seven constituencies) and of all 'splinter groups,' was more noteworthy than the transfer of votes between the main parties. Typical of the picture in Scotland was Glasgow, where Labour held a solid bloc in the north and east (eight divisions), leaving the equally solid south and west (seven divisions) to the Conservatives; at Edinburgh, to balance matters, the comparable holdings were three and four divisions.

Though the weakened Labour government went ahead with its project of nationalizing iron and steel, its precarious majority in the House made any fresh controversial legislation nearly impossible; in any case, the interest shifted at this stage to foreign affairs—to the outbreak of the Korean war and of disruptive Communist attacks in Malaya in 1950, and to the economic, military and diplomatic conflicts between Britain and both Iran and Egypt in 1951. At length the administration, finding its control over the parliamentary machine so tenuous and so uncertain as to make its continuance in office on the existing terms intolerably irksome (it was aptly described as 'government by sneeze'), went to the country again in October 1951. This time the pendulum, far from swinging, merely inched over to the right, so that Labour, with 295 seats, regretted its lost majority, and the Conservatives, with 321, found the margin in their favour much narrower than they had expected. The Liberals suffered a further decline to six seats in the entire United Kingdom (including one—Orkney and Shetland—in Scotland). The Conservatives gained two seats from Labour (Berwick and East Lothian, and Rutherglen) and one from the Liberals (Roxburgh and Selkirk), to make the representation of the two major parties in Scotland exactly equal at 35 —an occurrence without precedent in our political history. Contesting only two seats, the Scottish Nationalists polled fewer than 1,000 votes in the Western Isles, but nearly 6,500 in East Perthshire. The four Communist candidates (including one in West Fife) and the two I.L.P. candidates forfeited their deposits, as did the few 'independents.'

From a purely Scottish point of view (though its declared intention of denationalizing parts of the road haulage industry, decentralizing railway control, and 'unscrambling' the iron and steel business touched this country closely), the most interesting measures adopted during the early months of

Mr. (later Sir) Winston Churchill's new administration concerned the conduct of Scottish affairs. In pursuance of a pre-election pledge, the prime minister appointed, as the immediate deputy of the secretary of state, a minister of state, who would normally reside in Scotland and be available while his colleagues were in London (November 1951), and also a third under-secretary of state (February 1952). Scotland's ministerial 'team' (including the lord advocate and the solicitor-general) was thus brought up to a total of seven.

The municipal elections of the post-war era, fought on party lines in all the larger centres, and occurring regularly every year (in November until 1947, in May from 1949), in contrast to the longer intervals between general elections, followed a pattern which sometimes seemed to anticipate parliamentary changes, and sometimes ran counter to them, almost as though there were a perverse law of compensation at work. At the first resumption of these contests, in 1945, Labour, while confirming its hold on Glasgow and Greenock, gained control of Aberdeen, Dundee, Paisley and Kilmarnock, but met with set-backs in 1947, when its majorities disappeared at Dundee, Paisley and Hamilton (though the capture of Falkirk in that year was a consolation), and again in 1949, when Glasgow and Dumbarton slipped out of its control (though here Hamilton moved in the other direction). In 1950 Aberdeen (the last of the cities to hold out) and Dunfermline were regained by the Moderates. It was 1952 (when the central government was Conservative) before the trend back to Labour became appreciable in the municipalities; in that year Glasgow and Aberdeen once more got Labour administrations, and in 1953 Dunfermline followed suit. Throughout these eight years Edinburgh, with only minor fluctuations, remained in the Moderate camp; and it was noticeable that the swing of the pendulum, first to the left (1945–46), then to the right (1947–51), and again to the left (from 1952), affected, in the main, those cities and towns which had a substantial working-class element in their population.

From the parliamentary, and even the municipal, history

of the post-war era, one might conclude that Scotland had gone over body and soul to 'the big battalions' of Labour and Conservatism; but these returns tell only one side of the story. In particular, the inference that the nationalist movement had reached its modest peak about the year 1945, to suffer a steady decline thereafter, is only part of the truth, since, from soon after that date, extra-parliamentary agitation on the issue of self-government was growing rather than waning; not only so, it was producing results by way of governmental action and reaction. The Scottish rate of unemployment was higher than that of England; 'remote control' and 'the English parties' were favourite objects of attack; as Labour unfolded its plans for wholesale nationalization, an over-centralized bureaucracy—'London government'—seemed to many to be sucking the life-blood from the more distant parts of the kingdom; and there were grievances in the limited use of Prestwick as a civil airport and of Rosyth as a naval dockyard, in the failure to provide adequate harbours and ferries in the Highland area, and in the postponement of the project of building a road-bridge over the Forth.

A substantial section of the nationalist movement, possibly disillusioned by the failure of its parliamentary efforts, became convinced that a wider, non-party approach might prove more fruitful. A representative National Assembly was convened, and in March 1948 it decided to start a nationwide campaign for a parliament to deal with Scottish affairs. In May 1948, and in the three following years, the General Assembly of the Church of Scotland expressed itself, in varying terms, as being dissatisfied with the existing arrangements, as endorsing the demand for a greater measure of devolution, and as favouring an inquiry, preferably by royal commission, into the question of self-government. Test plebiscites, carried out by postal ballot at Kirriemuir, Angus (February 1, 1949), and at Scotstoun, Glasgow (October 25, 1950), showed a majority of those who voted as approving a Scottish parliament for domestic affairs. In October 1949 the third National Assembly launched the Scottish Covenant, which pledged its signatories, 'in all loyalty to the Crown and within the framework of the United Kingdom,' to do every-thing in their power 'to secure for Scotland a Parliament with adequate legislative authority in Scottish affairs'; the desire for such a reform, it was affirmed, transcended 'all political differences and sectional interests.' The sponsors of the Covenant refrained from participating in the elections of 1950 and 1951, but claimed, in the latter year, to have obtained over two million signatures (the electorate then numbering about 3,420,000); and in October 1950 Mr. John MacCormick, chairman of the Covenant committee, repeated the nationalist success of 1931 by being elected rector of Glasgow University. On the fringes of the movement there was extremist talk of complete separation or Dominion status for Scotland, as well as irresponsible activity like the removal of 'the stone of destiny' from Westminster abbey on Christmas day, 1950 (to be returned on April 11, 1951), or the rejection, sometimes forceful, of the numeral in the new queen's title, Elizabeth II, in 1952–53. But the leadership of the Covenant group was studiously moderate, disavowing any aim other than orderly devolution as regards domestic legislation, and in imperial affairs adhering to the parlia-mentary union.

During these years several approaches were made to ministers of the crown and party chiefs. In March 1949 the Liberal party reaffirmed the old policy of separate parlia-ments for both Scotland and Wales, but the two major parties (though it was noticeable that each, while in opposi-tion, paid more heed to nationalist opinion) formally rejected the idea of legislative devolution and, for some time, even the need for an inquiry. Yet it is probably true that the decision, in 1948, to grant the Scottish Grand Committee real control of Scottish legislation and the power to discuss the estimates owed more than a little to the agitation of the times, as well as to considerations of parliamentary convenience. Late in 1949, while the Labour government still stood out against an inquiry, the Scottish Unionists promised, if re-turned to power, to appoint a royal commission to examine the financial aspects of the question. At length, in the early summer of 1950, Mr. Hector McNeil, the secretary of state, set up a committee, with Lord Catto as chairman, to report on the practicability of determining the financial and economic relations between Scotland and the rest of the United Kingdom. Two years later the Catto committee reported, in effect, that a separate return of governmental revenue and expenditure for Scotland could be made out, but that the task of estimating Scotland's share in the country's trade or her balance of payments was all but impossible (July 24, 1952). The Conservative government accepted these conclusions and at once appointed a royal commission, under the earl of Balfour, 'to review with reference to the financial, economic, administrative, and other considerations involved, the arrangements for exercising the functions of Her Majesty's Government in relation to Scotland, and to report.' The commission proceeded to take evidence, written and oral, and, as this book goes to press, its report is awaited with much interest.

Contradictory views and conflicting data render it very difficult to assess the real strength of the nationalist sentiment in mid-century Scotland. On the one hand, there is the lack of success of its avowed spokesmen in the ordinary political contests: one parliamentary victory, short-lived, and gained at an abnormal time in a somewhat unusual constituency, makes an extremely poor showing. On the other hand, the evidence of the local plebiscites, the reception of the Covenant, the backing of the General Assembly, the publicity accorded to the movement by the press, and, more particularly, the sympathy of such a reputable journal as *The Scotsman* (the *Glasgow Herald* being much more critical), all point to a far larger body of support among the Scottish public than is suggested by the election returns. The conclusion that seems best to fit both sets of facts is that, while the leaders are enthusiastic and single-minded in the cause of self-government, that cause creates in many, perhaps a majority, of the Scottish people a readiness to acquiesce in the justice of the claim for a separate parliament as the symbol of nationhood, but in such a mild degree, with such lack of fervency, as not to shake their political habits or their adherence to the two major parties, neither of which subscribes to legislative devolution.

For the rest, the political life of post-war Scotland has followed the trends that were foretold in the 1920s and 1930s. The voters' inclinations to one side or the other have hardened into fixed party loyalties, the economic and social character of each district—farming, residential or industrial—has more and more dominated the ballot-box, and it has become steadily easier to predict, with some confidence, the outcome of the 'normal' general election in a very large number of constituencies. Too much emphasis need not be placed on the fact that the two main parties reached absolute equality in 1951, for this obviously does not set the pattern for the future; but a closer examination of the record shows how nearly even is the distribution of the rival strongholds throughout the country.

Labour draws its support primarily from the cities and burghs. Seven of the divisions of Glasgow (Bridgeton, Central, Gorbals, Maryhill, Shettleston, Springburn and Tradeston), one each of those of Edinburgh (East) and Aberdeen (North), both of Dundee's seats, and all six lesser burghs (Paisley, Greenock, Coatbridge and Airdrie, Stirling and Falkirk, Dunfermline, Kirkcaldy) can be regarded as 'safe' for Labour; and the same may be said of some thirteen shire constituencies in the central lowland valley—Kilmarnock, South Ayrshire, four of the Lanarkshire divisions (Bothwell, Hamilton, Motherwell and North), East and West Dumbartonshire, both Stirlingshire divisions, West Lothian, Midlothian and Peebles, and West Fife. In each of these 30 divisions, with a marked preponderance of working-class population, Labour's hold, to judge from the post-war polls, appears to be nearly unshakable.

The strength of the Conservatives is derived from two sources—the mainly agricultural counties, with their county-towns and marketing centres, and the middle-class suburban areas, residential towns and 'resorts.' To the first category belongs a solid bloc of 12 constituencies, running from Ross and Cromarty, by way of Inverness, Moray and Nairn, Banff, all six divisions of Aberdeenshire, Angus and Perthshire, to East Fife and to Argyll, with a south-westerly extension to take in Dumfries and Galloway. The second group includes one of the Aberdeen seats (South), four of Edinburgh's (North, Pentlands, South, West), three of Glasgow's (Cathcart, Hillhead, Pollok), and also three constituencies which are to a large extent the dormitories and playgrounds of Glasgow—East Renfrew, Bute and North Ayrshire, and the Ayr division. Again, it is difficult to visualize circumstances in which the Conservatives would fail to carry any of these 25 divisions.

These calculations suggest that out of Scotland's 71 divisions no more than 16 can be classified as 'doubtful.' Of these five are in Glasgow (Camlachie, Govan, Kelvingrove, Scotstoun, Woodside) and two in Edinburgh (Central and Leith); in all seven middle-class and working-class elements are nearly balanced. Six others, all in south Scotland, are 'mixed' constituencies, where the farming and residential interests approximately equal the industrial—Central Ayrshire, West Renfrew, Rutherglen, Lanark, Roxburgh and Selkirk, Berwick and East Lothian. There remain the three divisions on the outer fringes, which form a special subcategory. At the time of writing, indeed, Caithness and Sutherland appear to be firmly Conservative, Orkney and Shetland Liberal, and the Western Isles Labour. But in all three majorities have been small, and their political bias is less fixed than is the case with most of the lowland divisions; here, more than anywhere else in Scotland, the personality of the successful candidate, rather than any tradition of party allegiance, has been the decisive factor. For this reason the three outermost seats should probably be put in the 'doubtful' column.

The record thus indicates 55 'safe' seats and not more than 16 that are marginal, and strikingly illustrates the impact of economic determinism on the voters' habits. Now, political arithmetic is notoriously not an exact science, and electors have been known to take an almost malicious delight in upsetting the most reasonable and likely predictions; even to-day, when an observer might be pardoned for believing that any retired colonel could hold a safe Tory seat, just as any superannuated trade union official could be sure of a socialist stronghold, a flagrantly unsuitable candidate *can* lose for his party what looks like a certainty. Apart from such individual vagaries, one of two sets of circumstances might nullify the entire analysis—an internal quarrel so serious as to split and wreck a whole party, or a national crisis or disaster, for which one of the parties might incur the blame. Since both of these conditions have in fact been realized in the recent past, they cannot be discounted as future possibilities.

Chapter 5

The Government of Scotland

THE hardest problem that confronted the commissioners for union in 1706—and the only one that called for a joint meeting of the Scots and English members—concerned the mode of fusing the two parliaments into one. As we have seen, the agreed scheme was that Scotland should send 45 commoners to join England's 513, and that 16 representative peers should sit along with the English lords, who then numbered about 190. These proportions meant deliberate under-representation. Scotland's population was then probably about 1,100,000, and England's about 5,500,000; in the absence of a census, contemporary guesses put the ratio from one-sixth to one-third. Little heed was paid to such reckonings, but Englishmen did not fail to point to the great disparity in national wealth and revenue: Scotland's land-tax was to be only £48,000 annually against very nearly £2,000,000 from England, while her customs and excise yielded £63,500 per annum, compared with England's total of close on £2,300,000. These figures indicated that England could and did pay nearly forty times as much as Scotland into the national exchequer. The agreed quota may thus be regarded as a not unreasonable compromise between the two proportions—one-fifth by numbers, one-fortieth by wealth; but the gravamen of the charge of ungenerous treatment on England's part is that, while an increase of Scotland's trade was confidently expected as 'the happy consequence of the Union,' no provision was made for a corresponding addition to her representation. (Electoral details were adjusted by the Scots Parliament in February 1707.)

The interpretation of the terms governing peerage representation caused much ill-feeling among the politically conscious Scots nobles. Their sons, from 1707 to 1832, might not sit in the Commons for a Scottish constituency, but, since this view seems to have been endorsed by Scots members as well as English, it cannot be termed a hardship. Real differences arose over the position of Scots peers who were given British peerages. From 1709 they were denied the right to vote in the election of the 16 representative peers; more serious still, the Tory Parliament decided in 1711 that such nobles might not sit as British peers, but only if elected among the chosen 16, and this rule was not rescinded till 1782. It was the possibility of handing over to the government of the day power to create a great *bloc* of Scots votes which inspired these minor infringements of the Union, but in course of time all grievances disappeared, to the point that nowadays the Scottish peerage is really over-represented. Most holders of surviving Scottish titles also hold United Kingdom peerages, and, of those who do not, 16 are elected to each Parliament, so that the number of those without any claim to a seat diminishes both through extinction of titles and acquisition of new ones: already it is below 20.

According to the allocation (by the Scottish Estates) of the 45 Commons seats, 30 went to the 33 shires, 27 of which elected one member apiece, while the other six were grouped in pairs (Bute and Caithness, Nairn and Cromarty, Clackmannan and Kinross) for representation in alternate parliaments only. The royal burghs, over two centuries senior to the shires in a parliamentary sense, and limited to 66 in number prior to the Union, were not merged in the shires, but were allowed to elect the remaining 15 commoners. This was done by means of reverting to a device adopted in Cromwellian times, when the burghs had been combined in 'districts' of varying numbers; though now the principle was applied with arithmetical rigidity and lack of imagination. Edinburgh returned one member, the other 65 composed fourteen districts of four or five burghs each, and the districts returned one member apiece. The burghs were grouped, not according to size or importance, but by geographical propinquity. Thus Glasgow, Rutherglen, Dumbarton and Renfrew sent one member between them, while the 13 rather small Fife burghs sent two, and helped to send other two. The Scots (like the English) would not in those days differentiate between substantial towns and mere villages: it was traditional status that mattered, and all royal burghs were treated alike.

The same conservative spirit determined that within the constituencies the old voting arrangements should be retained. The normal shire qualification was land worth £400 per annum, which gave the vote to some 2,500 in the whole of Scotland; even in 1821, when the population was just under 2,100,000, of whom about 1,600,000 lived in the shires, there were some 3,000 voters. It was possible to compile, as William Adam did in 1788, a list showing the political sympathies of every shire voter in Scotland. Each burgh member was chosen by the town council or its delegates, and, since this body was a co-optive closed corporation, averaging perhaps twenty in number, there would be about 1,300 burgh voters in Scotland. In the counties (where the influence of the great families was already paramount), many nobles increased their 'interest' by creating fictitious votes in the period 1770-90; the collusive transfer of superiority over land, without actual possession, conveyed to the landowner's friends the right to vote. In the burghs all attempts at reform were frustrated. Thus the 45 Scots M.P.s, from 1707 to 1832, derived their title from fewer than 5,000 electors, who were wealthy proprietors, or their relatives and dependents, or substantial burgesses.

The nineteenth century Reform Acts fundamentally altered the parliamentary terms of the Union; since their tendency was in the direction of representation according to population, and since Scotland, by 1832, had nearly 2,400,000 inhabitants, or about one-sixth of England's total of over 14,000,000, the changes told in favour of the northern country. In 1832 the Scottish representation was raised from 45 to 53 by the creation of eight new burgh seats. Edinburgh and Glasgow were given two members apiece; Dundee, Aberdeen and Perth were taken out of their districts to return one member each; a new category of non-royal 'parliamentary burghs' was recognized, and of these Paisley and Greenock each got separate representation, while others, including Falkirk, Kilmarnock and Leith, were added to the districts, which were unaltered in number (14), but reorganized. These arrangements reflect the growth of industry and commerce, especially in the cities and towns, since about 1760. No change was made in the shires except that, in place of alternate representation, six small neighbouring counties were paired, each pair returning one M.P.— Clackmannan and Kinross, Elgin and Nairn, Ross and Cromarty. The Act also substituted simple property qualifications for the archaic franchises of town and country; the vote was given to £10 householders in burghs, to £10 proprietors and £50 occupiers in the shires.

The second Reform Act (1867–68) gave Scotland 60 seats out of an unchanged total of 658. Of the seven additional members, two went to the shires, three to the burghs and two to the universities, which had been refused representation in 1832. The counties of Aberdeen, Ayr and Lanark were each split into two one-member divisions, while Peebles and Selkirk were joined. Glasgow got a third member, Dundee a second, and a new district, the Hawick burghs, came into being. The franchise was greatly extended, to include all rate-paying householders and £10 lodgers in the burghs, £5 owners and £14 occupiers in the shires.

The Gladstonian reforms began with the Secret Ballot Act (1872), and were completed with the third Reform Act (1884–85), which introduced adult male suffrage, alike to town and country. In the redistribution of seats, strict regard was had to the population figures. English boroughs and Scots burghs or districts of burghs with fewer than 15,000 inhabitants were merged with the counties; limits (50,000 and 165,000) were fixed for one- and two-member constituencies; and, for the future, no more double-member divisions were to be created. The Act, bold and logical, at last gave Scotland, with 72 members out of 670, just representation. The shires got seven new members, Fife, Perth and Renfrew joining the two-member category and Lanark having no fewer than six divisions. The big towns likewise gained, Glasgow getting seven seats instead of three, Edinburgh four instead of two, Aberdeen two instead of one, while the liquidation of the Haddington and Wigtown districts made the net gain in burgh members five.

The Representation of the People Act, 1918, gave the vote to men over 21 and women over 30, raised the membership of the House of Commons to 707, and (again in accordance with the population-ratio) allocated 74 M.P.s to Scotland. Of these, 38 went to the shires, 33 to the burghs, and three to the universities (all four returning them by proportional representation). Every effort was made in this ingenious statute to preserve the old electoral units (shire and burgh) and yet to erect new divisions that would be roughly equal in population. Single-member counties, like Argyll and Dumfries, offered no difficulty; nor did, on the one hand, either the big shires, such as Fife and Renfrew, each with two M.P.s, and Lanark, with seven, or, on the other, the small shires that could be conveniently paired—for example, Caithness and Sutherland, or Roxburgh and Selkirk. The novel device of the 1918 Act—and it was, and is, peculiar to Scotland within the United Kingdom—was the linking of two contiguous shires, one too small to be worthy of its own member, and the other so large as to deserve more than one M.P., and then splitting them in a new way, so that the small shire and part of the large one formed one constituency, and the remainder of the big shire returned one or more members. Thus the shires of Stirling and Clackmannan made two divisions—Clackmannan and Eastern Stirling, and Western Stirling. By a variant of this formula, the Western Isles were taken out of their two shires (Inverness, and Ross and Cromarty) to form a separate division. Among the burghs, Glasgow got 15 members, Edinburgh five, Dundee and Aberdeen each retained two, and Leith, Paisley and Greenock one each; six districts of burghs were left, the others going into shires or parts of shires.

The recognition of the Irish Free State in 1921 involved the withdrawal of the Irish M.P.s (except 13 Ulster members) from the Commons, which was thereby reduced to 615. The Equal Franchise Act of 1928 gave the vote on the same terms to men and women, on their attainment of the age of 21;

this raised the electorate in Scotland to nearly 63 per cent. of the population. By an interim measure passed in 1944, 25 M.P.s, all English, were added to the House, in order to give fairer representation to certain congested urban areas, especially near London; more general changes were needed, but were postponed until the end of the war.

The Representation of the People Act, 1948, on the principle of 'one man, one vote,' abolished the business and university franchises; it also made each of the 625 divisions a single-member one. Scotland, with 71 seats, was deliberately left with some degree of over-representation (possibly as a belated recompense for her mistreatment between 1707 and 1885): her constituencies averaged about 8,000 fewer electors than did those of the entire kingdom. City divisions were re-drawn to take cognisance of suburban growth, Dundee was split into two divisions, three districts of burghs were merged in their shires and one new one was created; but the only substantial change in the distribution of seats involved the transfer of one from the north-east to Ayrshire.

Under this Act Scotland returns 32 burgh members—15 from Glasgow, seven from Edinburgh, two each from Aberdeen and Dundee, one each from Paisley and Greenock, and one from each of the four remaining districts of burghs (those of Coatbridge and Airdrie, Dunfermline, Kirkcaldy, and Stirling and Falkirk). Of the 39 shire members, Lanark claims six; Aberdeen, Dumbarton, Fife and Renfrew, two each; Argyll, Banff, Dumfries and West Lothian, one each; and there are seven pairs of shires with one member to each pair—Berwick and East Lothian, Caithness and Sutherland, Kirkcudbright and Wigtown (Galloway), Midlothian and Peebles, Moray and Nairn, Orkney and Shetland, and Roxburgh and Selkirk. The remaining 14 county members are allocated to five pairs of disparate shires of the kind already mentioned in connexion with the 1918 Act—Angus and Kincardine (two members), Ayr and Bute (five), Inverness and Ross and Cromarty (three), Perth and Kinross (two), and Stirling and Clackmannan (two). To the five 'composite' divisions involved in these arrangements (North Angus and Mearns, Bute and North Ayrshire, Western Isles,

Kinross and West Perthshire, Clackmannan and East Stirlingshire) there are no parallels outside of Scotland save the wholly exceptional English constituency of Rutland and Stamford; again, though there are many paired borough seats in England, there is nothing like the Scottish district of burghs; and it is pleasing to note the preservation, despite the modern quest for uniformity and equality, of these characteristically Scottish departures from the type of British constituency.

One other recent change in our parliamentary system has been touched on in the preceding chapter. The idea of 'the Scottish Grand Committee' goes back to 1894, but it was only in 1907 that, by amendment of the standing orders, it was made a standing committee. For the first 40 years, it played a useful but subsidiary and far from spectacular role in legislative affairs, relieving the pressure on members' time by considering the committee stage of certain Scottish bills. By a further amendment of the standing orders, adopted in 1948, a bill may be referred to the Scottish Committee for second reading debate—that is, for consideration in principle—and the estimates for Scottish services may be discussed there during six days in each session. All 71 Scots M.P.s are members, along with 10–15 others (added to ensure that the balance of parties approximates to that of the whole House); another safeguard of Commons control permits any ten M.P.s to object effectively to the delegation of legislative powers. It is, however, vital to remember that usage and precedent, not formal rules, are what count in parliamentary affairs; and that both Labour and Conservative governments have respected and maintained the Committee's powers in legislation and in discussing the estimates.

The procedure is so new that its full significance may easily be missed: it is a fact that no other standing committee is entrusted with similar powers. In May, 1953, for example, while the Committee was debating the St. Andrews University bill, an amendment was proposed by Mr. Walter Elliot and supported mostly by Labour members but also by a few Conservatives. On a 'free vote,' the amendment—to make

F

the rector instead of the principal the chairman of the University Court—was carried by 29 votes to 16, and the government, accepting its defeat, altered its bill accordingly. Only on a Scottish bill could this have happened; only the Scottish members enjoy such an *imperium in imperio*. If the privilege is preserved—and, far from expecting any limitation, we might even see an extension—it embodies a kind of legislative devolution without parallel in constitutional experience; one, moreover, that (by using the members of the 'imperial' parliament) avoids the danger that hangs over all subordinate legislatures in a federal system—the taint of the provincial and second-rate. While a separate parliament in Edinburgh has a sentimental appeal for home rulers, they might do well to ponder the powers and potentialities of the Scottish Standing Committee, and to ask themselves whether they are pursuing the shadow and neglecting the substance of true self-government.

Between 1603 and 1707, while the king's commissioner represented the absentee monarch, executive government had been in the hands of the privy council, though an astute secretary in London, like Lauderdale, could exercise real control. After the Revolution, parliament took a more active part in administration, but the Treaty of Union expressly continued the privy council 'for preserving of public peace and order, until the Parliament of Great Britain shall think fit to alter it or establish any other effectual method for that end.' It was abolished in 1708, and soon after new arrangements were made. There were now two English secretaries of state, with a rather untidy division of labour between them, whereby they shared responsibility for domestic affairs, while in the sphere of foreign policy one took the 'northern department,' one the southern; not till 1782 were separate home and foreign secretaries appointed. During the first forty years of union, partly because of the importance of Scottish affairs, but mainly for political reasons, a third secretary of state, a Scottish noble in charge of Scottish administration, sometimes appears. But appointments were irregular, and the post was as often vacant as filled. The Tories let the office lapse between Queensberry's death in July 1711 and Mar's appointment in September 1713, and it was revived then by Harley as part of his manœuvres against Bolingbroke. Another vacancy occurred during the 'Fifteen rebellion, and the dismissal of Roxburghe from the secretaryship in 1725 led to a gap of seventeen years, during which Scottish affairs were 'managed' by Argyll and his brother (and eventual successor), the earl of Islay, and by Duncan Forbes of Culloden, as lord advocate (1725–37) and president of the Court of Session (1737–47). The last of the third secretaries, Tweeddale, was appointed in 1742 as a party move against Walpole; in the midst of the 'Forty-five rising, the post was abolished (January 1746).

The function of the third secretary had been not so much Scottish administration—there was not enough of that to justify such an appointment—as the control of parliamentary elections and the dispensing of government patronage in line with English practice; and different methods were now adopted with those aims in view. Official responsibility for Scotland fell to the northern secretary of state until 1782, and thereafter to the home secretary, who had the lord advocate, at first unofficially and later specifically, as his under-secretary for Scottish affairs. The government depended on either the lord advocate or a Scottish peer, with political talents and good family connexions, to 'manage' Scotland in such a way as to ensure the support of a majority of the country's elected representatives in both Houses. Skilful management involved the bestowal, for services rendered or to be rendered, of army and navy commissions, of clerkships in the East India company, of posts in the customs and excise, and of pensions and sinecures, the employment of family 'interest' and kinship in the shire elections, and the use of direct bribery in the burghs.

Scotland's most successful manager, with firm control over all but a few of its 45 members, was Henry Dundas, later Viscount Melville, and the trusted lieutenant of the younger Pitt from 1783 to 1806. Despite his despotic bearing towards reformers at the crisis of the French Revolution, and despite his cynical disregard for financial probity, his fame and popularity remained unshaken in thousands of Scottish homes.

But the political outlook changed with the approach of reform, and the second Viscount's death in 1827 marks the abandonment of the system of management.

Between 1827 and 1885 the home secretary, advised by the lord advocate, continued to hold the ministerial responsibility, but from time to time, with the expansion of the field of government, statutory boards were set up in Edinburgh, with somewhat arbitrary authority over specified branches of administration, and including both part-time *ex-officio* members and whole-time crown appointees. They comprised the Board of Supervision (for poor law) (1845), the General Board of Commissioners in Lunacy (1857), the Prison Commissioners (1877) and the Fishery Board (1882); the registrar-general, too, had his own department from 1854. The Scotch Education Department (it did not become 'Scottish' until 1918) was set up in 1872 on different lines: nominally a committee ('my lords') of the privy council, it was always a nebulous body, last meeting in 1913 but not abolished until 1939. After much agitation, the secretaryship for Scotland, a cabinet post, was instituted in 1885, with general responsibility for Scotland, although the *ad hoc* boards retained their independent statutory powers. The secretary's clerks and assistants came to be known as 'the Scottish Office'; and the secretary, as vice-president of the privy council committee, assumed ministerial direction of the Education Department.

From 1894 central administration of Scottish poor relief fell to the Local Government Board, and, from 1919, to the Scottish Board of Health, which also took over the Highlands and Islands medical service (enacted in 1913). The Board of Agriculture for Scotland was called into being in 1912 in connexion with the crofting legislation that culminated in the Small Landholders (Scotland) Act, 1911. The Scottish secretary became a secretary of state in 1926, but even more important changes came with the Reorganization of Offices (Scotland) Acts of 1928 and 1939, which, following the reports and recommendations of sundry committees of inquiry, substituted civil service departments, under ministerial control, for *ad hoc* boards charged with statutory functions. There thus emerged four major and equal departments—Home (absorbing fishery and prison administration), Health (covering, besides public health, housing, registration and lunacy), Education and Agriculture; the old Scottish Office was merged in the first of these, carrying with it central co-ordination of police and fire services, and liaison duties as regards local government, criminal justice, licensing and elections. By 1939 the staffs of all four departments had been transferred to Edinburgh and accommodated in St. Andrew's House. Each is headed by its own permanent secretary, and at the apex of the civil service hierarchy stands the permanent under-secretary of state. The ultimate responsibility (to Parliament) for the direction of policy rests with the political chiefs—the secretary of state, the minister of state, and (since 1952) three parliamentary under-secretaries of state, who answer to the secretary of state for a share of the work of the four departments. Assistance and advice on legal matters are obtained from the lord advocate and the solicitor-general.

The political and economic functions of the four departments located in St. Andrew's House constitute the larger part of the administration of Scotland, but there are other sectors of government and industry which, because of the closeness of Anglo-Scottish relations and the inseparability of the interests of the two countries, are placed under the control of 'Great Britain departments.' These include, most notably, the Post Office, Board of Trade, Ministries of Labour, National Insurance, Supply, Works, Food, Fuel and Power, and Transport, and the three Service departments; but there are many others. In each case the Scottish organization is headed by a controller, director, or similar senior officer, with what are deemed adequate powers of taking decisions without reference to London. Scottish opinion is not, however, unanimous that the optimum degree of devolution has been attained, that sufficient authority is allowed to 'the man on the spot,' or that Scotland's needs are always understood in Whitehall; among the more interesting administrative reforms that have been suggested are the institution of a Scottish Department of Commerce, to take over some of the functions of certain 'Great Britain' ministries, and the revival of the Scottish Privy Council, to serve as the formal and supreme agency of central government and executive power.

The financial relationships between Scotland and England have often demanded careful consideration and have on occasion caused friction. There was basic agreement in 1707 that the union should be as nearly 'entire' as possible, and this was helped forward by certain broad similarities in the fiscal systems of the two countries. In both, direct taxation, in the form of a land-tax, was traditionally the main source of extraordinary crown revenue; in both, too, this was beginning to yield in importance to the customs and excise (especially on malt liquors and on salt); and in both, finally, there was complete acceptance of the prevailing mercantilist notions, which underlay a complex and imposing array of tariffs, prohibitions, bounties and 'drawbacks' (rebates), all intended to serve the grand purpose of hoarding bullion as the real form of national wealth. There were, however, divergences in practice, mainly because of the limited commercial experience of the Scots. These historic differences necessitated the inclusion in the Treaty of many minor adjustments, and in fact rather more than half of that document dealt with fiscal and economic matters.

The land-tax was imposed in England as a levy of so many shillings in the pound of valued rent, but in Scotland as a grant to the crown of so many months' 'cess' or 'stent'—one month's cess yielding a fixed sum of £6,000 sterling. (The medieval rule had been that the clergy paid one-half, the nobles one-third, and the burghs one-sixth, but, the church lands having been secularized, the shires now paid five-sixths or £5,000, the burghs £1,000.) To find a just formula for equating the two systems, the commissioners examined the tax records since the Restoration and, finding that the highest rates imposed during the period were 4s. in the pound in England and eight months' cess in Scotland, reached the sensible agreement that these two rates, representing approximately equal burdens, should thenceforth be levied concurrently, and so *pro rata*; in point of fact, the land-tax became fixed at those levels and has so remained ever since (though commutation, in accordance with later legislation, has reduced Scotland's contribution to about £30,000 per annum). Since the English yield at 4s. in the pound was £1,997,763 8s. 4½d., it may be inferred (and Englishmen did infer) that their wealth, measured by the taxable value of land, was some 41 times greater than that of Scotland; but, inasmuch as a subsistence economy, divorced from money transactions at many points, still obtained in the northern country, this calculation probably exaggerates the real disparity.

Indirect taxation was more troublesome and involved. Scotland received 'full freedom and intercourse of trade and navigation' in the United Kingdom and the overseas dominions, and agreed to the adoption of the English customs and excise, subject to certain concessions intended to shield her trade and industry from the crippling effect of the heavier English duties. Thus, bounties were granted for the export of oatmeal, home-made salt was freed for seven years from the excise levied in England, drawbacks were allowed on imported foreign salt used for curing fish or meat, and Scotland was exempted from 'any imposition upon malt during this present war'—that is, from England's war tax. For the future, indirect taxation must be entrusted to the united Parliament, which would surely impose burdens only when necessary and 'with due regard to the circumstances and abilities of every part of the United Kingdom.'

Two money-payments were promised to Scotland. The first was the well-known 'Equivalent' (£398,085 10s. 0d.), to compensate her for undertaking joint responsibility for England's national debt (Scotland did not have one); it was reckoned according to the proportional revenue of the two countries. The second sum, not susceptible of nice calculation, was to be a return to Scotland for the great increase in her customs and excise revenue 'which will be the happy consequence of the Union.' Besides extinguishing the public debts of Scotland, the first Equivalent was to be used to make good private losses incurred through the change to English coinage, to repay the Darien stockholders and dissolve the company, and the second to provide £2,000 per annum for the encouragement of coarse wool manufacture during the first seven years, and thereafter for the promotion of fisheries and other industries.

Some of the formal and subsidiary provisions of the Treaty of 1707, and their sequels, are not without interest. Special commissioners, having their office 'within the limits of Scotland,' were to collect and disburse the Equivalents and be accountable to Parliament; twenty years later these funds, employed to set up the Royal Bank and the Board of Trustees for Manufactures, helped materially to develop banking facilities and to stimulate industrial expansion. English weights and measures, as well as English coinage, were to become standard throughout the United Kingdom; but the Scots, strongly attached to their own usages, preferred, until well on in the nineteenth century, their bolls and firlots as grain measures to the English quarters and bushels; to this day, indeed, the use of the peck and lippy (though not quite in their original sense) is not unknown in rural Scotland. The reform and strengthening of the Scottish Court of Exchequer, along English lines, and especially the grant of jurisdiction 'for deciding questions concerning the revenues of customs and excises there,' were included in the terms of the Union. These changes were put into force in 1708, and the reformed Court served as the clearing-house between the collectors of revenue and the government in London, scrutinizing accounts and checking receipts of feudal dues, court-fines, crown rents, burgh-fermes, customs, excise and taxation. Whitehall, however, had the last word, and in 1833 it was found convenient to transfer revenue control to the Treasury, the Court of Session taking over the Exchequer's judicial functions in 1856.

The financial provisions of the Treaty were just and even generous; it was the failure to live up to their spirit that was disillusioning. There was a delay of three months before the Equivalent was delivered, and then much of it came in unfamiliar 'paper money.' The new customs and excise officers, bound in any case to be unpopular, were far from being the best of their type; and they did not mend matters by gauging on Sundays in a country given to strict Sabbath observance. Next, as we have already seen, the linen export duty of 1711 and the proposed malt duty of 1713 evoked bitter opposition, while the Shawfield riot in Glasgow (1725) and the Porteous riot in Edinburgh (1736) indicated the wide diffusion (extending even to ministers of the gospel) of belief in the veniality of smuggling and of hostility to the revenue men. A generation after the Union, Duncan Forbes was still perturbed about Scotland's insolvency, which he attributed to the illegal importation of spirits and wines and to the growing social vice of tea drinking. From the middle of the century, however, the advance of trade and industry changed the picture, and by 1797 Scottish excise revenue alone amounted to £1,293,000—a forty-fold increase since the Union.

Scotland, indeed, became a financial asset in the nineteenth century. In 1868 Scottish taxation yielded £7,740,000, or much more than one-seventh of that of England. Little was spent, moreover, on social services and much on military and naval defences, and, since France was the chief enemy, Scotland did not even benefit locally from the presence of barracks or dockyards, which became concentrated in the south. No more Highland forts were built after the 'Forty-five and a century and a half elapsed before Redford barracks were put up to accommodate the last remaining cavalry unit, the Scots Greys (then in danger of losing their identity), and naval bases were developed at Rosyth, Invergordon and Scapa, conveniently located to deal with a German rather than a French threat. Meanwhile, a Treasury calculation in the year 1888 had shown that England and Wales contributed 80 per cent. of the United Kingdom revenue, Scotland 11 per cent., and Ireland 9 per cent.; and the 'Goschen formula' came to be adopted as a just basis for the allocation of Exchequer funds—Scotland getting 11/80ths of the sum granted to England and Wales, or 11/91sts of the total for Great Britain.

The Treasury figures show that Scotland steadily 'paid her way' between 1891 and 1922, contributing just over or just under 11 per cent. of the United Kingdom total; Ireland, meanwhile, was a wasting asset or a positive liability. In 1921–22, for example, Scotland found 11·06 per cent. of the national revenue, received 11·13 per cent. of the sums disbursed for 'local' purposes, and was accordingly to be credited with 11·05 per cent. of the balances available for 'imperial' expenses. The continued applicability of the Goschen figures, so far as Scotland is concerned, is impressive; but, as Ireland's contribution to the revenue was only 4·52 per cent. in that year, England's share was 84·42 per cent. Soon, however, the onset of industrial dislocation and distress —as was inevitable under modern budgetary principles— reduced Scotland's payments towards income tax, customs and excise, and increased her claims upon unemployment relief, public assistance and social service expenditure. After the establishment of the Irish Free State, in 1922, the Treasury returns ceased, but they were resumed for the years 1931–32 and 1934–35 in respect of the Scottish and English revenue and expenditure. The picture had by then become tragically different. In 1934–35, towards a total revenue of £775 millions Scotland paid nearly £67 millions, or 8·63 per cent., England and Wales the other 91·37 per cent. (Scotland's population was then about 10·8 per cent. of the whole.) Of this total over £383 millions went on local expenses, largely social services, and Scotland got £47½ millions thereof, or 12·39 per cent., England the remaining 87·61 per cent. This left £392 millions for 'imperial' purposes, towards which Scotland contributed £19½ millions, or 4·96 per cent., and England £372½ millions, or 95·04 per cent. In other words, Scotland, with almost one-ninth of Britain's population, paid just over one-twelfth of the revenue, was refunded to the extent of nearly one-eighth of the money spent locally, and so was able to pay a sum that was just short of one-twentieth of the common charge. The cessation of these Treasury returns from 1935 was due to the abandonment of free trade and the growing complexity of the national accounts that followed the adoption of tariffs, subsidies, bounties, bulk purchases and other state controls; historically, it was unfortunate that these returns (for long the latest available) referred to the years of depression and

showed Scotland's fiscal position in an exceptionally un-
favourable light.

Though economic conditions were markedly better after
1945 than in the 1930s, Scotland at mid-century still fell
short, not only of the Goschen formula, but also of the proportion which her population bore to that of Great Britain
(10·43 per cent. in 1951). Scottish unemployment was nearly,
or quite, double that of England. The inland revenue
figures for the year 1950–51 (published in February 1952)
showed the net receipt of income tax from Scotland to be
£97½ millions and from England £1,299½ millions—or 6·98
and 93·02 per cent. respectively. A special income census
for 1949–50, issued at the same time, credited Scotland
with £680 millions of assessed personal income, or 8·58 per
cent. of the United Kingdom total of £7,925 millions, and
showed the Scottish average to be lower than the English,
though higher than those of Wales and of Northern Ireland.

Despite the increased labour involved in sorting out
governmental revenue and expenditure between Scotland
and the rest of the United Kingdom, the Catto Committee
reported in July 1952 that separate returns were still practicable; and a white paper, published in January 1954, gave
the figures for the year 1952–53. Scotland's contribution to
the £4,227 millions of British revenue was under £410
millions (9·69 per cent.), and she received £207 millions
(12·34 per cent.) out of a total local expenditure of nearly
£1,678 millions; thus, her payments towards the balance,
available for common purposes, of £2,549 millions fell short
of £203 millions (7·95 per cent.). If still disappointing, the
picture was more cheerful than in 1935.

The financial relations between Scotland and England are
not necessarily the decisive argument for or against political
union; in the eyes of unionist and home ruler alike, there are
moral and spiritual values in the ideas of continued association, as of separation, of the two countries, which transcend
the lessons of the international balance-sheet. Thus, while
a viable Scottish economy would naturally appeal to the
separatist as a point in favour of self-government, he would
regard the insolvency of his country as a reproach to, and

a reason for terminating, the existing union. Similarly, if the believer in Anglo-Scottish unity sees a prosperous Scotland as an attractive partner, he might well contend that the northern country, having, in all probability, more than paid her way throughout the nineteenth century, deserves to be assisted by England, as a matter of historic justice, through the less happy conditions of the twentieth century. However the figures are presented and interpreted, the argument cuts both ways, and we have moved far from the days when angry patriots, defying the rules of arithmetic, denounced the union for its 'unfair' fiscal treatment of Scotland, and asserted that the northern country was paying more than her due share into the national exchequer and receiving relatively less in return. On the financial side, the debate as to the future of Scottish government hinges on more fundamental matters, and to-day's facts and figures, while interesting in themselves, are but one element among many.

The most remarkable departure from precedent in the Treaty of Union was the preservation of the separate identity of Scots law. Although the feudal structure of medieval Scotland had been, in large part, imported from Norman England—the *Laws of the Four Burghs*, for example, being borrowed directly from Newcastle-upon-Tyne—the legal systems of the two countries had diverged widely during the later middle ages. Scottish law students, debarred from Oxford and Cambridge by mutual feelings of national hostility, sought their professional education in the great schools of Italy, France and the Low Countries. Thus the model for the supreme civil court, the College of Justice (1532), was the University of Pavia, and it was the principles of Roman, or civil, law that were imparted to youthful Scots by the jurists of Leyden and Utrecht. While the pragmatic English, relying on precedent and avoiding mere abstractions, built up their common law on actual cases and past decisions, the Scots found it possible, by adapting the Roman code to their own needs, to produce many expositions, at once massive and detailed, logical and authoritative, of their maxims and procedure. *The Institutions of the Law of Scotland*, by Sir James Dalrymple, later Viscount Stair (1681), was followed shortly by a work of the same title by Sir George Mackenzie of Rosehaugh (1684); each of them was to run into numerous editions, and to inspire Lord Bankton's *Institute* (1751–53), John Erskine's *Institutes* (1773), and George Joseph Bell's *Principles* (1829)—the two last-named also being destined to appear in a very large number of revised editions.

In both countries judges and lawyers formed almost a closed corporation, with long and expensive training and slow promotion through well-defined grades, but in England the connexion with public life was more intimate, while the Scottish advocates, virtually controlling the judicial machinery, tended to form a narrower ring. But it was in the organization of the courts that Scotland was most different and most characteristically herself. Although the principles and practice of law had been systematically codified, the courts in existence in 1707 presented an untidy arrangement. For one thing, there were too many 'supreme' tribunals. Parliament was an important court for trying certain crimes, especially high treason, and it was claimed that, in civil cases, appeal lay to it from the Court of Session; though this opinion was unorthodox, it could and did review cases when 'protest for remeed of law' was made, and the whole question of Parliament's appellate jurisdiction was bound to be raised when the Scots Parliament, with all its rights and powers, was merged in that of the United Kingdom. Privy Council exercised supreme jurisdiction by way of summary prosecutions of public enemies of the peace of the realm. The normally supreme civil court was the College of Justice or Court of Session, then composed of president and fourteen ordinary lords, and sitting permanently in Edinburgh. The Court of Justiciary, having inherited the powers of the medieval justiciar, and comprising justice-general, justice-clerk, and five commissioners of justiciary who were also lords of session, was the highest tribunal in criminal matters; it was located in Edinburgh, but went on circuit to other towns. Maritime cases fell to the Admiralty Court, and the Court of Exchequer, under the chamberlain, had an archaic and ineffective jurisdiction in finance. Finally, there was the Commissary Court of Edinburgh, chief of all the commissaries which had inherited the functions of the old episcopal or consistorial courts, and especially important in cases affecting marriage, divorce, legitimacy and testaments.

The chief local court was that of the sheriff, competent for most civil and criminal causes, subject to appeals and remits to the central courts; its efficacy was gravely impaired by the fact that 22 of the 33 sheriffships were now heritable. To help and relieve the sheriff-court, justices of the peace had been introduced by James VI in 1609; attempts had been made to emulate English efficiency in the work of preserving the peace, but they had achieved little, and the J.P. courts were not important. The many special local courts—the heritage of feudalism—were a real rival to the dispensers of royal justice. Lords of regality had a heritable jurisdiction equal on the criminal side to that of the Justiciary and in civil cases to that of the sheriff; especially dangerous was their power of repledging from the royal courts. Baron-courts and burgh courts had, *ex antiquo*, ample powers in civil cases and in crimes (extending to 'pit and gallows,' the right to inflict capital punishment), but these had largely fallen into desuetude during the seventeenth century, and they were now petty tribunals. Local courts of special jurisdiction included constabularies (around royal castles), admiralties, and, most notably, some twenty or more commissary courts, which were favoured for the registration of deeds and held in high regard for their impartial and professional justice.

The Treaty stipulated 'that the laws which concern publick right, policy and civil government may be made the same throughout the whole United Kingdom, but that no alteration be made in laws which concern private right, except for evident utility of the subjects within Scotland.' The Courts of Session, Justiciary and Admiralty were continued, subject to regulation by the Parliament of Great Britain, and, as we have seen, provision was made for reform of the Court of Exchequer and for the possible abolition of the Privy Council (both of which were effected in 1708). All heritable jurisdictions and the rights of royal burghs were reserved. The real problem—appeals to Parliament—was cautiously evaded. The commissioners, aware that the House of Lords was competent for English appeals and unwilling to invalidate it, after Scottish peers had joined its membership, from the hearing of Scots cases, neither asserted nor denied the right of appeals from Scotland. They met the situation—rendered doubly delicate by the Presbyterian faith of Scotland and by the presence of Anglican bishops among the peers of England—by decreeing that 'no causes in Scotland be cognoscible by the Courts of Chancery, Queens-Bench, Common-Pleas, or any other Court in Westminster-hall'; as the House of Lords was not necessarily a Court in Westminster hall, it was not expressly excluded, and the issue was left open.

On the judicial side, the most interesting sequel to the Union concerns the three *causes célèbres* which have been the subjects of Scottish appeals to the Lords. James Greenshields had been imprisoned in Edinburgh for openly using the Anglican liturgy, and the Court of Session had supported the presbytery and the city magistrates in their actions against him; but the peers took the opposite view and ordered his release (March 1711). Whilst this may look like an enlightened decision, a protection of minority rights, it is fair to recall that the same legislature passed the Occasional Conformity Act (December 1711) to disqualify Protestant dissenters from office. In 1761, on the death of the duke of Douglas, his vast estates were claimed on behalf of Stewart Douglas, reputed to be the surviving twin son of Lady Jane Douglas, the duke's sister; his birth, in Paris, had been an obscure event, the lady was over fifty years old, and there were other suspicious circumstances. The Douglas name was popular in Scotland, the Hamiltons, who had a reversionary interest, were disliked, and the action was followed with passionate concern by the Edinburgh citizens. In 1767 the Court of Session decided against Douglas by the casting vote of Lord President Dundas, but the House of Lords, without a division, reversed the judgment in 1769. The third historic cause was that of the 'Wee Frees,' in which the Lords decided in favour of the non-uniting minority of the Free Church against the majority, who, they held, by combining with the 'voluntaries' of the United Presbyterian Church in 1900, had abandoned the principles of the Disruption and thereby forfeited any claim to the Church's property (1904). Possibly good in law, this judgment was certainly absurd in practice, but it led to a fair and sensible division of the endowments by statute (1905).

The judicial reforms that have been effected since the Union have had the sanction of public opinion, in so far as they have evoked any interest outside legal circles. Heritable jurisdictions were surrendered in 1748 in accordance with a statute of the preceding year. Compensation amounting to £152,000 was paid, instead of the £580,000 asked by 75 claimants; the greatest beneficiary was the duke of Argyll, who got £21,000. At once the sheriff-courts began to advance in power and prestige, and in 1787 the office of sheriff-substitute, until then permissive, was regularized, salaries being paid by the state. By a series of Acts passed between 1808 and 1830, the Court of Session was reorganized as an Inner House of two divisions, each of four lords, headed by the lord president and justice-clerk respectively, and an Outer House comprising the remaining, or junior, lords, reduced in number to five. The Admiralty Court, by now almost a sinecure, was dissolved in 1830, its remaining jurisdiction going to the English Admiralty Court, the Court of Session and the sheriffs. The Court of Exchequer, reduced in the same year from three 'barons' or judges to one, was merged in the Court of Session in 1856. Commissaries were abolished by Acts of 1824, 1830 and 1836, Court of Session and sheriffs sharing their work. In 1878 the sheriff-substitute became a crown-appointed judge, with one of the more populous areas as his province. In 1887 all lords of session became judges of the High Court of Justiciary. In 1892 town councils were empowered to appoint, if they so desired, a qualified stipendiary magistrate to sit in the police court with the burgh magistrates.

The twentieth-century reforms have included the institution of two new central tribunals. The Scottish Land Court—a chairman with the rank and tenure of a lord of session, and four other members—was set up in 1911 to hear and determine matters arising in connexion with small landholdings. A Court of Criminal Appeal, comprising three of the lords commissioners of justiciary, came into being in 1926, to hear appeals from the High Court (that is, single judges) and from sheriff courts. A statute of 1948 authorized an increase in the number of lords of session from 13 to the older total of 15. The corpus of Scots law has been changed in two ways. Specific statutory alterations have included the liberalization of divorce law in 1938 (the new grounds being cruelty, habitual drunkenness, criminality and incurable insanity, the old ones desertion—reduced from four years to three—and adultery), and the abolition, in 1949, of punishments deemed obsolete (drawing and quartering, corruption of the blood, eschcat, outlawry, penal servitude and hard labour). In the second place, Scots law has inevitably been influenced by English legal experience and has, as a matter of common sense, been drawn into conformity with the English practice in such relatively new fields as company law and mercantile law. Yet the 1707 promise not to change private law 'except for evident utility of the subjects within Scotland' has, on the whole, been well kept, and our lawyers are proud of their ancient heritage and resolved to safeguard it at every point—the distinctive titles of lord president, lord commissioner of justiciary, lord of session, dean of faculty and advocate; the majority rule of juries, the 'not proven' verdict, and the entrusting of all prosecutions to a state official, the procurator-fiscal; the purely contractual nature of marriage, the protection of widows' and children's interests against arbitrary testamentary settlements, and the compulsory registration of land deeds.

Local government at the time of the Union was in the hands of six agencies, which had been created or had developed with little reference to each other and at wide intervals of time. Sheriffs and burghs dated back to the twelfth century, baronies (including regalities) took shape under Robert Bruce, kirk sessions were set up at the Reformation, justices of the peace and commissioners of supply were introduced in the course of the seventeenth century.

The medieval sheriff had served as a link between the capital and rural Scotland, his administrative aspect appearing in the duties of collecting crown dues, executing royal writs, publishing statutes and, later, making the return of shire-members. But, as great nobles made the sheriffships their family heritages, the crown restricted their official functions. Thus, as the sheriffs gained in jurisdiction, they lost executive power, and since the Union their activities have become formal—executing parliamentary writs, registering voters and conducting elections.

The royal burghs were governed by 'setts' or constitutions, whereby power rested with provost, bailies and self-elective town councils. The system was notoriously riddled with abuses, especially fiscal ones, but was authorized by the Union, and the eighteenth-century reform movement failed to achieve results. The exclusive privileges of merchant guild and craft were largely abandoned before they were expressly abrogated (1846), but the royal burghs remained until the nineteenth century self-contained units of local government, often with considerable revenues; these would have been much greater but for the fraudulent disposal of common lands which became standard practice in the eighteenth century. Exchequer control reached the statute book, not for the first time, in 1822, but the law courts refused to enforce it, and in any case it was too late.

Baronies and regalities showed the opposite trend to the sheriffs: though their rights of justice were mostly laid aside by 1707, they had executive duties that were important locally—preserving common lands, pastures, woods and peat-mosses, maintaining dykes and ditches, keeping the assize of bread and ale, and in general upholding the law of 'gude nychtburheid.' After the abolition of heritable jurisdictions (1747) even the administrative functions of the baronies fell into desuetude, though they survived here and there till much later. The burghs of barony differed very widely one from another; extreme cases are Paisley, with complete self-government on the model of the royal burghs, and Kirriemuir, where a nominated baron-bailie exercised all power.

Kirk sessions had advantages that were not enjoyed by other agents of local government. They were small enough to be in close touch with the needs of ordinary men and women, and there were enough of them—nearly one thousand —to cover the whole country. They had a standard organization under the minister as moderator, elders as councillors, deacons to manage the parish funds, and kirk officers or beadles to report and to execute policy. And, in accord with Presbyterian polity, they were impelled as dutiful Christians to supervise the parishioners' morals, to attend to their education, and to administer the poor law. They had to act under the general guidance of the commissioners of supply, expenditure required the sanction of the heritors, and, in the burghs, they co-operated with the town councils; but it was the kirk sessions that attended to the details of managing schools, appointing teachers, and moderating salaries and pupils' fees; of keeping the poor's roll and paying pittances (often a shilling a month) to the aged indigent, to cripples, orphans and other disabled persons; and of distributing charitable relief after fires, floods and famines. Parish assessments (levied, since 1663, half from owners, half from occupiers) were permissive, but they were unpopular and little used; the weekly collections, helped out by certain court-fines and any available 'mortifications' (bequests), were the mainstay of parochial finance. Secession and schism, however, undermined the system, and by the time of the Disruption (1843) poor law urgently needed reform.

Though the justices of the peace never had the prestige of their English brethren, their administrative powers, especially after 1708, were considerable. They saw to the maintenance of roads and bridges (work which was shared with the commissioners of supply from 1718); they settled disputes as to work and wages, and enforced the use of proper weights and measures; they suppressed riots, supported customs officers and excisemen, and supervised prisons and almshouses. Their agents, the constables, haled vagabonds and suspects before the justices, who may be regarded as a rough and ready prototype of the county police.

The commissioners of supply, on the other hand (customary before 1667, statutory from that year), were the forerunners of the much later county councils. As a county committee of wealthy landowners, appointed to allocate the monthly 'cess' or land-tax, they had an organization including convener and clerk, and this made it convenient to entrust them with other duties—the enforcement of the Education Act of 1696 and (along with the justices) the control of vagabondage and the upkeep of highways. Further work was to come to them, and their command of local money made their influence great down to the late nineteenth century.

Local reform began with the burghs in 1833, when the magistrates and town councils of the 66 royal burghs and 13 parliamentary burghs were to be elected by the £10 householders. By another series of statutes, royal burghs and burghs of barony (1833), parliamentary burghs (1847), and mere 'populous places' (1850 and 1862) might adopt a system of 'police' (including watching, lighting, paving, cleansing and water supply) and so become 'police burghs.' This legislation, culminating in the Burgh Police (Scotland) Act, 1892, and the Town Councils (Scotland) Act, 1900, gave responsible government, ample local authority, and the duty of dispensing the growing social services, to 206 towns, large and small, old and new.

In rural Scotland evolution was slower. A first need was the creation of a regular paid county police force, and this was done by acts of 1839 and 1857, control going to the commissioners of supply. Poor law reform was taken in hand in 1845, when parochial boards were established, composed of elected members, kirk session delegates, heritors and burgh magistrates (if any). A Board of Supervision of nine members, mostly appointed, controlled all the Scottish parishes. Parochial boards were given fresh duties in connexion with registration (1854) and with public health and the water supply (1867). In 1872 popularly elected school boards were set up in each burgh and parish, with power to levy a special local rate and to compel attendance up to the age of thirteen. The boards did good work during the 46 years of their existence. In 1878 county road trustees were set up in each shire, road tolls and the older 'statute labour' being abolished; for this purpose elected trustees were joined with the commissioners of supply.

Police, poor law, education and the roads had thus been dealt with as separate problems. The first comprehensive plan came in 1889, when county councils, popularly elected in each shire, took over the work of commissioners of supply, justices of the peace, and county road trustees. They were given control of police in burghs with a population of under 7,000, and they administered public health services. The county council was authorized to impose a consolidated rate for all county purposes, but the last word, as regards the police and all capital works, was given to the standing joint committee, comprising seven county councillors and seven commissioners of supply (retained for this purpose), under the sheriff as chairman. In the larger shires district committees were to be the council's agents for roads and public health. In 1894 parochial boards were displaced by parish councils, elected by the ratepayers and charged with the administration of poor relief and all local affairs. The district committee, now composed of the county councillors for the district, together with one representative of each parish council and of any town council within the district, provided liaison between county and parish. All local authorities were empowered in 1899 to promote private legislation by way of provisional order, local inquiry and confirmation bill.

The twentieth century has seen this elaborate fabric of local government practically torn down and rebuilt on quite different lines. The process began modestly enough in 1909, when county and town councils were authorized to undertake town planning schemes, subject to central approval. The drastic changes started in 1918 with the replacement of the numerous and small school boards by *ad hoc* education authorites, endowed with much wider powers and put in charge of the 33 counties and the five largest towns. The Equal Franchise Act of 1928 gave women the local, as well as parliamentary, vote on the same terms as men.

Nothing less than a revolution was wrought by the Local

Government (Scotland) Act, 1929, the first statute to survey the whole field. Standing joint committees, parish councils, the *ad hoc* education authorities, and district boards of control (for lunacy) were swept away. County and town councils were retained, district committees were transformed into district councils, and to these three councils went all local powers, on the basic principle of grading responsibility according to the size and status of the governing body involved. For this purpose the burghs were divided into three categories—the four 'counties of cities' (Glasgow, Edinburgh, Dundee and Aberdeen), the 20 other 'large burghs' (with approximately 20,000 inhabitants), and the remaining municipalities or 'small burghs' (170 in number).

To the four cities and the counties went full responsibility for all branches of local administration, including education. The large burghs controlled public health, poor relief and all other services, major and minor, except education; but they were allowed a separate police force only if they had one at the time of the passing of the Act (five of them had none), or if they had 50,000 inhabitants. Small burghs remained as housing authorities, but otherwise their powers extended only to local duties like public buildings and parks, street lighting and cleansing. For matters beyond their competence, town councils were represented *ad hoc* on county councils, which thus comprised a fixed number of landward members and a varying number of town councillors, and would be at maximum strength for education and tend to diminish successively for police, social services, housing and petty affairs. District councils (including county councillors and specially elected members) became the agents of the county council, usually over a number of contiguous parishes; they inherited some of the work of the old parish councils, but their rating power was limited to one shilling in the pound. The statute provided for four unions of burghs, and stipulated that, for all major public services, the county councils of Perth and Kinross should be combined, as should those of Moray and Nairn.

Local finance came under review. A new and consolidated grant was made to the Scottish authorities to compensate them for the withdrawal of all former *ad hoc* Treasury grants, and also for the heavy loss of rating revenue incurred that year by reason of the 'de-rating' of agricultural, industrial and freight transport subjects; to this a new sum of £750,000 per annum was added in respect of their increased responsibilities under the Act. The allocation of the Scottish total between counties, cities and large burghs was made in accordance with a complex formula, which took into account total population, infant population, population in relation to road mileage, rateable value and unemployment.

Viewed either as a complete and logical scheme of 'rationalization' or as an exercise in parliamentary draughtsmanship, the 1929 Act must excite our admiration; its underlying motive—the equating, at several levels, of governing powers and governing units—is intelligible and possibly, in the abstract, justifiable. But experience has revealed certain defects and dangerous weaknesses in the 1929 system. The stripping of authority from the small burghs dried up a main source of civic pride and local patriotic enterprise in many a thriving town; and no method was provided, then or now, for the promotion of a small burgh to large burgh status. The abolition of parish councils, coming on top of the disappearance of the school boards, deprived the country dwellers of any intimate contact with the processes and personalities of local administration; and the district councils, with little to do and very little money, have proved no substitute for their forerunners. Above all, the trend away from local autonomy towards reliance on the central government was given a great impetus by the Act. As the taxpayer has come to the relief of the ratepayer, so the county and town councils more and more give the appearance of being merely the local agents of the state, charged with carrying out a national policy which is decided elsewhere.

These tendencies have been carried further by certain changes introduced since 1929. Unemployment assistance became a central responsibility in 1934, to be followed in 1948 by national assistance (the old poor relief). The Minister of Transport took over the main through routes, as 'trunk roads,' in 1936, and some of the public health duties went to regional hospital boards, under the national health service, in 1948. The Police (Scotland) Act, 1946, authorized voluntary amalgamations of police forces; the three south-western counties combined for this purpose in 1947, and the three south-eastern in 1948.

Minor alterations have been made by other statutes. Town planning schemes, which earlier legislation required to be undertaken on the initiative of the central government, became compulsory in the Town and Country Planning (Scotland) Act, 1947: all local planning authorities (county and certain town councils) were instructed to make a survey and prepare a development plan for approval by the secretary of state, and were empowered to acquire any necessary land by purchase. The Local Government (Scotland) Act, 1947, was mainly a consolidating measure, but local finance was thoroughly overhauled in the following year, when the Treasury 'bloc grant' of 1929 gave way to 'Exchequer equalisation grants,' arrived at by an even more complex calculation of 'weighted population'—weighted, that is, by allowance for the number of children under fifteen, and for a low density of population per road mile. This was an English system, applied to Scotland with a 25 per cent. addition to bridge the gap in the rating methods and yields of the two countries. From 1949 May became the month for holding elections for town councils (annually) as well as county councils (triennially).

That all is not well with local government—that, in particular, the raising of revenue by rates never designed to bear the burdens now placed upon them is wholly un-satisfactory—is implicitly admitted by the appointment, in May 1953, of the Sorn committee, to review the system of valuation and rating and to suggest changes. Among proposals that have been mooted are the adoption of the English principle of levying rates from occupiers only, not owners; the more radical idea of a supplementary local income tax in place of rates; the termination of 'de-rating' as unduly favouring farmers and industrialists and depriving local authorities of needed revenue; the institution of large

SHETLAND

Scale in Miles
0 20 40 60

ORKNEY

CAITHNESS

SUTHERLAND

ROSS

AND

CROMARTY

MORAY

BANFF

NAIRN

INVERNESS

ABERDEEN

NESS

KINCARDINE

ANGUS

PERTH

ARBROATH

DUNDEE

PERTH

FIFE

KINROSS

STIRLING

CLACK
MANNAN

KIRKCALDY

DUMFERMLINE

DUMBARTON

CLYDEBANK

COATBRIDGE

FALKIRK

WEST
LOTHIAN

EAST
LOTHIAN

GLASGOW

GREENOCK

PORTGLASGOW

PAISLEY

RENFREW

AIRDRIE

EDINBURGH

MIDLOTHIAN

RUTHERGLEN

MOTHERWELL
& WISHAW

HAMILTON

BERWICK

KILMARNOCK

LANARK

PEEBLES

BUTE

AYR

SELKIRK

AYR

ROXBURGH

DUMFRIES

DUMFRIES

KIRKCUDBRIGHT

WIGTOWN

COUNTIES, CITIES
AND LARGE BURGHS
OF SCOTLAND

☐ CITIES
● LARGE BURGHS

Scale in Miles
0 10 20 30 40

regions as more suitable planning units than counties and burghs; and, conversely, the entrusting of more power to district councils and town councils. It seems clear that some changes, possibly drastic and perhaps revolutionary, will be made in the not too distant future.

Chapter 6

Economic Conditions

A T the time of the Union with England much the greater part of the Scottish people were engaged in the basic industry of agriculture, and the primitive conditions that prevailed in farming had remained without change for many generations. Fields were cultivated, flocks and herds were raised, not for profit but for subsistence. The aim was to make each region, and, as far as possible, each estate, self-supporting: the land should provide a livelihood, not wealth or comfort, and the ideal was stability rather than progress.

The typical landowner was the laird, who might be a baron or a feuar, holding from the crown, or a 'goodman,' holding from a subject; the greatest of the barons, and the largest landowners, were nobles. The typical farmer was the 'kindly' tenant, occupying his holding by custom, or at will. Leases were very uncommon, and were indeed alien to the spirit of feudal agriculture, which held that the good and bad land should be shared and re-distributed by the periodic (originally the annual) 'deal' or 'daill.' This insecurity of tenure gave little incentive for improvement and confirmed the peasant's adherence to traditional practices. In addition to his stated rent, the tenant owed customary feudal services, especially work on the lord's land at seed-time and harvest (when his own holding most needed attention), the leading of peats, road-making and sundry carriages. The most onerous of the personal services related to milling, which was a dominical monopoly: all tenants living within the 'sucken' were 'thirled' to the lord's mill, whither they brought their grain for grinding and where they paid 'multure' to the laird and 'knaveship' to the miller. Money rents played a small part in the rural economy, and much was due in oats, bere (rough barley), meal, poultry, eggs and cheese. In the Highlands the tacksman, usually a kinsman of the chief, was a middleman in respect of the exaction of both rents and military service; he himself had a lease, but the clansman had none.

Methods of tillage and pasturage were equally defective. The arable land was traditionally divided into infield and outfield, the former lying near the farm-buildings. The infield got some manure—say, every third year—and was cropped continuously until the exhaustion of the soil obliged the farmer to leave it fallow for a year. The outfield was used partly for grazing cattle and sheep, partly for growing grain for as many years in succession as the land would bear; it received only the casual droppings of the animals. Cultivation was by 'run-rig': long, narrow strips, separated from each other by raised baulks of turf and weeds, were parcelled out among the tenants, not in contiguous holdings, but scattered over the estate to ensure the equitable distribution of all types of land. The staple crops were oats (for food) and bere (for drink); a little flax, peas and beans, and occasionally wheat and rye, were also sown. Eight oxen, with three or four men in attendance, dragged the heavy wooden Scots plough; each tenant contributed one or more beasts to the common ploughing team. Harrows were of wood, crops were cut by sickle, and the Highlander used the *cas chrom*, or foot-plough. In many parts of the Lowlands, owing to the lack of drainage, the 'dry-field' of the hillsides was preferred to the rich but moist carse-land.

Even small farms were mixed, but cattle and sheep got little help from man. No special feed-crops were grown, for, argued the farmer, why waste ground and labour raising feed for animals instead of food for men? Flocks and herds might be taken to distant hills for summer grazing and, after harvest, were turned on to the open fields to eat the stubble. In the winter, the weather being deemed too rigorous, the cattle were brought indoors, to be fed on heather mash, corn straw, or anything else that could be spared. Many beasts died from sheer starvation, and the survivors were so emaciated that, at the spring 'lifting,' they had to be carried to pasture. The womenfolk on the farms had their hands full with cheese-making, flax-spinning and the weaving of coarse cloth. The entire rural economy was laborious, unproductive and short-sighted; at times—as during the dreadful famine of 'the Seven Ill Years' (1696–1703)—it failed utterly and the countryfolk perished by the thousand.

As agriculture was shackled by feudal tradition and convention, industry and commerce were hampered by the chartered privileges of the burghs, which had originally been granted for their protection and encouragement, but had long operated merely to conserve existing monopolies and to thwart new enterprises. In each of the 66 royal burghs, and in most of the 150-odd burghs of barony, a number of crafts—14 in Edinburgh and Glasgow, but generally between four and nine—had been incorporated by 'seal of cause' or 'letter of deaconry' to supervise and safeguard their own sectors of urban industry. Baxters or bakers, fleshers and maltmen (who supplied the brewster wives) purveyed food and drink; tailors, cordiners or shoemakers, bonnetmakers and skinners (including furriers) dealt in clothing; hammermen or smiths, wrights and masons worked with metal, wood and stone products; websters or weavers, waulkers or fullers, and litsters or dyers were concerned with woollens. The larger towns had their specialists—goldsmiths in Edinburgh, gardeners in Glasgow, surgeons and barbers in both—while the lesser crafts were combined or non-existent in smaller places. In most cases masters and journeymen worked to order, not for a speculative profit. The general aim was to preserve the hereditary rights of a closed society, by fixing wages and prices, by maintaining the apprenticeship system, by favouring the entry of sons and sons-in-law of masters ('at the near hand'), and by adhering in all things to ancestral ways.

As regards the list of industries covered by the burgh crafts, the omissions are even more revealing than the inclusions. Though there had been attempts—not very successful—during the seventeenth century to encourage fisheries, and though the prices of curing-salt were fixed by statute, fishing was never a craft. It was carried out, with small boats, from almost every little haven along the east coast and in the south-west, while in the Highlands it was an adjunct to farming. Iron and lead were mined in small quantities in south Scotland, and surface seams of coal were worked along the shores of the firth of Forth, windmills being used for draining water; but peat was commonly used for domestic fuel, and there was neither an industrial demand nor means of transport for much coal. Exceptionally, a few salt-pans in the Forth and Clyde areas used local coal for the evaporation of sea-water and produced salt for fish-curing. Though agrarian serfdom had disappeared as long ago as the fourteenth century, colliers and salters were 'thirled' to their work, which, though degrading and brutalizing, brought them a daily wage of one shilling, or twice that of most labourers. Flax spinning, as we have seen, was a by-work on the farms, and further supplies of the fibre were imported, to be woven in many villages and towns into coarse cloth; only the Dunfermline linens were of better quality.

Sea-borne commerce was largely in the hands of the 'merchants,' or brethren of the merchant guilds of the royal burghs. Efforts had been made during the reign of Charles II to modify their statutory monopoly, and these had culminated in 1693 in the 'communication of trade,' whereby the right of foreign trade was to be conveyed to such of the 'unfree' burghs as undertook to relieve the royal burghs of ten per cent. of their 'cess,' or parliamentary tax. Some thirty of the greater burghs of barony, including Grangemouth, Bo'ness, Falkirk and Greenock, came into the scheme, but elsewhere the preference was for illegal trading. The relief to the royal burghs worked out at only about two per cent., and smuggling, as we have seen, retained its popularity long after the Union.

The main Scottish trade-routes lay from the eastern ports, especially Leith, Kirkcaldy, Dundee and Aberdeen, to the Baltic, the Netherlands, France and East England, and from the south-western ports, such as Glasgow, Greenock, Dumbarton and Ayr, to Ireland, to West England and (in a thin trickle of defiance of England's Navigation Acts) to America. Exports included linen cloth, coarse woollens such as plaidings and kerseys, cured herring and salmon, cattle, hides and sometimes oats, and the usual imports were timber, iron, salt, wine, flax, silks, spices and manufactured goods, while grain and butter were occasionally shipped from Ireland. Six or seven of the larger seaports had each about a dozen sea-going ships, and there were only about a hundred of them in all Scotland. The nation's greatest commercial adventure, the Darien scheme, had come by unparalleled disaster (1698–1700), and the loss of life and of capital probably hastened the decay of the smaller ports in Fife and elsewhere, which had already been declining in the seventeenth century. The sole bright spot in the picture was provided by Glasgow, whose merchant citizens had had the enterprise to build 'Newport' (Port Glasgow) in 1668, to import odd cargoes of Virginia tobacco from 1674, and, before 1700, to establish candle-houses in the 'rigs' west of the city (Candleriggs), as well as a 'soaperie,' sugar-works, a rope-walk and a glass factory.

The whole economy was in dire need of a powerful stimulus. This was afforded, before very long, by the Union, but the first effects of government from London were disillusioning. The new customs officers and excisemen, English or English-trained, threatened the pastime of smuggling and this led to much ingenuity in the landing and disposing of contraband cargoes of brandy, wine, tea and silks. The relatively high salt-duty practically killed the fishing industry, and in the middle of the century swarms of Dutch boats hovered off the Scottish coasts, while the natives could not afford to equip fishing-boats. Woollen manufactures suffered sadly from free trade with England, for the home products could not compete with the finer stuffs woven in England from superior wool. And the linen trade was treated with callous indifference or worse. Before a generation had passed, however, agriculture, linen and foreign trade began to make marked advances.

Changes in the aims and methods of farming were slow and uneven, but they amounted, cumulatively, to nothing less than an agrarian revolution, the effects of which could be appreciated by the end of the century. The actual changes were similar to those which occurred in England, with this difference that, feudalism having a tighter hold on Scotland, there were both more to be done and a greater resistance to reform. This explains the slow pace and the irregularity of the changes. The chief advocates of reform were noblemen and lairds, including the duke of Atholl, the earls of Haddington, Stair, Loudoun, Eglinton and Findlater, Lord Kames, Adam Cockburn of Ormiston and Sir Archibald Grant of Monymusk, whose familiarity with farming techniques abroad led them to interest themselves in the betterment of conditions at home. They came together in 1723 to form the Society of Improvers in the Knowledge of Agriculture in Scotland, important not only for its leadership and advice in all farming matters, but also as the forerunner and foster-father of the many local agricultural societies.

Enterprising landlords busied themselves with the enclosing of lands (especially of wastes for pasturage), the popularizing of the new crops, turnips, potatoes and artificial grasses, the introduction of horse-hoeing and drilling, the granting of long leases, the planting of millions of trees, the draining of marshes and bogs, and the utilization of the winnowing and threshing machines invented by the Meikles, father and son. Sometimes the changes were deeply resented, particularly if they involved cherished rights of 'commons,' as when, in 1724, the Galloway peasants rose against enclosures and 'levelled the dykes.' Again, tenants destroyed young trees in the belief that they impoverished the soil, stole the sunshine and harboured destructive birds. Often a curiously strong attachment to the archaic run-rig system was encountered, so that the proprietors' home-farms might be oases of 'improvement' set in a desert of old-fashioned wastefulness and sloth. The demands of the English cattle markets furthered the Scottish improvements, by inducing the farmers to grow turnips as winter-feed, for turnips needed hoeing and made for a sensible rotation of crops. Clover and grasses were another beneficial addition to the produce of the land, and more wheat was sown to cater to the growing urban taste for white bread. From the 1740s the cultivation of potatoes was spreading north, and from 1762 large sheep-farms began to appear in the Highlands, where the Cheviot and Blackface strains were acclimatized. The traditional drove-roads saw increasing numbers of black cattle making the long journey to the trysts, first at Crieff and later near Falkirk, to finish their lives, very often, in the rich pastures of East Anglia; it is estimated that, by 1800, as many as 100,000 beasts were driven from the Highlands and Galloway to England every year.

The uneven geographical distribution of the agrarian reforms is noteworthy. The main mechanical improvements —a light iron plough, various iron harrows, carts and threshing machines—were in common use in the Lowlands before the end of the century, but they had not superseded the older methods in the Highlands. So, too, with the leasing of land, which was facilitated by the Entail Act of 1770; nineteen years was the usual term in the southern counties by 1800, but leases were infrequent in the Highlands, where the effect of economic change was to transform the clan chiefs from patriarchal leaders into normal landowners, who relied on the tacksmen to extract rents from their tenants-at-will. The farmers of Berwickshire and the Lothians specialized in wheat and other grains, and were the most advanced in Scotland. There were many improved estates in Fife, Angus, the Mearns and Aberdeenshire, and farmers were beginning to follow the example offered by landlords on their home farms. Ayrshire was already earning fame for its dairy-farming, Galloway for its stock-breeding, the southern uplands for their sheep-rearing. By 1800 the agrarian revolution was about half-accomplished.

Industrial progress can be dated from the institution, in 1727, of the Board of Trustees for Manufactures, who were empowered to spend an annual sum of £6,000 (accumulated from the 'second equivalent' promised at the Union and from other funds), and allocated £2,650 to linen manufacture, £2,650 to the herring fisheries, and £700 to the wool trade. The Board did for linen what the Society of Improvers did for agriculture. They supervised and stamped cloth, imported skilled artisans from abroad, awarded premiums

G

for flax-growing and for bleaching-fields and prizes for inventions and new processes, set up spinning-schools, and gave advice on all aspects of the industry. In the 'forties production had increased sufficiently to warrant the grant of a state bounty on exports and the establishment of the British Linen Company, at first concerned with the financing of the growing industry, but destined to become the pioneer of branch-banking in Scotland and, indeed, in Britain. From 1752 to 1784 the Commissioners for the Forfeited Estates, entrusted with the revenues of the exiled Jacobite leaders and authorized to expend them upon Highland rehabilitation, attempted, as part of their task, to repeat in the north the achievements of the Board of Trustees in the Lowlands; besides husbandry and handicrafts, they tried to foster linen spinning and weaving, but without conspicuous success. Among the Lowland counties, Forfar easily led in output of linen cloth, followed by Fife, Perth, Renfrew and Lanark. In value of produce, however, there was little difference between the counties of Forfar, Renfrew and Lanark, since, while the Angus weavers made cheap and coarse cloth, fine fabrics like lawn and cambric were woven in the west country, where Christian Shaw's 'Bargarran thread' marks the beginning of Paisley's fame as a centre for quality textiles.

The rapid and steady progress of the industry may be seen from the facts that, when the Board of Trustees started operations, the annual output was two million yards, and by the end of the century it was 24 millions. More flax was now imported than was grown at home, and the expansion of the industry led to its reorganization. Water-driven lint-mills carried out the preparatory processes of scutching and heckling, the final stages of bleaching and dyeing came to be specialized and mechanized, but the basic work of hand-spinning and hand-loom weaving went on unchanged. And yet, though spinners and weavers owned their instruments and worked them in their cottages, the scale of the business demanded capital, so that all over the country, at Glasgow, Dunfermline, Kirkcaldy, Perth, Dundee, Montrose, Aberdeen and elsewhere, 'manufacturers' imported flax or bought it at home, distributed it to housewives for spinning, and collected and paid for the yarn; the same or other 'manu-facturers' often gave out yarn to be woven on hand-looms by wage-earning weavers. The independent craftsman was still to be found in 1800, buying his own material and selling fine cloth to local customers, but the industry at large was already 'big business.' The capitalist came long before the factory.

Overseas commerce benefited from the Union even more than farming and linen. The Navigation Acts were now a help rather than a hindrance, for they gave Scottish traders a favoured position in relation to the colonial raw materials and markets, and Glasgow found itself on the right side of the map *vis-à-vis* the American plantations. Her shipping rose from 15 vessels at the Union to nearly 400 before the War of American Independence. The most lucrative branch of commerce was the import and re-export to Europe of raw tobacco. This trade, starting about 1718, and changing about 1740 from a 'barter' system (the exchange of Scottish goods for tobacco crops) to a 'factor' system (the purchase, often in advance, of entire crops by the trader's agent on the spot), became by 1750 highly speculative, fiercely competitive and fantastically profitable. The Glasgow merchants gradually pushed ahead of those of Bristol and London, until, in 1772, 49,000 out of the United Kingdom's import of 90,000 hogsheads came to the Clyde. All but a fraction was for re-export (44 out of 46 million pounds in 1771). In 1773 there were 38 Glasgow firms engaged in the trade and the 'tobacco lords' were, along with the London 'nabobs' of the East India trade, among the wealthiest and most arrogant of British merchants. Sugar, rum, mahogany, lemons and limes were also imported, and return cargoes comprised mainly linen cloth, with some thread, stockings, and glass, leather and metal goods.

In 1775, on the outbreak of war with the American colonists, the bubble burst. The tobacco trade, an exotic luxury made possible by the monopolistic principles of the 'old empire' and by the continental craving for snuff and smoking, collapsed and never recovered. After 1783, however (the year of the foundation of the Glasgow Chamber of Commerce), mercantile prosperity was regained. The Atlantic trade in sugar and cotton enriched Glasgow and Greenock, while Leith, Dundee and Aberdeen benefited greatly from close intercourse with the continent. If the lesser seaports tended to decline into fishing villages, the greater harbours were thronged with traffic, and, instead of the 100 sea-going ships of 1707, Scotland had 2,000 by 1800.

By about 1780 Scotland could no longer be called a poor country. Capital had been accumulated in three main ways. Landowners like Sir Archibald Grant of Monymusk and George Dempster of Dunnichen knew that improved farming meant higher rent-rolls; other rich men, such as David Dale and James Monteith, got their start as linen weavers and then became linen merchants; of the third group the most out-standing is John Glassford, the tobacco lord, who owned 25 ships and traded for £500,000 per annum. The fortunes amassed from scientific agriculture, linen manufacture and foreign commerce were held, in many cases, by enterprising men, prepared to invest in promising new ventures. Thus Scotland was ready to enter the Industrial Revolution, which, in its first phase, depended on James Watt's invention of the separate condenser (1765), Richard Arkwright's water-frame for spinning (1769), Samuel Crompton's spinning-mule (1779), and Henry Cort's process for puddling iron (1784).

Scotland's first cotton-spinning mills were set up at Rothesay (1778) and Penicuik (1779); more important was James Monteith's mill at Anderston, near Glasgow (1780). Scotland's biggest mill, employing over 1,300 people, was opened by David Dale at New Lanark in 1786, and soon the west country had abandoned linen in favour of the new textile. Spinning was entirely mechanized but the hand-loom continued in use; the cotton weaver, with weekly wages sometimes as high as 30s., was the best paid worker. By 1800 the cotton industry, centred in Glasgow and Paisley, had an annual output of nearly £3,000,000, compared with just over £1,000,000 for linen.

The iron industry dates effectively from the establishment of the Carron works in 1759. Before that time charcoal-burning furnaces had operated in a very small way at remote spots like Bonawe, Invergarry and Loch Broom, where wood was plentiful. Coke-smelting was used at Carron, and soon 'carronades,' farming tools and domestic utensils were being distributed at home and abroad. In the 1780s the iron industry spread westwards, with the Clyde works (near Glasgow), Wilsontown and Omoa (in Lanarkshire), and Muirkirk (Ayrshire). Some twenty furnaces were in blast by 1800, with an annual output valued at over £100,000. About this time, too, stimulated by the rising domestic and industrial demand, and assisted by the invention of water-pumping and coal-raising engines, new coal-pits were being opened, especially in Lanarkshire, Ayrshire and Midlothian.

Other forms of economic activity underwent great changes during the eighteenth century. Banking facilities were provided by the Bank of Scotland (1695), the Royal Bank (1727), the British Linen Company (started in 1746 but confined to banking from 1763), and local banks set up at Glasgow from 1750 and at other towns from 1763 on. Apart from two failures (the notorious 'Ayr Bank,' in 1772, and the unlucky Glasgow Arms, in 1793), the Scottish banks were stable as well as progressive, and they helped to finance many industrial developments. Road transport improved with the building of General Wade's military roads in the Highlands (1724–36) and, after the Turnpike Road Act (1751), of hundreds of toll-roads throughout the country; by 1786 Edinburgh was only 60 hours from London by stage-coach. From 1759 (the first of many acts) the Clyde was being deepened to take ocean-going vessels. Two canals, the Forth and Clyde, and the Monkland, intended primarily for the carriage of coal and other bulky cargoes, were opened for traffic, after long delays, in 1790; and the wooden wagon-ways or tram-roads at the coalfields foreshadowed a yet greater change. Among the minor industries that were stimulated by the general economic advance were paper-making, printing and publishing, coach-building and glass-blowing (all at Edinburgh in particular), sugar-refining, pottery, rope-making and chemicals (in the west), and the weaving of coarse woollens, long established in the Borders

and now fostered by individuals and societies in the Highlands. Another ancient industry, the herring fishery, was of
special significance for the Highlands, but Dutch competition, based on large boats and efficient curing, had been
triumphant since the seventeenth century. In 1750, state
bounties, on a tonnage basis, were promised for 'busses'
(ships of 20 tons and upward, with standard equipment),
but still the industry languished. From 1786 the British
Fisheries Society set up three 'stations' or new villages,
Ullapool, Tobermory and Lochbay (Skye); though none of
them really answered the needs of the herring fisheries, the
Society's next venture, the building of a new harbour at
Pulteneytown, on Wick's doorstep (1806–11), was destined
to achieve dramatic success.

In the early nineteenth century, agriculture, employing
about one-third of the people, was still the country's economic
mainstay. The Napoleonic Wars gave an impetus and a
kind of unplanned protection to arable farming, with prices
high and imports scarce: the wheat acreage reached a peak
of 140,000 in 1814. The coming of peace threatened home
farmers with abundant imports and depressed prices, but
they were influential enough to obtain the artificial or state
protection of the Corn Laws (1815–46). Sheltered, therefore,
in one way or another, agriculture remained the leading
industry. The old improvements—long leases, enclosures,
rotation of crops, fallow, light ploughs and threshing
machines—spread to areas hitherto backward, while new
techniques—chemical fertilizers, tile drainage, artificial
cattle-feed (linseed and cotton-seed cake), reaping machines,
and the application of steam-power—were developed and
quickly taken up in the advanced districts. The 'high
farming' of the Lothians set a standard of efficiency (especially in wheat production) that impressed such a know-
ledgable visitor as William Cobbett, who found the farms
there 'factories for making corn and meat, carried on
by means of horses and machinery' (1832), while George
Robertson testifies that 'the markets were kept full of the
best beef the whole year round' (*Rural Recollections*, 1829).
By 1840 the best of the Lothian farms (running to several

hundred acres) might rent for as much as £7 an acre, and the farmer, entering on a lease of twenty-one years, required a large capital outlay, a substantial body of farm-workers, the most modern machinery, and a detailed knowledge of soil chemistry and climate, animal breeding, markets and accountancy; on that basis, he could expect to become or remain a man of wealth and standing in the community.

With the advent of free trade in 1846, Scottish farming was exposed to the open competition of Danish butter, Dutch cheese, American wheat, Argentine beef, Australian wool and New Zealand mutton. Only the soundest arable farming could survive, and the marginal and sub-marginal lands were driven out of cultivation. The 'great depression' (1873–92) was not without periods of recovery, but there was a steady tendency for prices to drop, for the farm area to shrink, and for the farm labourer to seek other work. There had been over 500,000 persons employed on farms, woods and gardens in 1801; by 1901, though the total population had nearly trebled, the number was down to 210,000, with other 27,500 engaged in fishing. The acreage under oats and barley, potatoes and turnips, declined slowly, but wheat, as an uneconomic crop, fell steeply between 1875 and 1932. Permanent grass, on the other hand, and the numbers of sheep and cattle maintained on it, increased. The trend was everywhere towards local specialization—Aberdeen-Angus cattle, Clydesdale horses and fruit orchards, Ayrshire and Galloway dairy-farming, Border and Highland sheep-rearing.

Apart from the conversion of small crofts into sheep-walks, which continued until about 1850, the Highland economy suffered amazing vicissitudes. In the period 1790–1820 the burning of seaweed to make kelp (valued for its iodine content, particularly while war cut off imports of barilla and potash) brought profits and attracted settlers to the western seaboard and islands, until the withdrawal of the import duty on barilla killed the industry (1823). About the same time, the migratory Highlanders who had sought seasonal labour on the Lowland farms began to find Irish immigrants undercutting them for this work. Fortunately, however, from about 1814 the north-eastern ports, from Wick to Peterhead, experienced a steady run of prosperity, one good herring season (lasting for six weeks each summer) following another. From the middle of the century free trade cut down the profitability of much Highland sheep grazing, and proprietors began to set aside vast estates for renting to sportsmen as deer forests or grouse moors. Admittedly these areas had already been depopulated with the coming of the sheep, and offered the poorest and roughest of grazing, but a small fraction was capable of better use. Overshadowing all other changes was the continued emptying of the inland glens of their inhabitants, to make sheep-walks, enlarge the holdings, or provide coastal settlements of fishermen-crofters. As varied as the motives behind the clearances were the methods of carrying them out—from 'the horrors of grinding oppression' and 'scenes of desolation' deplored by Donald Sage when writing (in *Memorabilia Domestica*) of the Sutherland evictions (1811–20), to the humane and enlightened conduct of the Campbells of Argyll in seeking the immediate relief of, and a lasting solution for, the congestion on the island of Tiree, at the time of the potato failure (1846). All depended on the will of the individual proprietor until, by the Crofters' Holdings Act of 1886, as we have seen (page 124), the small farmer for the first time gained security of tenure and other rights.

The nineteenth century witnessed the continued supersession of manual by mechanical labour in all branches of textiles. The transition was very slow, and varied greatly from one type of work to another, and also as between the different fabrics. Thus, spinning lent itself more readily to mechanization than did the more complex process of weaving, and flax was, for technical reasons (especially the sticky nature of the fibre), less suitable for the machine than was cotton. Two full generations passed before the hand-worker disappeared, or all but disappeared, in face of the advance of the mills, and the completion of the Industrial Revolution in respect of textiles cannot be dated earlier than about 1870.

The first practicable power-loom for cotton was in use at Catrine, in Ayrshire, in 1807, but it was not until the 1830s and 1840s that the hand-loom weaver, whose weekly wages dropped as low as 4s., was virtually squeezed out of the industry. In linen machine-spinning was generally adopted in the period 1825–35, and power-weaving only about 1860, when, again, the bewildered operator of the hand-loom experienced intense suffering, unemployment and starvation. Wool-spinning mills and stocking-frames appeared at Aberdeen, Hawick and Galashiels about 1800 and power-weaving was taken up from about 1850, but the mills were small (with, say, 50 workers apiece) and the paternalistic mill-owners saw to it that the change involved the least possible hardship.

Against the flowing tide of mechanization, the workers of Paisley—already famed for textile experimentation and variety, and used to lawns, cambrics, silk gauzes, incles (linen tape), thread, muslins and 'tambouring' (fine embroidery)—produced their celebrated shawls, woven entirely by hand, in imitation of the finest Oriental work, with a warp of 'Cashmere' (wool spun around a silk core) and a weft of fine Tibetan wool or worsted. The Paisley shawl trade lasted, with many fluctuations and depressions, from 1820 until 1870, when fashion changed and the demand ceased. Seven different colours were normally used, the patterns were delicate and precise, and the work was both arduous and finical; but the weaver was in some sense his own master—free to work, to play, or to discuss politics, as he chose—and he had the sense of fulfilment that comes only to the creative artist. His trade represents the most picturesque episode in the gallant and futile struggle of man against the all-conquering machine.

For fifty years cotton expanded slowly but steadily. The mills became larger, with an average labour force of about 200, and they were increasingly concentrated in the west country and subject to direction and financial control from Glasgow: of 192 cotton mills in 1839, 175 were in Lanarkshire and Renfrewshire, 98 of them in Glasgow and 41 in Paisley. Badly shaken by the economic crisis of 1857, cotton was ruined by the outbreak of the American Civil War in 1861, for it never recovered from the stoppage of supplies of raw cotton from the southern states, and after 1865 both capital and labour turned to the heavy industries. A few cotton mills survived—at Deanston (Perthshire), Bridgeton (Glasgow) and Catrine; otherwise what was once Scotland's premier industry came to be represented only by specialized offshoots, such as carpet-weaving at Glasgow and Kilmarnock, calico-printing and dyeing in the Vale of Leven, lace-making in the Irvine valley, and thread-manufacture at Paisley.

Linen too suffered a degree of localization and dispersal. Its chief centre, Dundee, began to change to jute, the cheapest of carriers and packers, in 1833, and by 1890 the shift was complete. From 1847 a large linoleum industry developed at Kirkcaldy, while Dunfermline specialized in fine table linens and damasks. The main industry itself was carried on principally in the towns of Angus, like Arbroath, Forfar and Kirriemuir. The woollen mills of the Borders gradually adopted quality fabrics; the renown of their typical product was furthered by the lucky misreading of the trade-name 'tweel' as the more romantic 'tweed.' Other woollen specialities included north-eastern 'overcoatings,' city knit-wear and hosiery, and the hand-woven and hand-knitted goods of Harris, Orkney and Shetland. The general trend was, however, one of contraction: in the second half of the century textile employment shrank from 250,000 to 175,000. Moreover, the order of magnitude of the several branches was reversed, for, whereas in 1800 cotton was easily first, linen second and wool third, by 1901 jute led, with 39,000 workers, followed by wool (25,000), linen (under 24,000) and cotton (nearly 15,000).

The central fact of Scottish economic history between the Napoleonic Wars and the first World War is the rise of 'heavy industry' to a position of dominance, and the most striking feature of that rise is the increasing inter-dependence of activities that were originally quite separate—coal-mining, iron-working, shipbuilding, engineering and steel-making. An expansion in one direction stimulated developments in others and confirmed their alliance, until they came to form a single closely integrated industrial group, heavily capitalized, employing a huge labour force, and exporting its products to all parts of the world. This second phase of the Industrial Revolution transformed the central lowland plain, stretching from Ayrshire to Midlothian and West Fife, and possessing, in proximity to each other, all the needful advantages—abundant supplies of coal and iron ores, navigable rivers and canals, enterprising capitalists and a sufficiency of labour, immediately available or within call: for, in so far as native workers fell short of requirements either in skill or in numbers, English experts, such as iron-workers, could be imported, or, on the other hand, thousands of hardy but untrained Irishmen could be induced to settle.

In certain lines, notably iron-smelting and shipbuilding, Scottish discoveries and pioneer work were basic. In 1801 David Mushet demonstrated the economy and usefulness of blackband ironstone, an ore containing a high proportion of coal and found in quantity in the Monkland area, and in 1828 James B. Neilson patented his hot-blast furnace, capable of smelting a ton of pig-iron with two tons of coal instead of the seven used by the cold blast. Almost at once iron-works sprang up in the Monklands—Gartsherrie (1828), Dundyvan (1833) and Summerlee (1837); the famous 'Dixon's Blazes' were lit at Govan in 1839. Long before the close of the century the annual output of Scotland's iron industry reached a million tons.

If William Symington's *Charlotte Dundas* (1802) and Robert Fulton's *Clermont* (1807) were the pioneers of the steamship, Henry Bell's *Comet* (1812) gave the Clyde a flying start and led at once to the building of large numbers of auxiliary steam vessels, for use first on rivers and coastal runs and, within a generation, for ocean voyages. And it was a Scottish shipowner, George Burns, and a Scottish engineer, Robert Napier, who made possible the founding of the world's most famous shipping line, the Cunard (1839), just as it was the Clyde that built its first four ships, the *Britannia, Acadia, Caledonia* and *Columbia* (1840). Like the railways, which began in Scotland in 1826, steamships were doubly linked to heavy industry, for they can be regarded either as metallurgical and engineering products, or as carriers of raw materials and of finished goods. The propeller-driven iron steamship very gradually displaced the 'wind-jammer' from the middle of the century. Iron itself gave way to steel in the 1880s and by 1889 all but a small fraction (97·2 per cent.) of Clyde tonnage was of steel. In 1900 the steel output was 960,000 tons, but, while steel had many advantages over iron, it had one great drawback in that three-fifths of the ores required by the Scottish furnaces had to be imported; there was thus a partial loss of the natural self-sufficiency on which the earlier prosperity of heavy industry had rested.

The exploitation of the central coal-fields was steadily intensified until, at the close of the century, the output neared 40 million tons, and the workers below and above ground exceeded 100,000. At that time iron and steel manufacture employed over 23,000, shipbuilding nearly 35,000, while no fewer than 119,000 were engaged in the multifarious activities of the engineering shops—making marine engines, locomotives, spindles and looms for the mills, and steam engines and constructional work of many kinds.

Transport was revolutionized along with industry in the course of the nineteenth century. For some time canals were favoured for the carriage of bulky goods. The Crinan canal (1801) provided a short cut between Loch Fyne and the open sea, another waterway was opened from Aberdeen to Inverurie in 1807, and a third (1811) joined Glasgow, Paisley and Johnstone, but was never continued, as originally intended, to the sea at Ardrossan. In 1822 two more important water routes were opened—the Union canal, linking Edinburgh and Falkirk (31½ miles), and joining the Forth and Clyde canal, and the Caledonian, following the line of 'the Great Glen' over a distance of 60 miles, only 22 of which had to be cut. But the deepening of the Clyde—to 15 feet by 1830, to 20 feet by the end of the century—made of that river, in effect, an artificial waterway that carried much more traffic than all the canals of Scotland.

The canals bore many passengers and much traffic until, in the 1840s and 1850s, they were superseded by the railways. The immediate forerunner of the new mode of transport was the Kilmarnock–Troon line, opened for horse-drawn wagons

in 1810, but the first true railway (though for a time it still
used horses) ran from the Monkland coal-field to the canal
at Kirkintilloch (1826); along with the Ballochney (1828),
Garnkirk–Glasgow (1831) and Coltness–Wishaw lines (1833),
it formed a rough cross centred on what came to be the new
town of Coatbridge. The movement of coal was the main
function of these early lines, as it was of the Edinburgh–Dalkeith railway (1831). Inter-urban services were supplied by
the Glasgow, Paisley and Ayr railway (1840), the Glasgow,
Paisley and Greenock (1841), and the Edinburgh and Glasgow (1842). Even more ambitious projects were realized
by the linking of Edinburgh with Berwick (the North British
railway, 1846), and so with London, the opening of the
'Caledonian' route between Glasgow and Carlisle (1848), and
the provision of the alternative line by way of Kilmarnock
(1850). Northward, Perth (1847) and Aberdeen (1850) were
reached, while the Elgin–Lossiemouth (1852) and Inverness–
Nairn (1853) lines were the first beyond the Grampians.
By 1870, through amalgamations, control had come into the
hands of five large companies—the North British, Caledonian,
Glasgow and South-Western, Highland, and Great North of
Scotland—and a few small ones. The Tay was bridged in
1879 (by a structure which collapsed in a gale on December
28 of that year and caused total loss of life on the train that
was in transit) and again, more durably, in 1887, and the
Forth (presenting harder engineering problems) in 1890. By
1900 the five Scottish companies had over 3,500 miles of
double or single track.

Banking developments were likewise ancillary to economic
evolution. The Commercial Bank (1810) and the National
Bank (1825) were added to the three older and larger
institutions; and in 1810 the first of many local savings banks,
accepting small deposits from the working classes, was set up
at Ruthwell by the Rev. Henry Duncan. The industrial
expansion of the 1830s was accompanied by the foundation
of many new banks, most notably the Union (1830), the North
of Scotland (1836), the Clydesdale (1838) and the City of
Glasgow (1839); but the Bank Acts of 1844–45 forbade the
formation of any new banks of issue and in effect closed the

list at 19. This number was reduced by way of seven amalgamations and two failures: the Western Bank collapsed, with a loss of nearly £3,000,000, in the financial panic of 1857, and the gigantic fraud of the directors of the City of Glasgow Bank (1878) cost the depositors over £6,000,000 and brought ruin and desolation to many a west country household. All ten remaining banks, as a precaution against such disasters, simultaneously adopted limited liability in 1881. Meanwhile, and in spite of these two exceptional lapses, such were the strength, stability and good repute of the Scottish banks that one of them, the Clydesdale, was able to 'invade' England in 1874, when it set up three branches in Cumberland; though by tacit agreement any further expansion of this kind was abandoned, all the Scottish banks secured the right of having London offices, and they closed the century as sound and solvent institutions. Their note-issuing powers (in denominations of £1 and upwards) made a sharp contrast with English practice; banknotes circulated as freely as gold in Scotland, and public confidence furthered industrial investment and commercial progress.

Though developments in heavy industry, textiles, rail transport and banking best typify the Industrial Revolution in nineteenth-century Scotland, there were other economic changes that were both dramatic and significant. In its stand against the coming of steam-power and the machine, the famous Aberdeen tea clipper might be compared with the Paisley shawl: construction was maintained from 1839 to 1869, and among the most celebrated products of the Aberdeen yards were the *Cairngorm*, *Black Prince*, and *Thermopylae*. Fishing by line from sail-boats, for both white fish and herring, was reasonably prosperous for the greater part of the century, but each branch was in turn revolutionized by the adoption of the steam-trawler at Aberdeen in 1882 and of the steam-drifter at Wick in 1898; the tendency now was in the direction of deep-sea rather than inshore fishing, and the use of larger vessels favoured the greater ports and more commodious harbours, at the expense of the tiny fishing villages. The annual catch rose steadily until the outbreak of the first World War. Another trade with romantic overtones is that of the yearly whaling expeditions sent out from Dundee and Aberdeen.

A very wide range of minor industries flourished, or survived, during the century—chemicals and soap-making at Glasgow, sugar-refining at Greenock, paper-making, printing and publishing at Edinburgh and elsewhere, granite-cutting at Aberdeen, and, scattered throughout the country, brewing and distilling, coach-building, glass-blowing, boot and shoe manufacture, and a host of 'service' trades. Commercial advance kept pace with industrial: channels were dredged, dangerous points around the coasts lighted, docks, piers and wharves built. Once again, the developments of the time brought advantage to the greater centres, so that the bulk of the freight passed into and out of Leith, Grangemouth, Dundee and Aberdeen, in the east, and Glasgow and Greenock, in the west. As has already been mentioned, the Cunard line owed its start to Scottish enterprise; and a number of other steamship lines that came to be well known on the sea-routes were Scottish concerns—the White Star (1825), the Clan line (1845), the Anchor (1852) and the Donaldson (1858).

The evolution of railways and banks was from small, independent concerns, by way of absorption and unification, towards ever larger combines, and this consolidation of capitalism is characteristic of the whole field of industrial organization. In the early years of the century leadership was taken by bold and venturesome pioneers, like James Ewing and Kirkman Finlay, who forged new commercial links with the West Indies and India; or Alexander Baird of Gartsherrie and his sons, who left farming to exploit their coal and iron resources; or Henry Houldsworth, who changed from cotton weaving to cotton machinery and set up the Anderston foundry (1839); or Charles Macintosh, transferring from chemicals to iron and finally to the waterproofed rubber that was to immortalize his name. Later in the century huge and impersonal companies, with wide and varied interests, took the place of the highly individualistic entrepreneur. The very titles are often significant. John

Elder's shipbuilding business grew into the Fairfield Ship-building and Engineering Company (1885), Robert Napier's marine engineering establishment was the nucleus for William Beardmore and Company, while the firm of J. and G. Thomson (1846) grew into the Clydebank Company, which was merged in John Brown and Company in 1899. In textiles, the United Thread Manufacturing Company was formed in 1896 from the rival concerns of Coats and Clark, and the identity of the Crums of Thornliebank was sunk in the Calico Printers' Association (1899). The chemical firms founded by Charles Tennant (1800) and others were brought together in 1890 as the United Alkali Company, Macintosh's interests formed a main element in the Dunlop Rubber Company (1895), while as early as 1877 six whisky producers had combined as the Distillers' Company Limited. And it was at Finnieston, about 1870, that a twenty-year-old Glasgow youth founded a small corner shop which was to grow into the world-wide commercial empire of Lipton's Limited (1885).

As we shall see in the next chapter, the seemingly irresist-ible march of economic progress was achieved by Victorian Scotland only at a fearful price in terms of living conditions and social welfare, but the same kind of prosperity lapped over into the twentieth century and continued until the first World War. From about 1910, in particular, there was a trade boom. The demand for luxury liners and for 'dread-noughts' and other warships was stimulated by international competition in both mercantile and naval shipping, and the highest output ever attained by the Clyde yards was recorded in 1913, when the figure of over 750,000 tons was one-third of the United Kingdom total and greater than that of all Germany. Shipbuilding was regarded, with some justice, as a rough measure of general industrial health, for busy yards meant the diffusion of work and orders throughout the hinterland. Nevertheless, it is clear enough in restropect, though it was not suspected by contemporary observers, that things were far from well with Scotland in 1913, that the face of her economy, indeed, showed a hectic and feverish flush.

The population was now 4,800,000, or three times that of 1800, and it naturally included fairly large numbers in the 'sheltered' trades and occupations—fully 200,000 in 'personal service,' over 140,000 bakers, butchers, grocers and other purveyors of food, some 125,000 transport workers by land and sea, and substantial groups in house-building, government posts, shop-keeping, the professions and clerical work. But the basic industries, which had made possible the great national increase in numbers and in wealth, and which supported the whole economic superstructure, were each showing serious flaws. Scottish farming was efficient: this is proved by the valuable international trade that had grown up in pedigree bulls (Aberdeen-Angus, Ayrshires and Shorthorns) and in seed potatoes. But that this primary industry of mankind gave employment to only 200,000, or one-tenth of the country's paid workers, indicated a serious lack of balance in the economy. The opposite criticism applies to the 400,000 workers in heavy industry (including rather more than a quarter of all 'gainfully employed' males), for this was an unduly large proportion in view of the troubles now being encountered: dependence on imports of foreign ores, serious competition from United States and Germany, and the growing preference, as a fuel, for oil (and later electricity) in place of coal, the basic commodity of the metallurgical group. Textiles employed nearly 165,000 in various localized branches, of which the largest, Dundee jute, faced a losing struggle with its offshoot, the mills of Calcutta. Other industries, like paper, leather, pottery, glass and chemicals, though well established, needed relatively few workers, and little or nothing in the way of new industry was in sight. Scotland had put her eggs in one basket: what had once brought her strength was threatening to become a source of weakness. Over-expanded and insufficiently varied, her economy was peculiarly exposed to trade depression and the vagaries of world-wide demand and supply.

The war of 1914–18 emphasized these points. In profits and wages it brought prosperity to both agriculture and industry. Shortages and rationing of foodstuffs, and the submarine blockade, put a premium on arable farming, and the government appealed in 1917 for the ploughing-up of grasslands. The result was an increase in the acreage under wheat and oats. Textiles were helped by large government orders for army shirts, uniforms and blankets. Coal was urgently needed for industrial and domestic use, and the output remained fairly constant at some 30 million tons a year. Iron and steel production was well maintained, but most of it went to the making of shells (12 millions of which came from Scotland), guns, cartridges, bombs and other munitions of war. The shipyards were hectically busy, but priority was given to naval contracts and to repair work, so that mercantile construction at first declined steeply. Later the blockade and the need to maintain food supplies caused a resumption of merchant shipbuilding, but, even so, the Clyde output, averaging under 500,000 tons a year, was far short of the 1913 figure. Other industries, such as locomotive- and bridge-building and chemicals, suffered through the diversion to munitions work.

Both labour and raw materials were scarce throughout the war, the former because of recruiting and conscription (which were conducted with little or no regard to the needs even of essential industry), and the latter because of the restriction of trade to food, iron-ores, military equipment and a few other war-time necessities. In consequence, unemployment practically disappeared, and nominal wages increased; coal-miners, for example, got 13s. a day in 1918, as against 7s. in 1914, and other workers had steeper rises. Yet there were 20,000 fewer miners in 1918 than at the start of the war. On the material side, exports were drastically curtailed, and the vital foreign markets for Scottish coal, textiles, ships and machinery were very largely abandoned; the outward trade from Glasgow (one of the safer ports) was cut almost in half. Thus the enormous expenditure of those years on unproductive ends (effected only by national borrowing) accentuated Scotland's pre-war lack of balance in two ways: it stimulated the already over-blown heavy industries to further expansion, in order to make articles that had little or no place in peace-time, and at the same time it obliged them to refuse the foreign orders that were their life-blood, and to invite their overseas customers to deal instead with their rivals in other countries. And, finally, the casualties of the war—74,000 Scotsmen, in the flower of manhood, killed, and hundreds of thousands physically weakened through wounds in greater or less degree—constituted a heavy economic loss as well as a major human tragedy.

The pre-war weaknesses, exaggerated by the damage inflicted by war-time dislocation, came out fully in the period between the German wars (1918–39), when Scotland in the material sense was in a worse state than she had been since the very early years of the eighteenth century. The premature removal of war-time controls was one of the causes which led to depression in the early 1920s, a condition that was chronic in agriculture throughout the decade. Heavy industry experienced wild fluctuations of fortune. The need to replace the merchant shipping sunk in 1917–18 brought something like a boom in 1919 and 1920, when the Clyde's annual output was about 650,000 tons. There was a three months' coal stoppage in 1921, the furnaces in blast fell to 40 (there had been 85 during the war), and one out of five insured workers was unemployed—a severe test for the new insurance scheme inaugurated in 1920. From 1922 onwards, though shipbuilding declined heavily, some of the export trade in coal, forfeited during the war, was recovered. The seven months' coal stoppage of 1926, which led to the general strike, affected all industry adversely, besides necessitating the importation of foreign coal. The metallurgical branches, meanwhile, were hampered by temporary stoppages, reduced shifts and unusable surplus stocks, but the deadliest blow was the impending exhaustion of the 'hard splint' coal of Lanarkshire, which had been the main field for a century and a quarter. While imports into Britain's open market of iron, steel and manufactures mounted, stagnation spread through towns like Motherwell, Coatbridge and Falkirk. Between 1921 and 1931, consequently, the skilled workers were drifting away from every branch of heavy industry, the decreases ranging from 18·7 per cent. in coalmining to 37·1 per cent. in shipbuilding. Only less severe were the sufferings in textiles: Italian and Czechoslovakian linens, and Japanese cottons, competed successfully with Scottish products, and Indian jute brought poverty and worklessness to Dundee. It is true that, at the close of the decade, the buoyant optimism of American investors brought another wave of orders to the Scottish yards, so that the Clyde output in the years 1928–30 averaged 500,000 tons per annum; but this was a fleeting ray of sunshine before the big storm broke.

In 1931 there began the most serious world-wide depression of modern times, and Scotland was affected with peculiar intensity. The fall of prices was general and steep: wheat, which had been 70s. a quarter during the war, dropped to 24s. 8d. Coal output in 1931 was 29 million tons—the lowest for the century with the exception of the great strike years of 1921 and 1926. Imports of steel actually exceeded exports, and there was a time in 1931 when only one out of 77 furnaces was in blast. Clyde shipbuilding declined to ever lower levels —150,000 tons in 1931, 67,000 in 1932, and 56,000 (out of 74,000 for all Scotland) in 1933. In those three years over a quarter of the insured workers were out of work, and in 1933 the total reached 407,000, a proportion in excess of 30 per cent. of the total. Symbolic of the frustration of the times was the giant new Cunarder lying half-completed at Clyde-bank, its construction suspended for want of money, while 31,000 workers in shipbuilding and marine engineering were unemployed—or nearly 65 per cent. of the area's total of 48,000, which had itself declined from a figure of 63,000 as recently as 1928.

Among the measures taken by the government to arrest and reverse economic decay was the adoption, by agreement with the dominions at the Ottawa Imperial Conference in 1932, of a full system of protection. Import-quotas were fixed for wheat, beef, mutton and bacon, and a tariff was imposed on imported oats. Iron and steel goods were subjected to a $33\frac{1}{3}$ per cent. duty. Textiles and other manu-factures were protected either by the general tariff of 10 per cent. or by higher specific duties, though many foodstuffs and raw materials were left on the free list. In this way free trade, under which British industry and commerce had thriven for three generations, was abandoned. Since state protection was enacted by a mainly Conservative administration, and since socialist philosophy leaned even more towards state control and, indeed, nationalization, it seemed that the days of *laissez-faire* were gone for ever, regretted only by the Liberal minority. For tariffs did not stand alone as the 'National' government's remedy for widespread depression; many other steps were taken in a similar direction. Marketing schemes were instituted for milk products, pigs, bacon and potatoes. The Herring Industry Board was set up in 1935, with a Treasury grant, for the purpose of reorganizing and modernizing that industry; warning was given, in effect, that the old individualistic practices would no longer suffice. Those areas which were suffering most from unemployment in Northern England, South Wales and Central Scotland were designated 'distressed areas;' they were later re-named 'special' and finally 'development' areas. Commissioners were appointed for each, and given funds to be spent in efforts to induce the newer and lighter industries (which had been consistently avoiding every region that could be called 'black country') to settle in their areas. As a logical sequel to this new policy, industrial estates, with ready-made factories for rent and all services provided, were laid out on chosen sites in these hard-hit areas; the first in Scotland was at Hillington, to the south-west of Glasgow (1937), and others followed in North Lanarkshire—Carfin, Chapelhall and Larkhall (1939). The newer industries were thus to be brought to the people who needed them.

A gradual improvement resulted from these measures, and from the rearmament orders which began to flow in 1936. It is, however, an index to the severity and duration of the trade recession of the 1930s that, as late as December 1939, three months after the start of the second World War, the Scottish unemployed numbered 177,000, or 10·6 per cent. of all insured workers. In many ways, the country's experiences during that war were a repetition of those of 1914–18, but the lessons of the earlier conflict had been learnt and the mistakes were for the most part avoided. The casualties of the second—and more protracted—war were happily fewer than of the first: about 34,000 were killed in the services (including the merchant service) and 6,000 civilians. In the economic sphere, there was a more intelligent use of man-power in the second war, and it was not followed by a hasty and unwise cancellation of the war-time controls. In any case, something had been achieved in the years 1932–39 to prepare the country for the damage and dislocation in-separable from global warfare, and the same could not be said of 1914. For one reason or another, Scotland weathered the storm reasonably well.

With ordered conscription in force before the actual outbreak of hostilities, the fighting services claimed one-third of the workers during the struggle: 446,000 men were in the armed forces of the crown, and to these should be added the 29,000 Scottish merchant seamen and 69,000 women in the auxiliary services. Unemployment naturally disappeared, but for a 'hard core' of the truly unemployable (numbering 16,000 in 1944). Arable farming, as before, was given a fillip, and was regarded as vital to the war effort. In 1938, indeed, in anticipation of war and its requirements, subsidies had been granted for the ploughing-up of grasslands. Farm labour was 'frozen' in 1940, with a guaranteed weekly wage of 48s. Other subsidies (2s. 6d. for a ewe, £2 for a heifer) were given from 1941 to encourage hill grazing. Both the arable acreage and the yield of crops were greatly increased: by 1943, the peak tillage year, 641,000 acres had been added to the pre-war total. And, in the winter of 1943–44, amid all the military demands upon transport, a record movement of seed-potatoes (470,000 tons) was carried out, coastwise and by land, from Scotland to England. Textiles again benefited from war orders, but also suffered under the planned 'concentration of industry,' which involved another loss of export contracts. The mining of coal showed a decline, but heavy industry in general increased its output to meet the needs of the armed forces and the merchant marine. Com-merce, like civilian life at large, was reduced to a level of bare and austere necessities. Imports were cut to less than half of those of 1938, exports to about one-tenth; but, since prudence dictated a shift to the safer seaports of the west coast, the Clyde more than doubled its share of what trade survived. War damage was, fortunately, slighter than might have been expected, and Clydebank was the only town that was severely hit; despite all her trials, shortages and disturbances, Scotland in 1945 was really in better shape than she had been in 1918.

It is as hard to write with any assurance of the post-war economic developments as of the political changes of the time; the two were, indeed, closely intertwined. The outlines, however, are clear enough. Under the Labour government of 1945–51, state policy was based on full employment and high wages, the nationalization of essential industry, sufficient taxation to finance 'the welfare state,' and the maintenance of rationing and price controls. In these circumstances, the Scottish economy showed a remarkable degree of stability. The agricultural gains of the war years were mostly retained, and there were larger acreages and better yields of the main crops than in the 1930s, as well as good figures for livestock (except for the vanishing horse). Coal output, on the other hand, beset by the progressive exhaustion of the older fields, fell away from the pre-war total of over 30 million tons to about 24 millions per annum. Pig iron production rose to 886,000 tons in 1952, while the yearly figures for steel ingots ranged between 2,100,000 and 2,400,000 tons. Shipbuilding was very steady at about 500,000 tons in each of the post-war years—five-sixths of it from the Clyde. Textiles suffered from recurrent trade depressions, though Border tweeds and hosiery did very well in exports. The most pleasing feature of the period was the fact that unemployment was of manageable dimensions, showing seasonal fluctuations within the limits of 42,000 and 75,000 (2·0 and 3·6 per cent.). Much of the credit for this condition must be attributed to the creation, by the end of 1952, of 50,000 new jobs on the 23 industrial estates, four of them established in the years 1937–39, and the remainder after 1945. 21 of these estates were in the Clyde valley region and two at Dundee, and to both areas they brought much needed diversification, relieving the chronic unemployment in heavy industry and in jute by fostering the manufacture of a wide range of 'consumer' goods, including light engineering products, aero-engines, electrical appliances, business machines, plastics, new textiles and processed foods.

To complete the picture of Scottish economic development since 1901 some account is needed of the growth and consolidation of those services which may be broadly defined as distributive and ancillary to industry. The ten Scottish banks were reduced to six by amalgamations: the Bank of Scotland absorbed the Caledonian Bank (1907), the North of Scotland, having combined with the Aberdeen Town and County (1907), was united with the Clydesdale (1950), and in 1952 the Bank of Scotland and the Union Bank announced an exchange of stock designed to lead to complete fusion. Meanwhile, some of the English joint-stock banks had obtained control of the share capital of certain Scottish banks, leaving their local management and note-issuing powers unaltered. The National Bank thus became 'affiliated' with Lloyds Bank (1919), the British Linen with Barclay's (1919), and the Clydesdale and North of Scotland with the Midland (1920–23); but, by way of counterpoise, the Royal Bank at this time acquired as 'associates' two of the smaller English concerns, Williams, Deacon's Bank, and Glyn, Mills and Company.

The five Scottish railway companies were taken over by the government during the first World War, were returned to private ownership at its end, and, by the Railways Act of 1921, were, along with those of England, re-grouped, so that, from January 1, 1923, the Caledonian, Glasgow and South-Western, and Highland systems were incorporated in the London, Midland and Scottish Railway, while the North British and Great North of Scotland became parts of the London and North-Eastern Railway. Taken over again in 1939, the railways were nationalized, as British Railways, by the Transport Act, 1947, and Scotland became one of six regions, with some devolved powers under the British Transport Commission and the Railway Executive.

A marked trend of the times was the transfer of both goods and passenger traffic from rail to road. Here again with growth went increasing central control. The maintenance of the main 'through' roads was entrusted by the Trunk Roads Act, 1936, to the Ministry of Transport, and the road haulage and passenger transport industries were largely nationalized by the Transport Act, 1947. Efforts were made to improve roads in the crofter counties, where, also, piers and ferries were generally inadequate, but the lack of local resources hampered developments. A road bridge across the Forth and a tunnel under the Clyde at Whiteinch were other post-war schemes which were deferred for financial reasons. The three surviving canals—Forth and Clyde, Caledonian and Crinan—carried little traffic and were run at a loss.

Throughout the half-century commerce tended to concentrate in about a dozen ports. Glasgow retained the lead, ranking fifth among United Kingdom ports. The remarkable rise of Grangemouth to second place was due to the addition of new traffic (for its oil refining, dyestuffs and chemical industries) to what already existed in coal, timber, scrap iron, cement and other heavy goods. Through these two ports, and through Leith and Aberdeen, passed a large variety of cargoes, including cereals, fish, timber, paper, oil, fertilizers and metal manufactures. Dundee and Greenock must now be reckoned secondary seaports. Coal shipments, though greatly reduced in volume, are still important for the lesser ports of the Forth (Methil, Bo'ness and Burntisland) and Clyde (Ardrossan, Ayr and Troon).

Some pioneer work in the newest mode of travel was done before 1939, but air transport got its big fillip from the second World War. Prestwick, a nearly fog-free airport, became the Transatlantic 'air-ferry' terminal, and was retained after the war as an international airport, second in Britain only to those of London. Internal air-routes have been developed between London and Scotland, and, within Scotland, to and from Edinburgh (Turnhouse), Glasgow (Renfrew), Aberdeen (Dyce), Inverness (Dalcross), Orkney (Kirkwall) and other places; and ambulance services (from Glasgow and Aberdeen) are maintained with the islands and remote parts of the north and west.

The general trend in the provision of light, fuel and power was from a local or urban to a regional, and finally a national, basis. Reference has already been made to the nationalization of coal (1946), electricity (1947) and gas (1948), and also to the establishment of the North of Scotland Hydro-Electric Board in 1943 (pages 143, 145-6). The commercial principle underlying this vast enterprise was the sale of surplus power to the Lowlands (where two Boards, for the South-East and South-West, were set up in 1948), and the use of such profits to finance improvements within the Highlands, which must often be uneconomic in themselves. Work went ahead from 1945 on a great net-work of dams, generating stations and power-lines, the backbone of the system running from Loch Sloy and Shira, in the south, by way of Lawers, Breadalbane and Tummel, to Fannich (Ross) and Loch Shin (Sutherland), with an eastward loop of transmission lines by Aberdeen and Dundee, and western spurs to utilize Affric, Moriston, Garry and other glens, and ultimately to serve the entire area, including the western isles.

It is possible, from the Census Report of 1951 and other official statistics, to assess the part played by Scotland in the British economy at mid-century. The population of Scotland in 1951 was 5,095,969, or 10·43 per cent. of that of Great Britain (48,740,893). The following table indicates the basic agricultural and industrial products in respect of which Scotland's output was in excess of her proportion of the population:—

1951	Scotland	Great Britain	Percentage
Barley (thousand tons)	131	1,019	12·9
Oats (thousand tons)	244	341	71·6
Potatoes (thousand tons)	652	5,181	12·6
Milk (million gallons)	231	1,895	12·2
Beef and veal (thousand tons)	104	532	19·5
Mutton and lamb (thousand tons)	39	141	27·7
Fish landed (thousand cwt.)	4,972	19,399	25·6
Coal (million tons)	24·3	222·3	10·9
Steel (thousand tons)	2,115	15,639	13·5
Ships (thousand gross tons)	491	1,196	41·1
Jute yarn (thousand tons)	112·1	113·7	98·6
Jute cloth (thousand tons)	69	69	100·0

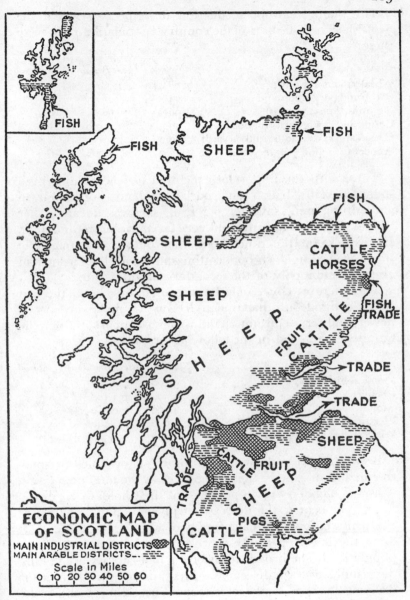

FISH

FISH

SHEEP

FISH

SHEEP

FISH

CATTLE
HORSES

SHEEP

FISH,
TRADE

S H E E P

CATTLE

FRUIT

CATTLE

TRADE

TRADE

SHEEP

CATTLE
FRUIT

TRADE

S H E E P

PIGS

CATTLE

ECONOMIC MAP
OF SCOTLAND
MAIN INDUSTRIAL DISTRICTS
MAIN ARABLE DISTRICTS
Scale in Miles
0 10 20 30 40 50 60

The main items of production in respect of which the Scottish share fell short of the country's population-ratio were these:—

1951	Scotland	Great Britain	Percentage
Wheat (thousand tons) . .	68	1,781	3·8
Bacon and pork (thousand tons) .	24	237	10·1
Pig iron (thousand tons) . .	790	9,669	8·2
Cotton and rayon yarn (million lbs.) .	50·3	1,410·0	3·6
Cotton and rayon cloth (million yards)	49·2	2,960·1	1·7
Woollens (million square yards) .	26·3	417·0	6·3

Thus, with the important exception of wheat, and (by a slight margin) bacon and pork, Scotland stood well in agriculture, and, save for pig iron, she was ahead of her 'quota' in heavy industry and very far ahead in shipbuilding. In textiles, on the other hand, her output was relatively small or very small in both cotton and wool, though she had almost a monopoly of the secondary product, jute.

These figures cover only basic commodities, and the fact that Scotland still had much leeway to make up in the newer, lighter, 'consumer' industries is apparent from the numbers employed in the following branches:—

	Scotland	Great Britain	Percentage
Motor vehicles and cycles . .	9,100	340,000	2·7
Chemicals, etc.	24,500	353,100	6·9
Aircraft	4,600	130,800	3·5
Electrical machinery . . .	1,900	107,500	1·8
Wireless and gramophones . .	2,100	52,300	4·0

Between 1901 and 1951 the number of 'occupied persons' rose in almost exactly the same degree as the total population —from 1,982,800 (44·56 per cent. of the whole) to 2,270,100 (44·55 per cent.); the decrease in juvenile employment was compensated by the greater supply of adult labour consequent upon the lowering of the death-rate and the ageing of the population. The broad trends of the half-century are readily discernible in two directions. First, there were significant declines in one group of occupations, and of these the following figures may be taken as a sample. (They are subject to some margin of error, since the methods of classifying persons under 'occupations' and 'industries' were rather different in 1901 and 1951.)

	(Thousands)	
	1901	1951
Farming and forestry	209·7	166·4
Fishing	27·6	12·5
Coal mining	108·1	82·2
Textiles	174·5	124·2
Railways	43·0	34·8
Domestic service	165·7	38·8

By contrast, the next table sets forth some of the more remarkable increases of these fifty years:—

	(Thousands)	
	1901	1951
Woodworking	39·0	54·8
Road transport	53·8	82·9
Education	25·4	58·7
Medicine and dentistry	12·7	64·8
Government service	21·4	90·1
Defence	8·0	50·8

There was thus a marked trend away from the basic and productive occupations towards the professions, processing trades and 'sheltered' services (except domestic service, now much more of a luxury than it was in 1901). It should be added that changes in the methods of enumeration make it impossible to measure the increase in the retail and service trades; in 1950 shops, restaurants and garages employed 262,250 persons whole-time and 47,500 part-time.

At mid-century the labour force on the farms (excluding self-employed persons) was just in excess of 100,000, and the average weekly wages were well over £5 for men, and between £4 and £5 for youths, women and girls. Small as was the farming community, in terms of land-use it was of primary importance: out of Scotland's 19,069,000 acres, about 3,200,000 (16·8 per cent.) were arable, other 1,200,000 (6·3 per cent.) were in permanent grass, and 10,900,000 (57·2 per cent.) were classified as rough grazings; thus, just over four-fifths of the land-area comprised agricultural holdings of one kind or another. Of the remainder, forestry claimed some 1,350,000 acres, about half in high forest and half in scrub.

Since 1932 farming has been characterized by state protection and assistance, intensive cultivation and a sustained drive for maximum productivity. The acreages under all main crops—oats, barley, potatoes and wheat (in that order) —have therefore increased, while the areas under the feed crop (turnips and swedes), and also under rotation grass and permanent grass, have diminished. But concentration on crops has meant no neglect of livestock; on the contrary, the animal population, with one exception, was stable or expanding at mid-century—over 1,500,000 cattle, more than seven million sheep, upwards of 400,000 pigs and nearly ten million poultry. Horses, declining in twenty years from 150,000 to 58,000, formed the exception. Here the reason was, of course, the advance of mechanization. By 1950 the number of tractor ploughs in use (40,520) exceeded that of horse ploughs (39,570), and the same is true of tractor-driven binders (16,790) against horse binders (13,430); by 1952 there were more tractor-mounted cultivators (25,330) than horse-drawn (23,370). The story is similar for stationary engines, milking-machines, the huge combined harvester-thresher, and other labour-saving devices, although one machine, of special importance for Scotland, is still, at the time of writing, in a stage of advanced experimentation— the potato harvester.

Mention has already been made of the state subsidies, begun in 1941, for the encouragement of hill grazing; from the 1940s other grants were paid to stimulate the ploughing of grasslands, food production from marginal farms, the use of fertilizers and lime, and the breeding of calves for beef, and for such schemes as land drainage, bracken control, and water supplies. A further significant step was the appointment, begun during the war and made permanent in 1948, of agricultural executive committees, charged with the duties of increasing food production and promoting good husbandry; each committee, comprising twelve members, acts for one of the eleven areas (varying from one to four counties) into which the country is divided. In the growing field of scientific research and education, much work has been and is being done by the Highland and Agricultural Society (founded in 1784), the two veterinary colleges (at Edinburgh and Glasgow), the three agricultural colleges (at Aberdeen, Edinburgh and Glasgow), and the three modern institutes, the Rowett (1920), the Macaulay (1930) and the Hannah (1931), concerned with animal, soil and dairy research respectively.

The rural industries most closely allied to farming have also had much state encouragement. Since its establishment in 1935, the Herring Industry Board has set up co-operative curing stations, kippering and quick-freeze plants, and fish-oil and meal factories (to utilize surplus catches and do away with the desperate remedy of dumping them in the sea), and has sponsored canning research. In 1951 it was joined by the White Fish Authority, with a Scottish committee empowered to reorganize and develop that branch. Rural crafts have been fostered by the Department of Agriculture, the Highlands and Islands Advisory Panel, and others, but the most promising of ancillary work is forestry. While their direct labour requirements run to only a few thousands, the 190 forests of Scotland are a national asset of great and growing value, and offer a natural and substantial contribution to economic diversification. Here the long-term view is the only possible one: the government-financed Forestry Commission was given in 1947 the task of planting a million and a quarter acres in fifty years. In six years (1947–53) some 161,000 acres of new Scottish woodland were planted by the Commission and private owners.

In industry more and more emphasis has been placed on organization and planning to ensure the efficient use of resources—human, financial and material—and maximum production, especially for the export market. Some of the measures to relieve unemployment and diversify industry are already matters of history—the scheduling of 'development areas,' including a central lowland belt and Dundee (from 1934), the establishment of industrial estates (from 1937), the harnessing of hydro-electric power under the Act of 1943, and the remarkable expansion of Grangemouth since the war. Other similar activities are, as this book goes to press, to be classified as 'current affairs'—most notably, the work of surveying, promoting and new thinking done by the Scottish Council (Development and Industry), under the inspiring leadership of Lord Bilsland, and the no less vigorous and successful enterprise of Mr. Thomas Johnston and his Scottish Tourist Board in attracting visitors ready to spend millions of pounds every year. Yet other schemes are in an even earlier stage of evolution, and on these, in some measure, the future well-being of the Scottish economy depends.

Foremost among these hopeful projects is the building of Scotland's two new towns, East Kilbride (Lanarkshire) and Glenrothes (Fife), for which development corporations were appointed in 1947 and 1948. East Kilbride is planned as a centre specializing in scientific research, mechanical engineering and aircraft production, and, in a social sense, as a receiving area for part of Glasgow's 'overspill.' The main purpose of Glenrothes is to accommodate the miners required for the newer coalfields of East Fife, but a secondary aim (suggested by the mistakes of the nineteenth century) is to attract a wide range of complementary and 'balancing' industries. The 'target' population for the two towns is 45,000 and 18,000 respectively. Of good augury, too, is the formation of a group of companies, under Ferranti Limited as 'parent contractor,' for research and development in electronics and precision engineering (June 1951). The need to retain, modernize and expand existing industry, and to promote suitable new ventures, is much in the minds of our planners and in their reports, which run the gamut from the three large regional plans (Clyde valley, Tay valley, and Central and South-East Scotland) to individual city, county and burgh surveys, and to projects for providing a variety of jobs in the Border woollen towns, the Buckie–Peterhead district, and other zones with special problems. Perhaps the greatest challenge to human ingenuity and foresight is offered by the necessity for an orderly transfer of redundant miners, with their families, from Lanarkshire to Fife, the Lothians and Ayrshire, where economic and social opportunities, superior to those left behind, must be furnished.

Most of these plans are little more than blue-prints, and financial considerations may enforce substantial modifications, but already much has been achieved, and more is on the way, towards broadening the base of the Scottish economy and rendering it less vulnerable to the winds of adversity than it was, say, in the early 1930s. Agriculture, steel-making and shipbuilding are sound and stable, but it is realized that these traditional lines must nowadays be reinforced by the production of such items as office equipment and plastics, nylons and processed foods; and recent advances in these directions are encouraging. Even more heartening is the general recognition of the close relationship that subsists between economic and social progress. Urban congestion and rural depopulation, the relief of unemployment and the fostering of a proper community spirit, are seen to be facets of the same theme of national well-being; and equal urgency attaches to the improvement of Highland communications and the supply of jobs for miners' women-folk, to the nurturing of ancillary trades in the fisher-towns of the north-east and the provision of adequate housing in the industrial belt. Both for what has already been accomplished and for its clearer view of desirable future developments, the Scottish economy is essentially healthier than was the case a generation ago.

H

Chapter 7

Social Life

THE population of Scotland at the opening of the eighteenth century may be estimated at about 1,100,000, and four-fifths of the people were country-dwellers, directly dependent for their living on the land. The primitive state of farming inevitably conditioned their lives and affected even the appearance of the countryside. Scottish scenery was not then admired, and the visitor was but too likely to express abhorrence for what met his eye—gaunt hills and treeless moors, miserable, ill-kempt cornfields and narrow, muddy lanes, the squalid hovels of the peasantry and the austere homes of the lairds. Travel was undertaken only when unavoidable, for the roads were fit for riding-horses and pack-horses, but scarcely for carriages (which, in any case, were almost unknown north of the Forth), and the inns were notoriously filthy and uncomfortable. Those who had to move around generally contrived to stay overnight at a country house, where they could rely on the rough and simple hospitality of a kinsman or friend.

Money, as we have seen, was a rare commodity in Scotland's subsistence economy. Landowners with £500 a year were indeed wealthy, and many of them had less than £100; often enough their lot was, in the words of an old proverb, 'a pickle land, a mickle debt, a doocot and a lawsuit.' Both they and their ladies dressed simply, in home-spun woollens, woven and cut by the women or by travelling tailors, and kept their gold braid, fine lace, three-cornered hats and silk gowns for ceremonial occasions. Most lairds kept servants, their wages running from £1 for maids up to £5 for tutors or governesses. The three daily meals, early breakfast, mid-day dinner and evening supper, were no doubt monotonous in many households, for fresh meat was nearly unobtainable from November to May, and tea (at 25s. a pound) and wheaten bread were expensive luxuries; the common fare thus consisted of bannocks or oatcakes, kail or meat-broth, salted beef and mutton, fish (though not in all districts), much home-brewed ale and some French claret. But the diet of the country laird, if he was a good manager with an imaginative wife, might well be such as to arouse envy rather than pity. The 'doocot,' as Scott reminds us, was more than a gentlemanly fad: 'This dove-cote, or columbarium, . . . was no small resource to a Scottish laird of this period, whose scanty rents were eked out by the contributions levied upon the farms by these light foragers, and the conscriptions exacted from the latter for the benefit of the table' (*Waverley*, chap. viii). Again, the Murrays of Ochtertyre, in the 1730s, not only enjoyed a wide variety of soups, meat, fish and poultry; their game included venison, hare, rabbit, woodcock, partridge, plover and moorfowl, they had artichokes and asparagus among their vegetables, and their dinners might end with gooseberry tart or custard posset, pancakes or apple fritters. What is, however, undeniable is the poor quality of the accommodation and furnishings in the country houses: everywhere were to be seen the smoky peat-fires on open hearths, bare, plastered walls, ill-fitting, draughty doors and the unhygienic box-bed.

Life was cruder and harsher for the tenant, whose work in the fields brought him, in another old saying, 'ane to saw, ane to gnaw, and ane to pay the laird witha'.' He rarely ate meat, and his regular diet was oatmeal, kail and fish, ale and milk. His working hours almost coincided with the daylight, whilst his womenfolk employed their leisure in spinning wool and linen yarn. His house, with one or two rooms, was thatched with heather, and lacked glass windows or even a chimney to carry off the peat-reek; in the winter it was occupied by cattle at one end and human beings at the other. Farm servants' yearly wages ran from 13s. 4d. for women to 30s. for skilled ploughmen (besides perquisites such as clothes and shoes). Often ill-nourished and filthy in habits—'the clartier the cosier'—they were vulnerable to skin-disease, as well as to ague (from working in wet weather and in undrained fields) and to rheumatism (from living in cold, damp houses). Both men and women wore coarse woollen plaiding, and donned shoes painfully on Sundays and holidays. Apart from weddings and funerals, their amusements were largely confined to feasting, drinking and dancing at the annual fairs, and the low level of their intelligence is suggested by their superstitious beliefs about witches and spells. It is, however, temptingly easy (as Grey Graham showed in his *Social Life of Scotland*) to depict the flaws and to overlook the good points of country life 250 years ago. The air was pure, the rivers were unpolluted and full of salmon. Hardships were numerous, but they were common to all in a society that lived very close to the soil. There were no absentee landlords among the gentry, or forgotten men among the tenant-farmers. Above all, the thorough mixture of classes, and the fact that the laird and his man, in every sense, spoke the same language, left no room for social snobbery or exclusiveness.

The towns of Scotland, over 200 in number, housed between 200,000 and 250,000 inhabitants. Edinburgh claimed some 40,000 of these, and, as the meeting-place for law courts and general assembly, and the city wherein country gentlemen had town-houses, was a real metropolis. The finest urban architecture was concentrated there—the tall, galleried and gabled houses, partly French and Flemish in origin, partly native, which were such a pleasing feature of old-time Scotland. Disinclination to build outside the imperfect, sixteenth-century city walls had determined the vertical direction of Edinburgh's expansion, in the same way as, much later, the confined space of Manhattan island produced the New York skyscraper. Those who lived in the capital were perforce crowded into the soaring 'lands' of the celebrated 'royal mile'—the High street and Canongate—the neighbouring Lawnmarket and Cowgate, and the adjoining closes, wynds and vennels. The life and habits of the citizens have often been described—the strange mixture of classes in the flats, with cobblers and poor clerks in cellars and attics, lawyers, merchants, ministers, judges and noblemen on the

intervening storeys; the busy, friendly thronging of all types of
people in the narrow, uneven, dirty streets; the great importance of the many taverns for social or business meetings,
since few private houses were roomy enough for them, and
beds had to be fitted into every available corner; the early
start of the daily round, the hearty eight o'clock breakfasts of
porridge, collops (minced meat), mutton and ale, the eleven
o'clock pause for nips of ale or brandy before midday dinner;
the ladies' afternoon parties, when claret or ale might be
served in drawing-room or bedroom; supper and the ten
o'clock curfew, marked by the cry of 'Gardyloo' as the day's
refuse was emptied out the windows, to the annoyance of
any insufficiently agile passer-by.

Glasgow, with 12,500 inhabitants, was the second city. In
contrast to Edinburgh, it won favourable comment from all
travellers, who praised its wide streets and its skyline full of
church spires, its simple rustic beauty and its fresh country
air, although here, as in all Scottish towns, the odours of
street garbage were to be deplored. Glasgow had little in
the way of fashionable society, and the merchants formed the
upper class. The Covenanting tradition was strong, and
the townsfolk were a more sober and devout body than in
Edinburgh.

Next after Glasgow came Dundee, Aberdeen and Perth,
each having between 5,000 and 8,000 inhabitants; there
were a few stone buildings and many mean hovels in these
towns. A dozen or more burghs had each a population of
two or three thousand, including Stirling and Inverness,
the gateways to the Highlands, with important fairs, Dunfermline and Paisley, the linen centres, Ayr, Dumfries and
St. Andrews, which were in some sense regional capitals,
some county towns like Haddington, Linlithgow and Elgin,
and the lesser ports, such as Kirkcaldy, Montrose, Greenock
and Irvine. Most of the others—burghs though they were
by chartered right—were in fact minor market towns, semi-
rural villages, or fishing centres, each with a few hundred
inhabitants.

The pace of social change was slow until about 1760, but
thereafter it gathered momentum. Many factors contributed

to the betterment of living conditions. The feudal order decayed, especially after 1747, and social relationships came to be governed by purely monetary contracts. The increased production of wealth meant more money to spend and there was a general rise in living standards. The agrarian improvements made available more varied foods—fresh meat, potatoes and turnips, and wheat-bread. Wages more than doubled, and ploughmen by the close of the century were getting £5–7, besides their customary 'gains,' while rent-rolls mounted steeply. The economic advance provided profits for the owners, high wages for skilled workers and craftsmen, and goods for all to buy—the new textiles, ironmongery and domestic appliances, the foreign luxuries imported by enterprising merchants. The triumph of the 'Moderates' in the Church made men more tolerant of customs and pastimes formerly deemed sinful—the theatre, dancing, card-playing and outdoor sports. Walpole's malt-duty of 1725, by making ale dearer, gave an impetus to the consumption of spirits, and, towards the end of the century, the Highland 'drug,' whisky, was finding favour among the poor in the Lowlands, while West Indian rum was preferred by the well-to-do; it is said, too, that the French wars, by rendering the traditional claret an 'unpatriotic' drink, encouraged the taste for the heavier port. From the 1780s, fast travel by stage-coach was becoming a common experience, and the canals, from 1790, helped to dispel the feeling of rustic isolation.

The total population increased by about 50 per cent. in a century, to become 1,608,000 at the first official census, in 1801. Edinburgh grew steadily, and Glasgow rapidly enough to overtake the capital: by 1801 each city, with its suburbs, had just over 80,000 inhabitants. Even more dramatic was the rise of Paisley, the centre of textile advance and experimentation, to third place; its numbers in 1801—31,200—put it just ahead of Aberdeen and Dundee. Urban growth was mainly healthy and manageable, especially in the linen centres, seaports and county towns; the comment of the minister of Ayr, in the *Old Statistical Account*, is typical— 'Upon the whole, the inhabitants have been increasing sensibly, though not rapidly, for more than 30 years past.' One of the planning measures undertaken towards the end of the century by improving landlords was the building of entirely new villages, or the re-founding of old and decayed ones, particularly for the fostering of textile manufactures among country dwellers. Thus the villages of Grangemouth (the eastern terminal of the Forth and Clyde canal), Johnstone, Larkhall and Letham (in Angus) were all deliberately 'begun' in the years 1776–81, while Blantyre, Longforgan and New Langholm were re-founded at the same period. In the prosperous farming districts, the population remained stable or increased slightly, for the savings in man-power made possible by scientific agriculture were offset, or more than offset, by the creation of new employments (wheelwrights, blacksmiths, slaters, joiners, ditchers and dykers) and the need for innkeepers and shopkeepers. There was an exodus from the Highlands in 1746, and there were post-war settlements of discharged Highland soldiers in 1763 and 1783, especially in New York, North Carolina and Canada, while throughout the century the folk of the glens felt, and responded to, the 'pull' of such towns as Glasgow, Greenock, Crieff, Perth and Dundee. Nevertheless, what we know as the seven Highland or 'crofting' counties, stretching from Argyll to Shetland, were substantially more populous in 1801 (303,000) than they had been according to Alexander Webster's unofficial enumeration of 1755 (257,000). There was thus as yet no general Highland depopulation, but the loss by migration and emigration of the more enterprising youth had begun.

Soon after the Union (which was expected to blight Edinburgh's gaiety and social graces) new amenities made life more pleasant in the capital. 'Assemblies' (fashionable subscription balls) were held from 1710. Two newspapers were started, the *Courant* (1718) and the *Caledonian Mercury* (1720), which, unlike earlier and short-lived journals, were to survive till the second half of the nineteenth century. A Musical Society was founded in 1728; from 1762 the evening concerts were to attract many citizens and their ladies to St. Cecilia's hall, in the Cowgate. Golf was played on Bruntsfield links by members of the Edinburgh Burgess Club (1735) and the Honourable Company of Edinburgh (1744). Stage-plays were being presented from 1740, and this form of entertainment achieved respectability once the uproar over John Home's *Douglas* (1756) died down. Another and yet more novel pastime appears for the first time in an advertisement in the *Courant* (May 30, 1761) of 'a proper house on wheels, with horse and servants,' to be hired for one shilling from the Royal Oak Inn at Leith for the purpose of sea-bathing. Most characteristic of the social innovations was the formation, from mid-century, of numerous clubs, some serious or cultural, like the Select Society and the Revolution and Union Clubs, others light-hearted or convivial, like the Hell-fire and Six-feet Clubs or the Bonnet Lairds; they brought literature, science and politics, or mere eating, drinking and roistering, into the night-life of the taverns, coffee-houses and streets of the capital. To the traditional Scottish fare there had now been added roast goose and turkey, crab-pies and potatoes, port and brandy, punch and toddy, while, from the 1760s, the oyster-cellars of the Cowgate beckoned the gourmet to sample their provender and to wash it down with draughts of porter.

Edinburgh had now entered on her most brilliant phase, her Athenian period, which was dominated by such lions of polite society as William Robertson and Alexander Carlyle, Adam Smith and David Hume. Physically, however, the city was cramped and confined within its royal mile, wherein growth might be inward or upward, but not outward; as late as 1769 there still lived in the Canongate two dukes, 16 earls, and many lords and judges. The first breach with the historic past came with the removal of the famous Nether Bow port, between the High street and Canongate, in 1764; the first portent of the great change to come was the building, in 1767, of a new house among the farmlands beyond the 'Lang dykes,' on the line of what was to be Princes street. Lateral expansion was at last made possible by the construction, in 1772, of the North bridge, connecting the old town with the area to be developed to the north. The Theatre Royal (1769) and the Register House (1774) were built at the east end of Princes street, and Queen and George streets were laid out parallel to that noble thoroughfare; George street was given graceful form and definition with St. Andrew's square

(1778) and lovely Charlotte square (1800) as its eastern and western terminals; the Nor' Loch was drained, and excavations provided materials, in a most original manner, for the 'Earthen Mound' (1781), another link between the old and new areas. In the opposite direction, the South bridge (1788) spanned the Cowgate, to give access to George square (1761–84), at Number 25 of which Walter Scott spent his first 21 years. By 1800 the New Town, exemplifying Georgian urban architecture at its best and embodying Scotland's most successful town planning of all time, was firmly established as Edinburgh's residential district; unhappily, this meant the abandonment, to neglect and dilapidation, of the no longer fashionable lands and tenements of the Old Town.

In social progress, as in education and cultural distinction, Glasgow followed some way behind the capital; the western city had the advantage of a more convenient, if less romantic, location. Here, too, a *Courant* was published, though only for two years (1715–17); it was followed by the hardier *Glasgow Journal* (1729) and the still more durable *Glasgow Advertiser* (1783), which, re-named the *Glasgow Herald*, has completed 170 years of existence. For the theatre the going was rougher in Glasgow than in Edinburgh: the first was destroyed by the weavers (1752), the second was burnt down (1764), and not till 1782 did one achieve a measure of stability. But Glasgow had its Literary Society (1755), its assemblies, concerts and fashionable new shops and coffee-houses; and from the 1770s onward it had many clubs—the Grog, the White Wine (whisky), the Gaelic, the Board of Green Cloth (cards), and so forth. Expansion was easy on all sides—over the river Clyde to the south, and into the surrounding fields on the other sides. The suburban villages of Calton (1731) and Anderston (1735) were built towards the east and west, outside the city limits, which were slowly stretched to cover the intervening spaces. 'Cow loan' became Queen street (1762), a new bridge was thrown across the river in 1772, and Jamaica street gave access to the southern suburb of Gorbals, which became the favoured residential area in the last two decades of the century. The Gallowgate port to the east and the Trongate port to the west were taken down in 1755 and 1760, and on their sites were built two hostelries which were to achieve fame, the Saracen's Head (with the Edinburgh stage-coach station) and the Black Bull (the Highlanders' meeting-place).

Till well on in the century Glasgow retained its pleasant and indeed handsome aspect. Edward Burt wrote, 'Glasgow is, to outward appearance, the prettiest and most uniform town that I have ever seen, and I believe there is nothing like it in Britain' (*Letters*, 1754); and, as late as 1777, John Gibson, the city's second historian, and perhaps the most modest and readable of all, asserted, 'Every stranger is charmed with the appearance of Glasgow.' Another of the local chroniclers, Robert Reid, who was to live long enough to assume the pseudonym of 'Senex,' was taken by his family, while he was still a boy, on a new kind of holiday—to remote and unfamiliar 'salt-water quarters' at Rothesay (1778), Dunoon (1779) and Largs (1782). The 1780s brought further stirrings of new life: the setting up of nine lamps on the south side of the Trongate, the laying out of George square, destined to be the municipal centre, the beginning of the use of hackney coaches in place of sedan chairs. As for the improvement of communications, it is recorded that, in 1787, a Glasgow mercer received goods from London within six days of ordering them by letter. Meanwhile, the impact of the College was strong enough to ensure that not all thoughts were of commerce, and cultural interests were advanced by the foundation of Stirling's Library (1791) and of Anderson's University (1796).

Similar changes were taking place in the other towns, though on a smaller scale and at a slower pace. More public buildings were made of stone, squares were planned, churches were given spires, and, wherever possible, the well-to-do citizens left the old and cramped quarters in town centres to live in new suburbs. The *Old Statistical Account* (1791–99) tells us of the richer opportunities for varied use of leisure—of hunting at Dumfries, of dancing and card-parties at Montrose, of the masonic lodges and weavers' societies in the western towns. Golf was played at Perth, and it was in 1754 that a St. Andrews society was formed, which later took the name of the Royal and Ancient Club and came to be recognized as the arbiter of the rules of the game throughout the world. The establishment of town libraries and the publication of local historical and antiquarian books suggests the wide diffusion of urban culture in eighteenth-century Scotland, as does the success achieved by many local newspapers, two of which—the *Aberdeen Journal* (1748) and the *Kelso Border Mail* (1779)—survive to this day, each amalgamated with a former competitor.

The prosperity of agriculture raised the standards of living in the rural households, where such articles as clocks, mirrors and wall-paper came into common use, china and glass displaced pewter, and the spinet gave way to the piano. The last Scottish famine occurred in the winter of 1782–83, and thereafter the whole country's food-supply was reasonably sure. Country-dwellers, as they have done always and everywhere, tended to follow city modes after a lapse of time. Thus, while in Edinburgh the dinner-hour was moved back to four or five o'clock, Glasgow might dine at three, and the country gentry even earlier. Tea-drinking, too, slowly percolated to the towns, villages and country houses, where at first it was conducted surreptitiously. Fashions in dress changed in the same slow and irregular manner, from the heavy and sparkling brocades, gold ornaments and gentlemen's swords that characterized the early years, to the more sedate modes that came in after mid-century—quieter tones and lighter fabrics, white linen shirts and stocks, cotton stockings and waistcoats, silk-lined plaids and walking canes. High and low, however, still relaxed at home in their old and worn garments, night-caps, night-gowns, and shirts of 'harn' (crude, home-spun linen).

The most reprehensible of the new practices of the times was that of intemperance. The nation had formerly been noted, with rare exceptions, for its sobriety or moderation, but, as the century drew to its close, the habit of heavy drinking spread to all classes, from the Glasgow merchants, who imported quantities of lemons, oranges and limes for their rum punches and toddies, to the tipplers of 'twopenny' ale or raw whisky (costing from 10*d.* to 1*s.* 8*d.* a bottle) in the public houses. The testimony of the ministers who wrote the parochial contributions for the *Statistical Account* is nearly unanimous on the excessive number and the evil effects of the dram-shops in city, town and village; typical of them is the incumbent of the parish of Kirkhill, near Inverness, who berated these 'seminaries of vice and idleness.' Along with much that was good and gracious, the century bequeathed to its successor a great and growing social problem of habitual drunkenness.

Between 1801 and 1901 the population of Scotland rose from 1,608,000 to 4,472,000—an increase of 178 per cent. More striking than the over-all rate of growth is its uneven distribution. The seven crofting counties, covering 47 per cent. of the land area, increased in population from 302,800 to 352,400. This meant a steep relative decline, from nearly 19 per cent. to under 8 per cent. of the whole nation. Moreover, all seven had passed their peak and were positively losing by 1901; the highest numbers for the entire region had been recorded in 1841 (396,100). By contrast, seven central counties (Ayr, Renfrew, Dumbarton, Lanark, Stirling, West Lothian and Midlothian), containing only 11 per cent. by area, had 522,400 inhabitants, or rather more than 32 per cent. of the Scottish total, in 1801; a five-fold increase brought their figures 100 years later to 2,673,000, or very nearly 60 per cent. of the whole population. Thus three out of every five persons had come to reside in one-ninth of the land.

The century's changes are even more startling on the level of towns than of counties, for the movement of population was due almost exclusively to a process of urbanization. Town and country were nearly balanced in the early years, and it was during the first intercensal period (1801–11) that the former passed the latter; thereafter urban gains were continuous and impressive. Edinburgh, annexing the suburbs of Canongate and Portsburgh in 1856, and taking in Portobello in 1896 and Granton in 1900, grew from 82,500 to 316,800— that is, rapidly rather than healthily. Most fortunate of the Scottish towns (though the fact was seldom appreciated in those days of admiration of the 'big battalions') were those which, with varied economic interests, residential advantages and such attractions as good schools, shops and theatres, saw their population increase at a steady pace and in a manageable manner; to this category belonged county towns like Stirling, Ayr, Dumfries, Perth, Inverness and Elgin. Very different was the case of Glasgow, with nearly a ten-fold growth (from 77,400 to 761,700); in the process it too swallowed the burghs on its perimeter, including Gorbals, Anderston and Calton (1846), Hillhead, Maryhill and Pollokshields (1891). Only less dramatic was the rise in numbers at Dundee (from 26,800 to 161,200) and at Aberdeen (from 27,600 to 153,500); while Paisley, Leith and Greenock likewise advanced rapidly. The demographic records were, however, made by the new, or almost new, industrial concentrations—by Airdrie, Johnstone, Coatbridge and Wishaw, in the first half of the century, and, after 1850, by Motherwell and Clydebank, by Cowdenbeath and Lochgelly, and, above all, by the two old villages of Govan and Partick, which grew to be the seventh and ninth towns of Scotland, with 76,500 and 54,300 inhabitants respectively. By 1901, 40 per cent. of the Scottish people lived in the ten largest towns.

The political and economic aspects of the Highland evictions and migrations have already been touched on (cf. pages 124, 199–200); less spectacular, but cumulatively more significant, than emigration, whether voluntary or by 'assisted passage,' were the coastward drift—to Oban, Campbeltown and Tarbert from inland Argyll, to Helmsdale and Brora from the Sutherland glens—and the constant 'seepage,' not only to Glasgow, Greenock, Edinburgh, Perth and Dundee, but also to the villages along the Lowland edge, like Callander, Crieff, Comrie, Methven and Longforgan. What gave an ironical twist to the departure, for Canada and other overseas lands, of thousands of Highlanders was the almost simultaneous settlement in Scotland of even larger numbers of destitute and famished Irish peasants. Seasonal migration, especially of shearers for the Lowland farms, had begun during the Napoleonic wars, and this was facilitated by the cross-channel steamer service started in 1818. From the 1820s work on canals and roads, railways and ditches, in mills and mines, attracted thousands of permanent settlers every year, and the movement became a stampede when the Irish potato crop failed in 1845–46. The fare was a shilling or less, and, while the parochial authorities might return hordes of paupers, there was nothing to prevent them coming back. On one trip in August 1849 the little steamship *Thistle* (of less than 300 tons) brought over 1,900 persons. The census of 1851 showed 207,000 Irish-born out of a total population of 2,889,000, or one in fourteen. In Glasgow the proportion was 18 per cent., and to this figure should be added the children of the immigrants, who, if born in Scotland, were reckoned Scottish; thus Mr. James Handley estimates that about 25 per cent. of the inhabitants of Glasgow were of Irish birth or extraction in 1851 (*The Irish in Modern Scotland*). There were also heavy concentrations of the Irish in Greenock, Paisley, Airdrie, Dundee and Kilmarnock. The number of immigrants declined in each decade after 1851, but the arrivals were still substantial, and in 1901 there were 205,000 Irish-born persons in Scotland, or 4·6 per cent. of the total population.

The writer just cited remarks temperately that, 'in general, the attitude of the majority of Lowland Scots towards the Irish immigrant was one of settled hostility.' Bred to a potato-and-herring standard, willing to work for pitiful wages, sometimes ready to be used as strike-breakers, and professing, for the most part, the widely detested Roman Catholic faith, the Irish, crowding into the already congested cities and towns, were indeed objects of fear and suspicion, and were often treated as sub-human beings. It did not mend matters that, from the start, a minority of them were Ulstermen and Protestants, or that this element formed much the greater part of the immigration from the year 1876 (when detailed statistics of emigration from Ireland become available), for this meant the importation to Scotland of the customary Irish faction fights. The first 'Orange walk' was held in Glasgow as early as 1821, and 'Orange-and-green' riots began soon after, to reach a climax of violence in the period 1854–83, when, in many of the western towns, the parade held on July 12 might be the signal for a savage tumult, in which firearms were frequently used and lives lost.

Alien in race and religion, prone to pauperism and an inexhaustible source of cheap labour the Irish may have been,

but the social problem which they presented was simpler:
there were too many of them in the densely populated industrial towns, where their appearance intensified the man-
made evils of the factory age. It is perhaps easy to over-
emphasize these evils and to forget that town life went on for
many in normal and pleasant ways. The Glasgow manu-
facturers had imposing mansions in the west end, the Edinburgh lawyers enjoyed gracious living in the New Town,
Dundee's merchants could live in their Newport villas and
travel to work by ferry steamer, and Aberdeen's large professional and middle class were housed in the College precinct
of Old Aberdeen or in the new granite-built drives and
terraces beyond the Den burn. There were theatres in the two
chief cities, and suburban tea-gardens, where tea, fruits, curds
and cream were dispensed. Other towns were visited by
travelling companies, circuses and menageries, penny concerts were popular, and horse-races had been instituted or
revived in the eighteenth century. During Glasgow's great
fair conjurers' stalls, marionettes, peep-shows and shooting-
ranges lined the Saltmarket and Stockwell street and attracted
thousands of visitors. Golf was played by some, quoits by
others, while prize-fights and cock-fighting were watched by
many. Although the fashionable dinner-hour moved between
1800 and 1850 from about 5 o'clock to 6.30, certain old
customs lingered on; until after mid-century, for example,
the 8 o'clock curfew warned the children to go home to bed,
just as the rising-bell had summoned their parents to work at
6 o'clock.

When George IV paid his state visit in 1822—the first
monarch to do so since the seventeenth century—it was to a
city (the city of Scott and Raeburn) and to a country that
were by no means deaf to cultural values and aspirations.
Apart from the universities and schools (to be considered in
a later chapter) there were sundry media for the diffusion of
knowledge in all the principal towns—libraries, reading and
itinerant, mechanics' institutes, philosophical, scientific and
antiquarian societies, and several publishing clubs, headed
by the Bannatyne at Edinburgh (1823) and the Maitland
at Glasgow (1828). The capital's famous periodicals, the

Edinburgh Review (1802) and *Blackwood's Magazine* (1817), led in the fields of literary taste and political criticism, but wider circles were reached by *Chambers's Edinburgh Journal*, the trailblazer for the cheap magazine (1832). Even more influential were the newspapers, although the paper duty, which was not abolished until 1861, made them expensive; thus the greatest of them, the *Scotsman*, founded in 1817, was at first a bi-weekly of eight small pages, and it cost 10*d*. an issue (including 4*d*. duty). Groups of readers got over the price difficulty by subscribing together for a single newspaper between them. The Reform movement gave birth to a large number of local journals, most of which were short-lived. Nevertheless, a very large number of local papers were successfully launched in the first half of the century; these included (to mention only a few of the thirty-odd that survive to-day, alone or in amalgamations) the *Dundee Advertiser* (1801), the *Ayr Advertiser* (1803), the *Aberdeen Free Press* (1806), the *Dundee Courier* (1816), the *Inverness Courier* (1817), the *Fife Herald* (1822), the *Elgin Courant* (1827), and the *Stirling Observer* (1836).

The other side of the picture of the factory age in Scotland is, however, all too well supported by facts. For most of the town-dwellers it was a time of uncertain employment and recurrent destitution, of overcrowding, filth and degradation, which brought in their train improvidence and intemperance, vagrancy and crime, disease and death. In those days of dark, damp closes, fetid rooms, privy middens and inescapable squalor, the necessities of decent living, to say nothing of amenities or comforts, did not reach the masses. Gas lighting, for example, was provided in Glasgow from 1818, in Edinburgh from 1820, in Aberdeen from 1824, in Dundee from 1825, but in each case it was supplied by a private company at a cost far beyond the means of all but the well-to-do. Dundee's water was 'bright, sparkling, and piquant to the palate,' but a royal commission found it to be 'nothing but a very thorough purified sewage, to the properties of decomposition of which it owes its pleasant flavour' (quoted by Professor Ferguson in *The Dawn of Scottish Social Welfare*). As late as 1861 27 per cent. of the population of Scotland lived in one-roomed houses (which might, in extreme cases, house

15 persons) and 38 per cent. in two rooms; in 1863 (to cite Professor Ferguson again) there were still 171 byres in the city of Edinburgh, and some of these, built under human dwellings, 'proved a source of discomfort to the inhabitants above.'

In the circumstances, both drunkenness and disease were inevitable. There were 17,200 licences by 1830, and Glasgow in 1834 had one spirit-dealer for every fourteen families. Cheap, foul whisky was for the Scottish slums what gin was for the stews and lodging-houses of London; 'it was,' in the words of the late Professor Saunders (in *Scottish Democracy*), 'a specific for a bad climate, domestic friction, economic misery and religious gloom, or simply a bad habit supported by befuddled sentiment and a cheap and copious supply.' Amid much malnutrition and general ill-health, typhus fever was prevalent in city and town from 1818, and smallpox (though vaccination was successfully practised from 1801) continued its ravages by reason of sheer neglect, or worse: as a check on the number of hungry mouths to feed, it was cynically termed 'the poor man's friend.' Worst of all was the new and deadly plague of cholera, which brought 20,202 cases, 10,650 of them fatal, in its first visitation (1832) and was only less severe in the three later epidemics (1848–49, 1854–55 and 1869).

Private charity and philanthropic endeavour did something to alleviate distress and suffering. Besides the work of trade unions (which were weak from 1825 to 1867), friendly societies and savings banks, all encouraging thrift among the poorer inhabitants, there were soup kitchens, coal funds, sickness and funeral societies, and dispensaries providing medicines for the working classes. Doctors did their heroic best, against crippling disabilities—the inadequacy of the general hospitals to cope with the fever cases during an outbreak, the low repute of the nursing profession, the public suspicion as to 'body snatching' created by the Burke and Hare scandal (1829). In 1829 there was set up in Glasgow what is believed to have been Britain's first temperance society, and it was soon followed by many others, as well as by total abstinence groups. 'Ragged' schools, starting at Aberdeen in 1841, did much to remedy juvenile vagrancy and delinquency, and parochial board assessments, from 1845, made systematic poor relief possible (though not yet for the able-bodied poor). Meanwhile, the statutory powers of the urban authorities in such matters as sanitation, water-supply and dangerous buildings were being widened, by local acts (Aberdeen, 1795, Glasgow, 1800, Edinburgh, 1805, and Paisley, 1806) and by the series of general 'police' acts that began in 1833, but little use was made of these enactments because of the expense involved, and the real advances in public welfare and social services were delayed until after mid-century.

Temperance reform, as we have seen (page 116), took its effective start with the Forbes-Mackenzie Act of 1853. Another milestone was Glasgow's 'epic of municipalization,' the harnessing of the waters of Loch Katrine in 1859, and a third was the appointment of medical officers of health at Edinburgh (1862) and Glasgow (1863), which was soon followed by the building of fever hospitals and the appointment of sanitary inspectors. A planned policy of slum clearance was initiated by the Glasgow City Improvement Trust (1866), which, in 25 years, demolished the older sections and re-housed 50,000 displaced inhabitants. A similar Edinburgh Trust removed 3,000 'unwholesome' houses, and parallel action was taken in other large towns. After the gas supply was taken over by town councils—in Glasgow, for example, from 1869—the price was steadily lowered to the consumer. Electricity was municipalized in Glasgow from 1891, at Aberdeen from 1894. Horse-tramways had been operated in the principal towns from the 1870s, and these were taken over by the town councils in the 1890s and electrified a few years later. Public parks, municipal baths and wash-houses, workmen's 'model' lodging-houses, and a limited number of town council dwelling-houses, were also provided in the second half of the century. A different type of collective action made possible the sale of groceries and other necessities at low cost; at Aberdeen, for example, the Northern Co-operative Company, from the opening of its first shop in 1861, achieved quite remarkable success.

The resulting improvements in living conditions were real

though slow in appearing; it was 1911 before the proportion
of persons dwelling in houses of one or two rooms fell below
half (to 49·6 per cent.). And the advance was very uneven,
for the proportion was 82·8 per cent. at Armadale, and over
70 per cent. in seven other industrial towns. The Scottish
death-rate, in excess of 22 per thousand in the 1860s, fell to
just over 17 forty years later. Mortality was higher in the
cities, but in the fifty years 1863–1913 Edinburgh's rate
declined from 25·8 to 14·3, while Aberdeen's figure was
18·2 in 1901, compared with 24·5 in 1860. Over the forty
years, too, infant mortality decreased from about one death
in six births to one in eight.

The social drama of the nineteenth century has as its twin
themes the grim deterioration of the first half and the rise of
curative and ameliorative services during the second, but
running through the spectacular changes are undertones of
stability and immutable custom. Basic wage rates altered
little (aside from the heart-breaking experiences of the hand-
loom weavers): the range was about 15s.–25s. a week in the
early years and 15s.–30s. in the later. Price changes, if any,
were downward, especially under the full impact of free trade
after 1870. Wheaten bread fell from 1s. to 6d. and less, tea
from 6s. or 8s. a pound to 2s. 6d., sugar from 9d. to 3½d.; consequently these commodities came into common use, along
with the traditional Scots fare of porridge and oatcakes,
potatoes and kail, kippered herring and 'finnan' haddocks.
Country life showed few departures from the old ways. The
typical farm-house was still the 'but-and-ben,' furnished with
box-beds, straight wooden chairs, table, press and chests, and
having a kail-yard and privy-midden attached. Single men—
and sometimes women too—lived in crude and primitive
'bothies,' but the married labourers had their cottages, often
single-roomed and comfortless; as late as 1861 there were
nearly 8,000 'black houses' (with one room, devoid of window
or chimney) in the Highlands and Islands, and fifty years
passed before these were eliminated. In the rural calendar
Hallowe'en (when kitchen games were played) and Hogmanay
(when 'guisers' presented rustic tableaux and friends went
first-footing) retained their place, as did the feeing-fairs

and harvest-home, funerals followed by prolonged 'draigies' and dancing to the fiddle at weddings; but Handsel Monday gave way to New Year as the occasion for family reunions and gifts, and 'Fastern's E'en,' the day for cock-fights at school, dropped out altogether. Horse-races and cattle-shows, ploughing matches and local fairs, remained popular, and the consumption of whisky (despite the temperance reformers) was apt to be prodigious on all such special occasions.

The general reduction of the daily hours of work from 11 or 12 to $8\frac{1}{2}$ or 8 left the people with more leisure to enjoy such amenities as theatres, concerts, libraries, museums and art galleries, and the press became truly popular late in the century, when morning papers cost 1d. and evening papers $\frac{1}{2}d$. A wide variety of sports and pastimes developed. In the Highlands the gentry took up deer-stalking, fishing and shooting, while shinty, curling and the annual games or gatherings appealed to greater numbers. Seaside 'links' became famous golf courses, at North Berwick, Prestwick and Troon as well as St. Andrews, and, late in the century, cricket and bowls came in from England. From 1885–86 the 'boneshaker' and the 'penny-farthing' gave way to the safety bicycle, with pneumatic tyres, and cycling became a common method of short-distance travel, instead of a nine days' wonder. Football, forbidden by medieval statutes as a frivolous waste of time, was revived as a game and as a spectacle, when, in 1873, the Scottish Rugby Union was formed to adminster the 'carrying' code, and the Scottish Football Association was made the governing body for the 'dribbling' game, or 'soccer.' Western clubs, like Queen's Park, Clydesdale, Vale of Leven, Renton and Third Lanark, for long dominated the competitions for the Scottish Cup (instituted in 1873–74) and the Scottish League (founded in 1890–91); and the feuds between Protestant and Catholic factions in Scotland were transformed into the strongly partisan support accorded to the Glasgow rivals, the Rangers and Celtic, and also, in Edinburgh, to the Heart of Midlothian and Hibernian teams.

The population of Scotland increased from 4,472,000 in 1901 to 5,096,000 in 1951, or by 14 per cent. in 50 years; the rate of growth was much slower than it had been in the preceding century, and the decade 1921–31, for the first time, showed an actual decline, the excess of emigration over immigration more than counter-balancing the natural increase. Nearly the whole of the difference for Scotland between 1901 and 1951 is accounted for by the rise in the number of the inhabitants of the seven central counties, from 2,673,000, or 60 per cent. of the total, to 3,266,000, or 64 per cent. The only other steep increase was recorded by Fife (from under 219,000 to nearly 307,000 inhabitants). The seven crofting counties suffered a further decline, from 352,400 (7·9 per cent. of the whole) to 285,700 (5·6 per cent.); each of the seven had a smaller population in 1951 than in 1901. Numbers were nearly stationary over the half-century in the other broad regions of the country; for example, the eight southern counties, stretching from Wigtown to East Lothian, had 301,400 in 1901 and 307,800 in 1951.

City growth during the period was due almost entirely to the extension of boundaries. Glasgow, annexing Govan, Partick and Pollokshaws in 1912, recorded an increase from 761,000 to 1,089,500, but it was established from other figures that she had reached her peak in 1939 and was losing a few thousand inhabitants each year. Edinburgh's total rose from 317,000 to 467,000, by virtue of the absorption of Leith and four suburban parishes in 1920. Aberdeen (182,700) pushed slightly ahead of Dundee (177,300). Among the large burghs, the most marked fluctuations were experienced by Clydebank, which grew from 18,700 in 1901 to no fewer than 48,100 by 1939, only to decrease very sharply after the air-raids of 1941, and to rise again to 44,600 in 1951. The 196 burghs contained in 1951 69·9 per cent. of the population, but even this high figure did not fully reflect the degree of urbanization that had been reached. For census purposes 'urban areas' comprise 180 burghs and 225 towns and villages, each with a population of 1,000 or more; on the basis of that definition, Scotland had been 74·3 per cent. urban in 1901, 25·7 per cent. rural; in 1951, the proportions were 82·9 and 17·1 per cent., which means that nearly five out of six persons were town-dwellers. The inter-dependent processes of urban gain and

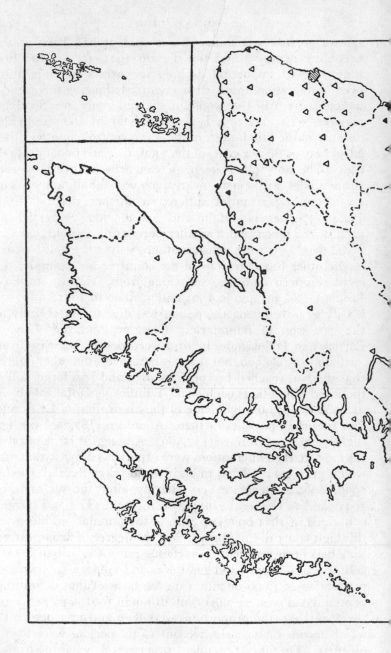

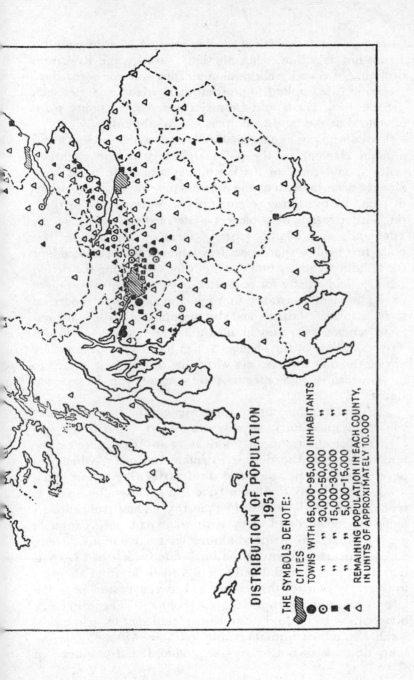

DISTRIBUTION OF POPULATION
1951

THE SYMBOLS DENOTE:
CITIES
TOWNS WITH 65,000-95,000 INHABITANTS
   ,,   ,,   30,000-50,000   ,,
   ,,   ,,   15,000-30,000   ,,
   ,,   ,,   5,000-15,000   ,,
REMAINING POPULATION IN EACH COUNTY,
IN UNITS OF APPROXIMATELY 10.000

rural depopulation were at work in most parts of the country. It was not only that, while Shetland, Orkney and Ross were declining, Lerwick, Kirkwall and Dingwall were growing; the same rule applied to prosperous Lowland counties such as Aberdeen, Perth and Dumfries, where the county town advanced as the landward areas lost inhabitants.

The continuous expansion of the state's social services forms a main element in the political history of the twentieth century, and most of the landmarks along the route have already been indicated: the introduction of old age pensions in 1908, the beginnings of unemployment insurance in 1912, the authorization of a pioneer state medical service in the Highlands and Islands (1913), 'local option' temperance polls (first held in 1920 under legislation of 1913), state aid for the building of many houses, chiefly for sale during the period 1920–39 and chiefly for rent after 1945, the centralization of unemployment assistance in 1934, the Beveridge report on social insurance (1942), and the inception in 1948 of a complete scheme of national insurance and universal health services. Some of the changes which have come over society during these fifty years, and which are due at least in part to these measures of conscious state control, can be assessed statistically.

The nineteenth century improvement in the death-rate was maintained fairly steadily after 1900, when it was just over 17 per thousand; it stood at 12 in 1952. Even more remarkable was the decline in infant mortality, which was never below 100 per thousand until 1916 (when it was 97·1), dropped gradually to 68·5 in 1939 and rapidly after 1945, to reach the record low figure of 35 in 1952. These truly encouraging movements did away with what had been causes of deep reproach to Scotland among civilized nations. There was a concurrent drop in the birth-rate (which had been as high as 35 per thousand in the period 1860–80) from about 29 in the early years of the century to between 17 and 18 in the late 1930s and again in the early 1950s. The difference between the birth- and death-rates is sufficient to yield a substantial, but not unmanageable, natural increase; but the sharp decrease of both rates has produced, and produces, an ageing population. In 1881, when the birth- and death-rates were still high, 37 per cent. of the population were under 15 years old and only 11 per cent. were aged 55 and up; but in 1951 these proportions were 24·6 and 19·7 per cent.; in other words, the changes in age distribution within two generations were such that fewer than a quarter, instead of more than a third, of the population were boys and girls, while nearly one in five, instead of one in nine, were old or elderly persons. By 1931 the expectation of life at birth was 56 years for males and 60 years for females, an increase of nearly 16 years compared with the 1860s, and by 1951 another striking advance had brought the figures up to 64 and 69 respectively.

The failure of the natural increase to produce a more rapid growth of the population has been due to the counter-acting loss by migration, chiefly to England, Canada and the United States. The net loss by migration in the fifty years, 1901–51, amounted to 1,105,000, or an average drain of 22,000 per annum; 'no country on the continent of Europe,' writes Mr. J. G. Kyd (in *Scottish Population Statistics*), 'has lost such a high proportion of her people as Scotland,' while England has experienced nothing resembling 'the great exodus of the Scots.'

Throughout the nineteenth and twentieth centuries poor housing presented the most damaging defect in Scottish social conditions; it was a contributory cause, and often the main source, of the prevalent evils of the time—squalor and disease, improvidence and intemperance, vagrancy and vice. In Scotland, unlike England, the housing problem was, and is, concentrated in one group of dwellings, the one-roomed and two-roomed houses, the great majority of which have for long been the notoriously cramped and sordid 'single-enders' and 'double-enders' of the congested cities, industrial towns and mining villages. Thus the success of the housing programmes, which yielded some 250,000 new dwellings in the period 1919–39 and rose after the second World War to an annual output of over 30,000 in 1952, may fairly be judged by the reduction of the numbers living in these small homes, for this factor implies their transfer to more commodious and more healthy surroundings. The following table sets out, for

Scotland and the four cities, the percentage of the population living in one or two rooms at twenty-year intervals:—

	1911			1931			1951		
	One Room	Two Rooms	1+2	One Room	Two Rooms	1+2	One Room	Two Rooms	1+2
Scotland .	8·7	40·9	49·6	7·1	36·9	44·0	6·2	23·5	29·7
Aberdeen	4·8	33·8	38·6	4·9	34·4	39·3	2·2	21·5	23·7
Dundee .	9·9	53·1	63·0	8·5	47·7	56·2	4·9	34·5	39·4
Edinburgh	6·1	31·1	37·2	4·8	32·3	37·1	2·5	20·7	23·2
Glasgow .	13·8	48·7	62·5	11·0	44·4	55·4	8·2	33·3	41·5

As a result of forty years' efforts, three instead of five out of every ten persons lived in small, and mainly unsatisfactory, homes; the improvement had been from over six to about four in Glasgow and Dundee, the heavily industrialized cities, and from under four to more than two in Edinburgh and Aberdeen, with their greater residential and middle-class elements.

New building had thus produced an undeniable amelioration in housing conditions, and other sets of statistics confirm this. For example, instead of (as in 1911) 45·1 per cent. of the total population living at a density of more than two persons to each room, there were in 1951 only 15·5 per cent. Yet the uneven distribution of the improvements is likewise striking. Whatever the standard of measurement, the lot of the inhabitants of, say, Moray and Kirkcudbrightshire was much happier as regards housing conditions than that of Lanarkshire or West Lothian, and the same contrast applies to 'resorts' like Carnoustie, Newport, North Berwick and Castle Douglas, on the one hand, and industrial centres such as Galston, Port Glasgow, Coatbridge and Armadale, on the other. Even wider is the gap between the older and newer parts of the same city. Out of Glasgow's 37 wards, Hutchesontown had in 1951 85·9 per cent. of its inhabitants living in houses of one or two rooms, and Dalmarnock's figure was 77·0 per cent., while the comparable proportions were negligible for residential wards on the perimeter, like Craigton (1·3), Pollokshields (2·2) and Knightswood (2·6); so, for Edinburgh, the extremes were Holyrood (56·1) and St. Giles (54·7), in the heart of the old city, and Pilton (0·7) and Corstorphine (2·0), on the outer fringes.

The Census of 1951, for the first time, collected information regarding the availability of five household conveniences— piped water, cooking stove or range, kitchen sink, water closet and fixed bath. It was found that 65·0 per cent. of all households in Edinburgh had exclusive or shared use of all five conveniences, but that the percentage was substantially less in the other cities—48·7 in Glasgow, 46·3 in Aberdeen, and only 40·7 in Dundee. Here again the over-all figures are somewhat misleading, for the proportion was very low in the poorer quarters at the city centres—St. Clement's (3·0) and Greyfriars (3·2) in Aberdeen, the twelfth ward of Dundee (7·5), and Hutchesontown (7·3), Cowcaddens (8·0), Gorbals (8·0) and Kingston (8·8), all in Glasgow.

Apart from the state's social services, a leading share in shaping the lives of the people and their mental attitudes must be attributed to the impact of the two World Wars, which, by uprooting two successive generations of young men and introducing them forcefully to new and hazardous careers in strange and far-off lands, inevitably slackened the ties of tradition, reduced the appeal of ancestral ways, and made change natural and innovation acceptable. The appearance of this new spirit coincided in time with a revolution in modes of transport, the invention of mechanical devices for the home, and the development of modern forms of entertainment. All this, moreover, happened at an epoch of inflation, which, after the great monetary stability of the Victorian and Edwardian periods, gave the mass of the people far more spending money than their forebears had commanded. By mid-century, the normal weekly minimum wage was about £5, and the more skilled workers had £7, £8 and upwards. The rise in prices, though substantial, did not quite keep pace with this increase: it was estimated that, in 1952, the cost of living was 3·4 times that of 1914, while wage-rates were 4·6 times those of the same year. And, working a 7½ or 8 hour day, for 5½ days a week, with a fortnight's paid holiday each year, most ordinary men and women had leisure for the enjoyment of their amenities and the cultivation of their tastes.

The increased mobility of all ranks is perhaps the most remarkable phenomenon of the age. Until the first World War the electrified tramways, municipally operated, offered the cheapest and fastest method of local transport, while the railways were available for longer journeys. From about 1920 motor buses gained steadily from their earlier rivals, to the extent that by mid-century many of the shorter railway lines had been closed and others were clearly uneconomic, while the tramways had been abandoned by some towns and elsewhere were being compared unfavourably with the bus and the trolley-bus. From the first decade of the century, too, the use of private transport grew year by year. Ownership of motor-cars spread from the wealthy to the middle classes and eventually to well-to-do artisans, and the bicycle became immensely popular with all. Parochial isolation almost disappeared, village and farm came into close touch with the town, and the city-dweller re-discovered the countryside. The holiday camp and the charabanc tour, the country weekend and the roadside picnic, works and office 'outings' and rambles through the new national parks—all came to form a big part of the life of the twentieth-century Scot, who knows the pleasures of the open air and the open road in a way that was denied to his grandparents.

More leisure has meant more demands on the agencies of enlightenment and entertainment. Much use has been made of free libraries, catering for the serious reader, and of commercial circulating libraries, offering light fiction, of the museums and art galleries which were built or extended during the half-century, of public lectures and of evening classes. Newspaper readers were numerous enough in 1953 to support six Scottish dailies (besides the Scottish editions of two London papers), nine evening papers, two Sunday papers (and the Scottish edition of a London one), and 145 local papers (mostly weekly, with a few bi-weeklies). Cultural and social as well as professional activities have been pursued by such occupational groups as the Women's Rural Institutes (starting at Longniddry, in East Lothian, in 1917), the National Farmers' Union, chambers of commerce, trade unions, and the many clubs (especially Rotary, Burns, Soroptimists and Young Farmers), while philosophical, anti-quarian, naturalist and horticultural societies profess more specialized aims. Cinema and wireless, however, dating from the 1900s and the 1920s respectively, have forged ahead of all rivals, bringing some loss of favour to older institutions— the 'live' theatre (in the commercial sense, but not amateur drama), the literary and debating society, the whist drive, the musical 'at home,' the oratorio and the choral concert. In 1952—the telephone meanwhile having come into use in most offices and many farms and middle-class homes— the latest of the series of inventions, television, progressed from the experimental stage into general service.

In the field of recreation, public ball-rooms and cheap dance-halls have had a great vogue; the emphasis has been since the 1920s on jazz music, the fox-trot and the slow waltz, and since 1945 on revived country dances. Among indoor pastimes, billiards, badminton and darts have won many friends, and table tennis, squash, dominoes, draughts and chess have their devotees, while, in the outdoors, bowling, tennis, putting and swimming have benefited from municipal as well as private patronage, and rugby, cricket and hockey from the sponsorship of schools and universities. Golf is both played and followed avidly, especially during the champion-ship tournaments, but one wonders, in view of rising costs, how long it can remain (as it has been, uniquely, in Scotland) a truly democratic game. For both players and spectators, football remains the national game above all others. Nearly all the large burghs maintain one or more of the 32 senior clubs—Glasgow has six, Edinburgh and Dundee two each— and most of these have supporters' clubs, who charter buses for 'away' matches; the mass-appeal of the game may be gauged from the attendance of 149,547 (a British record) at Hampden park, on April 17, 1937, for the Scotland v. England international. Junior, juvenile and amateur clubs have good followings, and football is easily first favourite among boys from an early age.

Dietary habits improved in the twentieth century through the increased use of fresh fruit, clean milk, and vitaminized bread and margarine, and the provision of cheap school meals. During and after the second World War priority foods were issued to mothers and children, and state subsidies lowered the price of essential foodstuffs. But the greatest change of the times was the decline in drinking, due in part to temperance propaganda and legislation, in part to the development of other ways of enjoying leisure, but above all to a budgetary policy which turned alcohol from a cheap narcotic into an expensive luxury for infrequent indulgence: the 'dram' became too dear to make its appearance on every social occasion, great or small. The hotel cocktail lounge began to be the meeting-place for friends, and the public house, sensing competition, was cleaned up and made more orderly, draught beer being the usual beverage. As addiction to strong liquor diminished, other growing habits aroused the alarm of observers of the social scene. Cigarettes ousted snuff, chewing tobacco and pipe tobacco, and were smoked, despite mounting taxation, in huge quantities by men and women of all classes. But it was gambling that was most roundly denounced as a social vice—on horse races, on greyhounds, and finally (from about 1930) on football pools; the desire for a 'flutter' on Saturday's results and the hope of making a fortune on one 'coupon' affected high and low alike, and may be taken as symptomatic of the restlessness of our war-torn generation and its reaction against continuing austerity.

Philanthropic and humane endeavour produced, long before the welfare state was officially born in 1948, many agencies striving to promote a richer community life—the British Red Cross Society, the British Legion, the two societies for the prevention of cruelty (to children and to animals), local charitable societies, incorporated trades and masonic lodges, friendly societies like the Rechabites and Oddfellows, old age pensioners' associations and the Church of Scotland's eventide homes, the Y.M.C.A. and Y.W.C.A., boy scouts and girl guides, boys' brigades, girls' guildry and lads' clubs, local nursing associations and community centres in the new housing estates. Special efforts were made, by lectures and discussions, indoor recreation and outdoor sports, to wean young persons from street-corner lounging and idle habits, but it is commonly asserted that the lowest and neediest youths fail to respond to all the 'uplift,' preferring to regard as their club the ice-cream saloon and the fish-and-chip shop. Like gambling, juvenile delinquency was exercising the minds of social reformers at mid-century; attributed in general to the loosening of the bonds of religion, moral training and parental discipline, it had been aggravated by the war-time experiences of civilian evacuation, broken family life, easy divorce and interrupted schooling, but it did not argue permanent demoralization of a generation.

From time to time rural depopulation is emphasized in a dramatic manner—by the abandonment of St. Kilda in 1930 and of Soay, off the coast of Skye, in 1953, and by the marked loss of inhabitants by the islands of Islay, Mull and Tiree alongside equally marked gains, within the same county, by the burghs of Dunoon, Campbeltown and Oban. The problem is economic as regards both cause and remedy (or palliative). Since the mechanization of agriculture must go on, some further decline in the farms' direct use of man-power seems inevitable, but the drift from country to town can be checked in other ways—by afforestation and hydro-electric power, by the fostering of rural crafts and food processing plants, by such projects as diatomite production in Skye and peat-burning for power in Caithness, by modernization of fishing and encouragement of tourism.

The health of the nation affords some grounds for satisfaction. Major epidemic outbreaks and the constant toll of fevers are things of the past. Diphtheria has been nearly eliminated by the immunization campaign started in Britain in 1941: Scotland had five deaths in 1951, compared with 356 in 1931. The fact that certain towns and villages, mostly in the central industrial belt, are 'under-doctored' is a routine challenge to the medical authorities to induce entrants to the profession to settle where they are most needed. The reduction

in the general, maternal and infant death-rates is truly grati-
fying, and may well be carried further : informed opinion hopes
and expects to see infant mortality fall from 35 to 25 per
thousand. But the ageing of the population itself presents new
complications in the high incidence of heart troubles and of
cancer and other degenerative diseases, which imply protracted illness and incapacity rather than sudden death. The
multiple problem, now and for the future, is that of keeping
the aged happy in pleasant homes, ensuring their well-being
by preventive medicine, and finding them, when possible, the
right kind of work. Other forms of disease that now attract
attention do so rather by reason of the retreat of deadlier
rivals than by their own advance. Thus the ravages of
pneumoconiosis among miners cannot be compared to the
appalling human wastage of the earlier factory age, while the
death-rate from tuberculosis was halved between 1931 and
1951; yet there is disquiet because of the suspicion that both
are preventible, the one by the use of coal-dust suppressors
and the other by the provision of adequate housing.

This brings us back to the central problem, and it is a
measure of the gravity of Scotland's plight that (to cite yet
another statistic) 32 per cent. of her houses, against only 4·2
per cent. in England, are of one or two rooms. There is little,
if any, exaggeration in the assertion that half of Britain's
urgent needs are in Scotland and half of Scotland's in Glasgow.
Any planning, for that city and other towns like it, which did
not involve the demolition of acres of gaunt slum tenements
and the rehousing of the displaced residents in more commodious premises, on the site or elsewhere, would be a cynical
mockery. But the double operation would be immensely
costly in money and labour, while even a single-ender is a
'house in being' and there are waiting-lists of homeless
families. How much easier, then, to build housing estates on
the perimeter and to let houses there, at the expense of the
taxpayer and ratepayer, at uneconomic rents! As over half of
Glasgow's 300,000 houses are, in the mild official phrase,
'unsuitable' and ought to be taken down within, say, twenty
years, planners contemplate an 'overspill' of as many as
450,000 persons, that is, the creation, outside the city limits,

of a community or communities of roughly the size of Edinburgh. Herein lies Britain's most pressing problem of slum clearance and rehabilitation, and whether national resources and local initiative can rise to such a gigantic enterprise is, at mid-century, an open and searching question, to which, as yet, no answer is in sight.

Other critics of current social trends are seized with the importance of a wholly different issue—the effect of the adoption of international standards of instruction, entertainment, speech, even food and dress. Is there danger to the Scottish way of life in B.B.C. refinement of thought and voice, in English public school manners, in Hollywood films, in French menus and *chic* tea-rooms, in canned goods and comic strips? A Scot may be pardoned for believing that his small nation had, and has, its own contribution to offer to western man in his social aspect, and for viewing askance the approach of a drab uniformity of spiritual values, mental habits and material things; but he may draw comfort from the reflection that, over a century ago, Lord Cockburn was deploring his generation's departures from the ancestral *mores*, and that now, as then, there are pointers in an opposite direction— facts that are small enough in themselves but cumulatively worthy of attention.

Never aspiring to gastronomic leadership, Scotland has nevertheless enjoyed a good name for homely and pleasant fare, like porridge and oatcakes, rich vegetable soups, kail and cockie-leekie, haggis, sheep's head and mince (collops), kippers and 'finnans,' and for a few more sophisticated dishes, such as salmon and trout, prime roast beef, grouse and pheasant; according to one's taste and purse, any or all may still be savoured in Scotland to-day. As for beer, the fact that in England some of it is excellent (alongside much that is indifferent or worse) has obscured a point that should be noted —that the Scottish product is unvaryingly good. Again, export trade records are surely 'chiels that winna ding,' and it is not only whisky that is sought by overseas customers (to an annual amount in excess of £30,000,000): biscuits and shortbread, jams and marmalade in large consignments find their way from Edinburgh, Glasgow and Dundee to many distant

I

lands. Next, the despondent patriot might recall the minor sartorial revolution which, since 1919, has transformed the kilt from the 'sporting' affectation that it largely was between 1822 and 1914 to an article of general civilian use, recognized to be eminently suitable for country wear; and he would do well to ponder how new and graceful country dances have been evolved in recent years, set to traditional airs, and taken up with infectious enthusiasm by young and old. Social *trivia* such data may be, but at least they do not suggest a decay of the national spirit, any more than do contemporary political and economic developments, or the purely native faults and virtues of such institutions as the Church of Scotland, Scots law, the schools and universities, and the two leading newspapers. The impact of alien influences need not unduly disturb the lover of his country and its distinctive ways. The tree of Scottish life is too deep-rooted to suffer from grafting; for centuries English shoots and French slips have 'taken' successfully, and the Scottish stock, far from wilting, has flourished in the past, and should flourish in the future, the more luxuriantly from being subjected to experimentation and hybridization.

Chapter 8

The Churches Yesterday and To-day

THE Church of Scotland at the opening of the eighteenth century was not quite the Kirk of Melville or of the Covenanters, but it did not differ in fundamentals. Its creed was the Westminster Confession, and its administration was conducted through general assembly, provincial synod, presbytery and kirk session; but, as a safeguard against a corrupt or compliant assembly, the Barrier Act (1697) empowered presbyteries to delay or veto 'overtures' (proposed new legislation). Under the Revolution settlement, the tacit abandonment of the Covenants and the formal abrogation of the civil penalties of excommunication, on the one hand, and the abolition of lay patronage (preferred by crown and nobility), together with the general duty of magistrates to support the censures of the Kirk, on the other, made the establishment a 'church of the middle'; while its independent and popular character was assured by the mode of election, whereby, after the heritors and elders had presented a candidate or candidates, it was the congregation alone that made the 'call,' though the presbytery inducted the new minister to the charge.

This was the Kirk that was secure in the hearts of the great majority of the people. True, it had its rivals. The 'Cameronians' of the south-west renounced it as unscriptural and uncovenanted. Episcopal sentiment was strong in Aberdeen and the north-east and among the nobles and lairds. The Roman Catholics were numerous in the west Highlands and the Hebrides, and there were small pockets of them elsewhere; but, debarred from citizenship as well as from open exercise of their devotions, they formed a proscribed 'underground' minority. By contrast, the Presbyterians were privi-leged and powerful, organized and vocal. They would not have accepted union with Episcopalian England in 1707 without the statute by which 'the true Protestant religion, as presently professed within this kingdom,' was 'effectually and unalterably secured'; and the declaration that that act (like the corresponding one in favour of the Anglicans) was 'a fundamental and essential condition' of the Treaty re-assured them as to the future of the Church 'as now by Law established.'

These hopes were soon dashed. The Kirk's betrayal forms part of our political history, and it is tempting at first sight to blame the whole process on the united Parliament, which, having shown itself unsympathetic to Scotland over the Greenshields case, passed legislation in 1712 permitting Episcopalian worship (provided the pastor abjured the exiled Stewarts) and restoring the rights of lay patrons to present to vacant churches (*cf.* p. 87). Though the Toleration Act was more bitterly denounced at the time, it was patronage that caused the subsequent damage, by precipitating the Original Secession in 1733, the formation of the Presbytery of Relief in 1761, and the great Disruption of 1843. Not till 1874 was the statute annulled, although the General Assembly protested against it each year from 1712 to 1783. The English Whigs must share responsibility with the Tories, the latter for passing the measure, the former for failing to repeal it when they had the power.

Thus might run the case for the prosecution, but it is not the whole story. Without reference to patronage, Scottish Pres-byterianism contained within itself the seeds of schism and disunion. The Cameronians remained stubbornly aloof and organized a separate Reformed Presbytery in 1743. As early as 1720 Thomas Boston and other evangelical divines opposed the Assembly's repudiation of the English Puritan treatise, *The Marrow of Modern Divinity*. The 'Marrow-men' were rigidly orthodox; at the other extreme stood Professor John Simson, of Glasgow University, who was deposed in 1729 for his ration-alist views. To the same era belong the beginnings of the sect of Glassites, Sandemanians, or 'Kailites,' who broke away to worship in their own strange fashion, somewhat after the manner of primitive Christian communists. The Church had thus to pick its way delicately between reaction and innovation. Among the seceders, too, divisive issues arose from an early date. Their 'Judicial Testimony' denounced, in addition to patronage, the dropping of the Covenants, the purely secular Union with England, and the toleration of episcopacy, heresy and witchcraft (1736). In 1747 came 'the Breach,' which split them into Associate Synod (Burghers) and General Associate Synod (Anti-burghers) over the propriety of taking the burgess oath, which included a reference to 'the true religion presently professed.' A minor and short-lived schism followed the 'Lifter' controversy as to whether the sacramental elements should be 'lifted' before or after the consecrating prayer (1783). A little later, a 'new light' led some of the seceders to question the right and duty of the civil magistrate to uphold the true faith and so to reject any state connexion, but their more orthodox brethren thought it sinful to view the Covenants in such a new light. In turn the Burghers (1799) and the Anti-burghers (1806) broke up into New Light and Old Light churches. Meanwhile, reaction against presbyterian order and discipline resulted in the separation from the Church of Scotland of the 'Old Scotch Independents' (1768) and the foundation by James Haldane of the first Congregational church (1799).

If, then, the Kirk, regardless of parliamentary intervention, was foredoomed to disunion, it remains true that patronage drew the clearest line of demarcation between opposing parties, and was itself a main cause of strife. Moreover, the hope that patronage might reconcile the nobility and gentry to a national church built around an enlightened and liberal-minded ministry was not realized: many patrons presented incumbents, with or without the goodwill of the parishioners, and themselves remained Episcopalians. For two decades, indeed, the rights of patrons attracted little attention and caused little trouble; it was not until 1732 that the Assembly, by ordering a return to the old system of popular election only when a patron failed to present a nominee, gave countenance to the legislative change of 1712. In due time, however, ministers themselves (many of them owing their livings to noble benefactors) came to regard patronage as essential to good order, and the Assembly's harsh proceedings against the founders of the Relief Church contrasts sharply with the temporizing attitude adopted towards the seceders a generation earlier.

By the third quarter of the century the gulf between the two main parties within the Church of Scotland was much wider than a mere difference on patrons' rights. Assembly policy came to be dominated by the Moderates, urbane and tolerant, abhorring 'enthusiasm' as vulgar, at home in polite society, resolved to make the Church count in the world of letters and learning. Their leaders were William Robertson, historian and principal of Edinburgh University, Alexander Carlyle, a great diarist as well as an unashamed *bon viveur*, and Hugh Blair, elegant preacher and professor of rhetoric; and among the familiar associates of these men were Adam Smith, the father of political economy, David Hume, philosopher and historian, and John Home, author of the controversial drama, *Douglas*. The minority party of Evangelicals or 'High-flyers,' though it included Alexander Webster, compiler of the unofficial census of 1755, and John Witherspoon, destined to achieve fame as president of New Jersey College, at Princeton (1768–94), could not compete with its rival's array of talents, but its members won wide popular support by the orthodoxy of their beliefs and the simple fervency of their sermons. The very fact that they avoided contact with high society, to devote their energies to the service of old-time religion, commended them to their humbler parishioners.

There was here more than a difference between two parties of manœuvre: it was a cleavage between two incompatible philosophies of life. In their anxiety to make their church worthy of the new age and its wider horizons, the Moderates were often in advance of their time. When Principal Robertson and his friends proposed, in 1779, to suspend the penal laws against the Roman Catholics, the mob rioted in Edinburgh and Glasgow, and the humane reform was defeated. Again, the Assembly found it expedient in 1784, when Mrs. Siddons the actress appeared in Edinburgh, to arrange its important sittings, in Carlyle's words, 'for the alternate days when she did not act, as all the younger members, clergy as well as laity, took their stations in the theatre on those days by three in the afternoon'; one wonders how such a decision would be received in towns and villages where the word of God was still preached with old-fashioned emphasis on worldly sins and eternal damnation. What happened was that many church members, reacting against the lukewarmness of their spiritual leaders, turned to the dissenters, in whom they found the orthodox sermons of the pastors and the simple piety of the congregations to accord better with the true faith as they and their forebears had understood it; and the gains of the Seceders (who were estimated to number 150,000 by 1800) were a protest against the Moderate drift to 'mere morality,' to deism and rationalism. While therefore the Church of Scotland became during the century a more tolerant and enlightened body, assuming the cultural as well as the religious leadership of the nation, the change cost it the loss to dissent of about a quarter of its membership.

For the Scottish Episcopalians it was a time of divided loyalties, dissension and weakness. The toleration offered to their clergymen in 1712 was conditional on their taking the same oath of allegiance (to the house of Hanover) and of abjuration (of the house of Stewart) as was required of the ministers of the Church of Scotland; and this many of them were unwilling to do. Its Jacobite leanings cost the church dear. In 1716 meeting-houses in which prayers were not offered for the royal family were ordered to be closed, and the measures taken in 1746 were more severe. Some of the sect's chapels were burnt and destroyed, and their pastors, besides praying for the reigning dynasty, were obliged, from September 1, 1746, to derive their orders from Anglican bishops. The episcopal succession was nevertheless maintained, though the line was thin: in 1784 there were five Scottish bishops and only about 40 other pastors, almost all in the north-east. A notable event occurred on November 14 of that year, when Samuel Seabury was consecrated bishop of Connecticut by three Scottish bishops; through him the whole Episcopal Church in America is linked with the Scottish Episcopal

Church. The death of Prince Charles (1788) made possible the repeal of the penal laws in 1792, though the clergy had to subscribe the oaths, pray for the royal family, and assent to the 39 Articles of the Church of England. The Episcopalians in 1800 therefore formed a small but free sect, inclining to move away, in an Anglican direction, from the doctrinal standards which they had held in common with Scottish Presbyterians.

Meanwhile, remote from the vital centres of the national life, a dwindling remnant—estimated to number in 1800 only 30,000—clung to the Romanist faith, in the teeth of popular dislike of their tenets, denial of all civil and religious rights, and detestation of their unwavering support of the exiled Stewarts. The ministrations of their persecuted clergymen were inevitably irregular, and the Society for Propagating Christian Knowledge made converts in their districts. Proposals for Catholic emancipation, as we have seen, came to nothing (1779), but Romanist priests received, from 1792, an annual money-grant from the government.

The new century brought new challenges to disturb the ecclesiastical peace that marked the long reign of the Moderates. Under their eyes the factory age was creating communities in which destitution and improvidence, hunger and intemperance, illiteracy and want of faith, stood forth as a reproach to Christian charity and benevolence—and the Church of Scotland was still responsible for poor relief and education as well as religion. But doubts were entertained as to whether the legal powers, customary practices and material equipment of the Kirk were equal to the needs of the new Scotland. There was controversy over the merits of the rival methods of poor relief—voluntary congregational offerings and compulsory assessments. Resentment of patronage, as an Erastian imposition on the church of Knox and Melville, had never died out and might again burst into flame. The parochial organization, transmitted from century to century with few changes, was becoming less and less adequate for the rapidly growing and shifting population, but in this respect, as with patrons' rights, the Church was not its own master. The remedy was to combine depopulated parishes and split

over-populated ones to bring the system up-to-date; but disjunctions, unions and erections of parishes involved prolonged
legal proceedings before the Court of Session (as 'Commissioners for the Plantation of Kirks and the Valuation of
Teinds'), and all that the Church could do of its own was to
set up 'chapels of ease,' the incumbents of which had no real
status before the law or in the church. Such problems raised
basic issues in the relations of church and state.

For a generation strenuous efforts were made to get the old
system to work. Henry Duncan launched what was to be a
national institution when he started the first savings bank at
Ruthwell in 1810. Thomas Chalmers, by his own inspiring
word and example, and with the devoted help of a band of
loyal admirers, demonstrated for eight years how voluntary
poor relief could succeed even in Glasgow's poorest parishes
(1815–23). Temperance societies, as we have seen, began in
1829 (cf. p. 241), and in that work the Kirk took the lead.
Other causes were warmly advocated and vigorously prose-
cuted—Assembly schools for poor and remote districts,
Sunday schools for the unlettered waifs of the streets, 'Church
extension' (into the new and unprovided industrial towns
and villages), home missions to seamen and fisher-folk, and
foreign missions to save the heathen.

The men behind these new movements belonged to the
revived Evangelical party, who now compared favourably in
every respect with the complacent and inert Moderates.
(There are economic undertones to the ecclesiastical disputes
of the time. Many a parish minister, drawing his stipend from
teinds and benefiting from the advance of prices, had over
£300 per annum, and the good livings were worth £500 and
upwards; the temptation was strong for the minister to
identify his interests with those of the gentry, to acquiesce in
existing conditions, and to lose 'the common touch.') The
Evangelical leaders were men of moral stature, spiritual
strength and academic distinction—Thomas Chalmers, David
Welsh, Thomas Guthrie and Robert Candlish. By 1833
they had won control of the General Assembly, and this
change precipitated the struggle between church and state
that was to assume epic dimensions in the folk-tale as

'the ten years' conflict' and 'the great non-intrusion controversy.'

The Assembly of 1834 passed two Acts which showed it to be in a militant and revolutionary temper. The Veto Act asserted the right of a congregation to refuse 'without reasons' a patron's nominee, and the Chapel Act admitted to membership of the church courts the incumbents of *quoad sacra* parishes and chapels of ease; together the Acts implied the power of the Kirk to interpret and modify its own statutory constitution. As was inevitable, the Veto Act led to litigation, and this involved long and bitter disputes. In the Auchterarder case (1834–39) the presbytery stood by a congregational veto and won the Assembly's approval. At Marnock (Banffshire) the patron's presentee was again vetoed, but the presbytery of Strathbogie, by a majority, accepted the state's view that the Veto Act was illegal; the Assembly deposed the majority and recognized the minority as the presbytery (1837–42). Each case went to the Court of Session and the House of Lords, which in turn found in favour of the patron and against the veto. The impasse could and should have been resolved by new legislation, but the government in London was apathetic or hostile to the reasonable representations of the church leaders, who fell back on the traditional expedient of issuing a Claim of Right (1842), in which the Assembly reaffirmed its position. The lack of a last-minute intervention by the government (which was expected by many) left the Evangelicals no alternative to secession, and the Disruption followed in May 1843, when some 450 ministers surrendered their churches, manses and assured stipends to form, with the ardent support of their congregations, the Free Church of Scotland.

The Original Seceders had meanwhile been moving with the times and weaving a complicated pattern of reunions and cross-unions. Most of the 'New Lights' of both branches, forgetting their old quarrel over the burgess-oath, came together in 1820 to form the United Secession Church, which combined with the Relief Synod in 1847 as the United Presbyterian Church. Openly 'voluntary,' the U.P. Church, with about 500 congregations, was roughly equal in size to the Free

Church at its inception, and had half the strength of the Church of Scotland. Among the 'Auld Lichts,' who adhered to the principle of establishment while repudiating the existing state connexion, there were unions in 1827 and 1842; many of them rejoined the Church of Scotland in 1839 (at a time when the fighting spirit of the Assembly accorded well with their own views), and most of the others threw in their lot with the Free Church in 1852, though a non-uniting remnant continued as the United Original Seceders.

The ecclesiastical history of the later nineteenth century was overshadowed by memories of the Disruption. That greatest of all Scottish schisms, while it called forth, from both ministers and congregations, a heroic spirit of self-sacrifice for the sake of conscience, was a tragedy in at least two respects. In the first place, it was preventable, had Parliament passed remedial legislation before instead of after the climax. As it was, the Benefices Act (1843) authorized presbyteries to give due weight to valid objections to presentees; the Quoad Sacra Act (1844) allowed disjunctions of parishes, subject to the consent of a majority of the heritors and the provision, from teinds or otherwise, of a competent living for the minister of the new erection; and eventually, in 1874, patronage was abolished and congregational elections were restored. Secondly, the Disruption left a legacy of sectarian bitterness which poisoned inter-denominational relations for two generations and ruled out thoughts of reunion even after Parliament had removed the original causes of strife. Spiritual energies were diverted from the exercise of Christian charity and reconciliation towards needless and often purely competitive church-building; in particular, those who had 'come out in 'Forty-three' were inclined to arrogate to themselves superior virtue on that account. The Free Church differed from previous seceding bodies in that it claimed to be national, so that it was headed by a general assembly (not, like the others, by a synod), it aimed to cover the whole country with a network of parishes, churches and schools, and it trained its ministers at its own colleges.

From mid-century, nevertheless, certain influences were working to soften the rigours of past animosities by obliging each of the three main Presbyterian churches, in turn, to modify its traditional beliefs, standards and practices. The changes were small, but all tended in the same direction and all helped to inculcate tolerance and mutual kindliness. In 1853 university professors, except the occupants of the divinity chairs, were absolved from the duty of subscribing to the Confession of Faith. Dr. Norman Macleod, minister of the Barony church, Glasgow (1852–72), preached and exemplified a more humane and gentler Christian faith, and Dr. Robert Lee, of Greyfriars, Edinburgh, another advocate of liberal ideas and usages, introduced stained-glass windows in 1857 and an organ in 1864. At the Free Church College, Aberdeen, Professor William Robertson Smith, a Semitic scholar of international repute, taught and wrote, during the 1870s, in favour of a new, historical approach to the Old Testament; his trial for heresy, and his removal by the Free Church Assembly (1881), were seen to be mistakes, for he was honoured in England and is one of the fathers of modern Biblical criticism. (The Church of Scotland had similar cause for regret, for, in deposing John McLeod Campbell, minister of Row, in 1831, for views on the nature of the atonement that were sufficiently advanced to be deemed heretical, it lost, but it did not silence, a sincere and devout evangelist.) In 1876 most of the Reformed Presbyterians joined the Free Church, though there was again a dissident minority to continue the name and existence of the parent body. Throughout all changes, the Westminster Confession of Faith had been retained as the doctrinal standard common to all Presbyterians, but opinion in all three churches now inclined towards a looser and more general form of subscription to that document. The desired relaxation was effected by declaratory acts passed by the United Presbyterians in 1879 and by the Free Church in 1892, and by an Act of Parliament of 1905, which empowered the Church of Scotland to settle its own formula. In the case of the Free Church, the change gave offence to a conservative minority, mainly in the Highlands and Islands, who seceded to form the Free Presbyterian Church, strictly orthodox and abiding by the traditional form of belief (1893).

Conciliatory gestures by the Church of Scotland during the

1870s and 1880s were disdainfully repulsed by the Free Church, which, in the closing years of the century, turned instead towards the United Presbyterians, 'voluntaries' though these were. In 1900 the amalgamation of the two bodies was effected, and the United Free Church, combining over 1,100 Free Church parishes and more than 600 United Presbyterian congregations, was about as strong as the Church of Scotland, which had just over 1,400 parishes. Once again, *more Scotico*, a minority stood aloof from the union and assumed the title of the whole church; this time the little schism had an interesting sequel. The vestigial Free Church (derisively called 'the Wee Frees') claimed the entire property of the parent body, on the grounds that the union was on a voluntary basis, that the majority had therefore departed from the testimony of the church, and that it alone was faithful to the principles of the Disruption. The surprising decision of the House of Lords in favour of the claim led, as we have seen, to an equitable division of the endowments in 1905 (*cf*. pp. 175–76).

The century brought changes to the non-Presbyterian churches. Congregationalism has been described as 'presbyterianism without the presbytery,' and the phrase aptly summarizes the evolution of the movement in Scotland, by way of separation, in the direction of 'independency,' from the national faith. In 1841 James Morison left the United Secession Church, and he and other like-minded ministers formed the Evangelical Union (popularly called 'the Morisonians') in 1843; their beliefs included the universality of the atonement and the doctrine of free will. Most of their churches were absorbed in 1896 by the Congregational Union, founded nearly a century earlier by Haldane (p. 261).

In the Scottish Episcopal Church the trend of the late eighteenth century continued. Canons of 1809 and 1811 restated its organization and confirmed its Anglican affinities in worship and doctrine (including the 39 Articles). An Act of 1864 declared all Scottish Episcopal clergy eligible for benefices in the Church of England. The fact that the body was now visibly and audibly 'high church' no doubt made it congenial to many of the English settlers who came in as industry and trade developed, but, while it retained its hold on the landed gentry and its large popular following in Aberdeenshire and the north-east, its growth does not seem to have kept pace with that of the whole population. By the end of the century, with 170 charges and over 50 missions, it had 46,000 communicants.

If the Episcopal Church became more English in spirit and sympathy during the nineteenth century, the Roman Catholic Church came to be preponderantly Irish in membership. Apart from the Scottish chapels (which were mainly in the Highlands and the north-east), the first Irish Catholic church was set up as early as 1808 at Paisley, and schools were opened in the Gallowgate and Gorbals (Glasgow) in 1818. A papal brief of 1827 divided Scotland into three districts, each under a vicar apostolic, so that there was a rudimentary organization before the passing of the Catholic Emancipation Bill (1829) removed civil disabilities. By the middle years of the century the native Romanists (estimated at 30,000) were being swamped by the immigrants, not without bitter Scoto-Irish quarrels over the control of church policy. Scottish Protestant feeling was strongly anti-Catholic and anti-Irish, the most outspoken journal in this respect being the Evangelical and Free Church organ, *The Witness*, under the able and eloquent editorship of Hugh Miller. As time passed, however, a more liberal and charitable sentiment prevailed among all Presbyterian groups, and the restoration, in 1878, of the Catholic hierarchy, based on territorial dioceses, evoked opposition only from extremist elements. There were then 252 priests serving a Roman Catholic population of nearly 333,000 by means of 129 missions and parishes.

Both before and after 1900, as has been mentioned, disestablishment was a political issue, if not a very lively one (*cf.* pp. 118, 121); but it was utterly silenced at the opening, in 1909, of serious negotiations for the reunion of the two great Presbyterian communions. By 1912 they had agreed to draw up a plan of union to be submitted for parliamentary ratification. Discussions were suspended in 1914 and resumed soon after the armistice of 1918. They were protracted, mainly because the spokesmen of the United Free Church took exception to two features of the existing establishment. They feared the possibility of Parliament dictating to the Church on matters of purely spiritual or ecclesiastical concern, and they disliked the Kirk's financial system, whereby teinds (a land-tax which varied in incidence according to the annual fiars prices) provided most of the revenue. The Church of Scotland undertook to promote legislation to meet these objections. The General Assembly adopted declaratory articles which ex-pressed the Kirk's loyalty to the principles of the Reformation, admitted its obligation to promote church union, affirmed the mutual duties of church and state, and asserted the right of the Church to legislate on doctrine, worship, government and discipline without interference by civil authority. The Church of Scotland Act, 1921, confirmed these articles. To the spiritual autonomy thus fully and graciously conceded by Parliament, another statute four years later added financial independence. The Church of Scotland (Property and En-dowments) Act, 1925, provided for the redemption of teinds and the management of all revenue by a new body, the General Trustees of the Church. The way was now clear, and the greatest of Scottish church unions was finally accom-plished in 1929.

The union was not quite unanimous; it was perhaps in-evitable, in the light of our ecclesiastical history, that a minority, too firmly wedded to voluntary religion to contem-plate joining even a reformed establishment, should continue the name of the United Free Church. But the magnitude of the achievement, as well as the scrupulous care with which it was prepared, is still impressive. The Church of Scotland brought in to the amalgamation nearly 760,000 communi-cants and 1,457 parish churches, while all but a handful of the 538,000 members of the United Free Church (in 1,441 con-gregations) also came in; the reunited Church was, of course, very much stronger numerically than it had ever been in the past. The union involved consequential arrangements for the co-ordination of ministerial training through the four divinity faculties of the universities and the three theological colleges. Provision was made for the raising of the minimum stipend, which stood at £300 per annum in 1929. But the hardest of the new problems arose from the fact that the Church was the heir of three denominations, whose nineteenth-century rivalries bequeathed many churches and charges which were now redundant. The national union needed to be implemented by local unions, both in town centres and in over-churched small communities. The strong ties that linked minister, congregation and place of worship obstructed the way for many a promising project, for local sentiment, as well as vested right, might oppose their severance on a point of mere convenience. Over-all church policy had therefore to wait upon casual vacancies and congregational consent. The drive towards a more rational parochial organization, despite such limitations, was reasonably successful; by 1953, 657 unions had been achieved, and the total number of churches (including new buildings) had fallen from about 2,900 to just over 2,300.

For the minor and non-established churches the twentieth century has brought no changes comparable in significance to the union of 1929. The five small presbyterian churches still clung to their divergent paths, though between some of them it was not easy for the outside observer to detect differences real or deep enough to supply a compelling reason for their continued and separate existence. The youngest of them, the United Free Church, was, of all five, perhaps the most thoroughly at home in the modern world, unafraid of innovations, inclining towards 'independency,' and disposed to closer association with the Congregational Union than with another presbyterian body; and it, alone of the five, seemed to be making headway. The other four stood far apart from the main stream of the national life. The Free and Free Presbyterian Churches, drawing their strength chiefly from remote congregations in the north-west Highlands and the Hebrides, remained faithful to the principles of the Disruption in a nation that was overwhelmingly in favour of forgetting that unhappy dispute. Living in an even more distant past were the two minute and rigidly orthodox sects of the Lowlands, the Reformed Presbyterians and United Original Seceders, both professing strict adherence to the Solemn League and Covenant. The Free Church was, and is, the strongest of the four. It is also the readiest with downright denunciation of what it regards as deplorable trends in the Scotland of to-day; these include not only gambling and drinking, but likewise dancing, whist drives, dramatic performances, Sunday sport and other secular activities such as are acceptable to, or even enjoyable by, the generality of the people.

The Scottish Episcopal Church adopted in 1929 a Book of Common Prayer based on the prayer-book of 1637—a document of evil memory in the annals of Covenanting Scotland, but one which, naturally, wears a more pleasing aspect in episcopalian eyes. The church, cultivating intimate relations with the renowned and powerful Church of England, has in the recent past made a strong appeal to various select groups of Scotsmen and their families; it has won converts, for example, among those who are attracted to ritualism and ceremony, those who have been educated at English public schools, and those who cherish social ambitions. Its gain in prestige has not been accompanied by any marked expansion in number of adherents. Its historian, Mr. F. Goldie, shows that, while its membership increased until 1921, it suffered a net loss of some 4,000 communicants between that year and 1950 (*Short History of the Episcopal Church in Scotland*, 1951). For the allegiance of the English settlers (who outnumbered those of Irish birth in Scotland from 1921) the Episcopalians must face (to say nothing of the appeal of the national church) the rivalry of the dissenting sects, as 'church' faces that of 'chapel' south of the Border. Besides the Congregational Union, with its roots, as we have seen, going back into Scottish history over more than 150 years, the non-native Methodist Church and Baptist Union developed as institutions intended primarily to meet the spiritual requirements of English and Welsh immigrants and their descendants.

The other mainly alien church, that of the Roman Catholics, did rather more, in the first half of the twentieth century, than hold its own. It was not that the tide of immigration still flowed strongly in its favour. The Census of 1931 recorded only 124,000 persons of Irish birth, and of these over half were above fifty years of age, and more than half came from Northern Ireland, the staunchly Protestant part of the country; Mr. James E. Handley, indeed, showed, in *The Irish in Modern Scotland* (1947), that incomers from Ulster during the first two decades of the century were between four and five times as numerous as those from the rest of Ireland. Yet the rate of increase of the Roman Catholic population seems to have outrun, by a rather wide margin, that of the Scottish people as a whole. One contributory factor in this respect is suggested by Mr. Handley's argument that infant mortality was relatively less among Irish settlers than native Scots; another, and more potent, cause would appear to be a higher birth-rate (kept high, *inter alia*, by clerical opposition to birth-control); and, in general, the stern discipline of the church has minimized lapses and defections among a section of the people with living standards, educational attainments and independence of mind below the average. It would be idle to pretend that the advance of Catholicism, or even its continued vitality, was a matter of indifference to most Scotsmen. Not that there was much danger of a widespread revival of the nineteenth-century persecution, discords and petty harassments; few were disposed, *pace* Mr. Handley, to cry, 'Rome on the rates,' when Catholic schools were brought into the educational system in 1918, or to regard as anything more than a diverting *jeu d'esprit* Mr. Thomson's apocalyptic anti-Irish essay, *Caledonia* (*cf.* p. 133). Again, in 1952, not many would endorse the view of the moderator of the synod of the Reformed Presbyterian Church, that Home Rule would open the door to 'Rome rule,' though more would no doubt sympathize with a report presented to the General Assembly of the Church of Scotland that year, which labelled Catholicism simply as a 'menace.' It was certainly a challenge to the national faith, just as the heavy concentration of the Scoto-Irish in the poorer quarters of the cities and towns was a challenge to the social reformer. Perhaps, after all, the two problems would turn out to be one: social betterment and educational improvement might in the long run, and incidentally, remove the 'menace.' It can at least be recorded that, by mid-century, more and more of the descendants of Irish Catholic immigrants were proving happily less resistant to the process of assimilation than had been the case with their forebears.

The Church of Scotland had in 1953 2,322 charges, organized in 66 presbyteries, 12 synods and a general assembly; and, in full communion with the Church, there are, 'furth of Scotland,' one presbytery in England, three on the Continent, six in India, six in Africa, and three elsewhere. The Free Church (with 14 presbyteries) and the United Free Church (with nine) are each governed by a general assembly, but the smaller presbyterian churches are organized under a synod. The Episcopal Church in Scotland, with over 400 congregations and more than 300 clergymen, is headed by a hierarchy of seven bishops, each with a diocese corresponding to one, two or three of the 14 ancient sees (Aberdeen and Orkney; Argyll and the Isles; Brechin; Edinburgh; Glasgow and Galloway; Moray, Ross and Caithness; St. Andrews, Dunkeld and Dunblane); one of the seven, elected Primus, presides over their conferences, but without archiepiscopal powers. (And the historic cathedrals of Scotland, where still in use, are, to the naïve surprise of some visitors, places of presbyterian worship belonging to the national church.) In 1952 the Roman Catholic Church had 333 missions or parishes in Scotland, served by 1,023 priests—803 seculars and 220 regulars. In this case the territorial division into dioceses (eight in number) bears no relation to the pre-Reformation system, but is simply devised with regard to the distribution of the Catholic population within the civil counties. St. Andrews and Edinburgh form one archbishopric, and Glasgow another; four bishops—of Aberdeen, Argyll and the Isles, Dunkeld, and Galloway—are suffragan to the former, while the incumbents of the two sees erected in 1948 (Motherwell and Paisley) are subject to the metropolitan authority of Glasgow.

The relative strength of the several denominations in Scotland is in certain respects hard to determine. Official statistics are not always available and, when they are, they do not constantly relate to the same thing. The Roman Catholic Church reckons the entire population of the faithful as her own; the Episcopal Church counts as members all who are confirmed, at an age of twelve to fourteen; for Presbyterians full membership is limited to adults and, in some districts, where the traditional warning anent worthily partaking of communion is still literally obeyed, to a chosen few of them. And methods of keeping church records may vary as widely as do the tests of church membership. Comparable figures must therefore be treated as tentative and approximate.

At the end of 1951 the Church of Scotland had on its rolls the names of 1,273,027 communicants, or 36·5 per cent. of the adult population of the whole country. (The Sunday schools contained 291,259 scholars, and it is interesting to note that this figure is equivalent to just over 37 per cent. of the age group 5–14.) The Episcopal Church had some 56,000 communicants in 1950, and a total baptized membership of 108,000, while the official estimate of the Roman Catholic population (of all ages) in 1952 was 748,463. United Free Church membership in 1951 was 24,528. Figures are elusive for the four smaller presbyterian bodies; here one may guess (bearing in mind the generally reticent attitude to full membership) that communion rolls short of 20,000 would suggest as many as 40,000 adherents. Similarly, the Congregational Union has about 35,000 members and claims 107,000 adherents; and the 33,000 official Baptists and Methodists should probably be inflated to 80,000 by the inclusion of supporters. Fluctuating numbers are characteristic of the work of the Salvation Army, and little is known of some of the smaller evangelical sects, such as Quakers, Unitarians, Christian Scientists and Plymouth Brethren. Thus the following composite table, based in part on church membership expressed as a percentage of adult population, in part on numbers of adherents at all ages stated as a proportion of total population, cannot be regarded as other than an approximate picture of the percentage distribution of the inhabitants of Scotland among the various religious organizations:—

Church of Scotland	36·5
United Free Church	0·7
Other Presbyterian Churches	0·8
Total Presbyterians	38·0
Episcopal Church in Scotland	2·1

Congregational Union	2·1
Methodist Church and Baptist Union	1·6
Salvation Army (say)	1·0
Other Christian Sects (say)	1·0
Total Protestants	45·8
Roman Catholic Church	14.7
Total Christians	60·5
Jews	0·4
Total for Religious Organizations	60·9

The figures reveal the very great extent to which the Church of Scotland is the guardian and spokesman of the spiritual life and aspirations of the nation. On its left, so to speak (and to borrow the political phrase), presbyterian and evangelical dissent is confined to small groups—relatively smaller, in all probability, than in any other Protestant country in the world to-day. While the surviving remnants of past schisms have been, and are, noted for sincerity, reverence and scholarship (those erudite historians, Thomas McCrie and Hay Fleming, were both strictly orthodox seceders), their attenuated followings, viewed in proper perspective, denote that not one in forty Scottish Presbyterians has any desire for a return to 'theocracy,' moral censure and the Sabbatarian discipline of Covenanting times. It is tempting to conclude that the days of ecclesiastical conflict and disruption are over. Evangelical protest, mainly in the Lowlands, has tended to move in a different, indeed in the opposite, direction, and it can scarcely be called a typically Scottish movement. As we have seen, Methodists, Baptists and (despite their Scottish origins) Congregationalists have drawn most of their support from the English and Welsh settlers; and names like Halliday, Griffiths and Morgan are of common occurrence among their clergymen. These three sects and, to some extent, the United Free Church are closely akin to English dissent in worship and government, in the directness of their approach and in their insistence on congregational autonomy.

It is on the other flank, and among those who incline towards authority and discipline in government, and ritualism and ceremony in the service, that the Church of Scotland finds its two chief rivals. The Episcopal Church and the Roman Catholic Church, each in its own way, cherish their links with

Scotland's past; and, of course, each claims descent from what was, at different times, 'the Church of Scotland.' While the continuity of the record of Scottish episcopacy—nearly complete among the people of the north-east, certain landed families and their retainers, and a few city congregations—is a reminder of its native roots, its chosen path has diverged widely from any Scottish road; its services and its membership both lean towards England and Anglicanism—there are, for example, many more episcopal clergymen with English names than a cross-section of any Scottish community would yield. It offers a spiritual 'home-from-home' not only to English settlers and their descendants, but also to all Scotsmen who, whether through education or by personal preference, are more comfortable in an English than a Scottish environment. It is thus a pardonable inaccuracy for the untutored Scot to speak of it as 'the English Church.' The Roman Catholics, too, have their traditional strongholds, in such places as South Uist, Barra and Morar, almost untouched by the Reformation, and they have made some converts in high places (though very few among the commonalty). But the great immigration of the nineteenth century gave their church such a new and alien character that (apart from the fact that its higher control is, as it has always been, in foreign hands) it can never expect to be regarded as a Scottish institution; in the eyes of most Scotsmen it is bound to remain the church of the Irish in Scotland.

The non-native membership, practices or affinities of all its potential rivals serve to enhance the stature of the Church of Scotland as a national asset of enduring value. Transmitted, like the systems of law and education, as a heritage from the days of Scottish independence, it shares with them the distinction of having preserved the worthiest of the national traditions, while being open to external influences and ready to adapt itself to the needs of a changing world. Thus, while the fundamentals of its faith and of its government—Calvinist theology, the Westminster Confession, administration through graded courts—are unaltered, its usages and its attitudes as to less essential matters have been profoundly modified and liberalized. It has welcomed the contribution of the higher

criticism to a broader and more humane understanding of the
scriptures. It has acquiesced in the movement for beautifying
church buildings and improving the musical content of
services. It offers full membership to adults on easier terms
than formerly—for example, by dispensing with the rather
uninviting formalities of the catechumen stage. In many
communities it gives a lead in the enrichment of social life and
in the youth movement: an indication of the extent of one
aspect of this work is conveyed by the fact that the women's
guilds had 150,000 members in 1951.

The modernization of old ideas, and the participation of the
Kirk in new activities, have been carried out with the full
approval of the great mass of its following. Nothing proves
this more clearly than the fact and the manner of the most
resounding triumph of presbyterianism in modern times—the
two unions which, in 1900 and 1929, gathered into one body
three communions with sharply contrasting views on the
ancient and still vital problem of the connexion between
church and state. Real and deep differences were truly reconciled in a tolerant and charitable spirit; and, at the end,
the united Parliament, in giving its blessing to the united
Church, made ample and honourable amend for past injuries
and blunders. It thus became possible for the Church of
Scotland to be acclaimed as 'the outstanding example of a
Church which is Established and yet is Free'; the words were
those of Archbishop Garbett, and in them there was perhaps a
shade of wistfulness, for recent experiences have shown the
Church of England to be much less the master within its own
house than is the sister church.

The two unions called for the exercise of good sense and
sympathy as well as hard work; that the church which
emerged from the processes of negotiation and compromise
enjoyed the overwhelming support of the nation is shown by
the small price that had to be paid by way of two minor
secessions. The same truth is reiterated each year at the time
of the General Assembly. It is not only, or mainly, that the
pageantry, the royal associations and the social festivities that
mark the occasion bring to Edinburgh, for a week in the
month of May, some of the ceremonial and external trappings

of a capital city; the meeting of the General Assembly has a deeper significance as a forum for the free expression of public opinion and informed criticism on a wide range of topics, secular as well as ecclesiastical. The debates of the ministers and elders still touch on matters which impressed their predecessors as having an impact on religious life—intemperance and gambling, Sunday travel and sport—but, in addition, they may discuss political and social questions on the moral plane—for example, the challenge of Communism, Britain's responsibility for colonial peoples, executive and legislative devolution in Scotland, and Glasgow's need of better housing. On such issues the Assembly's views and conclusions are reported in full by the press, treated with respect by civil authorities, and heard or read with interest by the people at large.

Its good repute as the mouthpiece of Scottish Protestantism, and its notable place in the life of the nation, do not make the Kirk complacent about the responsibility which it bears, as the state church, for the spiritual well-being of the entire people of Scotland. It realizes that, apart from the foreign mission field—somewhat shrunk, perhaps, from the Victorian concept, which took little heed of the merits of 'heathen' religions and philosophies,—it must direct its evangelistic efforts, not towards seeking converts among the other Christian sects of Scotland, but principally to proselytizing among the very large numbers who have no church connexion of any kind. The fact that nearly two out of every five persons in the country appear to refrain from membership of any religious body does not accord well with the traditional view of the Scots as a devout and God-fearing people, but it is useful to relate Scotland's case to that of other countries to-day. In England and the United States of America, with which comparison may most aptly be made, religious statistics suggest that more than half of the inhabitants are not church members. In Scotland, as elsewhere, this large element includes many different sorts of people—atheists, agnostics and sceptics, the followers of Darwin and Huxley, those who favour other methods of employing their day of rest and leisure, or scorn the church as a middle-class institution, or are merely lazy, some who must constantly travel or work on Sunday, and, again, many regular worshippers who are diffident about joining the church or prefer to vary the form of their devotions. Whatever their motives, the non-church-members invite the missionary endeavours of the Church, which has striven, especially since 1945, to bring religion to home and factory by the building of churches in housing estates and (as the most recent development) the appointment of industrial chaplains. Both church-membership and church attendance, it is well to remember, have become voluntary and personal in the past hundred years: the compulsive pressure of public opinion is largely a thing of the past. As one consequence, in the words of Professor G. D. Henderson (in *The Claims of the Church of Scotland*), 'there is better, if less, church-going.'

The Kirk is far from being free of domestic troubles. One of these, a basic one, has already been mentioned—the need for further local church unions, which exists alongside the opposite need to expand into the under-churched districts. The simple arithmetical problem of too many churches is thus complicated by the fact that a number of them are in the wrong places; transfers, like unions, are hard to achieve harmoniously, and restrictions on capital expenditure have since 1945 limited the amount of new building. It looks as if difficulties are likely to remain, to harass church planners and builders, for another generation.

The organization and higher direction of the Church are admittedly imperfect. The General Assembly, with over 1,600 members (half clerical, half lay), is too large for efficient administration, and this makes for a top-heavy structure. There is some danger of central bureaucracy, of the creation of an official caste, in the multiplication of committees, boards and agencies. And the incapacity of women, not only for the ministry, but also for membership of the Assembly, seems to many a poor return for their important part in the real work of the Church; this attitude to women is, to quote Professor Henderson again, 'not only un-Christianlike but definitely pre-Christian.'

The hardest problem that faces the Church to-day concerns

finance and the level of church livings. It is paradoxical that, while during the period 1830–1950 the prestige of the Kirk was maintained or enhanced, the material standards of its pastors were sharply depressed. Before the Disruption, as we have seen, many ministers were wealthy men, with £300 per annum and upwards; Lord Cockburn mentions the sacrifice of some who gave up incomes of £600 and more, and the extreme case of Dr. Patrick Macfarlane, minister of the West Kirk of Greenock, who 'has abandoned the best living in the Church, worth about £1,000 yearly.' Social and economic changes, and sectarian rivalries (which literally cheapened the ministerial office), produced a relative decline in clerical emoluments. In 1929 the minimum stipend was fixed, for the reunited Church, at £300 per annum (with a manse); by this time teachers were nearly on a parity with ministers (instead of, as formerly, receiving about a quarter as much), and other professions (especially the medical and legal), to say nothing of scientific and technical occupations, had forged far ahead.

The plan of union (1929) envisaged the raising of the minimum stipend to £400, but this modest aim was not achieved until 1947, and by then inflation was on such a scale as to render the change since 1929 retrogressive; the advance to £500 by 1952 still left the charges that were at the minimum level (fully one-third of the whole) worse off, in purchasing power, than was the case in 1929. No comfort lay in the thought that the dilemma was a general one. The minimum stipend was raised to £550 in the Church of England only in 1953, and it then stood at £400 in the Scottish Episcopal Church, the United Original Secession, and the Congregational Union; while the Free Church's 'equal dividend' was £375 in 1953.

The solution appears to be twofold. In the first place, the number of charges should be reduced, since there are assuredly still too many of them, and since it was their multiplication (in the hands of the sects) which led to the depreciation of emoluments. The obstacles to church unions have been mentioned; one way out (of which more use is likely to be made) is that of 'linkage,' whereby two congregations, while retaining separate identity, agree to share one minister, who may conduct services at each church, morning and evening alternately, over short periods. Secondly, the churchgoer, who often gives less than he should, must learn to adjust his donations to the financial realities of the times, for devaluation has cut sharply into the true worth of the endowments of the Church, which thus depends more than ever on congregational liberality. The cleavage between clergy and laity has never been as deep in Scotland as elsewhere: anti-clericalism is, and has been since the Reformation, virtually unknown. To-day the call for solidarity between minister and parishioner is clear and urgent. It is not that the clergy crave affluence or imagine that material rewards could ever be a substitute for a true vocation; but they feel that the dignity of their calling demands a modest competence, without which intending entrants may turn aside to other careers. Already the rate of recruitment of ministers is falling behind the rate of incidence of vacancies, and it seems that what is at stake in this matter is nothing less than the survival, as a national institution of the first rank, of a Church which has deserved the utmost loyalty and support of all its members.

Chapter 9

Scottish Education

THE paucity of our information about the schools of medieval Scotland makes it almost impossible to judge their worth, and those who have studied the subject have in fact been led to sharply conflicting conclusions. Long ago James Grant, with admirable industry, made the most of the slender evidence and produced, in *The Burgh Schools of Scotland* (1876), a generally favourable picture. More recently Dr. J. C. Jessop, in *Education in Angus* (1931), and Dr. G. G. Coulton, in *Scottish Abbeys and Social Life* (1933), have emphasized, each in his own field, the shortcomings of the system. Probably the truth lies about midway between these extreme views.

There are references (as a rule quite brief and cryptic) to schools at Abernethy (Perthshire), St. Andrews, Roxburgh, Perth, Stirling, Lanark and Linlithgow, in the twelfth century; at Ayr, Aberdeen and Berwick, in the thirteenth; at Cupar and Haddington, in the fourteenth; and at Brechin, Dundee, Peebles and Dumfries, in the fifteenth. Besides cathedral schools, for example at Glasgow and Elgin, there were schools in connexion with the greater abbeys, such as Holyrood and Dunfermline, and with some of the collegiate churches (Crail and Biggar). The chance survival of such notices in our records, and their wide geographical distribution, suggest that schools were maintained in all the leading burghs and in the chief religious centres (which sometimes coincided).

Two kinds of education were offered. A knowledge of Latin, the language of literature and learning, of church and university, was inculcated at the grammar school, while the 'sang schule' taught the elements of sacred music. The former was more closely associated with the greater burgh, the latter with the greater church, but no hard line can be drawn: in James I's reign Brechin had a grammar school and Dundee a song school. Moreover, the teachers at both were clergymen, for the educated layman was rare indeed; and what they taught was largely professional training for the priesthood or for a monastic order. Yet the town councils, at all events in the later middle ages, controlled the burgh schools, appointing the schoolmaster, paying his salary (which varied between 5 merks and £10 per annum) and fixing the scholars' fees. At this time, too, a third type, the English school, is found in a few large burghs; its province was reading and writing in the vernacular tongue. Occasionally two, or even all three, branches of instruction were combined in the one 'school'; but private schools were suppressed as threats to a valued monopoly. An unusually close look at daily routine is afforded by the rules which were in force at Aberdeen grammar school in 1553: the scholars were assembled, for 'prelections' (formal readings) or disputations, from 7 to 9, 10 to 12, 2 to 4, and 5 to 6 o'clock.

Much more is known of the three universities, all founded in the fifteenth century—St. Andrews (1412), Glasgow (1451), and King's College, in the city of Old Aberdeen (1495)—by papal bull, on the initiative of the local bishop, who was in each case perpetual chancellor. St. Andrews eventually had three colleges—St. Salvator's (1450), St. Leonard's (1512) and St. Mary's (1537)—but the others only one. At each college three or four regents, of whom the senior was principal or provost, conducted an entire class through the arts course, which led to graduation, as bachelor of arts, after two years, and as master after four. The curriculum was based on the scholastic system of Aristotelian philosophy—the seven 'liberal arts' derived from the Roman *trivium* (grammar, logic and rhetoric) and *quadrivium* (geometry, arithmetic, music and astronomy). Prelections were delivered in Latin, in which language all were presumed to be proficient and fluent. Since a degree might be a passport to preferment in state as well as church (the clergy supplying the civil service of the time), parsons and monks matriculated as members (*suppositi*) of the university, along with young students in training for an ecclesiastical career. The rector was elected by the whole corporation—regents, doctors, masters and students—voting in their four 'nations,' which comprised Alban, Angus, Fife and Lothian at St. Andrews; Clydesdale, Teviotdale, Rothesay and Alban at Glasgow; and Mar, Buchan, Moray and Angus at Aberdeen. Forty matriculations in the year would be normal at St. Andrews, but well above the average at the others.

Much can be said on behalf of medieval Scottish education. The most pleasing feature of the universities was their welcome to the poor scholar. Fees were low (as were living expenses), but a student who was unable to pay was entered on the roll as *pauper*, a word that conveyed an exact meaning but no social stigma: he promised to pay later, when things had mended for him—'no honest seeker after knowledge,' in the words of Maitland Anderson, editor of *The Early Records of the University of St. Andrews* (1926), 'being turned away from the best the University could give him, whether he could afford to pay for it or not.' One item of legislation was at least creditable in aim, though there is no evidence that it was ever operative: the famous Education Act of 1496 directed all barons and freeholders of substance to send their eldest sons and heirs to grammar school from the age of eight or nine till they 'have perfite Latyne,' and thereafter for three years to 'the sculis of art and jure,' so that, knowing the laws, they may do justice and relieve the poor people of any need to seek the king's principal courts 'for ilk small iniure.' The year 1522 saw an achievement rather than a mere good intention— the publication (at Paris) of Scotland's first Latin grammar, the *Rudimenta* of the Aberdonian, John Vaus.

Schools and universities are judged by the men they produce, and pre-Reformation Scotland passes the test comfortably. The distinguished alumni, graduates and regents of the three universities form, indeed, a fair academic procession, as they parade before the mind's eye in the traditional pairs— Bishops James Kennedy and William Elphinstone, educational pioneers and wise counsellors; the brother poets, Robert Henryson and William Dunbar; John Major and Hector Boece, historians as well as heads of colleges; James and David Beaton, uncle and nephew, in turn champions of the old church and the French alliance; and, on the other side of the Reformation divide, but educated under the old system, John Knox and George Buchanan, each a master of prose and a great historian as well as a founder of Scottish Protestantism.

Yet some damaging criticisms of medieval education must be admitted. Despite a few gifts of lands and rents by pious benefactors, clerical and lay, the universities were poorly endowed, and consequently unable to live up to the resounding promises of the papal bulls. The higher faculties of law and medicine were really non-existent, and even theology was neglected. The main aim of the church schools and colleges was to give a basic, minimum training, of a narrow, professional nature, to intending priests and monks; that even this modest ambition was being frustrated in the middle years of the sixteenth century by the general corruption of the church rests on Catholic evidence, and more particularly on the acts of the provincial councils denouncing, and proposing remedies for, the 'crass ignorance of literature and all the liberal arts' on the part of the clergymen. At lower levels the position was even worse, for secular education and an enlightened laity did not come within the scope of the system. The burgh schools were too small and the new English schools too few to achieve much; and, though here and there a conscientious parish priest or monk may have instructed children in the elements of the faith, the lack of parish or primary schools left the mass of the people sunk in illiteracy.

In attempting to strike a balance between these seemingly irreconcilable conflicts of fact and opinion, it is well to recall that Scotland suffered much in the middle ages from a backward economy, internal and foreign warfare, and uncertain contacts with the centres of European civilization. To such retarding factors were added the limited outlook and, latterly, the gross failings of the Catholic Church. We might conclude that, while the nation produced, in the circumstances, a creditable number of inspiring teachers and sound scholars, its educational development was essentially one-sided, weak and fitful, because of the want of a solid base of elementary schools.

It was here—in the lack of parish schools—that Knox and his fellow-reformers pressed home their attack. The First Book of Discipline (1560) described an elaborate superstructure of higher education, including grammar schools in the towns of any repute, arts colleges in 'every notable town,' and the three existing universities; but its fundamental and revolutionary claim was that in every parish—even if it be 'upland' (rural)—the children and youth must be instructed 'in their first rudiments.' The avowal of the Kirk's responsibility for education, popular as well as professional, and its resolve to establish one school in every parish, determined the course of events for some 300 years.

The Knoxian ideal was reaffirmed in the legislation of the seventeenth century. The Privy Council decreed in 1616 that there be a school in every parish, where the youth might learn to read and write English (and, *inter alia*, the Irish language, one of the principal causes of the continuance of Highland barbarity and incivility, might be abolished). This act was ratified by Parliament in 1633, when the bishops were empowered, as visitors, to stent the inhabitants for the maintenance of the schools. Parliament further enacted in 1646 that in every parish a schoolmaster's stipend of not less than 100 merks (£5 11s. sterling) or more than 200 merks (£11 2s.) be provided by a stent imposed by the heritors; if they failed in their duty, the presbytery should appoint twelve honest men within the bounds, to establish the school, modify the stipend and set down a stent. This statute was the model for the act of 1696, which repeated its terms, save that, in the event of a lapse by the heritors, the duty of intervention was laid upon the commissioners of supply for the county; each heritor might claim relief from his tenants for one-half of his stent.

Statutory machinery for the parish schools was thus adequate, but from the Reformation to the Union progress was hampered by lack of money and aversion to taxation, by civil strife and the alternation between presbytery and episcopacy. Still, there was some advance. The records suggest that, in such counties as Aberdeen and Forfar (which would be rather better than the Scottish average), fully half of the parishes had schools by 1650, although in some of these there might be no settled 'provision,' and thus no guarantee of continuity. Other types of school experienced similar vicissitudes. An act of 1579 was aimed at the revival and reform of song schools, but they seem to have died out in the course of the seventeenth century. Even the burgh schools had their troubles. Between 1560 and 1625 the crown made grants from the revenues of the old Church in favour of the schools of Dundee, Irvine, Renfrew, Elgin, Dunfermline, Paisley and Musselburgh, but as a rule the schoolmaster's stipend (at a rather higher rate than obtained in the parish) and his house-rent were defrayed out of the burgh funds. Neither in burgh nor in parish was there security of tenure, appointments often being made for only one year. Any odd room or even a barn might do duty as the school. The schoolmaster was usually a petty pluralist, eking out his stipend and the pupils' fees by filling one or more of the offices of session-clerk, registrar, precentor and reader.

The scholars attended the parish school between the ages of seven and nine or ten, and a few of them went on to the grammar school, to remain there until they were about fourteen years old, by which time, having acquired Latin, they were ready for the university. School hours were very long: at Stirling in 1613 they ran from 6 o'clock to 9, from 10 to 12, and from 1 to 6. The Saturday half-day appears at Elgin in 1649, but not till the 1670s do we hear of the opening hour being put back (at Dundee) to 7 o'clock in winter. By the 1690s, however, many schools were starting at 7 in summer and at 9 in winter. The boys paid their quarterly fees (one shilling or upwards) directly to the master, and also brought straw for the floor, peats for the fire, and fighting-cocks at Fastern's E'en.

University development during this period followed the same pattern of mixed success and retreat. Andrew Melville, while principal of Glasgow (1574–80), taught, and inspired the teaching of, a curriculum of dazzling scope and variety, from Astrology to Syriac; it was through his efforts that Greek won a permanent place among academic studies. It was thanks to him, too, that all three universities were reorganized at this time and endowed with new revenues;

K

but another of his innovations, that of 'fixed' or specialist professors, failed to take root, and the traditional system of 'rotating' regents prevailed. Two new universities were founded—Edinburgh 'Toun's College' (1583), and Marischal College, in the royal burgh of Aberdeen (1593).

In the seventeenth century, Scotland's five universities, sharing a few hundred students who were still for the most part training for the ministry, struggled against financial difficulties. These were eased from 1641 to 1660, and again after 1690, by grants to each of them from the episcopal revenues released by the triumph of presbytery, though the Restoration naturally dried up this source of income (but not before Glasgow's lovely 'Old College' buildings on the High street had been nearly completed). There were therefore alternating phases of expansion and contraction, and a change in church and state involved reversal of policy and depriva-tion of the principal and regents. New chairs—in mathe-matics, theology and medicine—were mostly short-lived, and the normal arts course, as fixed by tradition and subject only to local variations of a minor kind, comprised Greek, Logic, Ethics and Natural Philosophy. Each regent conducted his boys—their usual age at entry was fourteen, though some were older—through their four years, delivering formal Latin readings from Aristotelian texts and Dutch commentaries; classes met from 6 or 7 o'clock until 9, and again from 10 to 12, and the afternoons were given over to disputations, examinations and recreation.

College discipline was strict. Students boarded with regents or lived in bare and austere college chambers, which were inspected at dawn and curfew by the 'hebdomadar' (a kind of 'orderly regent'). The fare was homely and simple at the common tables. The boys were obliged to wear their gowns at all times and to speak only Latin (a rule that held also for the grammar school pupils); they might play 'at the gowff' or practise archery, but cards and dice, gambling, drinking and all forms of 'vageing or vice' were forbidden. The cloistered life and presbyterian piety appealed to Scottish fathers, and also to the English and Irish dissenters, who, late in the century, sent their sons, debarred from their own universities by religious tests, to Glasgow and Edinburgh; each of these had from 200 to 300 students by 1700.

The internal peace and economic advance of the eighteenth century brought gradual, but in the end impressive, improvement in the schools. In the absence of any amending legislation, the statutory stipend remained within the limits fixed in 1646 and 1696 (100–200 merks), but the schoolmasters' average income from all sources did rise—to about £11 per annum, according to their memorial in 1748, and to £13 by 1782, when there were some 900 parish schools in Scotland. The standard of teaching benefited from the increased flow of graduates from the universities; in Aberdeenshire, with its strong classical and academic tradition, all the parishes had schools by the end of the century, and most of these were grammar schools, which could prepare a boy for the university.

The formidable Highland problem—caused by remoteness, poverty, lack of communications, unduly large parishes, and the language barrier—was the special province of the Society in Scotland for Propagating Christian Knowledge, set up by royal charter in 1709. By 1732 it had provided 'English' schools for 109 parishes, almost all in the Highlands. From 1738, too, it was authorized to establish spinning schools for girls; in this work a share was taken by the Board of Trustees for Manufactures (1727) and by the Commissioners for the Forfeited Estates (1752–84). Changing its attitude on the language question, the Society in 1758 published the New Testament in Gaelic; by 1795 it had 229 ordinary (or parish) schools, with 12,010 scholars, and 94 spinning schools, with 2,360 girls.

For the 1790s we have evidence, in the *Old Statistical Account*, of hardships and weaknesses, but also of solid achievement, in the schools. Glassford (Lanarkshire) had five schoolmasters in six years, and the dominie at Glenholm (Peeblesshire) kept a shop to supplement his income; while at Coylton (Ayrshire) and Bathgate parents preferred the loom to the schoolroom for their children. At Anstruther Wester, on the other hand, and at Speymouth, all the children, however poor, could read; and at Campsie, Renfrew and Newburgh (Fife), the illiterate adults, ashamed of their lack, attended the parish school with the children to make good their deficiency. Since at the close of the century only ten parishes in all Scotland were without a school, it can be said that, though there were wide variations from one parish to another in teaching, attendance, accommodation and remuneration, the ideal laid down by Knox in 1560 had at last been broadly realized.

In the burghs, the grammar (or high) schools confined themselves to intensive classical instruction. Henry Mackenzie, attending Edinburgh High School from 1752 to 1757, had six hours a day (7 to 9, 10 to 12, and 2 to 4) under the one master for four years, studying such authors as Horace, Cicero and Virgil, and then went on to Livy in the rector's, or fifth, year class. Greek was introduced in 1772, so that Henry Cockburn, in his turn (1787–93), spent two years with the rector, learning Greek as well as advanced Latin. As early as 1761, the rector's class at Ayr covered Greek and mathematics, in addition to Latin. Stipends were higher at the grammar schools than at the parish schools: at Glasgow, in the 1780s, each of the four masters had £25 per annum; there was no rector, but, as his class in turn became the top class, each got other £10 as 'presiding teacher.' Fees were also higher (they were raised at Glasgow at this time from 5s. to 10s. a quarter), and still higher for country scholars, whose parents contributed nothing to the burgh revenues. But the old hostility to private schools died out from about 1750, as it was found that there was room for all. The town councils of Brechin, in 1759, and of Montrose, in 1773, actually made grants to 'adventure' teachers of English. And the 'academy,' an endowed school charging rather high fees, made its appearance to meet the need for a more modern, less severely classical, institution than the high school: its curriculum included linguistic, scientific, commercial and practical subjects. The first academy opened at Perth in 1760, and others followed at Dundee (1786) and Inverness (1788).

For the universities the eighteenth century was outstanding as an age of reform and enlightenment. The radical change from rotating regencies to fixed professorships was made at Edinburgh in 1708, at Glasgow in 1727, at St. Andrews in

1747, at Marischal College in 1753 and at King's College in 1798. At Glasgow, about 1730, Frances Hutcheson was lecturing in English, a new mode which eventually displaced the formal Latin prelection. Discipline was relaxed, and reports by student censors on their fellows' conduct were dropped, as was compulsory Latin conversation. College chambers—unable in any case to accommodate the increasing number of students—went out of favour, residential bursaries were commuted into money grants, and the youths lodged in town 'digs.' The abandonment of the common tables at St. Andrews in 1820 extinguished the last flicker of the old collegiate way of life. The provision at Glasgow of professors' houses, begun in 1722 and ultimately numbering 13, completed the 'Old College,' while Edinburgh's Adam-designed College buildings were constructed between 1789 and 1834.

The advance of learning was marked by the foundation of new chairs in arts, divinity and law, but more particularly in medicine, by the provision of facilities for clinical work through the opening of infirmaries at Edinburgh (1736), Aberdeen (1739) and Glasgow (1794), and by the study of new authors like Newton in physics and Locke in philosophy —until Frances Hutcheson and Thomas Reid developed a native system ('the Scottish philosophy') and Adam Smith evolved the new science of political economy. To the brilliance and sophistication of Edinburgh society, which have already been glanced at (cf. pp. 232, 262), its University, with no fewer than 27 chairs by 1800, made a notable contribution, but Glasgow and Aberdeen were not far behind in academic distinction. All had their active members of the commonwealth of letters. It was at Edinburgh that the three Alexander Monros, father, son and grandson, filled the chair of anatomy for well over a century (1720–1859); but it was Glasgow that gave her, in William Cullen and Joseph Black, two of her leading teachers of chemistry and medicine; it was from Aberdeen that Reid went to Glasgow, and the northern town also sent, to Edinburgh and Oxford, the amazing mathematical and medical dynasty of the Gregorys. Only St. Andrews, sinking into lethargy and decay in a city stripped of its ecclesiastical glories, did not share in the forward movement. But at least its top-heavy constitution, including three small and far from rich colleges doing much the same work among a few dozen students, was amended by the combination of two of these—St. Salvator's and St. Leonard's—as United College (1747), with professors instead of regents; and it survived, albeit as something of a cultural backwater.

In all four university centres the door was still wide open for the poor student. Fees were low, the session was short (from November to May), and both food and lodgings were simple; if obliged to do so, the student could live and learn for as little as £10 a year, though many spent £15–20. This was no doubt one reason why the several hundred students at Edinburgh and Glasgow throughout the century included English, American and foreign youths; but the other, and more potent, attraction was the quality of the teaching. Adam Smith (who knew Oxford and some of the continental universities) declared in 1785 that Edinburgh was superior to 'any other Society of the kind I ever knew'; and large numbers of ministers of taste and refinement, of physicians well grounded in theory and practice, of cultured lawyers and sound teachers, were the living proof of the worth of the universities to the nation.

The nineteenth century opened with a long overdue reform. The Schoolmasters' Act of 1803 fixed a new minimum salary of 300 merks (£16 13s. 4d.) and a maximum of 400 merks (£22 4s. 5d.), and provided for the adjustment of these figures, at 25-year intervals, in accordance with the movement of fiars prices. In 1828, therefore, the maximum was raised to £34 4s. 4d., and this became the usual stipend of the parochial schoolmaster, who also received customary perquisites, additional emoluments, and an income from fees which varied very widely from parish to parish—say, from £10 to £50 per annum. The Act of 1803 allowed the schoolmaster a house of two rooms (including the kitchen as one). Opponents of the measure promptly dubbed these modest abodes 'palaces for dominies'; in fact house and school were often combined as one two-storeyed building.

Many new types of school came into being in the first half of the century. A parliamentary report of 1834 showed only some 1,000 parish schools out of a total of over 4,000. There were over 300 'Society' schools, mostly founded (as we have seen) by the Society in Scotland for Propagating Christian Knowledge, but including some set up by other societies of a similar kind. 'Assembly' schools, provided by the General Assembly in the neediest localities, out of a fund established in 1823, numbered 146 by 1833, and 302 by 1872. 'Sessional' schools were maintained in cities and large towns by the 'general sessions' (unions of kirk sessions). The 270 endowed and subscription schools included the academies of Dumfries (1802), Montrose (1815), Edinburgh (1824), and many others, with the emphasis always on the 'modern' side. Leading the sectarian field in 1834 were the Secession and Relief Churches, with some 350 schools; but the Free Church, building about 600 in less than 40 years, was to outstrip the others in the long run. Episcopalian and Catholic schools were not numerous (36 and 32 respectively in 1851). Much the largest group in 1834 comprised the 2,000-odd 'adventure' schools, many of them unpretentious 'dame' schools which afforded a precarious livelihood for decayed gentlewomen.

A variety of specialist schools completes the picture. Evening classes for adults grew into mechanics' institutes, and these were the forerunners of the technical colleges. David Stow began the 'normal' or training school in Glasgow in 1824. The industrial or 'ragged' school owed its start to Sheriff Watson of Aberdeen (1841) and its development to Thomas Guthrie, at Edinburgh (1847). There were Sunday schools and infant schools early in the century. From about 1850 the girls' schools of the S.S.P.C.K. gave up spinning and weaving in favour of sewing, knitting, and ordinary 'subjects.'

The state was bound to intervene in this tangled domain. Parliamentary grants-in-aid, authorized in 1833, were given from 1839 to build schools open to state inspection, and from 1846 to pay salaries and other running costs. The system of grants, inspection and teaching qualifications was overhauled by the Parochial and Burgh Schoolmasters (Scotland) Act, 1861, which abolished religious tests and raised the maximum salary to £70 for male teachers and £30 for females. The

logical conclusion came in 1872, when the Education
(Scotland) Act transferred the presbyterian schools to elected
school boards in parishes and burghs. The boards' main
function concerned the elementary education (reading,
writing and arithmetic) that was now compulsory between
the ages of 5 and 13; but they might also maintain infant and
evening schools, as well as 'higher class' (later 'secondary')
schools for advanced pupils (approximately 12 to 17).
The Scotch Education Department, a committee of the
privy council charged with the distribution of the parliamentary grants and, from 1885, controlled by the Scottish
Secretary, instituted, in 1888, a leaving certificate examination as a university entrance standard. Machinery was set up
in 1892 for the allocation of a grant-in-aid to the secondary
schools. The unsatisfactory little 'adventure' schools disappeared. By the close of the century the school curriculum
had been extended to include such subjects as history, geography, French and the natural sciences, and the teachers
had both better qualifications and higher salaries—over £100
for men and £80–90 for women.

In an entirely different way, conditions at the universities
also called for state intervention in the course of the nineteenth century. It was not that the quality of the teaching or
research invited criticism or reform: from beginning to end,
from the days of Edinburgh's great philosopher, Dugald
Stewart, to those of Glasgow's even greater physicist, Lord
Kelvin, each generation of students could listen to some
inspiring lectures and to flashes of brilliance from the outstanding academic luminaries. It was the government and
internal administration of all the universities that demanded
drastic alteration. At Edinburgh bitter town-and-gown disputes over the medical curriculum in 1825 and 1845 convinced the professors that continued civic control was intolerably irksome and unsatisfactory. Glasgow suffered from the
opposite vice—the concentration of power in the self-styled
'Faculty,' composed of the incumbents of the thirteen oldest
chairs. Aberdeen's two colleges, each constituting a separate
university, represented needless and wasteful duplication of
work. St. Andrews, still far behind in intellectual distinc-

tion, was also the worst offender in the matter of conferring degrees on absurdly easy terms. In each case there were administrative irregularities, financial irresponsibility, nepotism in appointments, and imprecise requirements as to curriculum, examination and graduation.

A royal commission, appointed in 1826 and reappointed in 1830, collected much information and proposed sensible reforms. Strangely enough, no action was taken at this time, though the reports and recommendations were of real value and, indeed, foreshadowed many later changes. These came with the Universities (Scotland) Acts of 1858 and 1889, and with the ordnances made by the royal commissions set up under the terms of the two statutes. Each of the four universities (Aberdeen's two colleges being united in 1860) became an independent corporation. Administration, patronage and (from 1889) finance were committed to a new and supreme governing body, the university court, representing the academic and civic authorities, the senate, and the graduates (through the general council). The senate, including all professors, became solely responsible for matters of teaching, examining, graduation and discipline; and, under it, faculties of arts, divinity, medicine and law were organized. As a basic degree, the M.A. finally displaced the B.A. (which was abolished in 1861); and exact regulations were made for the bachelor's and doctor's degrees in the other faculties. The new faculty of science was established in 1893. In 1892, too, women students began to be admitted to the universities, and Queen Margaret College, founded as a separate institution in 1883, was incorporated in Glasgow University. Another initially independent centre of higher learning, University College, Dundee, had been set up in 1881; the commissioners brought it into the St. Andrews system in 1897, but unhappily left it, with its original trust deed still operative, as an *imperium in imperio.*

Throughout the century a college education remained within the reach of the 'lad o' pairts' from a humble home (though not from the very poorest). Duncan Dewar, an arts and divinity student at St. Andrews from 1819 till 1827, spent about £15 per annum, but was able to afford bed and board, books, clothes and fees, and also little luxuries like spats, snuff, beer, whisky, black sugar, peppermint drops and a breast-pin. Thus living was cheap at St. Andrews, as it was at Aberdeen: Edinburgh and Glasgow cost rather more (the total fees for an arts course at Aberdeen in 1813 were only 11 guineas, against 27 at Edinburgh). The way of life at all four was altogether simpler and much less expensive than at the Oxford and Cambridge colleges; and so it remained and remains. The number of students increased fairly steadily, to reach 6,000 by the end of the century—some 2,800 at Edinburgh, 2,000 at Glasgow, 800 at Aberdeen and over 400 at St. Andrews. From 1885 students' unions were established as centres for their social, recreational and extra-curricular activities, while students' representative councils became official spokesmen for their collective interests. The expansion in their numbers, as well as the growth of old and the addition of new departments of study, posed for Glasgow and Edinburgh problems of accommodation, which they solved in different ways. In 1870 Glasgow, having sold the graceful but dilapidated Old College to a railway company, moved to what was deemed a spacious site at Gilmorehill, in the more fashionable west end, while Edinburgh in 1883 initiated a policy (since carried much further) of dispersing its newer departments to more commodious though scattered quarters, while retaining its old building as the heart of the university.

The twentieth century educational reforms began in 1901 with the raising of the school-leaving age to 14; a further rise, to 15, was enacted in 1918 and again in 1936, but did not take effect until 1947. School boards were empowered in 1908 to provide meals and transport, medical inspection, continuation classes for pupils over 14, and teachers' superannuation. The legislation of 1918 and 1929, as we have seen (pp. 181–2), abolished the small school boards, numbering about 1,000, and replaced them by education committees of county councils and of town councils of the four cities (35 in all). In 1918 the Episcopalian and Roman Catholic schools were brought (subject to religious safeguards) into the field of public education, which now extended to university bursaries for poor but promising scholars, and a county library service for public use. By the Education (Scotland) Acts of 1945 and 1946—the second incorporating and superseding the first— the school age was to be raised without delay to 15, and as soon as practicable to 16, and midday meals and milk, free books and stationery were to be supplied. All public schools —apart from special schools (for the handicapped) and approved schools (for the delinquent)—were organized as nursery (from 2 to 5), primary (5 to 12), junior secondary (12 to 15) and senior secondary schools (12 to 17 or 18).

The 1946 Act dealt also with 'further education' (beyond the school-leaving age); it proposed to set up junior colleges, although financial stringency has, up to the time of writing, postponed the realization of this aim. The Act contemplated the supplementing, not the over-riding, of the existing agencies, which have grown out of such nineteenth-century creations as the evening class, the mechanics' institute, and a few more ambitious projects, like 'Anderson's University,' established for the benefit of Glasgow's working men by the bequest of Professor John Anderson (1796). As it is, further education to-day falls into two broad categories. On the one side are the 16 'central institutions'—colleges of technology, agriculture, commerce, art, music and domestic science—and the various local schools giving basic training in such branches as building, engineering and nursing. On the other side, adult education, starting in its modern form in 1911 through the initiative of the Workers' Educational Association, and now forming the main part of the extra-mural activities of the universities, offers, generally in evening lecture-and-discussion classes, a wide range of non-specialized courses of a cultural, scientific, or recreational character.

The latest age has seen the work of the universities growing and adapting itself to modern needs in a great variety of ways. The older faculties have been subjected to a high degree of specialization: typical of the new departments are education and Scottish history, bacteriology and ophthalmology. There has been expansion into entirely new fields, like psychology, genetics and applied economics, and Glasgow set up a faculty of engineering in 1923. Just after the end of the second World War, dentistry and veterinary medicine became university

responsibilities, and at the same time relations became intimate with the higher schools of fine art, music and agriculture.
One consequence of the increased activity was the addition of
new chairs (the mid-century total being 72 at Edinburgh and
67 at Glasgow) and of even more non-professorial posts
(which number about 500 at each of these two). Another was
the influx of students, which was especially marked after the
end of the two major wars. From 6,000 at the opening of the
century, the number of matriculations at the four universities
nearly reached 12,000 in 1921–22, passed that total at the
inter-war peak of 1930–31, declined somewhat in the later
1930s, and rose again to an all-time high record of 18,700 in
1948–49. The most recent trend shows the figures settling
down to something not far short of 16,000—under 6,000 for
each of the two larger universities and 2,000 for each of the
smaller.

In the changed circumstances of the present century the
ancient tradition of helping the poor scholar on his way was
maintained, partly by means of privately endowed bursaries,
partly by county and town council grants, partly by government assistance to ex-servicemen, but above all, perhaps, by
the work of the Carnegie Trust for the Universities of Scotland,
which, from its inception in 1901, devoted a large part of its
great resources to the payment of students' fees, and much
also to the improvement of teaching, research and social
amenities like playing-fields and residences. This policy no
doubt had much to do with the fact that Scotland's student
numbers remained at a high level in relation to the total population: her proportion at mid-century (over 0·31 per cent.)
was nearly double that of England and Wales (not quite 0·16
per cent.). One of the four universities, however, diverged
slightly from the normal Scottish pattern of a body of students
living at home or in 'homely' lodgings. St. Andrews, always
nearer than the others to the 'residential' ideal, happily recovered its academic standing in the first quarter of the
century, to become perhaps the best-loved and the most
intensely 'regional' of our universities; during the second
quarter it developed its student hostels on such a scale as to
prove attractive to the sons and daughters of families living far

afield. Its constitutional difficulties were resolved by Parliament in 1953, when, after both a committee of inquiry and a royal commission had reported, its government was remodelled on a federal basis, which allowed the St. Andrews and Dundee elements equal representation on the university court, and defined the academic province of each.

The questions that trouble Scotsmen who are conscious of the nation's proud heritage in education—Have we boasted too much of our former pre-eminence?—And is any such superiority (if it ever existed) now becoming a thing of the past?—are hard to answer factually. To-day there are rather more than 3,100 public schools, and over 200 private (or 'independent') schools, and the 33,500 teachers have charge of a school population slightly in excess of 800,000. The pupil-teacher ratio (just under 24) is deemed unsatisfactory, despite some recent improvement, inasmuch as it permits the existence of many over-crowded classes and indicates the need for further school building and the recruitment of more teachers—in each case at the expense of the heavily burdened national and local finances. A peculiarly disturbing shortage is that of teachers of scientific and mathematical subjects; this is clearly due to the higher material rewards offered by alternative careers, and yet it is extremely doubtful if the state can afford, or will be able within measurable time to afford, to offer truly competitive salaries to teachers. The present basic scales in the secondary schools are £620–960 for men and £507–807 for women, while they are lower by £100, more or less, in the primary schools. Whether such stipends represent, in modern conditions, an adequate return for the professional training and work involved; whether, if they do not, the economy can bear the cost of the desirable increases; whether, on the other hand, if such a measure is dismissed as uneconomic, society can contemplate with equanimity the lasting damage which, it is feared, will flow and is indeed flowing from the lowering of teaching standards;—such are the problems which, far transcending matters of the moment like the provision of new schools to replace outmoded buildings or to meet the requirements of housing estates, are causing anxiety (and look like continuing to do so) among all who are concerned with the future of the Scottish schools.

The universities, too, are no more free from doubts and worries than they ever have been. Each of the four has its individual troubles, whether of building, equipment, staffing, residences or amenities, but perhaps the most fundamental question facing all of them concerns their relations with the government, which have become increasingly intimate with the extension of state responsibility for public education and the national health service, and, since 1945, with the clearer recognition of the nation's need for trained scientists and technologists. The growth of state interest in the work of the universities has been accompanied by a comparable rise in the amount of the parliamentary grants allocated, through the University Grants Committee, to the maintenance and expansion of that work. Each of the two larger universities now receives over one million pounds annually from this source, while the two smaller ones get over half a million each; these sums represent rather more than two-thirds of the total revenues of the four institutions. If there is here a latent threat to the status of the universities,—if there is a danger (as has happened elsewhere) that they might gradually be brought under complete political control,—it can at least be said that there has hitherto been no sign of undue state influence upon their academic standards or internal administration. Both government and parliament, on the contrary, have wisely refrained from vexatious intervention and have shown themselves to be zealous for the preservation, as national assets of inestimable value, of our traditionally independent universities.

Chapter 10

Art and Letters

THE architectural, sculptural and literary remains of the first millennium in North Britain are evidence of the faint and tentative stirrings of the creative impulse among peoples struggling to emerge from the dark ages into the light of European civilization. They suggest a 'culture' in the archæological rather than the artistic sense, as is true of the artifacts of other tribes and nations in the long interval between the collapse of the Roman *imperium* and the establishment of the feudal order. Scotland, the exposed, storm-tossed and war-riven north-western bastion of medieval society, yet yields some notable monuments. The Celtic church is commemorated by its bee-hive cells and tiny, square-ended chapels, and Celtic art by the elaborate, interlacing patterns carved on crosses. The famous round towers of Abernethy and Brechin are of uncertain date, but in spirit at least they relate to primitive times when clergy as well as laity needed refuges from the barbarous sea-raiders. The far north contains the ruins of hundreds of brochs (the best of them being at Mousa, in Shetland), the massive circular strongholds of the Pictish lords. And at Iona Scottish literature had its modest beginnings in the seventh century essay in filial piety, the *Life of St. Columba*, written in Latin by the missionary's successor, Adamnan. But probably the most remarkable product of the age is the celebrated cross of Ruthwell, which, intricately and beautifully sculptured with pictures and symbols, and singularly well preserved over its entire height of eighteen feet, stands to-day with the parish church built around it.

St. Margaret and her sons, introducing Anglo-Saxon and Norman ways and 'Gothic' styles, brought the country into the mainstream of European culture, but Scotland's participation therein, and her literary and artistic achievements during the whole of the middle ages, were governed by the facts of geography and history; much the same thing, as we have seen, applied in the case of her educational attainments (*cf.* p. 287). The limiting conditions, as regards arts and letters, included the poverty and remoteness of the land, chronic baronial turbulence and royal minorities, recurring English wars in the period 1296–1550, sacerdotalism and spreading corruption within the church, the absence of secular education and, therefore, of informed public opinion or enlightened taste; even such materialist factors as the harsh climate and the abundance of stone had their influence. Among the undertones that became noticeable from time to time were the lack of any direct or substantial heritage from the Roman empire and the deep dichotomy between the linguistic halves of the nation.

Prior to the War of Independence English ideas were borrowed and adapted for church building as well as for ecclesiastical reorganization. The Scottish architects took kindly to the round arch, small window and massive pillar of the Romanesque and Norman styles, and, modifying these features in the direction of simplicity, strength and small dimensions, produced structures admirably suited for a rugged land, severe climate and plain people—the tiny chapel of St. Margaret on Edinburgh castle rock, the little parish churches of Dalmeny and Leuchars, the abbeys of Dunfermline, Jedburgh and Kelso, St. Regulus tower in St. Andrews and St. Magnus cathedral in Kirkwall. So, too, the characteristic early Gothic features of vertical lines, pointed arch, better lighting and delicate tracery are found in Scotland from about 1200, but in smaller churches than their English counterparts—the 'transitional' abbey of Holyrood, the cathedrals of Elgin and Glasgow (the latter with its unique vault which came to serve as 'the laigh kirk'), and the abbeys of Arbroath and Dryburgh. After 1300, however, English influences waned as political relations worsened, and it is the flamboyant style of the Continent rather than English perpendicular that finds an echo in the late Gothic architecture of Scotland. The typical buildings of this phase are again small, since the pious founders—kings and queens, barons, bishops and burgesses—now favoured modest collegiate churches rather than monasteries or cathedrals: the vogue was at its height in James II's reign (1437–60). Among them were St. Salvator's College, St. Andrews, and King's College, Old Aberdeen; Trinity, Kirk-o'-Field, Corstorphine and Crichton, in or near Edinburgh; Bothwell and Biggar, in the west; and the three 'Lamps of the Lothians,' each with its open-crowned spire (St. Michael's, Linlithgow, St. Giles', Edinburgh, and St. Mary's, Haddington). In such churches, in the words of Mr. Robert Hurd, 'certain French details become fused with a national idiom'; but the luxuriant stone carving of the most celebrated and most exotic of them all, Roslin chapel, points rather to Spanish and Portuguese models and perhaps workers.

The Scottish castle, on the whole, shows more native and fewer foreign features than does the church. Primarily a military 'strength,' the castle was also the residence of king, bishop or baron, and the *caput* (administrative centre) of his estate. The earliest castles were earthworks, with timber and clay buildings within a wooden stockade and a ditch; from these evolved, just before 1300, Bothwell, Dirleton and Kildrummy, with stone keep, smaller towers and 'curtain' wall enclosing wooden hall and lesser buildings. At a later stage the stressing of the hall produced the 'courtyard' castles of Doune, Tantallon and St. Andrews, the royal fortresses of Edinburgh and Stirling, and the royal 'palaces' of Falkland and Linlithgow (to each of which James IV and James V, employing French master-masons, gave grace and symmetry along with Renaissance details). Meanwhile, small barons and lairds, unable to afford courtyard or palace, developed the free-standing tower as combined home and fortlet. To the original design (a simple rectangle in plan), like that of the gaunt fourteenth-century Douglas stronghold of Threave (Galloway), or of the later towers of Elphinstone (near Tranent) and Rusco (in Kirkcudbrightshire), was added a wing, as at Dunnottar (near Stonehaven), Dunvegan (in Skye), and Portincross (North Ayrshire). Exceptionally for pre-Reformation times, Borthwick tower (Midlothian), with two wings, foreshadowed the later refinements of the

'Scots Baronial' style, which was to give the country its chief
claim to architectural distinction. Of the medieval burghs
the remains are pathetically small: Provand's Lordship, in
Glasgow, is the one outstanding building to-day. Possibly
there was not very much that was worth preserving, for, as
late as 1544, as Dr. H. M. Paton reminds us, 'even the larger
houses of Edinburgh and Canongate had no more than two
storeys and an attic.'

Some of the minor arts and crafts—the medieval mind did
not differentiate between them—benefited from the patronage
of crown and church, and to a lesser degree of baronage and
burgh. Church organs seem to have been in use from about
1250, and the song schools helped to maintain choral services
at a professional level. Of folk-music a few songs and titles
survive, like *Ha, now the Day dawis*, *The Wyf of Auchtermuchty*,
and *The Wooing of Jok and Jenny*, and others, under heavy
Protestant disguise, were included by the brothers Wedderburn, of Dundee, in *The Gude and Godlie Ballatis* (1567). We
have many references to minstrels, harpers, fiddlers, pipers
and drummers, and we know that dancing was popular with
high and low. The Jameses commissioned painting, both as
portraits and for heraldry, and the fourth of the name licensed
the printing press of Walter Chepman and Andro Myllar at
Edinburgh in 1507. Little of the wood carving and metalwork
that decorated the churches survived the Reformation, but
certain of the illuminated manuscripts which we still have are
of artistic as well as palæographical interest—most notably
the great charter of Kelso abbey (1159), embellished with
brilliant pictures of David I and Malcolm IV worked into the
initial letter.

The literary output of medieval Scotland was at first
wholly, and later partly, in Latin, the tongue of theologians,
teachers and philosophers. After Adamnan, fully four centuries elapsed before the next contribution was made, in the
form of another brief essay in hagiology, the *Life of St. Margaret*,
written before 1115 by her confessor, Bishop Turgot of St.
Andrews. The twelfth and thirteenth centuries saw the
compilation of two anonymous and collaborative monastic
chronicles, those of Melrose, which runs down to 1275, and

of Holyrood, which ends at 1356. Of the fourteenth and fifteenth century chronicles, the best is the work known as the *Scotichronicon*, begun by John of Fordun, an Aberdeen priest who died about 1384, and continued to the year 1437 by Walter Bower, abbot of Inchcolm. If these somewhat jejune annals are of limited appeal, true æsthetic values at last appear in the reign of James V: John Major's *Historia Majoris Britanniae* (1521) was, as we have seen, a milestone in diplomacy because of its warm advocacy of Anglo-Scottish union (*cf.* pp. 43–4), while the elegant Latinity of Hector Boece's *Scotorum Historia* (1527) marks it, despite his credulity and superstition, as a product of the humanist revival. The patent defects of the Latin chronicles should not blind us to their real merits: without them, the record of the times anterior to the rise of Scottish poetry and prose would be completely blank, and they helped to instil or foster a quality that was characteristic of the nation and its writers—the spirit of patriotism and of pride in the country's history.

Vernacular poetry, indeed, owed its rise to the awakening, during the English wars, of a truly national sentiment. Apart from a few fragmentary survivals from the early fourteenth century—a lament for the death of Alexander III and a Bannockburn battle-song—and a few poetic exercises in Arthurian legend a little later, it began with the *Brus*, a long, romantic poem in octosyllabic couplets, completed about 1375 by John Barbour, archdeacon of Aberdeen, in celebration of the exploits of King Robert and Sir James Douglas. Using the same metre, Andrew de Wyntoun, prior of St. Serf's, wrote, in the reign of James I, his *Orygynall Cronikil*, tracing the course of history, universal and Scottish, fabulous and real, from the creation to the death of Robert III. Some time before 1488 Blind Harry, or Henry the Minstrel, compiled his *Wallace* in the more ambitious and flexible metre of the heroic couplet. Between Barbour's time and that of Blind Harry, vernacular prose was steadily displacing Latin as the medium for statutes and other official records, and ultimately it was also used for translations of literary works. In 1536 John Bellenden, by command of James V, completed a version of Boece's *Historia* in Scots, while the anonymous *Complaynt of Scotland* (*c.* 1549), a lament about Scotland's woes and English oppression, was a free adaptation from the French of Alain Chartier. Again, it is easy to find flaws in these works—childish acceptance of the legendary and the miraculous, distortion of fact, insensate hatred of 'the auld enemy,' Barbour's frequent and Wyntoun's constant descent into doggerel—but these are redeemed by the poetic inspiration of the best passages of Barbour, Blind Harry and the *Complaynt*, and by the burning patriotism of all five.

Creative and imaginative poetry flourished throughout the fifteenth and sixteenth centuries. The line of 'makars' owed something to Chaucer—the allegorical form and other conventions—but more to their observation and faithful representation of Scottish life and nature, especially in sombre mood. Most of them were versatile artists, seeking different and sharply contrasting modes of self-expression.

James I certainly wrote *The Kingis Quair*, an allegory of love illumined by the emotional afterglow of his own wooing of Joan Beaufort, and also possibly *Peblis to the Play* and *Christis Kirk on the Grein*, vivid pictures of the gaiety and revelry of the traditional folk-festivals, and the first of many such in Scottish literature. The poetry of Robert Henryson, the Dunfermline abbey schoolmaster who survived, as a septuagenarian, well into the reign of James IV, is reflective and didactic, tinged with the melancholy resignation of the ageing scholar. These qualities are conspicuous in *The Bludy Serk*, *The Prais of Aige* and *The Abbay Walk*; and, in his best-known Chaucerian work, *The Testament of Cresseid*, he continued the master's *Troylus and Cryseyde*, rounding off the tale of infidelity by inflicting the horrible punishment of leprosy on the fickle heroine. The ideas of individual responsibility and retributive justice inform his finest poems—*The Morall Fabillis of Esope*, in which human frailty is depicted under animal disguises, and *Robene and Makyne*, an almost painfully realistic little pastoral.

William Dunbar, court-poet to James IV, immortalizes, in his moving elegy, the *Lament for the Makaris*, the names of many brother poets, including Henryson and Blind Harry, Walter Kennedy, his opponent in that poetic contest in vituperation and malevolence, *The Flyting of Dunbar and Kennedy*, and Gavin Douglas, who wrote two allegories, *The Palice of Honour* and *King Hart*, and translated the *Æneid* into Scots verse, using the heroic couplet and inserting, as original prologues, vivid descriptions of scenery and season; but the writer of the *Lament* far outshone not only his contemporaries, but all other poets of the middle ages in Scotland. A faithful recorder of court and city life, in all its showy glitter and rude vitality, at the dawn of the Renaissance, he was a technical perfectionist, with a variety of metres to match his diversity of mood, which ranged from the chaste allegorical fancy of *The Thrissill and the Rois* (celebrating the king's marriage in 1503 to Margaret Tudor) and of *The Goldyn Targe* (romanticizing the conflict between love and reason), or from the disillusioned serenity (reminiscent of Henryson) of *All Erdly Joy returnis in Pane*, through a number of self-seeking *Petitions* and *Complaynts*, and occasional poems in praise of London and Aberdeen or in disapproval of Edinburgh, to the audacious blasphemy of *The Testament of Mr. Andro Kennedy*, the bawdy candour of *The Tua Mariit Wemen and the Wedo*, and the wild conceits of his mordant satire, *The Dance of the Sevin Deidly Synnis*.

Sir David Lyndsay, Lyon king of arms under James V, never joined the reformers—he died in 1555—although he was destined to become their favourite poet for the large volume of propagandist verse in which he satirized the failings of church and state, of crown, court and burgh,—in *The Dreme*, *The Testament and Complaynt of our Soverane Lordis Papyngo*, *Kitteis Confessioun*, *The Tragedie of the Cardinall*, *Ane Dialog betuix Experience and ane Courteour*, and many others, but above all in *Ane Pleasant Satyre of the Thrie Estaitis*, the only complete morality-play that survives from pre-Reformation times. Although very long, verbose and prosaic, the *Satyre* has its dramatic moments, especially in the interludes which show Pauper deluded by the clergy, the Pardoner faking relics, burgess-wives banishing Chastitie, and Follie delivering a sermon; its latent possibilities as 'theatre' were revealed in Mr. Robert Kemp's shortened version, presented at the Edinburgh Festival in 1948.

The cultural achievement of medieval Scotland had both substance and variety—the comely native adaptation of church Gothic, the evolution of courtyard, castle, palace and baronial tower, some skilful and pleasing craftsmanship, the patriotic histories, romantic and factual, in Latin prose and Scots verse, the creative poetry of James I, Henryson and Dunbar, and the beginnings of the drama. New influences, both beneficial and adverse, came in with the Reformation, but the religious disputes of the seventeenth century were generally baleful in their effects upon artistic and literary endeavour.

Large churches did not find favour in the eyes of the reformers, and there is little of note in the ecclesiastical architecture of Protestant Scotland, although a few churches, like Drainie (Moray), Walston (Lanarkshire) and Terregles (Galloway), were built in the Gothic style, with Renaissance details added, and some others, such as those of the Anstruthers, of Pittenweem and of St. Michael's, Cupar, show affinity with the castles of the time. It was now the turn of lairds and burgesses to vindicate the national taste, and in fact the first century after the Reformation was the heyday of the baronial tower. One or two wings were built on, to produce a variety of plans (the L-, T-, Z- and E-types), and the barons strove for elegance rather than strength in their homes. While the towers were left severely plain near the ground, the higher levels were enriched with much pleasing ornamentation—corbels and spired turrets, crow-stepped gables, pack-saddle roofs and great coped chimneys. Among the best examples are Hatton, Greenknowe, Claypotts, Amisfield, Coxton, Craigievar and Scotstarvit, but scores of others were constructed out of the wealth derived from the secularization of church lands. 'They are,' declared James Fergusson in his monumental *History of Architecture* (1865-67), 'as remarkable as any class of buildings erected after the Middle Ages, both for originality and picturesqueness.' The 'Scots Baronial' inspired the urban architecture of the period 1560-1700, most notably in Huntly House, Acheson House, Gladstone's Land and George Heriot's Hospital, all in Edinburgh, the Tolbooth of the Canongate and other burghs, Loudoun

Hall in Ayr, Glasgow Old College, Argyll's Lodging in Stirling, and some of the still surviving houses and 'ports' (town-gates) of St. Andrews and Culross.

Portrait-painting as an art really began in the seventeenth century, with the work of George Jamesone, who was a pupil of Rubens and died in 1644, and of his contemporary, John Scougall, the first of several of that surname; and some good craftsmanship went into the making of such diverse products as wrought-iron staircases, chased pistols, engraved glass and the famous pewter 'tappit hen.'

In the late sixteenth century Sir Richard Maitland both wrote and collected Scots poems; Alexander Scott's love poems include some in the six-line stanza that Burns was to make his own; and Alexander Montgomerie, court poet to James VI and 'the last of the makars,' left two allegories, *The Cherrie and the Slae* and *The Bankis of Helicon*, a *Flyting* with Sir Patrick Hume of Polwarth, and, in his version of *Ha! now the Day dawis*, one of our finest sixteenth-century songs. The stream of Scots verse became a mere trickle in the seventeenth century—*The Life and Death of Habbie Simson, Piper of Kilbarchan*, and the *Epitaph on Sanny Briggs*, written about 1640 by Robert Sempill, one of a family of Renfrewshire poets, the anonymous *Blythesome Bridal*, and little else. Sempill's contemporaries mostly wrote in English, and of these Sir William Alexander, William Drummond of Hawthornden, and the great marquis of Montrose won some distinction in their chosen medium, particularly the last two for their sonnets and love-poems.

Prose underwent a similar change. The cult of literary Latin survived in Bishop John Lesley's *De Origine, Moribus et Rebus Gestis Scotorum* (1578), George Buchanan's *De Jure Regni apud Scotos* (1579) and *Rerum Scoticarum Historia* (1582), and Sir Thomas Craig's *Jus Feudale* (1603) and *De Unione Regnorum Britanniae Tractatus* (1605); but later works of such calibre appeared in English. Scots prose was also ousted (the authorized version of the Bible, 1611, operating powerfully in this direction), but not before a few substantial contributions had been made to the nation's literary heritage. The greatest of them—though written in a blend of Scots and English prose—is John Knox's *Historie of the Reformatioun of Religioun*, which, as the classic account of an important chapter of history, compiled by the chief actor therein, can be compared only to Caesar's *Gallic War*. But at least two other of the many vernacular works of the time are noteworthy for their attractive style and diction and the likeable character of their authors—Robert Lindsay of Pitscottie's *Historie and Croniclis of Scotland*, and James Melville's *Autobiography and Diary*. By the reign of Charles I, the presbyterian historians and diarists, David Calderwood and Robert Baillie, wrote in English with some Scotticisms, while Archbishop John Spottiswoode's *History* and William Lithgow's *Rare Adventures and Painful Peregrinations* are in pure English, and the same is true of such later works as Sir Thomas Urquhart's translation of Rabelais (1653), the essays and pamphlets of the anti-unionist Andrew Fletcher of Saltoun, and Robert Wodrow's *History of the Sufferings of the Church of Scotland from the Restoration to the Revolution*.

If the effects of the Reformation and the subsequent religious conflicts upon Scottish culture were thus mixed, the wider horizons, the tolerance and enlightenment, and the material prosperity, which were the long-term results of the Union, were almost wholly beneficial. The spirit of the age found expression in graceful 'Palladian' buildings, which called for the services of the professional architect. Even before the Union, the neo-classical style had appeared in the country mansions built about the turn of the century by Sir William Bruce, the 'restorer' of Holyroodhouse (1671–79). The cult was carried further by his pupil, William Adam, whose sons, and more particularly Robert (1728–92), achieved fame in England as in Scotland as the most tasteful exponents of Georgian classical architecture and interior decoration. Though the basic design of Edinburgh New Town was that of another architect, James Craig, its finest single feature— the façade of Charlotte square—was the work of Robert Adam, who was also responsible for the Register House, in Edinburgh, for Glasgow Royal Infirmary, and for Culzean castle, in Ayrshire; he began Edinburgh University, but it was completed by another eminent classicist, the builder of the National

Gallery and the Advocates' Library, William Henry Playfair (1789–1857).

In another of the arts, painting, the distinction attained by Scotsmen was in part due to the improvement in living conditions and in educational standards, which meant, on the one hand, patrons of wealth and taste, and, on the other, opportunities for study both in Italy and at home, for Edinburgh had its art school and Glasgow its academy of the fine arts (the latter founded in 1753 by Robert and Andrew Foulis, in whose classical texts Scottish printing touched its peak). There was no lack of encouragement for Scotland's line of portraitists, from William Aikman, who owed much to Sir Godfrey Kneller and Sir John Medina, through Allan Ramsay the younger, whose renderings of ladies of fashion, in their elegant silks and brocades, were much in demand in the middle years of the century, to Scotland's greatest artist of all time, Sir Henry Raeburn, who, between 1787 and his death in 1823, painted so many masterpieces that the whole of his distinguished generation, with the exception of Burns, lives for us to-day in his bold and vivid brushwork—Dr. Nathaniel Spens, Sir John Sinclair, Lord Newton, Viscount Melville, Sir Walter Scott, Macdonell of Glengarry, The Macnab, Mrs. Scott Moncrieff, Mrs. William Urquhart, Lord Braxfield, Dugald Stewart, and scores of others. Raeburn had followers and disciples in Andrew Geddes and Sir John Watson-Gordon, but more interest attaches to the work of two younger contemporaries in branches other than portraiture: the landscapes of John Thomson of Duddingston (1778–1840) and the *genre* paintings of Sir David Wilkie (1785–1841), whose *Pitlessie Fair, Blind Fiddler, Rent Day, Penny Wedding, Blind Man's Buff* and *Highland Family* brought him wealth and a reputation that long outlived him.

The chief feature of the literary history of the period, the vernacular revival, which carried Scots poetry from a seemingly moribund state about 1700 to its greatest height with the poems and songs of Burns, began when the rediscovery of old makars led to the encouragement of new. James Watson, an Edinburgh printer, published his *Choice Collection of Comic and Serious Scots Poems* in the years 1706–11, and William

Hamilton of Gilbertfield issued a modernized edition of Blind Harry's *Wallace* in 1722. Allan Ramsay, the Edinburgh wig-maker and bookseller who was to win renown with his pastoral, *The Gentle Shepherd* (1725), republished the Scots classics in *The Evergreen* (1724), and included many new songs in his *Tea-Table Miscellany* (1724–27). Among the original writers of the time, besides Ramsay and Hamilton, were two well-born songstresses, Lady Grizel Baillie and Lady Elizabeth Wardlaw, the grim satirist Alexander Pennecuick, who was a rival of Ramsay's, and, a little later, Robert Fergusson (1750–74), the gifted and unhappy forerunner of Burns and author of *Auld Reekie, Leith Races, Hallowfair* and *The Daft Days*.

Robert Burns (1759–96) thus owed much both to the earlier makars and to his immediate predecessors. He was able to find just the right words for his matchless songs, but the traditional airs were in many cases still current. Some of his verse is frankly imitative, and most of it shows his close kinship of mood and spirit with the older poets. There are echoes of James I in *Hallowe'en*, of Henryson in *Duncan Gray* and *Man was made to Mourn*, of Dunbar in *Tam o' Shanter, Address to the Deil* and *Death and Doctor Hornbook*, of Lyndsay in *The Twa Dogs, The Ordination, Address to the Unco' Guid* and *Holy Willie's Prayer*, of Sempill in *Tam Samson's Elegy*, of Ramsay in *The Jolly Beggars* and *The Holy Fair*, and of Fergusson in *Scotch Drink* and *The Inventory*. In turn, too, a host of successors have paid him the compliment of treading in his footsteps, and some of them, writing soon after his death, are still remembered for a favourite song or poem—Lady Nairne (*The Land o' the Leal, Caller Herrin'* and *Charlie is my Darling*), Robert Tannahill (*Jessie, the Flower o' Dunblane*) and William Tennant (*Anster Fair*). Yet, if the work of Burns—easily contained within the covers of a single volume—sums up all that was best and most characteristic in the whole range of Scottish poetry, it was given to him alone to stir to their depths the hearts of his fellow-men of all ages and conditions: the memory is truly immortal.

It is indicative of the many-sided life, the boundless verve, of the eighteenth century that the nation, while recovering and revitalizing its distinctive poetic heritage, was making a solid contribution to 'polite letters.' The leading Scottish writers in English form a very varied group—James Thomson, author of *The Seasons* (1726–30), an early and vigorous protest against formalism in verse, and of *Rule, Britannia* (1740), the philosopher David Hume, the historian William Robertson, the novelist Tobias Smollett, the diarist Alexander Carlyle, the political economist Adam Smith, the greatest of British biographers, James Boswell, and Henry Mackenzie, whose best-known work, *The Man of Feeling* (1771), received extravagant praise. The quest for refinement and the fear of appearing provincial led some aspirants to critical approval into ludicrously self-conscious attitudes. Boswell concluded that 'I ought not to keep too much company with Scotch people, because I am kept from acquiring propriety of English speaking,' and recorded that 'the Scotch tones and rough and roaring freedom of manners which I heard to-day disgusted me a good deal' (*London Journal*, February 3 and June 3, 1763). James Beattie, the Aberdeen philosopher-poet, counselled ambitious writers to study the English classics and avoid such Scotticisms as 'allenarly' for 'only' and 'airt' for 'direction'. If consequently Scotsmen's prose often had a 'bookish' ring, it was nevertheless sufficiently distinguished to excuse such vagaries.

Scotland's amazing record of multilingual virtuosity is completed by the appearance in print of a few slender but meritorious collections of Gaelic verse—the martial poetry of the Jacobite Alexander Macdonald, published in 1751, the popular hymns of Dugald Buchanan, and the scenic descriptions and Jacobite songs of Duncan Ban MacIntyre (who had fought on the Hanoverian side in 1745–46). It was, however, in another and more controversial manner that 'the romance of the Highlands' made its first impact on the outside world. Now generally accepted as very free adaptations and expansions of Celtic legends, James Macpherson's Ossianic 'translations' (*Fingal*, 1762, and *Temora*, 1763) were the literary sensation of their day, and they prepared England and Europe for Scott's sentimental interpretation of the Highland way of life.

Only in one department of letters did real success elude the

versatile Scot. Though many plays were written and produced, though there are dramatic passages in much of the
poetry of the age, though John Home was acclaimed a second
Shakespeare for his *Douglas* (1756), Scotland and the stage, so
far as first-class work is concerned, remained strangers to
each other.

Although in the opening years of the nineteenth century
Thomas Campbell and John Galt both took the high road to
London—the one to become the poet of war and patriotism,
the other to present authentic pictures of Scottish life in *The
Ayrshire Legatees, Annals of the Parish, The Provost* and *The
Entail* (1820-24)—the afterglow of the enlightenment still
shone on 'the Athens of the North.' The new generation of
literati—most of them contributors to the *Edinburgh Review* or
to *Blackwood's Magazine*—included James Hogg, 'the Ettrick
Shepherd' and composer of Scots songs, ballads and prose
tales, Francis Jeffrey the critic, Lord Cockburn, whose
memoirs faithfully mirror the age, Susan Ferrier, whose three
novels, *Marriage, The Inheritance*, and *Destiny* (1818-31), are
shrewd commentaries on Scottish society, Christopher North
(Professor John Wilson), the main writer of the once highly
esteemed *Noctes Ambrosianae* (1822-35), John Gibson Lockhart,
Scott's son-in-law and biographer, and David M. Moir,
author of *Mansie Wauch*. But head and shoulders above his
associates stood Sir Walter Scott, who showed forth to the
world the mind and spirit of Scotland in four several ways—
first, in rescuing from oblivion and immortalizing, in *The
Minstrelsy of the Scottish Border* (1802-03), many ballads
anciently recited to the accompaniment of the harp; next, in
presenting romantic chapters from the country's past in his
long, narrative poems (*The Lay of the Last Minstrel, Marmion*
and *The Lady of the Lake*, 1805-10); above all, in creating the
historical novel, especially in his Scottish masterpieces,
Waverley, Guy Mannering, Old Mortality, Rob Roy and *Heart of
Midlothian* (1814-18); and, finally, in surmounting the disaster of the Constable crash (1826) with courage, honour and
integrity worthy of the noblest hero of fiction.

The brilliance of Edinburgh's Athenian age was fatally
dimmed by the death of Scott in 1832. The culture of

Victorian Scotland was uneven, strangely rootless, dogged by the crass materialism and class divisions of industrialism. In architecture the vogue was for revived Gothic or a bastard form of Scots Baronial. Typical of the taste of the time were the Scott Monument at Edinburgh, Balmoral and Glamis castles, Marischal College at Aberdeen, the new Glasgow University buildings at Gilmorehill, and Fettes College; yet classical styles were handled with distinction by Alexander ('Greek') Thomson at Glasgow and by Sir Rowand Anderson at Edinburgh. In the closing years of the century Charles Rennie Mackintosh, the designer of the Glasgow Art School and a pioneer of modern functionalism, was protesting vigorously against artificiality and elaboration; recognition of his great talent was to come slowly, and mainly for his work on the Continent.

In painting the record is very much better. In the middle years of the century the sentimental Highland scenes depicted by Horatio McCulloch, the historical pictures and landscapes of Sir George Harvey, and the homely, nostalgic paintings of the Gallovidian brothers, John and Thomas Faed, were all popular; a little later, Sir William Orchardson and John Pettie executed fine *genre* or took their subjects from the past, while John MacWhirter again romanticized the mountains and glens of the north. From about 1880, in a revolt against the academic and conventional that was parallel to that of the French impressionists, the Glasgow School was developing the bold use of colour and exploring the qualities of light and shade. This group (which dominated Scottish art until 1914) included W. Y. Macgregor, William McTaggart, E. A. Hornel, Alexander Roche, E. A. Walton and George Henry; associated with them was the sculptor, James Pittendrigh Macgillivray, and they influenced the early work of Sir James Guthrie, who was later a successful and fashionable portrait painter.

In Thomas Carlyle and Robert Louis Stevenson Victorian Scotland produced two writers who were nearly, if not quite, of the first rank. If both of them left Scotland (and it is of interest that each was in turn an unsuccessful applicant for a Scottish chair), their Scottish heritage was, and remained, fundamental. Underlying his admiration of Germany and his feeling for the great man as the shaper of destiny was the self-righteous 'dourness' of the Covenanting forebears of 'the sage of Chelsea'; and, besides his stylish verse (which he himself deprecated), the author of *Dr. Jekyll and Mr. Hyde* and *A Lodging for the Night* drew on Scottish themes for some of his best work—*Kidnapped* (1886), *The Master of Ballantrae* (1889), and the unfinished masterpiece, *Weir of Hermiston* (published posthumously in 1897).

The mid-century prose favourites—none of them now as well thought of as they were in their own day—included James Grant's historical novels, *The Romance of War* and *The Yellow Frigate*, the military and sporting novels of George Whyte-Melville, Dr. John Brown's immensely popular *Rab and his Friends* (1859), and the north-eastern dialect stories of George Macdonald. Sir James Barrie's early Scottish work—*Auld Licht Idylls, A Window in Thrums* and *The Little Minister* (1888–91)—had, despite some idealization, greater fidelity to the Scottish scene as well as higher literary merit, but the administration of prodigious over-doses of sentiment by his inferior imitators produced the 'Kailyard' novels of S. R. Crockett (*The Stickit Minister*, 1893), of Ian Maclaren (*Beside the Bonny Brier Bush*, 1894), and, at a still lower level, of Annie S. Swan.

Some good prose literature was contributed by the scholars and specialists of the period. Among the best were Thomas Chalmers, the divine, Hugh Miller, the geologist (whose autobiography, *My Schools and Schoolmasters*, 1852, is a classic), David Masson, the biographer of Milton, Andrew Lang, historian and folklorist, two 'lay' philosophers in the world of politics, the earl of Balfour and Viscount Haldane, and Sir James Frazer, whose monumental *Golden Bough* was first published in 1890.

The passage of time has been unkind to the poetry of the age, which ranged from W. E. Aytoun's *Lays of the Scottish Cavaliers* (1848), Alexander Smith's ambitious *Life Drama* (1853), and the voluminous original work and translations of John Stuart Blackie, through the light verse of Stevenson and Lang, to the melancholy James Thomson's *City of Dreadful*

Night (1880) and to the metrical counterpart of Kailyard fiction—*Horace in Homespun* (1886) and *Ochil Idylls* (1891), by Hugh Haliburton (J. Logie Robertson). The thin stream of Gaelic verse continued, from Ewen Maclachlan at the opening of the century to Mary Mackellar near its close, but it did not pierce the language barrier. The Highland impact on Scottish letters was much stronger in other directions—in works of scholarship like W. F. Skene's *Celtic Scotland* (1876–80), or in the glamorized legends, in prose and verse, of Fiona Macleod (William Sharp).

It is still too soon to attempt a final evaluation of Scotland's varied and tumultuous record in arts and letters in the present century, but it is at least clear that creative work of value and perception has been produced in several fields. Sir Robert Lorimer, the leading architect, is happily commemorated by his Thistle chapel (St. Giles, Edinburgh), his restoration of Dunderave castle (Argyll) in the best Scots Barional style, and his controversial but much admired National War Memorial, within Edinburgh castle. Sir Patrick Geddes, the professor of botany who took up the study of civics, was one of the founders of modern town planning. During the half century three Scotsmen gained world-wide renown for their etchings —Sir D. Y. Cameron, Sir Muirhead Bone and James McBey —and three others, whose art was strongly influenced by Cézanne and the French post-impressionists, came to be known as 'the Scottish colourists'—S. J. Peploe, Leslie Hunter and F. C. B. Cadell.

In both music and drama the stirring of new life is unmistakable, especially by way of the organization of communal effort. Important landmarks were the formation, as early as 1891, of *An Comunn Gaidhealach*, dedicated to the promotion of the use of the Gaelic language and the cultivation of Gaelic literature, music and art; the foundation, in 1905, of the Glasgow Orpheus Choir, under Hugh (later Sir Hugh) Roberton as conductor; the inception, in 1927, of the Scottish Community Drama Association's annual one-act play festivals, which evoked, from towns and villages throughout the land, tremendous interest in the amateur theatre; and the holding, each year from 1947, of Edinburgh's astonishingly successful International Festival of Music and Drama. In music, it is true, individual achievement still lagged somewhat: Scotland has still to produce a great composer. Yet Marjorie Kennedy Fraser, by collecting, just in time, her *Songs of the Hebrides*, did for Celtic folk-song what Burns, Scott and others had already accomplished for Lowland tunes and Border ballads. And as regards the output of original dramatic work the record of the half-century far outshines that of any previous age, for it embraces the careers of two outstanding writers for the stage as well as a number of other competent craftsmen. Sir James Barrie's fine sense of theatre was exemplified, perhaps at its best, in *The Admirable Crichton* (1902), *Peter Pan* (1904), *What Every Woman Knows* (1908), *Dear Brutus* (1917) and the unfinished *Shall We Join the Ladies?* (1921); and, while the plays of James Bridie (Dr. Osborne Mavor) were of uneven merit, he attained rare dramatic power and coherence in his finest works, *The Anatomist* (1931) and *A Sleeping Clergyman* (1933), and there are memorable passages in such others as *Tobias and the Angel* (1931) and *Mr. Bolfry* (1943).

The prose literature of the period is remarkable for its range and versatility; especially noteworthy are the historical romances of Neil Munro and John Buchan (Lord Tweedsmuir), the short stories of R. B. Cunninghame Graham and Naomi Mitchison, the cosmopolitan novels and Highland skits of Sir Compton Mackenzie, the satires and fantasies of Eric Linklater, the sensitive North of Scotland tales of Neil Gunn, and such signal successes as Norman Douglas's *South Wind* (1917), A. J. Cronin's *Hatter's Castle* (1931) and George Blake's *The Shipbuilders* (1935). All of these, and more besides, have their merits; but two works of deeper significance demand special mention. (A harsh fate linked them, for both writers were cut off in early manhood, while their talents were still developing.) George Douglas Brown's *The House with the Green Shutters* (1901) was more than a counterblast to the saccharine sentimentalities of the Kailyard school; a grimly realistic study of the seamy side of life in a Scottish village, informed by a Greek sense of tragic destiny, it has taken its place among our classics of fiction. An even more penetrating analysis of the Scottish scene is presented in *Sunset Song, Cloud Howe* and *Grey Granite* (1932–34), forming the trilogy, *A Scots Quair*, by Lewis Grassic Gibbon (J. Leslie Mitchell). In exquisite prose, marked by lilting cadences which echo the rhythmic speech of the east country, and by the unobtrusive but always apt use of vernacular words and phrases, Gibbon recaptured the feel of countryside, village and town, the nuances and rich variety of Scottish life, in a masterpiece which, while true to the best native traditions, is, like all great fiction, universal in its appeal.

The task of assessing the poetry of the first half of the century is rendered uncommonly difficult by conflicting views, and even some strife, as to the choice of the linguistic medium. Gaelic poets include Sorley Maclean and George Campbell Hay, while John Davidson, Edwin Muir and many others have written solely or partly in English; but chief interest has centred in the use of Scots. From the 1920s the poets of the Scottish Renaissance have evolved a frankly artificial but, to their minds, appropriate diction, sometimes called 'plastic' or 'synthetic' Scots, but latterly, and perhaps less felicitously, 'Lallans,' compounded of the spoken dialect, Middle Scots archaisms, foreign words and neologisms, and characterized by new vowel symbols (*aa* and *ü*), the use of *i* for *in* and *o* for *of* or *o'*, and the present participle ending in –*an*. The most admired exponents of the new medium have been Hugh MacDiarmid (C. M. Grieve), Maurice Lindsay, Douglas Young and Sydney Goodsir Smith; and comparable 'literary' overtones are to be found in the vernacular as practised by Lewis Spence, Pittendrigh Macgillivray, William Jeffrey, William Soutar and Alexander Scott. Meanwhile, another group of poets, while arousing no controversy, has produced pleasing work by adhering to the genuine spoken vernacular: recognizably and attractively Scottish is the verse of Charles Murray, Violet Jacob, John Buchan, Sir Alexander Gray and Marion Angus. Whether it is in their songs and ballads, translations and adaptations, or in the more self-conscious and 'bookish' art of the Lallans poets, that the authentic voice of the modern makar is to be heard, is still open to argument.

L

If there is here a large question, that question will probably be unanswered for some time, for past experiences suggest that a full generation must elapse before the shifting patterns of literary fashion can be appreciated at their true worth. So it is with the multifarious strivings and accomplishments in the allied branches of contemporary culture. It is hard to make a final—possibly even a tentative—assessment of such varied activities as the architectural designs and ideas of Robert Hurd, the paintings of William Crosbie, J. D. Fergusson or William Gillies, the musical compositions of F. G. Scott and C. T. Davie, the dramatic works of Robert Kemp and Robert McLellan, and the documentary films of John Grierson. It can, however, be said that individual achievements look like matching the fruitful communal enterprises of recent times that went to the establishment of the Scottish Orchestra, the Saltire Society, the several 'little' theatres, and the great Edinburgh Festival.

The same general comment will apply as well to arts and letters as to the other main aspects of the national life— political, economic, social, religious and educational—in the middle years of the twentieth century: while there are failings to be redeemed, gaps to be filled or at any rate acknowledged, and certainly no grounds for complacency, the practice of self-criticism, the quest for fresh formulæ, the readiness to embark on new projects, together with a determination to retain or revive what is best in the heritage of bygone ages, are sufficiently evident to be hailed as symptoms of present health and as good auguries for the Scotland of to-morrow.

Bibliographical Note

(The following note is not intended to be complete in itself, but rather to indicate the more important of the recent books and to show how they supplement the older authorities. That something of the sort is called for is suggested by the fact that our fullest bibliographies were compiled a generation ago.)

General Works

The soundest of general histories is still P. H. Brown, *History of Scotland* (3 vols., 1900–09; Library edition, 1911); more colourful in parts, but less balanced, is A. Lang, *A History of Scotland* (4 vols., 1900–07). The best of the one-volume works are R. S. Rait, *History of Scotland* (H.U.L., 1914; new edition, 1946), C. S. Terry, *A History of Scotland* (1920), and R. L. Mackie, *A Short History of Scotland* (1930). A. M. Mackenzie's six-volume history (various titles, 1934–41), the same writer's *The Kingdom of Scotland* (1940; new edition, 1947), and G. M. Thomson, *A Short History of Scotland* (1932), are lively 'nationalist' versions that challenge the traditional view at many points; they are more remarkable for literary style and fluency than for sound documentation or historical accuracy. W. C. Dickinson, G. Donaldson and I. A. Milne, *A Source Book of Scottish History* (vols. i and ii, 1952–53; vol. iii in the press), is a balanced and scholarly selection from records and literary authorities. A. M. Mackenzie, *Scottish Pageant* (4 vols., 1946–50), is an eminently readable and entertaining anthology, coming down to 1800.

Publication of the basic national records proceeds, albeit slowly; the latest to appear are *The Register of the Privy Seal*, vol. iv, 1548–56 (ed. J. Beveridge, 1952), and *The Calendar of Scottish Papers*, vol. xii, 1595–97 (cd. M. S. Giuseppi, 1952).

The fullest bibliographies are G. F. Black, *List of Works relating to Scotland* (1916), and Sir A. Mitchell and C. G. Cash, *A Contribution to the Bibliography of Scottish Topography* (Scot. Hist. Soc., 2 vols., 1917). A good select list is in Brown's *History*, vol. iii (1909), and the latest pamphlet on the subject is H. W. Meikle, W. Beattie and H. H. Wood, *Scotland—A Select Bibliography* (C.U.P., 1950). Mention should also be made of *Bibliotheca Scotica*, the catalogue of John Smith and Son, of Glasgow (1926), which, as every Scottish historian knows, is one of the handiest of helps. Indispensable guides for the student are C. S. Terry, *A Catalogue of the Publications of Scottish Historical and Kindred Clubs and Societies* (1909), and its continuation to 1927, by C. Matheson (1928); and C. S. Terry, *An Index to the Papers relating to Scotland . . . in the Historical MSS. Commission's Reports* (1908).

For a quarter of a century (1903–28) articles on every subject and period appeared in the *Scottish Historical Review*, and its resumption in 1947, after a long suspension, was a welcome event. The Scottish History Society continues its fruitful work of publishing manuscripts; and a few local societies are still active, notably the Third Spalding Club, the Dumfriesshire and Galloway Natural History and Antiquarian Society, the East Lothian Antiquarian and Field Naturalists' Society, and the Ayrshire Archæological and Natural History Society. Noteworthy among recent works of reference are W. J. Watson, *History of the Celtic Place-names of Scotland* (1926), M. Stuart, *Scottish Family History* (1930), and G. F. Black, *The Surnames of Scotland* (1946). Of books of general interest and wide appeal, two are outstanding: H. W. Meikle (ed.), *Scotland: A Description of Scotland and Scottish Life* (1947), a comprehensive survey with historical overtones, and W. Notestein, *The Scot in History* (1947), a shrewd and perceptive appraisal by a kindly American scholar.

Pre-Union History—Chapters 1 and 2

On pre-history and the Roman occupation, the new facts and interpretations (suggested by air-photography as well as 'digs') are presented in Sir G. Macdonald, *The Roman Wall in Scotland* (new edition, 1934), V. G. Childe, *The Prehistory of Scotland* (1935) and *Scotland before the Scots* (1946), H. M. Chadwick, *Early Scotland* (1949), and O. G. S. Crawford, *The Topography of Roman Scotland* (1949). Those concerned with the earliest period of truly 'Scottish' history should see W. D. Simpson, *The Historical Saint Columba* (1927) and *The Celtic Church in Scotland* (1935), D. A. Mackenzie, *Scotland, the Ancient Kingdom* (1930), J. A. Duke, *The Columban Church* (1932), and G. A. F. Knight, *Archæological Light on the Early Christianizing of Scotland* (2 vols., 1933), as well as A. O. Anderson, *Scottish Annals from English Chroniclers* (1908) and the monumental *Early Sources of Scottish History* (2 vols., 1922).

For the medieval background, certain older works still hold the field—Sir A. H. Dunbar, *Scottish Kings, 1005–1625* (1899), Sir

A. C. Lawrie, *Early Scottish Charters* (1905) and *Annals of the Reigns of Malcolm and William* (1910), and J. Dowden, *The Medieval Church in Scotland* (1910) and *The Bishops of Scotland* (1912); but F. M. Powicke and others, *Handbook of British Chronology* (1939), gives Scottish as well as English data. Constitutional studies have been greatly advanced by R. S. Rait, *The Parliaments of Scotland* (1924), D. Murray, *Early Burgh Organisation in Scotland* (2 vols., 1924, 1932), T. Pagan, *The Convention of the Royal Burghs of Scotland* (1926), R. K. Hannay, *The College of Justice* (1933), Lord Cooper, *Select Scottish Cases of the Thirteenth Century* (1944), and W. M. Mackenzie, *The Scottish Burghs* (1949). Aspects of political history are dealt with in E. M. Barron, *The Scottish War of Independence* (1934), E. W. M. Balfour-Melville, *James I, King of Scots* (1936), and M. W. Stuart, *The Scot who was a Frenchman* [the Regent Albany] (1940). To the wide field of overlap between medieval politics and religion belong A. I. Dunlop, *The Life and Times of James Kennedy, Bishop of St. Andrews* (1950), D. E. Easson, *Gavin Dunbar* (1947), Lord E. Percy, *John Knox* (1937), and W. C. Dickinson, *John Knox's History of the Reformation in Scotland* (2 vols., 1949). On purely ecclesiastical affairs, besides A. R. MacEwen, *A History of the Church in Scotland* (to 1560) (2 vols., 1913, 1918), there is J. A. Duke, *History of the Church of Scotland to the Reformation* (1937).

For the period between the Reformation and the Union, the older works need to be supplemented by A. V. Dicey and R. S. Rait, *Thoughts on the Union* (1920), W. C. Mackenzie, *Andrew Fletcher of Saltoun* (1935), and G. S. Pryde, *The Treaty of Union* (1950); on the religious side, by J. G. Macgregor, *Scottish Presbyterian Polity in the Sixteenth Century* (1926), and G. D. Henderson, *Religious Life in Seventeenth Century Scotland* (1937); and, on the economic and social side, by J. Davidson and A. Gray, *The Scottish Staple at Vere* (1920), J. Warrack, *Domestic Life in Scotland, 1488–1688* (1920), G. P. Insh, *Scottish Colonial Schemes* (1922) and *The Company of Scotland* (1932), and, above all, I. F. Grant, *The Social and Economic Development of Scotland before 1603* (1930).

Political History since the Union—Chapters 3 and 4

The older histories deal sketchily, if at all, with the nineteenth century. The newer short surveys include G. P. Insh, *Scotland and the Modern World* (1932), and J. Scotland, *Modern Scotland* (1953). A. M. Mackenzie, *Scotland in Modern Times, 1720–1939*, forming the sixth volume of her general history (1941; new edition, 1947), and A. D. Gibb, *Scotland Resurgent* (1950), are nationalist re-statements, which, because of their selective approach to the facts, must be used with caution. *The Annual Register* (continuous from 1758) is useful, and is particularly helpful when Scottish affairs receive separate treatment (as they do from 1889 to 1914, and again since 1947). Illustrative extracts from the main sources are provided in J. G. Fyfe, *Scottish Diaries and Memoirs, 1550–1746*, and *1746–1843* (2 vols., 1928, 1942).

The theme of the Jacobites still fascinates many writers; notable among the books of the last generation are A. Cunningham, *The Loyal Clans* (1922); W. Duke, *Lord George Murray and the Forty-Five* (1927) and *Prince Charles Edward and the Forty-Five* (1938); Sir C. Petrie, *The Jacobite Movement* (1932; expanded into 2 vols., 1948, 1950); A. and H. Tayler, *1715: the Story of the Rising* (1936) and *1745 and After* (1938); Sir J. Fergusson, *Argyll in the Forty-Five* (1951); and G. P. Insh, *The Scottish Jacobite Movement* (1952). Also vital for this period are D. Warrand, *More Culloden Papers* (5 vols., 1923–30), and G. Menary, *The Life and Letters of Duncan Forbes of Culloden* (1936); and, for rather later times, J. Fergusson, *Letters of George Dempster to Sir Adam Fergusson* (1934); H. W. Meikle, *Scotland and the French Revolution* (1912); and two biographies of *Henry Dundas, first Viscount Melville*, one by H. Furber (1931), the other by C. Matheson (1933).

For Scottish political history during the last 150 years, no recent work can compare with Lord Cockburn, *Memorials of his Time* (1856; new edition, 1910) and *Journal* (2 vols., 1874), or with J. B. Mackie, *The Life and Work of Duncan McLaren* (2 vols., 1888); but L. C. Wright, *Chartism in Scotland* (1953), and the Marquess of Crewe, *Lord Rosebery* (2 vols., 1931), should be consulted. For the newer nationalism there are, on the favourable side, Sir A. M. MacEwen, *The Thistle and the Rose* (1932), and M. McLaren, *The Scots* (1951), and, on the critical, A. C. Turner, *Scottish Home Rule* (1951).

The Government of Scotland—Chapter 5

Scottish legislation may be studied in the *Public General Acts* (annual vols.) or, rather more conveniently, in *The Public General Statutes affecting Scotland* (3 vols., 1707–1847; annual vols., 1848–1947) and *The Scots Law Times* (annual). For 'The Scottish Standing Committee,' the student should see an article with that title in *Parliamentary Affairs*, vol. v (1952); for central government and the Scottish departments, the official *Handbook on Scottish Administration* (1950); for Scottish finance, the *Report of the Com-*

mittee on Scottish Financial and Trade Statistics, July 1952 (Cmd. 8609); and for *Local Government in Scotland*, two short studies with that title, one by J. D. Mackie and G. S. Pryde (1936), the other by J. E. Shaw (1942). Scottish legal history is the field of the S air Society, founded in 1934; its first volume, *The Sources and Literature of Scots Law* (1936), is especially valuable.

Economic Conditions—Chapter 6

The basic histories are H. Hamilton, *The Industrial Revolution in Scotland* (1932), and I. F. Grant, *The Economic History of Scotland* (1934). Supplementary works dealing with special aspects include T. Johnston, *History of the Working Classes in Scotland* (1920), A. W. Kerr, *A History of Banking in Scotland* (new edition, revised by F. H. Allan, 1926), W. H. Marwick, *Economic Developments in Victorian Scotland* (1936), T. B. Franklin, *A History of Scottish Farming* (1952), A. R. B. Haldane, *The Drove Roads of Scotland* (1952), and J. E. Handley, *Scottish Farming in the Eighteenth Century* (1953). Much information is to be gleaned from the annual white paper on *Industry and Employment in Scotland* (since 1946) and from other official publications, like the *Ministry of Labour Gazette*, occasional surveys by the Board of Trade, and periodic reports by the Department of Agriculture for Scotland. (See also the following section.)

Social Life—Chapter 7

H. G. Graham, *The Social Life of Scotland in the Eighteenth Century* (first published, 1899, illustrated edition, 1937), has now the standing of a classic. It has neither equal nor sequel, but parts of the story are amplified or continued in E. S. Haldane, *The Scotland of Our Fathers* (1933), T. Ferguson, *The Dawn of Scottish Social Welfare* (1948), L. J. Saunders, *Scottish Democracy, 1815–1840: The Social and Intellectual Background* (1950), and M. Plant, *The Domestic Life of Scotland in the Eighteenth Century* (1952). For public health, there are J. D. Comrie, *History of Scottish Medicine* (new edition, 2 vols., 1932), and J. H. F. Brotherton, *Observations on the Early Public Health Movement in Scotland* (1952). The *Census Reports* (decennial, 1801–1931; the 1951 figures now in course of publication) are indispensable for such matters as geographical distribution, age structure, housing and occupations; and the annual and quarterly *Reports of the Registrar-General* bring the vital statistics up to date. Among cognate works are D. F. Macdonald, *Scotland's Shifting Population, 1770–1850* (1937), J. E. Handley, *The Irish in*

Scotland, 1798–1845 (1943), and *The Irish in Modern Scotland* (1947), and J. G. Kyd, *Scottish Population Statistics* (1952).

The greatest of the original sources for the eighteenth and nineteenth centuries, *The [Old] Statistical Account of Scotland* (21 vols., 1791–99), and *The New Statistical Account of Scotland* (collected edition, 15 vols., 1845), are now being reinforced by *The Third Statistical Account of Scotland*: four volumes have, at the time of writing, been issued—*Ayrshire* (1951), *Fife* (1952), *East Lothian* and *The City of Aberdeen* (1953)—and it is planned to complete the survey for Scotland in 38 county and city volumes, which will present an incomparable picture of social (and also economic) conditions at mid-century.

The Churches Yesterday and To-day—Chapter 8

The older church histories require supplementing by Sir T. Raleigh, *Annals of the Church in Scotland* (1921), J. R. Fleming, *A History of the Church in Scotland, 1843–1929* (2 vols., 1927, 1933), F. Goldie, *Short History of the Episcopal Church in Scotland* (1951), and G. D. Henderson, *The Claims of the Church of Scotland* (1951); but A. Carlyle, *Autobiography* (new edition, 1910), still provides the best illustration of the mind and spirit of eighteenth-century 'Moderatism.' H. Scott, *Fasti Ecclesiæ Scoticanæ* (new edition, 7 vols., 1915–28, with supplementary vol., 1950), is standard for biographical details, while M. B. MacGregor, *The Sources and Literature of Scottish Church History* (1934), is a handy bibliography.

Scottish Education—Chapter 9

Various aspects of university affairs are examined in Sir P. Scott Lang (ed.), *Duncan Dewar's Accounts, 1819–1827* (1926); A. Morgan, *Scottish University Studies* (1933) and *The University of Edinburgh: Charters, Statutes and Acts* (1937); W. R. Scott, *Adam Smith as Student and Professor* (1937); R. G. Cant, *The University of St. Andrews: a Short History* (1946) and *The College of St. Salvator* (1950); W. C. Dickinson, *Two Students at St. Andrews, 1711–1716* (1952); and the *Report of the Royal Commission on University Education in Dundee* (1952). Outstanding among contributions to the history of the schools are J. C. Jessop, *Education in Angus* (1931); J. Mason, *A History of Scottish Experiments in Rural Education* (1935); and I. J. Simpson, *Education in Aberdeenshire before 1872* (1947). H. M. Knox, *Two Hundred and Fifty Years of Scottish Education, 1696–1946* (1953), is especially useful for legislation and state action in relation to both schools and universities. The annual reports and occasional publications of the Scottish Education Department (e.g., *Public Education in Scotland*, 1952) are often suggestive. (While this book was in the press, one notable addition to the above list appeared, namely, J. D. Mackie, *The University of Glasgow, 1451–1951* (1954).)

Arts and Letters—Chapter 10

In architecture, to take their place alongside MacGibbon and Ross's standard works of reference (1887–97), the no less substantial *Reports of the Royal Commission on the Ancient Monuments of Scotland* have been published periodically since 1910: the thirteenth report (on the city of Edinburgh) appeared in 1951; and, on a much more modest scale, the Ministry of Works official guides, especially in respect of the larger abbeys, castles and palaces, are helpful and attractive. Useful books are I. G. Lindsay, *The Cathedrals of Scotland* (1926); W. M. Mackenzie, *The Mediæval Castle in Scotland* (1927), and I. C. Hannah, *Story of Scotland in Stone* (1934). As regards painting, I. Finlay, *Art in Scotland* (1948), and S. Cursiter, *Scottish Art to the Close of the Nineteenth Century* (1949), should not be missed; nor, in related subjects, should H. G. Farmer, *Music in Mediæval Scotland* (1931), G. G. Coulton, *Scottish Abbeys and Social Life* (1933), and I. Finlay, *Scottish Crafts* (1948).

The literary histories of J. H. Millar (1903) and T. F. Henderson (1910) are still valuable, but they may be supplemented by A. M. Mackenzie, *An Historical Survey of Scottish Literature to 1714* (1933), and J. M. Reid, *Modern Scottish Literature* (Saltire pamphlet, 1945). Among recent anthologies (often with a useful introduction) are J. Buchan, *The Northern Muse* (1924), W. H. Hamilton, *Holyrood: a Garland of Modern Scots Poems* (1929), M. Lindsay, *Modern Scottish Poetry, 1920–1945* (1946), J. W. Oliver and J. C. Smith, *A Scots Anthology from the Thirteenth to the Twentieth Century* (1949), and D. Young, *Scottish Verse, 1851–1951* (1951).

Index

Abbay Walk, The (Henryson), 308

Abbeys, Scottish, 18–19, 22–3, 48, 284, 304

Abercromby, Sir Ralph (1734–1801), 108

Aberdeen, bishopric, 17, 275; burgh, 22, 34, 92, 140, 148, 157, 159–60, 182, 242; education at, 223, 241, 284–5, and *see* University; *Free Press*, 240; housing in, 239, 250–1; industry and trade, 47, 69, 191, 196, 201, 205–7; *Journal*, 235; North, 152; population of, 229, 230, 237, 245; Royal Infirmary, 293; social life in, 240–3, 259, 309; South, 153; Town and County Bank, 216; University, 40, 43, 285–6, 293, 296, 300, 302, and *see* King's College and Marischal College

Aberdeen, George Gordon, fourth earl of (1784–1860), 109

Aberdeen and Orkney (diocese), 275

Aberdeen-Angus cattle, 199, 209

Aberdeen-Inverurie canal, 204

Aberdeenshire, 21, 91, 152, 158, 160, 193, 257, 288, 291

Abernethy (Perthshire), 284; round tower, 303

Academies, 292, 295

Acadia colonial scheme (1621), 60

Acadia (steamship), 203

Acheson House (Edinburgh), 310

Act against Wrongous Imprisonment (1701), 79, 101

Act of Annexation (1587), 58, 61

Act of Revocation (1625), 63

Act of Security (1704), 81

Act of Toleration (1712), 87, 260, 263

Ada, Countess (d. 1178), 25

Adam, Robert (1728–1792), 293, 312

Adam, William (1689–1748), 312

Adam, William (1751–1839), 157

Adamnan (c. 625–704), 303

Adamson, William (1863–1936), 131

Address to the Deil (Burns), 314

Address to the Unco' Guid (Burns), 314

Administration, Scottish (central), 95, 99, 103–5, 117, 120, 162–6

Admirable Crichton, The (Barrie), 320

Admiralty Court, 173–4, 176

Adult education, 299

Adventure schools, 295, 296

Advocates' Library (now the National Library of Scotland), 313

Æneid (translated by Douglas), 309

Africa, 77, 275

Age distribution of population (1881, 1951), 249, 256

Agincourt, battle of (1415), 37

Agrarian Revolution, 191–3, 198–200

Agricultural colleges, 223

Agriculture, 19–20, 187–9, 191–3, 198–200, 209–10, 212–15, 218–23

Aikman, William (1682–1731), 313

Airdrie, 237, 238, and *see* Coatbridge and Airdrie

Air transport, 217

Alban, 12; nation of, at St. Andrews and Glasgow Universities, 286

Albany, Robert Stewart, duke of (c. 1340–1420), 37; Murdoch Stewart, duke of (1362–1425), 37; Alexander Stewart, duke of (c. 1454–1485), 41; John Stewart, duke of (1481–1536), 44

Albyn (Grieve), 133

Alexander I (c. 1077–1124), 16–19, 23, 25

Alexander II (1198–1249), 20, 23–5, 27

Alexander III (1241–1286), 13, 24–5, 27–9, 307

Alexander, elder son of Alexander III (1264–1284), 28

Alexander, Sir William, earl of Stirling (c. 1567–1640), 311

Aliens Act (1705), 81, 82

All Erdly Joy returnis in Pane (Dunbar), 309

Alnwick, skirmish at (1093), 15; fight at (1174), 26

America, trade with, 78–9, 191, 195–6, 199

American Civil War (1861–1865), 201

American War of Independence (1775–1783), 98–100, 108, 195

Amisfield tower (Dumfriesshire), 310

An Comunn Gaidhealach, 319

Anatomist, The (Bridie), 320

Anchor line, 207

Anderson, J. Maitland (1852–1927), 286
Anderson, Professor John (1726–1796), and Anderson's University, Glasgow, 234, 299
Anderson, Sir Robert Rowand (1834–1921), 317
Anderston (Glasgow), 196, 207, 233, 237
Angles of Northumbria, 11, 12
Anglo-Saxon Chronicle, 26
Anglo-Saxon influences, 12–15, 303–4
Angus, 91, 152, 160, 193–4; nation of, at St. Andrews and Aberdeen Universities, 286
Angus, Archibald Douglas, sixth earl of (c. 1489–1557), 44
Angus, Marion (1866–1946), 321
Angus, North, and Mearns, 160
Annals of the Parish (Galt), 316
Annandale, 20, 33
Anne of Denmark, queen of James VI (1574–1619), 59
Anne, Queen (1665–1714), 79–82, 84, 86, 88
Annuity-tax, 118
Anselm, Saint (1033–1109), 17
Anster Fair (Tennant), 314
Anstruther (Fife), 69, 291, 310
Anti-Burgher (General Associate) Synod, 261
Anti-Corn-Law League, 114–15
Antoninus Pius (86–161), 11
Appeals to House of Lords, 87, 126, 173–6, 266, 269
Arbroath, 46, 202; abbey, 18, 22, 33, 304; Letter of (1320), 33, 34
Architecture, 228, 232–3, 303–6, 310–13, 317, 319, 322
Ardrossan, 204, 217
Argathelians, the, 95
Argyll, 12, 139, 142, 152, 159, 160, 237; bishopric of, 17, 46
Argyll, Archibald Campbell, ninth earl of (1629–1685), 73; John, second duke of (1678–1743), 85, 89–90, 92, 95–7, 107, 163; Archibald (earl of Islay), third duke of (1682–1761), 91, 95–6, 163, 176; John (of Mamore), fourth duke of (c. 1693–1770), 91, 93, 107; John, fifth duke of (1723–1806), 107; George, eighth duke of (1823–1900), 120
Argyll and the Isles (diocese), 275
Argyll in the Forty-Five (Fergusson), 90
Argyll's Lodging (Stirling), 311
Aristotelian philosophy, 285, 290
Arkwright, Richard (1732–1792), 196

Armadale (West Lothian), 250
Arran, James Hamilton, second earl of, and duke of Chatelherault (c. 1515–1575), 50–1
Articles of Perth, Five (1618), 62–3
Asquith, Herbert H. (later earl of Oxford, 1852–1928), 125–7, 129–30
Assembly, General, origin of, 53
Assembly of Divines (Westminster), 65–6
Assembly schools, 295
Associate Synod, 261
Atholl, 23, 93; John Murray, first duke of (1659–1724), 85, 93, 192
Atholl brigade (1745), 93
Attlee, Mr. Clement (b. 1883), 144, 146
Auchterarder (Perthshire), 92, 266
Auld Alliance, the, 30, 35–7, 39–40, 42–3, 48–52, 287
Auld Licht Idylls (Barrie), 318
'Auld Lichts,' 261, 267
Auld Reekie (Fergusson), 314
Aumale, William of (d. 1260), 22
Austin canons, 18
Austria, 138
Autobiography and Diary (Melville), 312
Ayr, 22, 47, 69, 190, 205, 217, 229, 230, 237, 284, 292; *Advertiser*, 240; Bank, 197; district of burghs, 140; division of Ayrshire, 153
Ayrshire, 158, 160, 193, 197, 199, 236, and *see under* Central counties; Central, 153; North, *see* Bute and North Ayrshire; South, 145, 152
Ayrshire Legatees, The (Galt), 316
Aytoun, William E. (1813–1865), 318

Badenoch, 30
Baggot's Hussars (1745), 92
Baillie, George, of Jerviswood (1663–1738), 85
Baillie, Lady Grizel (1665–1746), 314
Baillie, Robert (1599–1662), 65, 312
Baird, Alexander, of Gartsherrie (1799–1862), 207
Baird, Sir David (1757–1829), 108
Baldwin, Stanley (1867–1947), 131, 137–8
Balfour, Arthur J., first earl (1848–1930), 124, 128, 318; Robert A., third earl (b. 1902), 151.
Balliol family, 22, 25, 29–31; John (d. 1269), 22; John, king of Scotland (1249–1315), 29–31; Edward (d. 1363), 34–5
Ballochney railway, 205
Ballot Act (1872), 117, 158

Balmerino, Arthur Elphinstone, sixth Lord (1688–1746), 97
Balmoral castle (Aberdeenshire), 317
Balquhidder, braes of, 91
Baltic trade, 47, 190
Banff, 22, 92
Banffshire, 91, 152, 160
Bank Acts, 1844–1845, 205–6
Banking, 168, 194, 197, 205–6, 216, 265
Bankis of Helicon, The (Montgomerie), 311
Bank of England, 145
Bank of Scotland, 197, 216
Bankton, Andrew MacDowall, Lord (1685–1760), 173
Bannatyne Club (Edinburgh), 239
Bannockburn, battle of (1314), 33, 307
Baptist Union, 273, 276–7
Barbados, 78
Barbour, John (c. 1316–1395), 32, 307–8
Barclay's Bank, 216
Bargarran thread, 194
Barlow, Sir Montague (b. 1868), and the Barlow Report (1940), 143
Barony and baron-court, 33–4, 174, 178
Barony church (Glasgow), 268
Barra (Hebrides), 278
Barrie, Sir James M. (1860–1937), 318, 320
Barrier Act (1697), 258
Bathgate (West Lothian), 291
Baugé, battle of (1421), 37
Beardmore, William, and Company, 208
Beaton, Cardinal David (1494–1546), 49–50, 287; Archbishop James (c. 1474–1539), 286–7
Beattie, Professor James (1735–1803), 315
Beaufort, Lady Joan (c. 1399–1445), 308
Bell, Professor George J. (1770–1843), 173
Bell, Henry (1767–1830), 203
Bellenden, John (flor. 1533–1587), 307
Benedictine order, 18
Benefices Act (1843), 267
Berlin, 107
Bernicia, 11
Berwick, 19, 22, 24, 29–30, 34, 37, 39–41, 205, 284; Treaty of (1560), 52
Berwick and East Lothian, 147, 153, 160

Berwick and Haddington, 141, 145
Berwickshire, 193
Beside the Bonny Brier Bush (Maclaren), 318
Beveridge, Sir William (later Baron) (b. 1879), 143–5, 248
Bible, 50, 51, 311
Biblical criticism, 268, 278–9
Biggar (Lanarkshire), 284, 305
Bilsland, Steven, Baron (b. 1892), 224
Birmingham, 114
Birth rate, 248–9
Black, Professor Joseph (1728–1799), 293
Black Acts, the (1584), 58
Black Bull inn (Glasgow), 234
Blackface sheep, 193
Blackford (Perthshire), 92
Blackfriars division (Glasgow), 126, 128
Blackie, Professor John Stuart (1809–1895), 318
Black Prince (clipper ship), 206
Black Watch, The, 89, 98
Blackwood's Magazine, 104, 240, 316
Blair, Rev. Hugh (1718–1800), 262
Blake, Mr. George (b. 1893), 320
Blantyre (Lanarkshire), 231
Blind Fiddler (Wilkie), 313
Blind Harry, or Henry the Minstrel (flor. 1460–1492), 307, 308
Blind Man's Buff (Wilkie), 313
Bludy Serk, The (Henryson), 308
Blythesome Bridal (anon.), 311
Board of Agriculture for Scotland (1912–1928), 164
Board of Green Cloth (Glasgow), 233
Board of Health, Scottish (1919–1928), 164
Board of Supervision (1845–1894), 164, 180
Board of Trustees for Manufactures (1727), 168, 193–4, 291
Boece, Hector (c. 1465–1536), 22–3, 286, 307
Boer War (1899–1902), 125
Bolingbroke, Henry St. John, Viscount (1678–1751), 88, 163
Bone, Sir Muirhead (1876–1953), 319
Book of Common Order (Knox's), 62
Book of Common Prayer (Anglican), 64, 70; (Scottish Episcopal), 273
Book of Discipline, First (1560), 53, 288
Border tweeds, 202, 215
Borrowstounness (Bo'ness, West Lothian), 68–9, 190, 217
Borthwick tower (Midlothian), 305–6

Boston, Rev. Thomas (1677–1732), 260

Boswell, James (1740–1795), 315

Bothwell, James Hepburn, fourth earl of (c. 1536–1578), 55

Bothwell bridge, battle of (1679), 72; castle, 305; collegiate church, 305; division of Lanarkshire, 152

Bower, Walter (d. 1449), 307

Braxfield, Robert Macqueen, Lord (1722–1799), 101; Raeburn portrait of, 313

Breadalbane, 218; John Campbell, first earl of (1635–1716), 77

Brechin, diocese, 17, 275; schools of, 284–5, 292; round tower, 303

Brewster, Patrick (1788–1859), 114

Bridgeton (Glasgow), 135, 152, 202

Bridie, James (Dr. Osborne H. Mavor, 1888–1951), 320

Brigham-on-Tweed, Treaty of (1290), 29

Bright, John (1811–1889), 114–17, 122

Bristol, 12, 195

Britannia (steamship), 203

British Fisheries Society, 198

British Legion, 254

British Linen Bank, 194, 197, 216

British Railways, 216

British Red Cross Society, 254

British Transport Commission, 216

Britons of Strathclyde, 11, 12

Brora (Sutherland), 237

Brown, George Douglas (1869–1902), 320

Brown, Dr. John (1810–1882), 318

Brown, John, and Company, 208

Brown, P. Hume (1849–1918), 83

Bruce family, 25, 29; Edward, king of Ireland (c. 1276–1318), 32; Marjory (c. 1296–1316), 35; Robert (c. 1078–1141), 20; Robert the Claimant (1210–1295), 29–30; Robert, earl of Carrick (1253–1304), 30; Robert the king, *see* Robert I

Bruce, James (1730–1794), 106

Bruce, Sir William (d. 1710), 312

Brude, king of the Picts and victor of Nechtansmere (685), 12

Bruntsfield links (Edinburgh), 231

Brus (Barbour), 307

Buchan, nation of, at Aberdeen University, 286

Buchan, John Stewart, earl of (c. 1381–1424), 37

Buchan, John, later Lord Tweedsmuir 1875–1940), 320, 321

Buchanan, Dugald (1716–1768), 315

Buchanan, George (1506–1582), 99, 287, 311

Buckie (Banffshire), 224

Burgh court, 174, 176

Burgher (Associate) Synod, 261

Burgh-on-Sands (near Carlisle), 32

Burgh Police (Scotland) Act, 1892, 180

Burgh schools, *see* Grammar schools

Burghs, early, 21–2, 306; parliamentary, 157–60, 180; police, 180–2, 183–4, 245; royal, 46–7, 68, 83, 105, 156–8, 174, 177–8, 180, 189–90; burghs of barony, 46, 178, 180, 189–90

Burke and Hare scandal (1829), 241

Burns, Sir George (1795–1890), 203

Burns, Robert (1759–1796), 102–3, 106, 311, 313, 314, 320

Burns clubs, 253

Burntisland (Fife), 69, 217

Burt, Edward (d. 1755), 234

Burton, John Hill (1809–1881), 83

Bute, 157, 162; John Stewart, third earl of (1713–1792), 98, 107

Bute and North Ayrshire, 141, 153, 160

Butler, Mr. R. A. (b. 1902), 143

Cadell, F. C. B. (1883–1937), 319

Cairngorm (clipper ship), 206

Caithness, 13, 156; diocese, 17, 275

Caithness and Sutherland, 137, 139, 145, 153, 159, 160

Calcutta, 209

Calderwood, David (1575–1650), 312

Caledonia (steamship), 203

Caledonia (Thomson), 133, 274

Caledonian Bank, 216

Caledonian canal, 204, 217

Caledonian Mercury, 231

Caledonian railway, 205, 216

Caledonians, ancient, 11

Calico Printers' Association (1899), 208

Callander (Perthshire), 237

Caller Herrin' (Nairne), 314

Calton (Glasgow), 233, 237

Cambridge University, 172, 298

Cambuskenneth, 34

Cameron, Clan, 91; and *see* Lochiel

Cameron, Sir D. Y. (1865–1945), 319

Cameron, Richard (d. 1680), 75

Cameronians, *see* Reformed Presbyterians

Camlachie (Glasgow), 153

Campbell, Alexander (*flor.* 1836–42), 114
Campbell, Clan, 91, 200
Campbell, Rev. John McLeod (1800–1872), 268
Campbell, Robert, of Glenlyon (1632–1696), 77
Campbell, Thomas (1777–1844), 316
Campbell-Bannerman, Sir Henry (1836–1908), 118, 124, 125–7
Campbeltown (Argyll), 237
Camperdown, battle of (1797), 108
Campsie (Stirlingshire), 291
Canada, 106, 108, 231, 237, 249
Canals, 197, 204, 217
Candida Casa (Whithorn), 17
Candleriggs (Glasgow), 191
Candlish, Rev. Robert (1806–1873), 265
Canning, George (1770–1827), 105
Canongate (Edinburgh), 22, 228, 232, 306; Tolbooth, 310
Canons Regular, 18
Canterbury, 14, 17, 25
Cape of Good Hope, captures of (1795 and 1806), 108
Carberry hill (Midlothian), 56
Carfin industrial estate (Lanarkshire), 213
Carham, battle of (1018), 12
Carlisle, 30, 92, 205
Carlyle, Alexander (1722–1805), 232, 262, 315
Carlyle, Thomas (1795–1881), 317–18
Carnegie Trust for the Universities of Scotland, 300
Carnoustie (Angus), 250
Carolina, North, 98, 231
Carron (Stirlingshire), 105, 197
Carteret, John (Earl Granville, 1690–1763), 95, 97
Cas chrom (foot-plough), 188
Casket Letters, the, 55
Castle, the Scottish, 22, 174, 305–6, 310
Castle Douglas (Kirkcudbrightshire), 250
Cathcart (Glasgow), 153
Catholic emancipation, 99, 105, 110, 270
Catrine (Ayrshire), 202
Catto Committee report (1952), 150–1, 171
Celt and Saxon, conflict of, 13–20, 22–4, 27
Celtic church, 14–19, 303
Celtic football club (Glasgow), 244
Celtic Scotland (Skene), 319

Census report, 1951, 218, 244–51
Central and South-east Scotland regional plan, 224
Central counties (seven), population of, 236, 245
Cézanne, Paul (1839–1906), 319
Chalmers, Thomas (1780–1847), 265, 333
Chamberlain, Joseph (1836–1914), 126; Neville (1869–1940), 138, 142
Chamber of Commerce (Glasgow), 195–6
Chambers's Edinburgh Journal, 240
Chapelhall industrial estate (Lanarkshire), 213
Charles I (1600–1649), 63–7
Charles II (1630–1685), 67, 70–3, 75
Charles VII of France (1403–1461), 37
Charles Edward, Prince, *see* Stewart, Charles Edward
Charlie is my Darling (Nairne), 314
Charlotte Dundas (steamship), 203
Charlotte square (Edinburgh), 233, 312
Chartier, Alain (1385–1433), 308
Chartist Circular, 114
Chartists in Scotland, 110, 114, 115
Chaucer, Geoffrey (*c.* 1340–1400), 308
Chepman, Walter (*c.* 1473–1538), 306
Cherrie and the Slae, The (Montgomerie), 312
Chester, 12
Cheviot sheep, 193
Choice Collection of Comic and Serious Scots Poems (Watson), 313
Cholera, 241
Christis Kirk on the Grein (James I?), 308
Churchill, Sir Winston (b. 1874), 142, 145, 148
Church of England, 66, 83, 264, 269, 273, 279, 282
Church of Scotland, pre-Reformation, 14–15, 17–19, 25–6, 46, 48, 49, 284–7, 304–6; Protestant, 52–75 *passim*, 83, 87–8, 111, 118, 121, 127, 230, 254, chapter 8 *passim*, 288, 295
Church of Scotland Act, 1921, 271
Church of Scotland (Property and Endowments) Act, 1925, 271
Cinema, 253, 322
City Improvement Trusts (Glasgow and Edinburgh), 242
City of Dreadful Night (Thomson), 318
City of Glasgow Bank, 205
Civil Law, 172
Clackmannanshire, 38, 156, 158, 160; and East Stirlingshire, 159, 161

Claim of Right (1689), 76; (1842), 266
Claims of the Church of Scotland, The (Henderson), 281
Clan Chattan, 91
Clan line, 207
Clans, Highland, 20–1, 89–94, 97–8, 188
Clark, George A. (1823–1873), 208
Claverhouse, John Graham of, Viscount Dundee (1649–1689), 72, 75
Claypotts tower (Angus), 310
Clerk, Sir John, of Penicuik (1684–1755), 80
Clermont (steamship), 203
Cloud Howe (Gibbon), 321
Club life in Edinburgh, 232; in Glasgow, 233
Clyde, river and firth, 11, 12, 28, 195, 197, 203–4, 208, 210–12, 214–15, 224
Clydebank, 212, 215, 237, 245
Clydebank Shipbuilding Company, 208
Clyde iron works, 197
Clydesdale, 199; nation of, at Glasgow University, 286
Clydesdale Bank, 205–6, 216
Clydesdale football club, 244
Clyde Workers' Committee (1916–1922), 129
Coalition government (1915–1922), 129–30, 135, 141
Coal-mining, 19, 138, 143, 145, 190, 197, 202–3, 209–12, 215, 217, 218, 221, 224
Coatbridge, 205, 211, 237, 250
Coatbridge and Airdrie, 152, 160
Coats, James (1774–1857), 208
Cobbett, William (1762–1835), 198
Cobden, Richard (1804–1865), 114, 116
Cockburn, Adam, Lord Ormiston (1656–1735), 192
Cockburn, Henry, Lord (1779–1854), 104, 106, 257, 282, 292, 316
Coldingham abbey, 18, 19
College discipline, 290, 293
College of Justice, 45–6, 172; and see Court of Session
Coltness-Wishaw railway, 205
Columba, Saint (521–597), 12
Columbia (steamship), 203
Comet (steamship), 203
Commerce, 13, 19, 21–2, 46–7, 68–9, 75–6, 77–8, 86, 88, 115, 190–1, 195–6, 206–7, 210, 212–13, 214–15, 217
Commercial Bank of Scotland, 205

Commissary courts, 173–4
Commissioners for the Forfeited (or Annexed) Estates, 97, 194, 291
Commissioners for the Plantation of Kirks and the Valuation of Teinds, 265
Commissioners of Supply, 118, 177, 179, 180
Commonwealth, Scotland under the (1651–1660), 67–9
Common Wealth party, 142
Communication of trade (1693), 190
Communists in Scotland, 131, 133, 135, 137, 144–5, 147, 280
Community Drama Association, Scottish, 319
Complaynt of Scotland, The (anon.), 307–8
Comrie (Perthshire), 237
Comyn family, 22, 29, 31–2; John (d. 1306), 31
Confession of Faith (1560), 53, 73; and see under Westminster
Congregation, lords of the, 52
Congregational Union, 261, 269, 272, 273, 276–7, 282
Connecticut, 263
Conservatives and Conservatism in Scotland, chapter 4 passim
Constable, Archibald (1774–1827), 316
Convention of Royal Burghs, 46
Cooper, Lord, cited, 34
Cope, Sir John (c. 1689–1760), 90, 92
Corn Laws, 110, 114–15, 198
Corstorphine (Midlothian), 251, 305
Cort, Henry (1740–1800), 196
Corunna, retreat to (1809), 108
Cottar's Saturday Night, The (Burns), 103
Cotton industry, 196, 200–2, 220
Coulton, Dr. G. G., cited, 284
Counties of cities, 182, 185 (map), 298
Country life, 226–8, 230, 235, 237, 243–4, 255
Country (or Patriot) party, 81, 85
County councils, 123–4, 181–6, 298
Courant, Edinburgh, 231; Glasgow, 233
Court of Criminal Appeal, 177
Court of High Commission, 62
Court of Session, 45–6, 87, 173–7, 265
Court party, 84–5, 87, 95
Covenant, National (1557), 52; (1581), 58; (1638), 64, 70, 259, 261; and see Solemn League and Covenant, and Scottish Covenant (1949)
Cowcaddens (Glasgow), 251

Cowdenbeath (Fife), 237
Cowgate (Edinburgh), 228, 231, 232
Coxton tower (near Elgin), 310
Coylton (Ayrshire), 291
Crafts and craft privilege, 178, 189
Craig, James (d. 1795), 312
Craig, Sir James (1748–1812), 108
Craig, Sir Thomas (1538–1608), 60–1, 311
Craigievar tower (Aberdeenshire), 310
Craigton ward (Glasgow), 251
Crail (Fife), 284
Crawar, Paul (d. 1433), 48
Crawford (Lanarkshire), 22
Crichton church (Midlothian), 305
Crieff (Perthshire), 92, 193, 231, 237
Crimean War (1854–1856), 116
Crinan canal, 204, 217
Crockett, Samuel R. (1860–1914), 318
Crofters' Holdings Act, 1886, 124, 200
Crofting counties, population of, 231, 236, 245
Cromartie, George Mackenzie, third earl of (c. 1702–1766), 91
Cromartyshire, 92, 156, 158; and see Ross and Cromarty
Crompton, Samuel (1753–1827), 196
Cromwell, Oliver (1599–1658), 66–9
Cromwellian Union (1651–1660), 67–8, 75, 156
Cronin, Mr. A. J. (b. 1896), 320
Crosbie, Mr. William (b. 1915), 322
Cross Creek rising (1775–1776), 98
Crums of Thornliebank, 208
Culdees, 14–15, 18–19
Cullen, William (1710–1790), 293
Culloden, battle of (1746), 91, 93–4, 98
Culross, 69, 311
Culzean castle (Ayrshire), 312
Cumberland, 89, 206; William Augustus, duke of (1721–1765), 90, 92, 97
Cumbria, 12
Cunard line, 203, 207, 212
Cupar (Fife), 284, 310
Czechoslovakia, 138, 211

Daft Days, The (Fergusson), 314
Dalcross airport (Inverness), 217
Dale, David (1739–1806), 196
Dalkeith (Midlothian), 205
Dalmarnock (Glasgow), 250–1
Dalmeny (West Lothian), 304
Dalriada, 12
Dalry (Argyll), fight at (1306), 32
Dance of the Sevin Deidly Synnis, The (Dunbar), 309

Dancing, 230, 231, 234, 244, 253, 258
Darien Company (1695–1700), 77–9, 167–8, 191
Darnley, Henry Stewart, Lord (1545–1567), 44, 54–5
Darwin, Charles (1809–1882), 280
David I (1084–1153), 16, 18–21, 23–7, 29, 306
David II (1324–1371), 34–6
David, son of Alexander III (1273–1281), 28
Davidson, John (1857–1909), 321
Davie, Mr. Cedric Thorpe (b. 1913), 322
Dawn of Scottish Social Welfare, The (Ferguson), 240–1
Deanston (Perthshire), 202
Dear Brutus (Barrie), 320
Death and Doctor Hornbook (Burns), 314
Death-rate, 243, 248
Deer forests, 200
De Jure Regni apud Scotos (Buchanan), 311
Dempster, George, of Dunnichen (1732–1818), 196
Den burn (Aberdeen), 239
De Origine, Moribus et Rebus Gestis Scotorum (Lesley), 311
Department of Agriculture for Scotland, 165, 223
Department of Health for Scotland, 165
De-rating, 183, 184
Derby, 90
Derwentwater, James Radcliffe, third earl of (1689–1716), 96
Destiny (Ferrier), 316
Dettingen, battle of (1743), 108
De Unione Regnorum Britanniæ Tractatus (Craig), 311
Development areas, 136, 213, 223
Dewar, Duncan (1801–1868), 297–8
Dialog betuix Experience and ane Courteour, Ane (Lyndsay), 309
Dingwall (Ross), 248
Dirleton castle (East Lothian), 305
Disestablishment (Irish), 118; (Scottish), 118–19, 121, 123, 124, 126–7, 270
Disraeli, Benjamin, earl of Beaconsfield (1804–1881), 112, 117, 119, 123
Disruption (1843), 115, 118, 176, 179, 260, 265–7, 269, 272, 282
Distillers' Company Limited, 208
District committees, 181–2
District councils, 182, 186
Dixon's Blazes (Govan), 203

M

Does Haughty Gaul Invasion Threat (Burns), 102

Dr. Jekyll and Mr. Hyde (Stevenson), 318

Dominica, capture of (1761), 108

Donald Bane, king of Scots (c. 1033–1100), 16

Donaldson line, 207

Douglas, Sir James (c. 1286–1330), 33, 307; Archibald, fourth earl of (c. 1369–1424), 37; William, sixth earl (c. 1423–1440), 39; William, eighth earl (c. 1425–1452), 39; James, ninth earl (1426–1488), 41; Margaret, mother of Darnley (1515–1578), 44; Archibald, duke of (1694–1761), 175; Lady Jane (1698–1753), 175; Stewart, Baron Douglas (1748–1827), 175

Douglas, Admiral Sir Charles (d. 1789), 108

Douglas, Gavin (c. 1474–1522), 309

Douglas, Admiral Sir James (1703–1787), 108

Douglas, Norman (1869–1952), 320

Douglas (Home), 232, 262, 316

Douglas cause, the (1767–1769), 175

Douglases, the, 36, 39–40

Doune castle (Perthshire), 305

Drainie church (Moray), 310

Drama, *see* Theatre

Dreme, The (Lyndsay), 309

Dress, 226, 228, 235, 258

Drumclog, battle of (1679), 72

Drummond, William, of Hawthornden (1585–1649), 311

Drummonds, in Jacobite risings, 91

Dryburgh abbey, 19, 304

Dumbarton, 22, 92, 148, 156, 190; district of burghs, 140

Dumbartonshire, 139, 152, 160, 236, and *see under* Central counties

Dumfries, 22, 31, 229, 234, 284

Dumfries Academy, 295

Dumfriesshire, 34, 89, 139, 152, 159, 160

Dunbar, 22; battle of (1650), 67

Dunbar, William (c. 1460–1520), 286, 308–9, 314

Dunblane, bishopric of, 17, 275

Duncan I (c. 1001–1040), 12, 13

Duncan II (c. 1061–1094), 16

Duncan, Abram (*flor.* 1832–1848), 114

Duncan, Adam, Viscount (1731–1804), 108

Duncan, Rev. Henry (1774–1846), 205, 265

Duncan Gray (Burns), 314

Dundas, Robert, Lord Arniston (1713–1787), 175; Henry, first Viscount Melville (1742–1811), 99–100, 103, 108, 163; Raeburn portrait of, 313; Robert, of Arniston (1758–1819), 100; Robert, second Viscount Melville (1771–1851), 104, 108, 164

Dundee, burgh, 126, 128, 137, 139, 140, 145, 148, 152, 158, 159–60, 182; fealty of clergy at (1310), 32; housing, 229, 250–1; population of, 229, 230, 237, 245; schools, 284–5, 289, 292; social life at, 231, 238, 239, 240, 251; trade and industry, 47, 69, 190, 194, 202, 207, 209, 212, 215–16, 217, 218, 223

Dundee, University College, 297, 301

Dundee, Viscount, *see under* Claverhouse

Dundee Advertiser and *Courier*, 240

Dundee Whig Club, 100

Dunderave castle (Argyll), 319

Dundyvan iron works (Lanarkshire), 203

Dunfermline, 16, 136, 148, 190, 194, 202, 229, 289; abbey, 19, 22, 284, 304, 308; district of burghs, 140, 152, 160

Dunkeld, diocese, 17, 275

Dunlop Rubber Company, 208

Dunnichen (Angus), 12

Dunning, John (1731–1783), 99

Dunnottar tower (Kincardine), 305

Dunoon (Argyll), 234

Dunvegan tower (Skye), 305

Dupplin, Thomas Hay, Viscount (later earl of Kinnoull, 1710–1787), 107

Dupplin moor (Perthshire), battle of (1332), 34

Dutch wars, 68–9, 76

Dyce airport (Aberdeen), 217

Eadmer (d. c. 1124), 17

Early Records of the University of St. Andrews (Anderson), 286

East Anglia, 193

East Indian trade, 163, 195

East Kilbride (Lanarkshire), 224

East Lothian, 245; and *see under* Berwick

Ecgfrith, king of Northumbria (d. 685), 12

Edgar, king of England (944–975), 26

Edgar, king of Scots (1072–1107), 16, 17, 24, 27

Edgar the Atheling (*flor.* 1066-1106), 14

Edinburgh, burgh and city, 16, 34, 43, 64, 68, 83, 96-7, 99, 104-5, 111, 114, 116-18, 132, 140, 145, 147, 148, 157-60, 164, 165, 182; castle, 22, 56, 304, 305, 319; Central, North, South and West, 153; diocese, 275, and *see* St. Andrews and Edinburgh; East, 140, 152; industry and trade, 68, 189, 197, 207, 217; population of, 46, 228, 230, 236, 245; social life in, 228-9, 232-3, 235, 237, 239-43; streets and buildings, 42, 228-9, 232-3, 306, 310, 312-13

Edinburgh Academy, 295
Edinburgh and Glasgow railway, 205
Edinburgh Burgess Club, 231
Edinburgh-Dalkeith railway, 205
Edinburgh High School, 292
Edinburgh International Festival of Music and Drama, 309, 319-20, 322
Edinburgh regiment (1745), 92
Edinburgh Review, 103-4, 240, 316
Edinburgh Royal Infirmary, 293
Edinburgh University, 262, 290-1, 292-4, 296, 298, 300, 302, 312-13
Edmund, prince of Cumbria (*flor.* 1094-1097), 16
Education Act (1496), 286; (1646), 288; (1696), 180, 288
Education Department, 'Scotch' or Scottish, 164, 296
Education (England) Act, 1944, 143
Education in Angus (Jessop), 284
Education (Scotland) Act (1872), 118, 180, 296; (1918), 181, 298-9; (1945 and 1946), 146, 299
Edward the Confessor (d. 1066), 16
Edward I of England (1239-1307), 14, 28-32, 34
Edward II (1284-1327), 29, 32-4
Edward III (1312-1377), 33-5
Edward IV (1442-1483), 41
Edward VI (1537-1553), 50
Edward, son of Malcolm III (d. 1093), 15
Eglinton, Alexander Montgomerie, ninth earl of (*c.* 1660-1729), 192
Egypt, 108, 147
Elcho, David Wemyss, Lord (1721-1787), 91
Elder, John (1824-1869), 207-8
Elementary (primary) schools, 296, 299, 301
Elgin, 22, 229, 237, 284, 289, 304
Elgin Courant, 240

Elgin-Lossiemouth railway, 205
Elginshire, *see* Moray
Eliott, Sir George (1717-1790), 108
Elizabeth, queen of England (1533-1603), 52, 53-6, 58
Elizabeth II, Queen (b. 1926), 150
Elliot, Mr. Walter (b. 1888), 161
Elphinstone, Bishop William (1431-1514), 43, 286
Elphinstone tower (East Lothian), 305
Emigration, 98, 200, 231, 237, 245, 249
Engagement, the (1647), 66-7, 69
Engineering, 204, 207-8, 210, 212, 216, 220, 224, 299
English schools, 285, 287, 288, 292
Entail, The (Galt), 316
Entail Act, 1770, 193
Episcopal Church in Scotland, 97, 259, 263-4, 269-70, 273, 275-6, 277-8, 282
Episcopal Church in U.S.A., 263-4
Episcopalian schools, 295, 298
Epitaph on Sanny Briggs (Sempill), 311
Equal Franchise Act, 1928, 159-60, 181
Equivalent, the (1707), 82-3, 86, 167-8, 193
Eric, king of Norway (d. 1299), 28
Ermengarde de Bellomonte (d. 1234), 25
Erskine, Henry (1746-1817), 101, 103
Erskine, Professor John (1695-1768), 173
Erskine, Thomas, Lord (1750-1823), 103
Esk, river, 49
Ettrick forest, 33
Ettrick Shepherd, the (James Hogg), 316
Evangelical party in the Church, 262-3, 265-6, 270
Evangelical Union, 269
Evening classes, 295, 296, 298-9
Evergreen, The (Ramsay), 314
Ewart, Joseph (1759-1792), 107
Ewing, James (1774-1853), 207
Exchequer, Scottish, 105, 168, 173, 174, 176, 178
Expectation of life at birth (1861, 1931 and 1951), 249

Factory Act (1833), 114
Faed, John (1819-1902), and Thomas (1826-1900), 317
Fairfield Shipbuilding and Engineering Company, 208

Falaise, Treaty of (1174), 26
Falkirk, 128, 148, 158, 190, 193, 204, 211; battle of (1298), 31; (1746), 93; and see Stirling
Falkland palace, 49, 305
Fannich power-stations (Ross), 218
Fastern's E'en, 244, 289
Ferguson, Professor Thomas, cited, 240–1
Fergusson, James (1808–1886), 310
Fergusson, Sir James, cited, 90
Fergusson, Mr. J. D. (b. 1874), 322
Fergusson, Robert (1750–1774), 314
Ferranti Limited, 224
Ferrier, Susan (1782–1854), 316
Fettes College (Edinburgh), 317
Feudalism, 19–21, 33–4, 93, 97, 174, 176, 178, 187–9
Fife, 23, 69, 92, 158, 160, 191, 193–4, 224, 245; Malcolm, earl of (d. 1228), 20; East, 139, 152, 224; nation of, at St. Andrews University, 286; West, 128, 137, 144–5, 147, 152
Fife Herald, 240
'Fifteen rising, the, 89–94, 95–6
Finance, Scottish, 45, 117, 155, 166–72
Findlater, earl of, see Seafield
Fingal (Macpherson), 315
Finlay, Kirkman (1773–1842), 207
Finnieston (Glasgow), 208
FitzAlans, 20, 22
FitzRoland, Alan, lord of Galloway (d. 1234), 22
Fleming, David Hay (1849–1931), 277
Flemish traders, 13, 21–2
Fletcher, Andrew, of Saltoun (1655–1716), 85, 312
Flodden, battle of (1513), 43
Flyting of Dunbar and Kennedy, 309
Flyting of Montgomerie and Polwarth, 311
Fontenoy, battle of (1745), 98
Food and drink, 42, 227, 229, 230, 232, 235–6, 239, 240–1, 242–4, 254, 257–8
Football, 244, 253–4
Forbes, Duncan, of Culloden (1685–1747), 91, 96, 98, 163, 169
Forbes-Mackenzie Act (1853), 116, 242
Fordun, John of (d. c. 1384), 307
Forestry Commission, 223
Forfar, 22, 202
Forfarshire, 139, 194, 288–9, and see Angus
Forfeited Estates (1752–1784), 97, and see under Commissioners

Forster, Thomas (c. 1675–1738), 92
Fort Augustus and Fort William, 89
Forth, river and firth, 11, 16, 19, 68, 90, 149; bridge (railway), 205; (road—projected), 217
Forth and Clyde canal, 197, 204, 217, 231
'Forty-Five rising, 90–4, 97–8, 107
Foulis, Robert (1707–1776), and Andrew (1712–1775), 313
Fox, Charles James (1749–1806), 107
France, 30, 35–7, 39–40, 86–7, 90, 169, 172, 190
Francis I of France (1494–1547), 48
Francis II (1544–1560), 51–2
Franco-Scottish alliance, 30, 35–7, 39–40, 42–4, 48–52, 287
Fraser, Clan, 91; Simon, Lord Lovat (c. 1667–1747), and his son, Simon (1726–1782), 91, 93
Fraser, Mrs. Marjorie Kennedy (d. 1930), 320
Frazer, Sir James G. (1854–1941), 318
Free Church, 117, 118, 126, 175–6, 266–9, 270, 272–3, 275, 282, 295
Free Church College, Aberdeen, 268
Freeman, Edward A. (1823–1892), 14
Free Presbyterian Church, 268, 272
Free trade, 114–15, 136, 199, 212–13, 243
French influences (cultural), 40, 172, 304–5, 317, 319
French Revolution, 100–3, 107, 163
Fulton, Robert (1765–1815), 203
Further education, 299
Fyvie abbey (Aberdeenshire), 18

Gaelic language, 11, 13, 15, 22–3, 288, 291, 315, 319, 320, 321
Gaels, 11–14, 22
Galashiels (Selkirkshire), 201
Gallic War (Caesar), 312
Galloway, 16, 18, 22, 23, 27, 30, 139, 152, 160; diocese of, 17, 46, 275; farming in, 193, 199; 'Levellers' of (1724), 99, 192
Gallowgate (Glasgow), 233–4, 270
Galston (Ayrshire), 250
Galt, John (1779–1839), 316
Gambling, 254, 290
Garbett, Archbishop, cited, 279
'Gardyloo' (Edinburgh), 229
Garnkirk-Glasgow railway, 205
Gartsherrie iron works (Lanarkshire), 203, 207
Gas lighting, 240, 242
Geddes, Andrew (1783–1844), 313

Geddes, Sir Patrick (1854–1932), 319
General Associate Synod, 261
General strike (1926), 132
Gentle Shepherd, The (Ramsay), 314
George I (1660–1727), 88, 94, 95
George II (1683–1760), 94, 108
George III (1738–1820), 98, 107
George IV (1762–1830), 239
George, D. Lloyd (1863–1945), 129, 135
George square (Edinburgh), 233; (Glasgow), 234
George street (Edinburgh), 232
Gibbon, Lewis Grassic (J. Leslie Mitchell, 1901–1935), 320–1
Gibraltar, defence of (1779–1782), 108
Gibson, John (flor. 1760–1780), 234
Gillies, Mr. William G. (b. 1898), 322
Gilmorehill (Glasgow), 298, 317
Gladstone, William E. (1809–1898), 110, 117–20, 122, 124, 158
Gladstone's Land (Edinburgh), 310
Glamis castle (Angus), 317
Glasgow, burgh and city, 22, 64, 92, 96, 99, 105, 125, 132, 134, 135–7, 139–40, 145, 147, 148, 157–60, 182; Central, 152; diocese and cathedral, 17, 46, 275, 304; population of, 46–7, 229, 230, 237, 245, 250–1; schools and colleges, 223, 270, 284, 292, 295; social life in, 224, 229, 233–5, 237–42, 251, 253, 265, 280; trade and industry, 69, 189, 191, 194–7, 201–2, 204–8, 226
Glasgow Advertiser and Journal, 233
Glasgow and Ayr railway, 205
Glasgow and Ayr synod, 70
Glasgow and Greenock railway, 205
Glasgow and South-Western railway, 205, 216
Glasgow Arms Bank, 197
Glasgow Art School, 317
Glasgow Herald, 113, 122, 126, 151, 233, 258
Glasgow Orpheus Choir, 319
Glasgow, Paisley and Johnstone canal, 204
Glasgow Royal Infirmary, 293, 312
'Glasgow school' (painting), 317
Glasgow University, 40, 135, 150, 234, 260, 285–6, 289–91, 292–4, 296–8, 299, 302, 317, and see Old College, Glasgow
Glassford (Lanarkshire), 291
Glassford, John (1715–1783), 196
Glassites, sect of, 260–1
Glen Affric, Glen Garry and Glen Moriston (Inverness-shire), 218
Glencoe, massacre of (1692), 77, 89

Glenelg, Charles Grant, Baron (1778–1866), 108.
Glengarry regiment (1745), 93
Glenholm (Peeblesshire), 291
Glenrothes (Fife), 224
Glenshiel, skirmish at (1719), 89
Glyn, Mills and Company, 216
Godolphin, Sidney, earl of (1645–1712), 86
Godwin, Earl (d. 1053), 16
Goidels, 11, 12
Golden Act (1592), 59, 75
Golden Bough, The (Frazer), 318
Goldie, Mr. F., cited, 273
Goldyn Targe, The (Dunbar), 309
Golf, 231, 234, 239, 244, 253, 290
Gorbals (Glasgow), 140, 152, 233, 237, 251, 270
Gordon family, 21, 91
Gordon, Lord George (1751–1793), 99
Goschen formula (1888), 169–71
Gothic architecture, 304–5, 310, 317,
Govan (Glasgow), 140, 153, 203, 237, 245
Government of Scotland bills (1913 and 1914), 128
Graham, Henry Grey (1843–1906), 228
Graham, R. B. Cunninghame (1852–1936), 123, 133, 320
Grammar (burgh, high, Latin) schools, 284–7, 289, 292, 295; and see Secondary schools
Grampian mountains, 205
Grangemouth (Stirlingshire), 190, 207, 217, 223, 231
Grant, Sir Archibald, of Monymusk (1696–1778), 192, 196
Grant, Clan, 91
Grant, James (1822–1887), 318
Grant, James (1840–1885), 284
Grant, William, Lord Prestongrange (c. 1701–1764), 97
Granton (Edinburgh), 236
Gray, Sir Alexander (b. 1882), 321
'Great Britain departments' in Scotland, 165–6
Great Glen, the, 204
Great North of Scotland railway, 205, 216
Greek, study of, 289, 290, 292
Green, John Richard (1837–1883), 14, 31
Greenknowe tower (Berwickshire), 310
Greenock, burgh, 136, 139, 148, 152, 158, 160; economic and social conditions, 190, 196, 205, 207, 217, 231, 237, 238; West Kirk of, 282

Greenshields, Rev. James, and his case (1711), 87, 175, 260
Gregory family, 293
Greyfriars church (Edinburgh), 268; churchyard, 72
Greyfriars ward (Aberdeen), 251
Grey Granite (Gibbon), 321
Grierson, Mr. John (b. 1898), 322
Grieve, Mr. C. M. (b. 1892), 133; and see MacDiarmid, Hugh
Grouse moors, 200
Gude and Godlie Ballatis (Wedderburn), 306
Guild, merchant, and guild privilege, 178, 190
Gunn, Mr. Neil (b. 1891), 320
Gustavus Adolphus (1594–1632), 64
Guthrie, Sir James (1859–1938), 317
Guthrie, Rev. Thomas (1803–1873), 265, 295
Guy Mannering (Scott), 316

Habeas Corpus Act (1679), 79, 101
Haco IV of Norway (1204–1263), 28
Haddington, 34, 229, 284, 305; district of burghs, 159; and see under Berwick
Haddington, Thomas Hamilton, sixth earl of (1680–1735), 192
Haldane, James A. (1768–1851), 261, 269
Haldane, Richard, Viscount (1856–1928), 131, 318
Haliburton, Hugh (J. Logie Robertson, c. 1850–1922), 319
Halidon hill, battle of (1333), 34
Hallowe'en, 243
Hallowe'en (Burns), 103, 314
Hallowfair (Fergusson), 314
Hamilton, 72, 148; division of Lanarkshire, 141, 153
Hamilton family, 54, 84, 175; James Douglas, fourth duke of (1658–1712), 82, 84, 85, 88
Hamilton, Patrick, abbot of Ferne (c. 1504–1528), 48
Hamilton, William, of Gilbertfield (c. 1665–1751), 313–14
Hamilton, Sir William (1730–1803), 107
Hampden park (Glasgow), 253
Handley, Mr. James E., cited, 238, 274
Handsel Monday, 244
Hannah Institute (Ayrshire), 223
Hanover, house of, 80–1, 84–5, 94, 263

Ha, now the Day dawis (anon.), 306; (Montgomerie), 311
Hapsburg, house of, 53
Harlaw, battle of (1411), 37
Harley, Robert, earl of Oxford (1661–1724), 163
Harris tweed, 202
Harvey, Sir George (1806–1876), 317
Hatter's Castle (Cronin), 320
Hatton tower (Angus), 310
Hawick (Roxburghshire), 201; district of burghs, 158
Hay, Mr. George Campbell (b. 1915), 321
Heart of Midlothian (Scott), 316
Heart of Midlothian football club (Edinburgh), 244
Heavy industry, 203–4, 206, 207–13, 214–15, 218, 220–1, 224–5
Hebrides, 27–8; and see under Isles and Western Isles
Helmsdale (Sutherland), 237
Henderson, Arthur (1863–1935), 131
Henderson, Professor G. D., cited, 281
Henry I of England (1068–1135), 17, 24, 26
Henry II (1133–1189), 24–7
Henry III (1207–1272), 25, 28
Henry IV (1367–1413), 37
Henry V (1387–1422), 37
Henry VII (1457–1509), 42
Henry VIII (1491–1547), 42–3, 48–50
Henry, George (1858–1943), 317
Henryson, Robert (c. 1430–1506), 286, 308, 309, 310, 314
Henry the Minstrel, see Blind Harry
Heresy trials, 48, 260–1, 268
Heriot's Hospital, George (Edinburgh), 310
Heritable jurisdictions, 97, 174, 176
Herring Industry Board, 213, 223
Hertford, Edward Seymour, earl of, and duke of Somerset (c. 1506–1552), 50
Hibernian football club (Edinburgh), 244
High schools, see under Grammar schools
High street (Edinburgh), 228, 232; (Glasgow), 290
Highland and Agricultural Society (1784), 223
Highland education and culture, 23, 60, 288, 291, 295, 315, 319–20, 321
Highland Family (Wilkie), 313
Highland railway, 205, 216

Highlands, economic and social life in, 60, 97–8, 124, 143, 149, 164, 188, 193, 194, 197–8, 199–200, 218, 223, 225, 230–1, 237, 243, 245, 255; political life in, 19, 20–1, 30, 42, 77, 89–94, 97–8, 153; *see also* Emigration

Highlands and Islands Advisory Panel, 223

Highlands and Islands Medical Service (1913), 164, 248

Hillhead (Glasgow), 140, 153, 237

Hillington industrial estate, 213

Historia Majoris Britanniæ (Major), 43–4, 307

Historie and Croniclis of Scotland (Lindsay of Pitscottie), 312

Historie of the Reformatioun of Religioun (Knox), 311–12

History of Architecture (Fergusson), cited, 310

History of the Burgh Schools of Scotland (Grant), 284

History of the Sufferings of the Church of Scotland (Wodrow), 312

Hitler, Adolf (1889–1945), 137

Hogg, James (1770–1835), 316

Hogmanay, 243

Holland, 68, 73, 76, 190

Holy Fair, The (Burns), 314

Holyrood abbey, 18, 22, 284, 304

Holyrood Chronicle, 306–7

Holyrood palace, 55, 73, 312

Holyrood ward (Edinburgh), 251

Holy Willie's Prayer (Burns), 314

Home, John (1722–1808), 232, 262, 316

Home Department, Scottish, 165

Home rule (Irish), 119, 121–2, 127–8; (Scottish), 120–2, 124–5, 126, 127–8, 132–3, 135, 149–51, 162, 274

Honourable Company of Edinburgh, 231

Houldsworth, Henry (1774–1853), 207

House of Lords, *see under* Appeals

House with the Green Shutters, The (Brown), 320

Housing, 42, 227–9, 232–3, 235, 239, 240–1, 242–3, 249–51, 256–7, 280

Hume, David (1711–1776), 232, 262, 315

Hunter, George Leslie (1879–1936), 319

Huntingdon, earldom of, 17, 25–6; Henry, earl of (c. 1114–1152), 25; David, earl of (c. 1144–1219), 25, 29

Huntly, George Gordon, fourth earl of (1514–1562), 51

Huntly House (Edinburgh), 310

Hurd, Mr. Robert (b. 1905), 305, 322

Hutcheson, Francis (1694–1746), 293

Hutchesontown (Glasgow), 251

Huxley, Thomas H. (1825–1895), 280

Hydro-electricity, *see under* North of Scotland

Icolmkill, statutes of (1609), 60

Improvers, *see under* Society

Inchcolm abbey, 307

Inchkeith island, 119

Independent Labour party, 134, 135–7, 141, 144, 147

India, 207, 212, 275

Indulgence, Letters of (1687), 73

Industrial estates, 213, 215–16, 223

Industrial Revolution, 121, 196–7, 200–8, 240–1, 243–4

Infant mortality, 243, 248, 255–6

Infant (nursery) schools, 296, 299

Ingibjorg (d. c. 1065), 16

Inheritance, The (Ferrier), 316

Institute of the Laws of Scotland (Bankton), 173

Institutes of the Law of Scotland (Erskine), 173

Institutions of the Law of Scotland, The (Stair), 172

Intemperance, 116, 230, 235–6, 244; and *see* Temperance reform

Inventory, The (Burns), 314

Inveraray (Argyll), 91

Invergordon naval base (Ross), 169

Invergowrie (Perthshire), 16

Inverness, 22, 47, 69, 91, 229

Inverness Academy, 292

Inverness Courier, 240

Inverness-Nairn railway, 205

Inverness-shire, 90, 92, 139, 152, 160

Inverurie (Aberdeenshire), 204

Iona (Argyll), 12, 303

Iran, 147

Ireland, 11, 18, 47, 112, 169, 190; Northern, 171, and *see* Ulster

Irish Free State, 130, 159, 170

Irish in Scotland, 199, 203, 237–9, 244, 270, 273–5, 278

Iron industry, 146, 147, 190, 196–7, 202–4, 207–8, 210, 211, 212, 215, 217, 220

Irvine, 229, 289; valley, 202

Islay, earl of, *see under* Argyll

Isles, bishopric of the, 17, 46; and *see* Argyll and the Isles

Isles, lords and lordship of the, 35, 37, 42; Donald, second lord (d. *c.* 1420), 37; John, fourth lord (d. *c.* 1498), 41, 42
Is There for Honest Poverty (Burns), 103
Italo-Abyssinian War (1935), 137
Italy, 172, 211–12

Jacob, Violet (1863–1946), 321
Jacobites, 81–3, 85–94, 97–8, 194, 263–4, 315
Jamaica, trade with, 78
Jamaica street (Glasgow), 233
James I (1394–1437), 19, 37–9, 307, 308, 309, 310, 314
James II (1430–1460), 39–40, 305
James III (1451–1488), 28, 40–1
James IV (1473–1513), 41–4, 46, 48, 305, 308
James V (1512–1542), 44, 48–9, 305, 307
James VI and I (1566–1625), 55, 57–63, 65, 75, 77, 311
James VII and II (1633–1701), 72–5
James, Prince, 'the Old Pretender' *see* Stewart, James
Jamesone, George (*c.* 1588–1644), 311
Japanese cottons, 212
Jedburgh (Roxburghshire), 19, 33, 304
Jeffrey, Francis, Lord (1773–1850), 102, 106, 316
Jeffrey, William (b. 1894), 321
Jessie, the Flower o' Dunblane (Tanna-hill), 314
Jessop, Dr. J. C., cited, 284
Jews in Scotland, 277
Joan, queen of James I, *see* Beaufort, Lady Joan
Joanna, queen of Alexander II, 25
John of England (*c.* 1167–1216), 24, 27, 28
John XXII, Pope (1249–1334), 33
Johnston, Rt. Hon. Thomas (b. 1882), 224
Johnstone (Renfrewshire), 204, 231, 237
Jolly Beggars, The (Burns), 103, 314
Jus Feudale (Craig), 311
Justices of the peace, 60, 86, 174, 177, 179, 180, 181
Justiciary court, 173, 174, 176, 177
Juvenile delinquency, 255

'Kailyard' fiction, 318, 320
Kames, Henry Home, Lord (1696–1782), 192
Keith, Sir R. M. (1730–1795), 107

Kelp burning industry, 199
Kelso abbey, 18, 19, 22, 304; its great charter (1159), 306
Kelso Border Mail, 235
Kelvin, William Thomson, Lord (1824–1907), 296
Kelvingrove (Glasgow), 153
Kemp, Mr. Robert (b. 1908), 309, 322
Kenmure, William Gordon, sixth Viscount (d. 1716), 96
Kennedy, Bishop James (*c.* 1406–1465), 40, 286
Kennedy, Walter (*c.* 1460–1508), 308–9
Kenneth MacAlpin (d. 860), 12
Kerrera island (Argyll), 27
Kidnapped (Stevenson), 318
Kildrummy castle (Aberdeenshire), 305
Killiecrankie, battle of (1689), 75, 89
'Killing Time' (1680–1687), 72–3, 75
Kilmarnock, 148, 158, 202, 204, 238; division of Ayrshire, 137, 141, 152
Kilmarnock-Troon railway, 204
Kilwinning abbey (Ayrshire), 18
Kincardine, 160; and *see* Mearns
Kincardine and West Aberdeenshire, 145
King Hart (Douglas), 309
Kinghorn (Fife), 28
Kingis Quair (James I), 308
King's College (Old Aberdeen), 285–6, 293, 297–8, 305
Kingston ward (Glasgow), 251
Kinloss priory (Moray), 23
Kinross-shire, 38, 156, 158; and West Perthshire, 161
Kintyre (Argyll), 16
Kirkcaldy (Fife), 69, 190, 194, 202, 229; district of burghs, 140, 142, 152, 160
Kirkcudbrightshire, 19, 250; and Wigtownshire, 160; and *see* Galloway
Kirkhill (Inverness-shire), 236
Kirkintilloch (Dumbartonshire), 22, 205
Kirk-o'-Field (Edinburgh), 305
Kirk session, 62, 177, 179–80
Kirkwall (Orkney), 217, 248, 304
Kirriemuir (Angus), 149, 202
Kitteis Confessioun (Lyndsay), 309
Kneller, Sir Godfrey (1646–1723), 313
Knightswood (Glasgow), 251
Knox, John (*c.* 1514–1572), 52–4, 99, 264, 287–8, 292, 311–12

Korean War (1950–1953), 147
Kyd, Mr. J. G., cited, 249
Kyle (Ayrshire), 20

Labour party in Scotland, 123–54, *passim*
Lady of the Lake, The (Scott), 13, 22, 316
Laissez-faire, 121, 213
'Lallans' poets, 321
Lament for the Makaris (Dunbar), 308–9
Lanark, 22, 284; division of Lanark-shire, 153; New Lanark, 196
Lanarkshire, 145, 158–60, 194, 197, 201, 211, 224, 236, 250, and *see under* Central counties; North, 152; North-west, 123
Land Court, Scottish, 176–7
Land o' the Leal, The (Nairne), 314
Land-tax, 45, 155, 166–7, 180
Land-use in 1951, 221–2
Lanfranc, Archbishop (c. 1005–1089), 14
Lang, Andrew (1844–1912), 318
Langholm, battle of (1455), 39
Langholm, New (Dumfriesshire), 231
Langside, battle of (1568), 56
Largs (Ayrshire), 234; battle of (1263), 28
Larkhall (Lanarkshire), 213, 231
Lateran Council (1139), 14
Latin language, 284–5, 286, 289, 290, 292, 293, 306–7, 311
Lauder bridge (Berwickshire), 41
Lauderdale, John Maitland, second earl and first duke of (1616–1682), 72, 162
Law, Andrew Bonar (1858–1923), 124, 130
Law, Scots, and law courts, 172–7, 258
Lawers power station (Perthshire), 218
Lawnmarket (Edinburgh), 228
Laws of the Four Burghs, 172
Lay of the Last Minstrel, The (Scott), 316
Lays of the Scottish Cavaliers (Aytoun), 318
League of Nations, 130
Lee, Dr. Robert (1804–1868), 268
Leighton, Robert, archbishop of Glasgow (1611–1684), 71
Leith, burgh, 139, 145, 159, 237, 245; district of burghs, 139, 158; division of Edinburgh, 153; port of, 47, 68, 190, 196, 207, 217; sea-bathing at (1761), 232
Leith Races (Fergusson), 314

Lennox, Matthew Stewart, earl of (1516–1571), 44, 56; Esmé Stewart, duke of (c. 1542–1583), 56
Lerwick (Shetland), 248
Lesley, Bishop John (1527–1596), 311
Leslie, Alexander, first earl of Leven (c. 1580–1661), 64
Lesmahagow priory (Lanarkshire), 18
Letham (Angus), 231
Letters from a Gentleman in the North of Scotland (Burt), 234
Letters of Malachi Malagrowther (Scott), 105
Leuchars church (Fife), 304
'Levellers' of Galloway (1724), 99, 192
Leven, earl of, *see* Leslie
Leyden University, 172
Liberal Federation, Scottish, 127, 133
Liberal League (1902), 125
Liberal National party, 145
Liberals and Liberalism in Scotland, chapter 4, *passim*
Liberal Unionists, *see* Unionists
Life and Death of Habbie Simson, Piper of Kilbarchan (Sempill), 311
Life Drama (Smith), 318
Life of St. Columba (Adamnan), 303
Life of St. Margaret (Turgot), 306
'Lifter' controversy (1783), 261
Lindores abbey (Fife), 18, 22
Lindsay, Mr. Maurice (b. 1918), 321
Lindsay, Robert, of Pitscottie (c. 1500–1565), 312
Lindsays, family of the, 22
Linen industry, 88, 190, 191, 193–5, 200–1, 202, 211–12
Linklater, Mr. Eric (b. 1899), 320
Linlithgow, 22, 34, 49, 62, 68–9, 229, 284, 305; and *see* West Lothian
Linton, Bernard de, abbot of Arbroath (d. 1331), 33–4
Lipton, Sir Thomas (1850–1931), and Lipton's Limited (1885), 208
Lismore, or Argyll, bishopric of, 17, 46
Literary Society (Glasgow), 233
Lithgow, William (c. 1582–1645), 312
Little Minister, The (Barrie), 318
Liverpool, Robert Jenkinson, second earl of (1770–1828), 108
Lloyds Bank, 216
Local government, 177–86
Local Government Board (1894), 164
Local Government (Scotland) Act (1929), 181–3; (1947), 184
Lochbay (Skye), 198
Loch Fyne (Argyll), 204

Lochgelly (Fife), 237
Lochiel, Donald Cameron of (c. 1695–1748), 93
Loch Katrine water supply (1 859), 242
Loch Leven castle, 56
Loch Lomond, 92
Loch Shin power stations (Sutherland), 218
Loch Sloy power stations (Dumbartonshire), 218
Locke, John (1632–1704), 293
Lockhart, George, of Carnwath (1673–1731), 85, 88
Lockhart, John G. (1794–1854), 316
Lodging for the Night, A (Stevenson), 318
Lollards of Kyle (1494), 48
London, 36, 99, 114, 149, 160, 165, 168, 191, 195, 197, 217, 234, 266, 309, 316
London and North-Eastern railway, 216
London Journal (Boswell), 315
London, Midland and Scottish railway, 216
Longforgan (Perthshire), 231, 237
Longniddry (East Lothian), 253
Long Parliament (1642–1652), 65–7
Lords of the Articles, 45, 60
Lorimer, Sir Robert (1864–1929), 319
Lossiemouth (Moray), 205
Lothian, East, see East Lothian and also Berwick
Lothian, nation of, at St. Andrews University, 286
Lothian, West, see West Lothian and also Linlithgow
Lothians, 12–13, 15–16, 18, 193, 198
Loudoun, Hugh Campbell, third earl of (d. 1731), 192; John, fourth earl of (1705–1782), 91, 93
Loudoun Hall (Ayr), 310–11
Loudoun hill, battle of (1307), 32
Loughborough, Alexander Wedderburn, Lord (later earl of Rosslyn) (1733–1805), 108
Louis XIV of France (1638–1715), 80, 86
Lovat, Lord, see Fraser, Simon
Low Countries, 47, 172, 190, and see Holland
Lumphanan, battle of (1057), 13
Lyndsay, Sir David (1490–1555), 309, 314

Macaulay, T. B. (1800–1859), 77, 111, 115

Macaulay Institute (Midlothian), 223
Macbeth (c. 1005–1057), 13, 14
Macbeth (Shakespeare), 12
McBey, Mr. James (b. 1883), 319
MacCormick, Mr. J. M. (b. 1904), 133, 150
McCrie, Thomas (1772–1835), 277
McCulloch, Horatio (1805–1867), 317
MacDiarmid, Hugh (Mr. C. M. Grieve, b. 1892), 321
Macdonald, Alexander (c. 1700–1780), 315
Macdonald, Clan, 91; of Keppoch, 93; of Sleat, 91
Macdonald, Flora (1722–1790), 98
Macdonald, George (1824–1905), 318
MacDonald, J. Ramsay (1866–1937), 124, 131, 134
Macdonell of Glengarry (Raeburn portrait), 313
MacEwen, Sir Alexander (1875–1941), 137
Macfarlane, Dr. Patrick (1781–1849), 282
Macgillivray, James Pittendrigh (1856–1938), 317, 321
Macgregor, Clan, 91, 92
Macgregor, W. Y. (1855–1923), 317
Macheth, Malcolm (flor. 1130–68), 23
Macintosh, Charles (1766–1843), 207–8
MacIntyre, Duncan Ban (1724–1812), 315
McIntyre, Dr. Robert (b. 1913), 143
Mackay, Clan, 91
Mackellar, Mary (1834–1890), 319
Mackenzie, Clan, 91
Mackenzie, Sir Compton (b. 1883), 135, 320
Mackenzie, Sir George, of Rosehaugh (1636–1691), 173
Mackenzie, Henry (1745–1831), 292, 315
Mackie, Professor J. D., cited, 94
Mackinnon, Professor James, cited, 83
Mackintosh, Charles Rennie (1868–1928), 317
Mackintosh, William, of Borlum (1662–1743), 89
Maclachlan, Ewen (1775–1822), 319
McLaren, Duncan (1800–1886), 114–15, 116–23, passim
Maclaren, Ian (Rev. John Watson, 1850–1907), 318
Maclean, Clan, 91
McLellan, Mr. Robert (b. 1907), 322
Macleod, Clan, 91

Macleod, Fiona (William Sharp, 1856–1905), 319
Macleod, Dr. Norman (1812–1872), 268
Macnab, The (Raeburn portrait), 313
McNeil, Mr. Hector (b. 1907), 150–1
Macpherson, James (1736–1796), 315
McTaggart, William (1835–1910), 317
MacWhirter, John (1839–1911), 317
Madeleine of France, queen of James V (1520–1537), 48
Magna Carta (1215), 24
Magnus, king of Man (d. 1266), 28
Magus moor (Fife), 72
Maitland, Sir Richard (1496–1586), 311
Maitland Club (Glasgow), 239
Major, John (1469–1550), 43–4, 286, 307
Malaya, 147
Malcolm II (c. 954–1034), 12
Malcolm III (c. 1031–1093), 13–16, 18, 23–4, 26, 27
Malcolm IV (1141–1165), 18, 23, 25–7, 306
Malt duty, 88, 96, 167, 169, 230
Man, isle of, 28
'Manager' of Scotland, 96, 99, 103–4, 105, 163–4
Manchester regiment (1745–1746), 92
Man of Feeling, The (Mackenzie), 315
Mansfield, David Murray, second earl of (1727–1796), 107
Mansie Wauch (Moir), 316
Man was made to Mourn (Burns), 314
Mar, John Stewart, earl of (c. 1457–1479), 41; John Erskine, earl of (d. 1572), 56; John Erskine, earl of (1675–1732), 85, 89, 93, 162–3; nation of, at Aberdeen University, 286
March, earls of, 22
Margaret, Saint (d. 1093), 14–18, 19, 23, 306
Margaret of England, queen of Alexander III (1240–1275), 25, 28
Margaret of Scotland, queen of Norway (1261–1283), 28
Margaret, Queen (1282–1290), 28–9
Margaret of Denmark, queen of James III (c. 1457–1486), 28, 41
Margaret Tudor, queen of James IV (1489–1541), 42, 44, 309
Marischal College, Aberdeen, 290, 292–3, 296, 297, 317
Marlborough, John Churchill, duke of (1650–1722), 81, 107

Marmion (Scott), 43, 316
Marnock (Banffshire), 266
Marriage (Ferrier), 316
Marrow of Modern Divinity (by 'E.F.,' 1645), 260
Marston moor, battle of (1644), 65
Mary of Guise (1515–1560), 48, 51–2
Mary Tudor, queen of England (1516–1558), 48, 51
Mary, Queen (1542–1587), 49–56, 58
Mary II, Queen (1662–1694), 74–5
Maryhill (Glasgow), 152, 237
Masson, David (1822–1907), 318
Mr. Bolfry (Bridie), 320
Master of Ballantrae, The (Stevenson), 318
Matilda, queen of Henry I (1080–1118), 17
Matilda, queen of England (1102–1167), 24
Mavor, O. H., see Bridie, James
Maxton, James (1885–1946), 135
Maynooth College grant (1845), 116
Mealmaker, George (flor. 1790–1799), 101
Mearns, 16, 193; and see Kincardine and also Angus, North
Mechanics' institutes, 295, 299
Mechanization of textiles, 194, 196, 200–2; of farming, 192–3, 198–9, 222
Medina, Sir John (1659–1710), 313
Meikles, Andrew (1719–1811), and George (d. 1811), 192
Melrose abbey (Roxburghshire), 19
Melrose Chronicle, 23, 306
Melville, Andrew (1545–1622), 57–8, 59, 61, 259, 264, 289–90
Melville, James (1556–1614), 312
Melville, Viscount, see under Dundas
Memorabilia Domestica (Sage), 200
Memorials of his Time (Cockburn), 104, 316
Mersey river, 11
Methil (Fife), 217
Methodist Church in Scotland, 273, 276–7
Methven (Perthshire), 237; fight at (1306), 32
Midland Bank, 216
Midlothian, 197, 236; and see under Central counties; Northern, 142
Midlothian and Peebles, 152, 160
Midlothian campaign (1879), 119
Militia Act (1797), 101
Miller, Hugh (1802–1856), 270, 318
Minimum stipend, 271, 282–3

Minstrelsy of the Scottish Border, The (Scott), 316

Mitchell, Sir Andrew (1708–1771), 107

Mitchell, J. Leslie, *see* Gibbon, Lewis Grassic

Mitchison, Mrs. Naomi (b. 1897), 320

Moderate party in the Church, 230, 262–3, 264, 265

Moir, David M., 'Delta' (1798–1851), 316

Moncrieff, Mrs. Scott (Raeburn portrait), 313

Monkland-Kirkintilloch railway, 205

Monklands (Lanarkshire), 203, 205

Monmouth, James Scott, duke of (1649–1685), 72

Monro, Alexander, primus (1697–1767); secundus (1733–1817); tertius (1773–1859), 293

Monteith, James (1734–1814), 196

Montgomerie, Alexander (c. 1556–1610), 311

Montrose, 69, 118, 194, 229, 234, 292; Academy, 295; district of burghs, 139

Montrose, James Graham, marquis of (1612–1650), 64–6, 311; James, first duke of (1682–1742), 95; James, third duke of (1755–1836), 108; James, sixth duke of (1878–1954), 137

Moore, Sir John (1761–1809), 108

Morall Fabillis of Esope (Henryson), 308

Morar (Inverness-shire), 278

Moray (or Elginshire), 16, 24, 30, 158, 250; nation of, at Aberdeen University, 286

Moray, Angus, earl of (d. 1130), 23; Thomas Randolph, earl of (d. 1332), 33; James Stewart, earl of (c. 1531–1570), 54–6, 77

Moray and Nairn, 152, 160

Moray, Ross and Caithness, diocese, 275

Moreville, de, family of, 22

Morison, Rev. James (1816–1893), 269

Morley, John (1838–1923), 125

Morton, James Douglas, fourth earl of (c. 1516–1581), 56–7, 77

Motherwell, 211, 237, 275; division of Lanarkshire, 131, 143, 152

Motherwell and Wishaw, 136

Mound, the Earthen (Edinburgh), 233

Mousa broch (Shetland), 303

Muir, Mr. Edwin (b. 1887), 321

Muir, Thomas (1765–1798), 101

Muirhead, Mr. R. E. (b. 1868), 133

Muirkirk ironworks (Ayrshire), 197

Municipal elections, 128, 136, 139, 142, 148, 180, 184

Munro, Clan, 91

Munro, Sir Hector (1726–1805), 108

Munro, Neil (1864–1930), 320

Murray, Charles (1864–1941), 321

Murray, Lord George (c. 1700–1760), 90, 92–3

Murray, Sir George (1772–1846), 109

Murray, James (c. 1719–1794), 108

Murray, Sir John, of Broughton (1718–1777), 90, 97

Murrays, 91; of Ochtertyre, 227

Mushet, David (1772–1847), 203

Musical Society (Edinburgh), 231

Music in Scotland, 231, 235, 244, 253, 268, 279, 284–5, 289, 299, 306, 314, 316, 319–20, 322

Musselburgh (Midlothian), 22, 289

Myllar, Andro (*flor.* 1503–1510), 306

My Schools and Schoolmasters (Miller), 318

Nairn, 22, 205

Nairne, Caroline, Lady (1766–1845), 93, 314

Nairnshire, 139, 156, 158; and *see* Moray and Nairn

Napier, Robert (1791–1876), 203, 208

Naples, 107

Napoleon Bonaparte (1769–1821), 103, 108

Napoleonic Wars (1793–1815), 100–4, 198, 237

National Bank of Scotland, 205, 216

National Covenant, *see under* Covenant

National Farmers' Union, 253

National government (1931–1945), 134–8, 142–3, 144, 212–13

Navigation Acts (1651, 1660, etc.), 75, 190, 195

Nechtansmere, battle of (685), 12

Neilson, James B. (1792–1865), 203

Nesbit moor, battle of (1402), 36

Nether Bow port (Edinburgh), 232

Netherlands, *see* Low Countries

Neville's Cross (Durham), battle of (1346), 35

Newbattle abbey (Midlothian), 19

Newburgh (Fife), 22, 291

Newburn (Northumberland), fight at (1640), 65

Newcastle, 65, 66, 172

New Jersey College (Princeton), 262

New Light controversy (1799–1806), 261, 266
Newport (Fife), 239, 250
Newspapers, 231, 233, 235, 240, 244, 252; and see Glasgow Herald and Scotsman
Newton, Sir Isaac (1642–1727), 293
Newton, Lord (Raeburn portrait), 313
New Town (Edinburgh), 232–3, 239, 312
New York, 106, 228, 231
Ninian, Saint (d. c. 432), 11
Noctes Ambrosianæ (North), 316
Norham-on-Tweed, 29
Nor' Loch (Edinburgh), 233
Normal school, 296
Normans, 13–16, 22, 26, 172, 304
Norse (Northmen), 12–13, 26, 27–8, 303
North, Christopher (John Wilson, 1785–1854), 316
North, Frederick, Lord (second earl of Guilford, 1732–1792), 99, 107, 108
Northallerton, battle near (1138), 24
Northampton, Treaty of (1328), 33
North Berwick, 244, 250
North bridge (Edinburgh), 232
North British railway, 205, 216
Northern Co-operative Company (Aberdeen), 242
Northern Ireland, 171, 274; and see Ulster
North of Scotland Bank, 205, 216
North of Scotland Hydro-Electric Board, 143, 218, 223
Northumberland, 25–7, 32
Northumbria, 12, 14, 17, 24
Norway and Norwegians, 16, 17, 27–8
Notestein, Dr. Wallace, cited, 79
Nova Scotia baronetcies (1621), 60

Oban (Argyll), 237
Occasional Conformity Act (1711), 175
Occupations in 1901 and 1951, 220–1
Uchil Idylls (Haliburton), 319
Oddfellows, Independent Order of, 254
Ogilvies, 84, 91
Old Aberdeen, 239, 285
Old College (Edinburgh), 293, 298, 312; (Glasgow), 290, 293, 298, 311
Old Mortality (Scott), 316
Old Scotch Independents (1768), 261
Old Statistical Account (1791–1799), cited, 230, 234, 236, 291–2

Omoa iron works (Lanarkshire), 197
'Orange-and-green' riots, 238
Orchardson, Sir William (1832–1910), 317
Ordination, The (Burns), 314
Original Seceders, 260–2, 263, 266–7
Orkney, 28, 41, 60, 202, 217, 248; Patrick Stewart, earl of (d. 1615), 60; diocese of, 17, 46, 275
Orkney and Shetland, 125, 139, 145, 146, 147, 153, 160
Orr, Sir John Boyd (later Baron) (b. 1880), 143
Orygynall Cronikil (Wyntoun), 307
Ossianic poems (Macpherson), 315
Ottawa Imperial Conference (1932), 212
Otterburn, battle of (1388), 36
Output in 1951 (of Scotland and of Great Britain), 218, 220
Oxford Univeristy, 172, 293, 298

Paine, Tom (1737–1809), 100
Painting, 306, 311, 313, 317, 319, 322
Paisley, burgh, 92, 128, 137, 139, 145, 148, 152, 157–8, 159, 160, 289; economic and social life, 194, 196, 202, 204, 205, 229, 230, 237, 238; Roman Catholic church in, 270, 275; shawl trade, 201, 206
Palice of Honour, The (Douglas), 309
Palladian architecture, 312
Palmer, Thomas Fysshe (1747–1802), 101
Palmerston, Henry Temple, third Viscount (1784–1865), 117
Panama, isthmus of, 78
'Papal aggression' (1850), 116
Paris, 175, 286
Parish councils, 181, 182, 183
Parish schools, 288–9, 291–2, 294–6
Park, Mungo (1771–1806), 106
Parliament (English), 61, 65–7, 75–83; (Scottish), 29–30, 34, 36, 38, 45, 50–3, 56, 58–61, 62, 67, 70, 73–85, 95, 155, 173, 288; (of Great Britain), 68, 82–3, 86–8, 94–101, 155–7, 260; (of the United Kingdom), 103, 105–6, chapter 4, passim, 157–62, 267, 279, 302
Parliament Act (1911), 127, 146; (1949), 146
Parliamentary representation of Scotland, 29–30, 34, 36, 38, 45, 67–8, 75–6, 82, 105–6, 117–18, 119–20, 121, 127–8, 130, 132–4, 146, 155–61
Parochial and Burgh Schoolmasters (Scotland) Act, 1861, 295

Parochial boards, 181
Partick (Glasgow), 140, 237, 245
Paton, Dr. H. M., cited, 306
Patronage, lay, in the Church, 70, 87–8, 119, 259–62, 264–7
Pavia, University of, 172
Peace party (1853), 116–17
Peblis to the Play (James I?), 308
Peebles, 22, 284; shire, 34, 158, and *see* Midlothian and Peebles
Peel, Sir Robert (1788–1850), 105, 110, 112, 116
Peelites, 111–12
Peerage bill (1719), 96
Penicuik (Midlothian), 196
Pennecuick, Alexander (d. 1730), 314
Penny Wedding (Wilkie), 313
Pentland rising (1666), 71
Pentlands division (Edinburgh), 153
Peploe, Samuel J. (1871–1935), 319
Percys, the, 36
Perth, burgh, 22, 34, 37, 89, 157, 284; economic and social life, 194, 205, 229, 231, 234, 237
Perth, James Drummond, fourth earl of (1648–1716), 73
Perth Academy, 292
Perthshire, 139, 152, 158, 160, 194, 248; East, 147; West, *see* Kinross and West Perthshire
Peterhead (Aberdeenshire), 200, 224
Peter Pan (Barrie), 320
Pettie, John (1839–1893), 317
Philiphaugh, battle of (1645), 66
Picts, 11–12, 303
Pilton ward (Edinburgh), 251
Pinkie, battle of (1547), 50–1
Pitlessie Fair (Wilkie), 313
Pitt, William, earl of Chatham (1708–1778), 98, 107; the younger (1759–1806), 99, 100, 108, 163
Pittenweem (Fife), 310
Playfair, William H. (1789–1857), 312–13
Pleasant Satyre of the Thrie Estaitis, Ane (Lyndsay), 309
Pluscardine priory (Moray), 23
Pneumoconiosis, 256
Police (Scotland) Act, 1946, 184
Pollok (Glasgow), 140, 153
Pollokshaws (Glasgow), 245
Pollokshields (Glasgow), 237, 251
Pondicherry, capture of (1778), 108
Poor relief, 179, 180, 182, 242, 264–5
Population of Scotland, 46–7, 155, 157, 170, 209, 218, 226, 230, 236–7, 244–9; *see* also Crofting counties, Central counties, and Towns

Porteous, Captain John (d. 1736), and the Porteous riot (Edinburgh), 96–7, 169
Port Glasgow (Renfrewshire), 136, 191, 250
Portincross tower (Ayrshire), 305
Portobello (Midlothian), 236
Portsburgh (Edinburgh), 236
Portuguese influences (on architecture), 305
Prais of Aige, The (Henryson), 308
Presbytery, origin of, 57
Preston, battle of (1648), 67; (1715), 88
Prestonpans, battle of (1745), 90
Prestwick, 22, 149, 217, 244
Princes street (Edinburgh), 232
Princeton (New Jersey), 262
Principles of the Law of Scotland (Bell), 173
Prison Commissioners, 164
Privy Council, Scottish, 60, 71, 73, 86, 128, 162, 166, 173–4, 288
Proportional representation, 159
Protection, *see* Tariffs
Protectorate, Scotland under the (1653–1660), 67–9
Provand's Lordship (Glasgow), 306
Provost, The (Galt), 316
Pultneytown (Wick), 198

Quebec, capture of (1759), 108
Queen Margaret College (Glasgow), 297
Queensberry, James Douglas, second duke of (1662–1711), 85–6, 162
Queen's Park football club (Glasgow), 244
Queen street (Edinburgh), 232; (Glasgow), 233
Quoad Sacra Act (1844), 267

Rab and his Friends (Brown), 318
Rabelais (trans. by Urquhart), 312
Radical War (1820), 105
Raeburn, Sir Henry (1756–1823), 239, 313
'Ragged' schools, 295
Railways, 146, 205, 216
Railways Act (1921), 216
Ramsay, Allan, the elder (1686–1758), 314; the younger (1713–1784), 313
Randolph, Sir Thomas, earl of Moray (d. 1332), 33
Rangers football club (Glasgow), 244
Rare Adventures and Painful Peregrinations (Lithgow), 312
Reay, George Mackay, third Lord (1678–1748), 91

Rechabites, Independent Order of (established 1835), 254
'Red Clydeside,' 129–30, 134, 135
Redford barracks (Edinburgh), 126, 169
Reform Act (1832), 106, 110, 157–8; (1867–68), 112, 117, 158; (1884–85), 112, 158–9
Reformation, 49–53, 56–7, 278, 288, 306, 310, 312
Reformed Presbyterians, 75, 259, 260, 268, 274, 276
Reform Union (1839), 111
Regalities, 174, 177, 178
Regent system at universities, 285, 290, 292–3
Register House (Edinburgh), 232, 312
Reid, Robert, 'Senex' (1773–1865), 234
Reid, Thomas (1710–1796), 293
Reign of Terror (1793–1795), 100
Relief Church, 260, 262, 266, 295
Renaissance, 305, 309, 310
Renfrew, 156, 217, 289, 291
Renfrewshire, 20, 139, 158, 160, 194, 201, 236, and see under Central counties; East, West, 153
Rent Day (Wilkie), 313
Reorganisation of Offices (Scotland) Acts, 1928 and 1939, 164
Representation of the People Act, 1918, 159; 1948, 146, 160–1
Rerum Scoticarum Historia (Buchanan), 311
Resby, James (d. 1407), 48
Restoration, the (1660), 69–70, 290
Revolution, the (1689–1690), 73–5, 259
Rhineland, 138
Richard I of England (1157–1199), 26–7
Richard III (1452–1485), 41
Rights of Man (Paine), 100
Rizzio, David (c. 1533–1566), 54–5
Robene and Makyne (Henryson), 308
Robert I (Bruce) (1274–1329), 31–4, 307
Robert II (Stewart) (1316–1390), 35, 36
Robert III (1340–1406), 36, 37
Roberton, Sir Hugh (1874–1952), 319
Robertson, George (c. 1750–1832), 198
Robertson, J. Logie, see Haliburton, Hugh
Robertson, Principal William (1721–1793), 232, 262, 315
Robertsons of Struan, 91
Rob Roy (Scott), 316
Roche, Alexander (1861–1921), 317

Roman Catholic Church, 14–15, 17–18, 25–6, 32, 46, 48, 51, 53, 61, 73, 99, 105, 116, 238, 259–60, 264, 270, 274–8; schools, 270, 274, 284–7, 295, 298
Romance of War (Grant), 318
Romanesque architecture, 304
Roman Law, 172
Rome and Roman Empire, 11, 17, 26, 303–4
Rosebery, Archibald Primrose, fifth earl of (1847–1929), 120, 124–5
Roslyn chapel (Midlothian), 305
Ross, 37, 90, 92, 158, 248; diocese, 17, 275; Clan, 91
Ross and Cromarty, 139, 152, 160
Rosslyn, James Erskine, second earl of (1762–1837), 109
Rosyth naval dockyard (Fife), 126, 149, 169
Rotary Clubs, 253
Rothes, John Leslie, duke of (1630–1681), 71
Rothesay, 196, 234; David Stewart, duke of (1378–1402), 36; nation of, at Glasgow University, 286
Row (or Rhu), Dumbartonshire, 268
Rowett Institute (Aberdeenshire), 223
Roxburgh, 22, 34, 37, 39, 284
Roxburgh and Selkirk (shires), 135, 139, 145, 146, 147, 153, 159, 160
Roxburghe, John Ker, first duke of (1680–1741), 85, 95, 96, 163
Royal and Ancient Club (St. Andrews), 234
Royal Bank of Scotland, 168, 197, 216
Royal College of Surgeons (Edinburgh), 46
Royal Oak inn (Leith), 232
Rubens, Peter Paul (1577–1640), 311
Rudimenta (Vaus), 286
Rule, Britannia (Thomson), 315
Rural Recollections (Robertson), 198
Rusco tower (Kirkcudbrightshire), 305
Russell, Lord John (1792–1878), 116
Rutherglen, 72, 156; division of Lanarkshire, 147, 153
Ruthven, Raid of (1582), 58
Ruthwell (Dumfriesshire), 205, 265; cross of, 303
Rutland and Stamford division, 160

Sage, Donald (1789–1869), 200
St. Andrews, bishopric and cathedral, 17, 26, 46; castle, 50, 305; city and burgh, 22, 229, 234, 244, 284, 311; University, 40, 285–6, 292–4, 296–8, 300–1, 302

St. Andrews and Edinburgh, archdiocese of, 275
St. Andrews, Dunkeld and Dunblane, bishopric of, 275
St. Andrew's House (Edinburgh), 165
St. Andrew's square (Edinburgh), 232
St. Andrews University Act, 1953, 161–2, 301
St. Cecilia's hall (Edinburgh), 231
St. Clement's ward (Aberdeen), 251
St. Giles' cathedral (Edinburgh), 64, 305, 319
St. Giles' ward (Edinburgh), 251
St. Leonard's College (St. Andrews), 285, 294
St. Magnus cathedral (Kirkwall), 304
St. Margaret's chapel (Edinburgh castle), 304
St. Mary's church (Haddington), 305
St. Mary's College (St. Andrews), 285
St. Mary's Isle, priory of (Galloway), 19
St. Michael's church (Cupar), 310; (Linlithgow), 305
St. Regulus tower (St. Andrews), 304
St. Salvator's College (St. Andrews), 40, 285, 294, 305
St. Serf's priory (Kinross-shire), 307
Salisbury, Robert Gascoyne-Cecil, third marquess of (1830–1903), 120, 122, 123
Saltire Society (1936), 322
Saltmarket (Glasgow), 239
Salvation Army, 276–7
Samuel, Sir Herbert (later Viscount) (b. 1870), 136
Sandemanians, sect of, 260–1
Saracen's Head inn (Glasgow), 234
Saunders, Professor L. J., cited, 241
Savings banks, 205, 241, 265
Saxon and Celt, conflict of, 13–18, 19–21, 22–3, 27
Scapa flow (Orkney), 169
School boards, 118, 180–1, 296, 298
Schoolmasters Act (1803), 103, 294
Schoolmasters' stipends, 103, 288, 289, 291, 292, 294, 295–6, 301
Scone (Perthshire), 18, 31
Scotch Drink (Burns), 314
Scotichronicon (Fordun and Bower), 307
Scotorum Historia (Boece), 307
Scots Baronial style, 305–6, 310–11, 317, 319
Scots Greys, 126, 169
Scots Guards (French corps), 37
Scotsman, The, 104, 113, 122, 151, 240, 258
Scots National League (c. 1927), 133

Scots Quair, A (Gibbon), 320–1
Scotstarvit tower (Fife), 310
Scotstoun (Glasgow), 149, 153
Scots Wha Ha'e (Burns), 103
Scott, Alexander (c. 1525–1584), 311
Scott, Mr. Alexander (b. 1920), 321
Scott, Mr. Francis G. (b. 1880), 322
Scott, Sir Walter (1771–1832), 13, 22, 102, 105, 233, 239, 316, 320; Monument (Edinburgh), 317; Raeburn portrait of, 313
Scottish Abbeys and Social Life (Coulton), 284
Scottish Community Drama Association, 319
Scottish Council (Development and Industry), 224
Scottish Covenant (1949), 149–50
Scottish Cup, 244
Scottish Democracy (Saunders), 241
Scottish Diplomatists, 1689–1789 (Horn), 107
Scottish Emergency Organization (1926), 132
Scottish Football Association, 244
Scottish Grand Committee, 124, 127, 146, 150, 161–2
Scottish Home Rule Association (1886), 121
Scottish League, 244
Scottish National Assembly (1947), 149
Scottish Nationalist Committee (1910), 127
Scottish Nationalist party (1928), 133–4, 135, 137
Scottish National party (1934), 137, 141, 143, 145–7, 149
Scottish Orchestra, 322
Scottish party (c. 1932), 137
Scottish Patriot, 114
Scottish Population Statistics (Kyd), 249
Scottish Renaissance, 321
Scottish Rugby Union, 244
Scottish Tourist Board, 224
Scottish Trades Union Congress, 132
Scougall, John (flor. c. 1620–1640), 311
Seabury, Bishop Samuel (1729–1796), 263
Seafield, James Ogilvie, first earl of, and (from 1711) fourth earl of Findlater (1664–1730), 84, 85, 192
Seasons, The (Thomson), 315
Secondary schools, 296, 299, 301
Secretary (of State) for Scotland, 95–7, 120, 132, 162–5
Sedan, University of, 61
Select Society (Edinburgh), 232

Selkirkshire, 158; and *see* Roxburgh and Selkirk
Sempill, Robert (*c.* 1595–1665), 311, 314
Sessional schools, 295
Seven Ill Years (1696–1703), 189
Seven Years' War (1756–1763), 98, 108
Severus, Septimius (146–211), 11
Shaftesbury, Anthony Ashley Cooper, seventh earl of (1801–1885), 110
Shall We Join the Ladies? (Barrie), 318
Sharp, Archbishop James (1613–1679), 72
Sharp, William, *see* Macleod, Fiona
Shaw, Christian, of Bargarran (1686–*c.* 1740), 194
Shawfield riot (Glasgow, 1725), 96, 169
Sheep-rearing, 19, 193, 199–200, 218–19, 222
Sheriff and Sheriff-court, 21–2, 174, 176, 177–8
Sheriffmuir, battle of (1715), 89
Shetland, 28, 41, 202, 248; and *see* Orkney and Shetland
Shettleston (Glasgow), 135, 152
Shipbuilders, The (Blake), 320
Shipbuilding, 203–4, 206, 208, 210, 211, 212, 215, 218, 220, 225
Shira power station (Argyll), 218
Short History of the Episcopal Church in Scotland (Goldie), 273
Shorthorn cattle, 209
Simon, Sir John (later Viscount) (b. 1873), 136
Simson, Professor John (*c.* 1668–1740), 260
Sinclair, John, master of (1683–1750), 91
Sinclair, Sir John (Raeburn portrait), 313
Sinclair, Oliver (*flor.* 1537–1560), 49
Skene, William F. (1809–1892), 319
Slavery, abolition of (1833), 113–14
Slave trade, abolition of (1807), 103
Sleeping Clergyman, A (Bridie), 320
Small Landholders (Scotland) Act, 1911, 164
Smith, Adam (1723–1790), 232, 262, 293, 315
Smith, Alexander (1830–1867), 318
Smith, Mr. Sydney Goodsir (b. 1915), 321
Smith, Professor William Robertson (1846–1894), 268
Smollett, Tobias (1721–1771), 315
Snowden, Philip (1864–1937), 134

Socialism, early, in Scotland, 110–11, 123
Social Life of Scotland in the Eighteenth Century (Graham), 228
Society in Scotland for Propagating Christian Knowledge (1709), 264, 291, 295
Society of Improvers in the Knowledge of Agriculture in Scotland (1723), 192, 193
Society of the Friends of the People (1792), 100
Solemn League and Covenant (1643), 65–7, 69–70, 74, 259, 261, 272
Solway moss, battle of (1542), 49
Song schools, 284–5, 289, 306
Songs of the Hebrides (Kennedy Fraser), 320
Sophia, electress of Hanover (1630–1714), 81, 82
Sorn Committee (1953), 184
Soroptimists, 253
Soutar, William (1898–1943), 321
South bridge (Edinburgh), 233
South-East and South-West Scotland Electricity Boards, 218
South Wind (Douglas), 320
Spain, 59, 78, 89, 305
Spanish Armada (1588), 58
Spanish Civil War (1936–1939), 138
Spence, Mr. Lewis (b. 1874), 321
Spens, Dr. Nathaniel (Raeburn portrait), 313
Speymouth (Moray), 291
Sport, 200, 234, 244, 254
Spottiswoode, Archbishop John (1565–1637), 312
Springburn (Glasgow), 152
Squadrone Volante, 85–7, 95–7
Stair, James Dalrymple, first Viscount (1619–1695), 172; John, master, second Viscount and first earl (1648–1707), 77; John, second earl (1673–1747), 107–8, 192; John, sixth earl (1749–1821), 108
Standard, battle of the (1138), 24
Standing joint committees, 181–2
Stanhope, James, first earl (1673–1721), 95, 96
Steel industry, 146, 147, 204, 210, 211–12, 215, 218, 225
Stephen, king of England (*c.* 1097–1154), 24
Stevenson, Robert Louis (1850–1894), 317–18
Stewart, Professor Dugald (1753–1828), 296; Raeburn portrait of, 313

Stewart, house of, 20, 45, 80, 94, 260, 263, 264

Stewart or Stuart, James, 'the Old Pretender' (1688–1766), 80, 87, 89; Charles Edward, 'the Young Pretender' (1720–1788), 90, 92–4, 264

Stickit Minister, The (Crockett), 318

Stirling, burgh, 22, 35, 46–7, 90, 92, 229, 237, 311; castle, 22, 32, 94, 305; district of burghs, 118; high school, 284, 289

Stirling and Falkirk district of burghs, 140, 152, 160

Stirling bridge, battle of (1297), 30

Stirling Observer, 240

Stirlingshire, 152, 159, 160, 236; and *see under* Central counties; East, *see under* Clackmannan; West, 159

Stirling's Library (Glasgow), 234

Stobs military camp (Roxburghshire), 126

Stockwell street (Glasgow), 239

'Stone of destiny,' 30, 150

Stormont, Viscount, *see* Mansfield

Stow, David (1793–1864), 295

Strathbogie, presbytery of, 266

Strathclyde, 12–13, 16

Stuarts of Appin, 91

Summerlee iron works (Lanarkshire), 203

Sunday schools, 265, 276, 295

Sunset Song (Gibbon), 321

Sutherland, 13, and *see under* Caithness; Clan, 91

Swan, Annie S. (Mrs. Burnett Smith, 1859–1943), 318

Symington, William (1763–1831), 203

Tam o' Shanter (Burns), 103, 314

Tam Samson's Elegy (Burns), 314

Tannahill, Robert (1774–1810), 314

Tantallon castle (East Lothian), 305

Tarbert (Argyll), 237

Tariffs, 88, 114–15, 126, 131, 136, 166–9, 170, 191, 198–9, 212–13

Taxation, *see* Finance and Land-tax

Tay bridge (railway), 205

Tay valley regional plan, 224

Tea-Table Miscellany (Ramsay), 314

Tees, river, 11

Television, 253

Temora (Macpherson), 315

Temperance reform, 116, 128, 241, 242, 244, 248, 254, 265; and *see* Intemperance

Tennant, Charles (1768–1838), 208

Tennant, William (1784–1848), 314

Terregles church (Kirkcudbrightshire), 310

Testament and Complaynt of our Soverane Lordis Papyngo (Lyndsay), 309

Testament of Cresseid, The (Henryson), 308

Testament of Mr. Andro Kennedy (Dunbar), 309

Teviotdale, nation of, at Glasgow University, 286

Theatre in Scotland, 230, 231–2, 233, 253, 262–3, 309, 315–16, 319–20, 322

Theatre Royal (Edinburgh), 232

Theodosius (d. 376), 11

Thermopylæ (clipper ship), 206

Third Lanark football club, 244

Thirty-nine Articles, the, 264, 269

Thistle chapel (St. Giles, Edinburgh), 319

Thistle (steamship), **2**38

Thomson, Alexander ('Greek Thomson') (1817–1875), 317

Thomson, Mr. George M., cited, 133, 274

Thomson, James (1700–1748), 315

Thomson, James (1834–1882), 318

Thomson, J. and G., and Company (1846), 208

Thomson, Rev. John, of Duddingston (1778–1840), 313

Thornliebank (Glasgow), 208

Threave tower (Kirkcudbrightshire), 305

Thrissill and the Rois, The (Dunbar), 309

Tiree (Argyll), 200

Tobacco trade, 195

Tobermory (Argyll), 198

Tobias and the Angel (Bridie), 320

Tolbooth (Canongate), 310

Tory party, 87–9, 94, 98–9, 101–5, 108–13

Tourist Board, Scottish, 224

Towers, baronial, 305–6, 310

Town and Country Planning (Scotland) Act, 1947, 184

Town councils, 178–80, 182–4, 186; and *see* Municipal elections

Town Councils (Scotland) Act, 1900, 180

Town planning, 181, 184, 224–5, 233, 256–7, 319

Towns, population of, 46–7, 228–9, 230, 236–7, 245, 246–7 (Map), 248

Townshend, Charles, second Viscount (1674–1738), 88, 95

Trade, *see* Commerce

Tradeston (Glasgow), 152
Trades Union Congress, Scottish, 132
Tragedie of the Cardinall, The (Lyndsay), 309
Tranent (East Lothian), 101
Transport, 197, 203–5, 216–17, 226, 230, 242, 244, 251, 252
Transport Act, 1947, 146, 217
Treason Act (1709), 87
Treasury grants to local authorities, 182–3, 184, 295–6, 302
Treasury returns of Scottish revenue and expenditure, 169–71
Trevelyan, Sir George (1838–1928), 124
Trinity College church (Edinburgh), 305
Trondhjem (Norway), 17
Trongate (Glasgow), 233–4
Troon (Ayrshire), 204, 217, 244
Troylus and Cryseyde (Chaucer), 308
True Scotsman, The, 114
Trunk Roads Act, 1936, 138, 183–4, 217
Tua Mariit Wemen and the Wedo, The (Dunbar), 309
Tuberculosis, 256
Tucker, Thomas (flor. 1650–1660), 68–9
Tummel valley power stations, 218
Turgot, Bishop (d. 1115), 15, 17, 306
Turnhouse airport (Edinburgh), 217
Turnpike Road Act (1751), 197
Twa Dogs, The (Burns), 102, 314
Tweeddale, John Hay, second marquis of (1645–1713), 85; John, fourth marquis (c. 1695–1762), 97, 163

Uist, South (Hebrides), 278
Ullapool (Ross), 198
Ulster, 60, 159, 238
Unemployment, 130, 136, 138, 183, 210, 211–13, passim, 214, 215
Unemployment Assistance Board, 136, 183
Union Bank of Scotland, 205, 216
Union canal, 204
Unionists in Scotland, 122–3, 125–7
Union of Scotland and England (Mackinnon), 83
Union of the Churches (1929), 270–2, 279
Union of the Crowns (1603), 60–1
Union of the Kingdoms (1707), 79–86, 155–7, 162, 166–8, 172, 174–5, 177–8, 191, 260–1, 312

'Union of the Thistle and the Rose' (1503), 42, 309
United Alkali Company (1890), 208
United College, St. Andrews, 294
United Empire Loyalists, 106
United Free Church, 126, 269, 270–1, 272, 275, 276, 277
United Original Seceders, 267, 272, 282
United Presbyterian Church, 118, 124, 176, 266–9
United Scotsmen (1798), 101
United Secession Church, 115, 266, 269, 295
United States of America, 209, 212, 249, 280
United Thread Manufacturing Company (1896), 208
University College, Dundee, 297, 301
University Grants Committee, 302
Universities (Scotland) Acts, 1858 and 1889, 297
Universities, Scottish (parliamentary constituency), 143, 145, 158, 159, 160; and see under Aberdeen, Edinburgh, Glasgow and St. Andrews
Urquhart, Sir Thomas (1611–1660), 312
Urquhart, Mrs. William (Raeburn portrait), 313
Urquhart priory (Moray), 23
Urr, ancient burgh (Kirkcudbrightshire), 22
Utrecht, University of, 172

Vale of Leven, 202; football club, 244
Vaus, John (c. 1490–1538), 286
Verneuil, battle of (1424), 37
Veterinary colleges, 223
Veto Act (1834), 266
Victoria, Queen (1819–1901), 111, 125
Vienna, 107
Vienne, John de (c. 1342–1396), 36
Virginia, 191

Wade, Field-marshal George (1673–1748), 89, 97–8, 197
Wages in Scotland, 210, 214, 221, 226, 227, 230, 238, 243, 251–2
Wales, 12, 121, 134, 150, 171, 213
Wallace, Sir William (c. 1272–1305), 30–1
Wallace (Blind Harry), 307, 314
Walpole, Sir Robert (1676–1745), 89, 95–7, 163, 230
Walston church (Lanarkshire), 310
Walton, E. A. (1866–1922), 317

Warbeck, Perkin (1474–1499), 42
Wardlaw, Lady Elizabeth (1677–1727), 314
Warenne, William, earl of, and second earl of Surrey (d. 1138), 25
War Memorial, Scottish National (Edinburgh castle), 319
War of Independence, Scottish, 30–9, 304, 307–8
Wars of the Roses (1455–1485), 40
Waterloo, battle of (1815), 104
Water supply, 240, 242
Watson, James (d. 1722), 313
Watson, Rev. John, see Maclaren, Ian
Watson, Sheriff William (1796–1887), 295
Watson-Gordon, Sir John (1788–1864), 313
Watt, James (1736–1819), 196
Waverley (Scott), 227, 316
Webster, Rev. Alexander (1707–1784), 92, 231, 262
Weir of Hermiston (Stevenson), 318
Wellington, Arthur Wellesley, duke of (1769–1852), 105, 108–9
Welsh, Rev. David (1793–1845), 265
Western Bank, 206
Western Isles, 137, 145, 147, 153, 159–60
West Indies, trade with, 207, 230
West Lothian, 152, 160, 236, 250; and see under Central counties
Westminster, 30, 75, 83, 85, 94, 133, 150, 175; Assembly of Divines, 65–6; Confession of Faith, 66, 75, 259, 268, 278
What Every Woman Knows (Barrie), 320
Wheatley, John (1869–1930), 131, 134
Whigs, English, 80–1, 85, 88, 94–6, 98–9; Scottish, 100–6, 108–9, 111–13, 115, 117, 122
White Fish Authority, 223
Whiteinch tunnel project (Glasgow), 217
White Star line, 207
White Wine club (Glasgow), 233
Whithorn (Wigtownshire), 17
Whyte-Melville, George (1821–1878), 318
Wick (Caithness), 198, 199, 206

Wight, Isle of, 66
Wightman, Joseph (d. 1722), 89
Wigtown district of burghs, 159
Wigtownshire, 245; and see under Kirkcudbrightshire and Galloway
Wilkie, Sir David (1785–1841), 313
William the Lion (1143–1214), 23–7
William I, the Conqueror (1027–1087), 15, 16, 26
William II, Rufus (c. 1058–1100), 15
William III, of Orange (1650–1702), 73–80, passim
Williams, Deacon's Bank, 216
Wilson, Professor John, Christopher North (1785–1854), 316
Wilsontown iron works (Lanarkshire), 197
Winchester, Roger de Quincy, second earl of (c. 1195–1265), 22
Window in Thrums, A (Barrie), 318
Wireless telegraphy, 253
Wishart, George (c. 1513–1546), 50
Wishaw, 205, 237; and see Motherwell and Wishaw
Witherspoon, Rev. John (1723–1794), 262
Witness, The, 270
Wodrow, Robert (1679–1734), 312
Wolfe, James (1727–1759), 108
Women's Rural Institutes, 253
Woodside (Glasgow), 153
Wooing of Jok and Jenny, The, 306
Woollen industry, 19, 47, 191, 197–8, 202, 220
Worcester, battle of (1651), 67
Workers' Educational Association, 299
World War (1914–1918), 129–30, 209–11, 216, 251; (1939–1945), 138, 142–4, 213–15, 217, 251
Wyf of Auchtermuchty, The, 306
Wyntoun, Andrew de (c. 1350–1420), 307

Yellow Frigate, The (Grant), 318
York, 17, 25, 49
Young, Mr. Douglas (b. 1913), 321
Young Farmers Clubs, 253
Y.M.C.A. and Y.W.C.A., 254
Young Scots Society (1902), 125

Zetland, see Shetland

PRINTED IN GREAT BRITAIN BY J. AND J. GRAY, EDINBURGH